COUNT SERGEI WITTE
AND THE TWILIGHT OF IMPERIAL RUSSIA

COUNT SERGEI WITTE

AND THE TWILIGHT OF IMPERIAL RUSSIA

A BIOGRAPHY

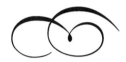

 SIDNEY HARCAVE

M.E.Sharpe
Armonk, New York
London, England

Library of Congress Cataloging-in-Publication Data

Harcave, Sidney, 1916–
  Count Sergei Witte and the twilight of imperial Russia : a biography /
Sidney Harcave.
   p. cm.
 Includes bibliographical references and index.
 ISBN 0-7656-1422-7 (alk. paper)
  1. Vitte, S., IU. (Sergei IUl'evich), graf, 1849–1915. 2. Statesmen—Russia—Biography.
3. Russia—Politics and government—1894–1917. 4. Russia—Economic policy—
1861–1917. I. Title.
DK254.W5 H37 2004
947.08′3′092—dc22

                                                                              2003019653

Printed in the United States of America

The paper used in this publication meets the minimum requirements of
American National Standard for Information Sciences
Permanence of Paper for Printed Library Materials,
ANSI Z 39.48-1984.

BM (c)   10   9   8   7   6   5   4   3   2   1

Contents

Acknowledgments

The volume of writing about Sergei Iulevich Witte is immense, but so far he has not been the subject of a biography in English. I was prompted to undertake such a project by my work in translating and editing his memoirs. I have sought to provide a picture of the man and his work in this comparatively short biography.

I owe special thanks to the Bakhmeteff Archive of Columbia University for allowing me access to its superb collection of Witte's papers. I am indebted to the many scholars who have written about him, notably B. V. Ananich, R. Sh. Ganelin, H. Mehlinger, T. von Laue, and J. M. Thompson. My thanks to Julianna Dranichak and Mark Kulikowski for their valuable bibliographic assistance.

In transliterating from the Russian I have followed the Library of Congress rules with some omission of diacritical marks, for the sake of euphony, anglicizing some given names (e.g., Nicholas, not Nikolai), and rendering surnames of non-Russian origin as their holders preferred to have them spelled in the Latin alphabet (e.g., Witte, Lamsdorff, Schwanebach). Dates are given according to the Julian calendar, which was used in Russia until 1918. Where appropriate, dates are given according to both the Julian and Gregorian calendars

COUNT SERGEI WITTE

AND THE TWILIGHT OF IMPERIAL RUSSIA

Chapter 1

The Formative Years, 1849–1865

He was acclaimed as "the one statesman who has arisen in Russia since Peter [the Great],[1] a Russian Colbert,[2] and "John the Baptist of the great Russian political reformation."[3] He was denounced as "Russia's evil genius"[4] and as a partner in a Jewish-Masonic conspiracy to make him president of a Russian republic.[5] No one ever called Sergei Iulevich Witte a mediocrity. Beyond question, he was the ablest and most influential minister to have served in the twilight years of the Russian monarchy.

Witte was born on June 17, 1849, in Tiflis, the administrative center of the viceroyalty of the Caucasus, at a time when the power of imperial Russia was at its zenith. Weeks earlier Field Marshal Prince Paskevich had led Russian troops across the Carpathian Mountains to help the Austrian emperor Franz Joseph crush the Hungarian revolution and thus extend the life of conservative monarchism, a cause to which the Russian emperor and Tsar Nicholas I devoted himself. It would be Witte's fate to spend much of his career shoring up the Russian monarchy and to die just as Russian forces were preparing to cross the Carpathian Mountains in a vain effort to defeat the aged Franz Joseph, an effort that would, despite its failure, speed the collapse of conservative monarchism.

The viceroyalty of the Caucasus, with an area about the size of Montana, was one of Russia's many borderlands, areas added, for the most part, by force of arms, inhabited at the time of annexation by non-Russians. It was dominated by the Caucasus Mountains, widely considered to constitute one of the borders between Europe and Asia. Its combination of towering mountains, highlands, plateaus, and occasional plains contributed to a bewildering assortment of ethnic groups—Azerbaidzhanis, Armenians, Chechens, and Georgians, just to name a few.

Tiflis, with a mix of Armenians, Georgians, Russians, and others, reflected some of the ethnic diversity of the Caucasus, the Russians being in large part civil servants or members of the considerable military force stationed there. For many centuries the crossing point of two major trade routes, it bestrode the Kara River for some seven miles. Not unexpectedly, ethnic groups tended to live in separate neighborhoods, with the Wittes living in the Russian quarter, where the residents tended to have no permanent commitment to the Caucasus.

Julius (né Christoff-Heinrich-Georg-Julius) F. Witte, the father of Sergei, was one such. Born in Courland, part of Russia's borderlands, a specialist in agriculture and mining, he was a civil servant in the province of Saratov when he met and sought the hand of Catherine Andreevna Fadeeva, daughter of the provincial governor, Andrei M. Fadeev. An obstacle to marriage was the fact that Julius was a Lutheran; he overcame it by conversion to the Russian Orthodox faith. In 1844 they were married. A son, Alexander, was born to them in the same year.[6]

Two years later Julius Witte and Andrei Fadeev, at the invitation of Prince Michael Vorontsov, viceroy of the Caucasus, moved to Tiflis with their families to assume major posts in the Caucasian administration. The Wittes and the Fadeevs had some land and serfs but were in debt and had to watch their kopeks if they were to cope with the high cost of living they found in Tiflis. To save money they set up a joint household in a large dwelling once owned by a Georgian prince.[7]

As the years passed, the household grew. After Alexander, Catherine Witte gave birth to Boris, Sergei, Olga, and Sophie. Elena Fadeeva (née Princess Dolgorukaia), wife of Andrei, was past childbearing age, but two of her children, Rostislav and Nadezhda, had not yet left the nest. Granddaughters Helena and Vera had joined the household on the death of their mother. Vera would gain fame as a children's writer, and Helena both fame and notoriety as Madame Blavatsky, one of the founders of Theosophism. A very colorful and controversial person, to say the least, she was given to holding séances and performing such feats as levitation, which she learned from D.D. Home, a spiritualist who had conducted séances for the tsar. Add governesses, wet nurses, tutors, and dozens of household serfs, plus occasional visits from the Fadeev grandchildren, and you have a household in which it was easy to get lost.

Like so many others of his class, Sergei spent his formative years under the supervision of servants, governesses, and tutors, with little time given him by his parents. But he was close enough to his father to develop both affection and respect for him. And indeed, there was much in the father to inspire respect: he was an able civil servant who was considered "the most learned man in Tiflis."[8] But Sergei barely mentions his mother in his memoirs and does not even refer to her death. He writes, however, with warmth and respect of his maternal grandmother, a gifted woman who imparted the rudiments of reading, writing, and religion to him and Boris.[9]

Of the five children of Julius and Catherine Witte, Sergei was the only one who distinguished himself. Alexander chose to make his career in the military, where he proved to be a courageous officer but no shining star. Boris, who lacked the drive that distinguished Sergei, had a respectable but unremarkable career in the judiciary. There is little to note about the girls except that they never married and that Sophie was the author of a minor novel.[10] Why Sergei stood out among them is a matter of fruitless speculation, but the what and why of his spectacular career are something else again.

In 1855 Julius Witte and his family were admitted to the ranks of the hereditary nobility. This class was proportionally more numerous than its counterpart in, let us say, Prussia, and the title of hereditary noble did not of itself confer material benefits. It did, however, confer prestige and a degree of privilege. Sergei would make much of the fact that he was a hereditary noble and that on his mother's side he was descended from the illustrious Princes Dolgorukii. His father's side did not provide such ammunition. What is more, he felt compelled to blur the truth that his father was a Baltic German by origin by stating that his paternal ancestors came from Holland.[11] He was brought up to identify himself as Russian by nationality and Russian Orthodox by faith, which probably explains why he dissociated himself from the Baltic Germans, so visible in the Russian civil and military service, who tended to hold fast to their ethnicity and Protestant religion.

As noted, Sergei and Boris learned their ABCs from their maternal grandmother. They were then given over to tutors, some of whom were not indifferent to the bottle, to be instructed in French, German, history, geography, music, and other elementary subjects. Finally, the time came for formal schooling, and they were enrolled in the local *gimnaziia* (secondary school) as auditors. They proved to be indifferent and undisciplined students who regularly cut classes. Their chief interest then was in music, leading them, among other things, to learn to play the flute. Sergei mistakenly thought he had a good voice and in later years, when out in the open country, would sing arias from Russian operas.[12] The two also enjoyed fencing, horseback riding, and hunting. Sergei would continue riding for decades and watching horsemanship even longer. In short, like many youngsters lacking parental discipline and not motivated by the need to earn a living, they did pretty much as they pleased.

Although the two were less than diligent, they managed to pass their yearly examinations, thanks to coaching by teachers from the *gimnaziia*. Finally, in 1865, they took their school-leaving examinations, the results of which would determine whether or not they graduated and whether or not they were eligible for admission to higher schools. They managed to pass all the examinations with mediocre grades, and each received a failing grade in deportment. Nonetheless, they were graduated and given school-leaving certificates entitling them to apply for admission to a university. The two were particularly galled by the low grades they received in French since they considered their command of the language to be superior to that of the two instructors who had examined them. Scamps that they were, they harassed the instructors.

Sergei was sixteen when he graduated from *gimnaziia,* quite tall for his age. A photograph of him together with Theodore Roosevelt and Komura, the Japanese plenipotentiary, taken in 1905, shows him a head taller than the president and at least two heads taller than Komura. His large torso and slender hips combined to give the impression of an "overgrown schoolboy," a bearded one, to be sure, in his later years. His was a commanding presence, yet one that lent itself to caricature by those hostile to him. His manners were rough and his accent provincial, and he did not soften with age. A British journalist wrote after seeing him in 1896: "In voice and manner he is rough and unsympathetic, and he has none of the *bonhomie* and suavity which are so common in Russia."[13] Sergei's French was not as good as he believed it to be: a Frenchman later wrote that Sergei's French was "rough, but at least intelligible," something he would not say about the French of most Russians who claimed mastery of that language. Sergei's German was slight indeed, and his Russian was marred by grammatical and spelling lapses. As indicated, he was musically inclined, played the flute, was a good horseman, and could fence. There is no indication then or later that he was bookish. Jeremiah Curtin, a renowned American Slavist who knew the Wittes in this period, later wrote: "I noticed in the boy [Sergei] the same remarkable energy, decision, and will power, imperious and strong, which later characterized Count Witte."[14] Curtin may or may not have been accurate in his recollection, but he certainly put his finger on the traits that Sergei was to show. Still, Sergei had yet to demonstrate that he was anything but a slightly spoiled teenager.

For Sergei these were carefree years, of privilege and what seemed like plenty, spent almost exclusively among civil servants and military officers and their families. Also, he felt touched by the aura of glamour that surrounded Field Marshal Prince Bariatinskii, who had replaced Vorontsov as viceroy and had brought with him from St. Petersburg officers who belonged to high society. And then there was the excitement surrounding Bariatinskii's campaign in the mountains to end the Moslem insurgency led by Shamil, a remarkable figure who was not captured until 1862. It was easy enough for Sergei to be caught up in the excitement, what with his uncle Rostislav Fadeev serving as an aide to the prince and playing a prominent role in the capture of Shamil. Years later, Shamil's banner, which had been given to Fadeev, would find a home in Sergei's library.

Life in the Caucasus had some resemblance to the life he would have had in India by being born and reared as part of the conqueror's establishment, one with a large military establishment that was frequently called to action. Like the English in India, Russian military and civilians from places such as Tiflis took to the mountains during the hot summers. As in India, so in the Caucasus the native nobility was brought into the establishment, their titles accepted by Russia and the ranks of the officer corps open to them. But unlike their counterparts in India, these nobles were white and Christian and, consequently, more socially acceptable. Sergei easily accepted the Armenians and Georgians with whom he was in contact. He also accepted the view that the Caucasus, like other borderlands won by Russian arms, should remain under Russian sovereignty.

The Caucasus was indeed remote from the center of power, but it was part of Russia. While Sergei was enjoying the pleasures of youth, Tsar Alexander II was enacting a series of major reforms triggered by Russia's shameful defeat in the Crimean War. The first of these, a milestone in the country's history, was the emancipation of the serfs on February 19, 1861. This historic step was followed by legislation establishing local elective governmental bodies, mitigating censorship, reforming the judicial system and the legal codes, and restoring university autonomy. These were accompanied by military reforms and measures to improve the economy, with railroad construction at the head of the list.

The reforms were intended to modernize the backward country, the chief aim being the regaining of great-power status without weakening the power of the autocratic sovereign or creating an urban proletariat. Alexander and his aides envisioned a future in which Russia remained essentially an agrarian country, with a strong landed nobility serving as the tsar's right arm. It was an unrealistic vision, at odds with both the forces at work and the expectations raised by the reforms. Those were exciting, if troubling, times in which Sergei Witte would soon be embroiled.

With graduation from the *gimnaziia* it became necessary for Sergei and Boris to leave the Caucasus if they were to receive a university education, as was their father's wish. This would be their first trip away from the Caucasus and a mighty long one at that, a jarring trip by horse and carriage, there being no railroad yet in the region, to a port on the Black Sea and then on to Odessa by ship. Like other adolescents going off to school, they were accompanied by their parents. The father would have preferred that the boys attend Kiev University, but circumstances led to the choice of the recently established Novorossiisk University, located in Odessa. The father had reason to believe that the superintendent of the Odessa Educational District would use his influence to get the boys into the university, but that was not enough. The father thereupon enrolled the boys in the Richelieu *gimnaziia,* where they could improve their records enough for them to be able to matriculate at the university. Odessa would be home to Sergei and Boris for a long time to come.[15]

Chapter 2

The Odessa Years, 1865–1879

Sergei and Boris had hardly begun their studies when the future premier decided that a change of venue and a change of lifestyle were required if he were to make something of himself. As he tells it:

> Now that we were on our own I began to take life seriously for the first time. I realized that I and Boris had wasted our years in play, had learned nothing but to chatter in French, and that if we continued in this way we would come to nothing. So I began to strengthen my character, began to become my own man and have been so ever since. It was a different story with Boris: having been my parents' favorite he was spoiled and he did not have as strong a character as I.[1]

Sergei does not exaggerate the change that took place, from a feckless youngster into a responsible young man, driven by ambition, determined to use his many talents to achieve whatever goals he set for himself. He would soon show that he had an iron will, an amazing capacity for work coupled with an equally amazing capacity to learn, be it in school or on the job. But he also had within him the ability to empathize and to agonize—in short, a combination of traits that one close observer called a mixture of iron and cotton wool combined into an almost "hysterical temperament."[2] One is reminded of Bismarck, the "Iron Chancellor" with whom he was often compared, who once said that, far from having an iron character, "I am all nerves, so much so that self-control has always been the greatest task of my life and still is."[3]

What lay behind the dramatic change in Sergei? His account clearly suggests sibling rivalry as well a sense of shame that he had failed in his father's eyes and a sudden realization that he was not the man that he had thought himself to be. He felt challenged and was determined to meet that challenge.

His first task was to improve his grades sufficiently to gain admission to the university. Accordingly, he took Boris in tow and, without waiting for permission from his father, decided to go to a place where they would be anonymous, and find a *gimnaziia* teacher who would take them in and help provide them with the coaching they needed. They decided on Kishinev, some hundred miles away, where they took up residence in the home of a bibulous instructor and spent six months cramming under the supervision of faculty members from the local *gimnaziia*. Their efforts bore fruit: they received satisfactory grades and were admitted to Novorossiisk University in 1866. Sergei, having done especially well in the science and mathematics examinations, enrolled in the Physico-Mathematical Faculty of the university, while Boris settled for the less demanding Faculty of Jurisprudence.

Early on in their studies the lives of the young men were abruptly changed by the deaths of their father and maternal grandfather. The father left an estate with few assets and some staggering debts occasioned by a mining venture into which he had been dragged. His widow now had to make ends meet with a small pension provided by the viceroy and some of the grandfather's estate, which Rostislav Fadeev kindly turned over to her. The viceroy also provided Sergei and Boris with small stipends that permitted them to remain in the university. Sergei supplemented his stipend by tutoring members of the Rafalovich family, about whom more later.

With Andrei Fadeev and Julius Witte gone, there was no longer a reason for Julius's widow to remain in Tiflis, where she had no roots. She pulled up stakes and moved to Odessa, where she could be close to Sergei and Boris, with her two daughters and a nursemaid and, so she thought, with the spirit of her late husband.[4] She was later joined by Nadezhda, her spinster sister, and by Rostislav, her brother, when he was terminally ill. From time to time she was visited by Madame Blavatsky. Quite a household, but it provided an anchor. From then on Odessa was Sergei's home base, a city to which he frequently returned in later years and on which he would confer many favors. (We say farewell here to Boris, who played no role in Sergei's later life, and shall henceforth refer to Sergei as Witte.)

Odessa presented a sharp contrast to Tiflis. A young city, established by Catherine the Great on the site of what had been a Turkish garrison, it was the seat of the governor-general of New Russia and Bessarabia. The very name "New Russia" was suggestive of the administrative policy toward the region, which was sparsely settled: the policy encouraged settlement by whoever was willing to move there, be he Russian, Greek, or Jew. It was even more of a cosmopolitan city than Tiflis, one that gave Witte a broadening taste of the world.

Odessa was a charming city with its well-laid-out streets and boulevards. More to the point, it was a lively and growing commercial and financial center, with the life of which Witte would become intimately acquainted. It was a boom town, with more new money than old, the kind of place in which financial hanky-panky could thrive, so well described by Sholem Aleichem in *Menachem Mendl*, a city with a busy stock exchange and many banking houses. One of the largest of the latter was owned by Fedor Rafalovich, a converted Jew, whose children Witte tutored. Witte would maintain ties with the family for the rest of his career.

Even more influential in Witte's development than the Odessa ambience was his university experience. He entered in 1866, at a critical time in the period of Alexander II's great reforms, the year when a student named Dmitrii Karakozov made an unsuccessful attempt on the life of the tsar. Influential conservatives at court, with some of whom Rostislav Fadeev was allied, had some success in convincing the tsar that his educational reforms had fostered the development of revolutionary ferment among students, particularly in the higher schools. Alexander was prompted to issue a statement declaring that "the youth should be taught in the spirit of the truths of religion, respect for property and the observance of the fundamental principles of the social order."[5] Conservatism gained strength at court, but the reforms already introduced remained in place, and additional reforms were still to come.

University reform had a liberating effect. Under Nicholas I, Alexander II's father, the universities had a barracks-like atmosphere. Typical of those times were the remarks that the curator of the University of Kiev delivered to faculty and students at a meeting he had called: "You professors can meet among yourselves, but only to play cards. And you students remember that I will look with an indulgent eye on drunkenness but that a soldier's uniform awaits anyone who is noted for free thinking."[6] A soldier's uniform meant twenty-five years of service.

Alexander II changed all that. His university reform got rid of restrictions that had severely limited admission. Also, he granted a fair degree of autonomy to university faculties. All this quickly changed the university climate, allowing considerable room for academic freedom, which, in turn, permitted the growth of leftist sentiment among students, much to the dismay of the powers that be.

Novorossiisk (New Russia) University started life as the Richelieu Lycée in 1805. In 1835 its upper classes were given university status, and in 1865 it became Novorossiisk University, with a student body of some four hundred. Its faculty was undistinguished at the time, but several were to gain distinction, notably the biologist I.I. Mechnikov, who would go on to win the Nobel Prize as well as some public attention for trumpeting the virtues of yogurt. N.I. Pirogov, the noted pedagogue and surgeon and the former superintendent of the Odessa Educational District, urged that a university in Odessa should disseminate Russian Orthodox influence in the Balkans to counter Catholic efforts in that area. That did not come to be, but the new minister of education, Count D.A. Tolstoi, did invite a Bulgarian professor, "a brother Slav," a man whom the students found to be obnoxious, to join the faculty.[7]

Witte chose to concentrate his studies on mathematics, for which he had already shown a gift. A combination of hard work and extraordinary intelligence indicated that he would be a top-notch mathematician, primarily in the theoretical aspects of the subject. The subject of the dissertation, "On Infinitesimal Quantities," is illustrative of his focus. The work was good enough to earn a French translation.[8]

Although he worked hard in his field, Witte did not abstain from the general life of the university. Like other Russian universities, Novorossiisk was a community where students from the various faculties rubbed elbows, argued about everything from their subjects to the nature of the universe, and flocked to hear popular professors regardless of the subject they addressed. These experiences left him with respect for universities as precious institutions devoted to a broad range of knowledge and to the concept of free inquiry. In later years he would defend what he called "the idea of a university" against those in the government who sought to restrict academic freedom, men who were themselves graduates of elite, specialized schools such as the Imperial School of Jurisprudence. Even though he deplored what he considered the excessive involvement of university students with politics, he would continue to identify himself with them, coming to their defense when the government took harsh steps against them, even though such a stand was not popular with his colleagues.

At the university he quickly noted that most students and some of the faculty were hostile to the established order, that "the idols of the students" were Chernyshevskii, Dobroliubov, and Pisarev, the ardent spokesmen of atheistic and antigovernmental views. Many of the students belonged to discussion groups called "circles." A fellow student writing anonymously many years later asserted that Witte was the head of one such group that included Andrei Zheliabov, who would head a terrorist group that would assassinate Alexander II.[9] That is not the case. Moreover, Witte, thanks to his upbringing and the influence of Uncle Rostislav, was one of the minority of students who were quite devoted to the throne and the Russian Orthodox faith.[10]

Fellow students remembered him for his extraordinary capacity for work, a trait that would be a hallmark throughout his career, and for his faithful execution of duties. For example, as an elected member of the Student Fund (a self-help organization), he and another student were the only ones never to miss a meeting. He was remembered too for his height.[11] Height, combined with drive and ability, make a powerful combination.

Hardworking though he was, Witte appears to have had time for play. He was, after all, only in his late teens. A fellow student remembered him as a leader of a group of "fast" well-to-do students.[12] Witte was far from well-to-do, but most likely he used his earnings from tutoring to splurge. Just what the members of this set did is not specified. Probably they drank some and chased female members of the demimonde, often actresses. In any case, he was so taken up with an actress named Sokolova that he did not participate in competition for a gold medal during his last year at the university. Nonetheless, he graduated at the top of his class. A gangling, gauche, and brilliant young man, he now had to choose a career.

As Witte tells it, his ambition was to become a mathematics professor, but his uncle Rostislav and his mother argued that an academic profession was déclassé.[13] Railroading, at least at the administrative level, was a different matter, so they said. In May 1870, about the time of his graduation, he was appointed to an administrative position with the Odessa Railroad, while still planning to continue efforts to enter academic life. What his thoughts were at the time we do not know. Surely he was torn between two very contrasting career paths. His own version of what happened may be a bit gilded.[14]

Whatever his mood may have been, he began work for the railroad, with Uncle Rostislav, by now a retired general, providing what Russians call *protektsiia* and what Americans call "pull." It was through Fadeev's efforts that, some months later, Witte met Count Vladimir Bobrinskii, minister of ways and communications, who happened to be in Odessa. Probably at Fadeev's urging, the count advised Witte to forget about academe and to devote himself to railroading instead. When Witte responded by saying that if he did as the count suggested, he would have to take time to acquire the degree of engineer of ways and communications, the count brushed the argument aside by declaring that such engineers already had too much power in railroading as it was, and that what the railroads needed was a man like Witte, a man with a good university specialization in mathematics and on-the-job experience.[15] Witte allowed himself to be persuaded.

By this time the Odessa Railroad, which had been government owned, had become a subsidiary of the Russian Steamship and Commercial Company, headed by Nicholas M. Chikhachev, a naval officer with ties to the imperial court. Uncle Rostislav thought he would aid his nephew's career by getting Prince Bariatinskii, now retired, to write a letter of recommendation to Chikhachev. In it the prince praised Witte and urged Chikhachev to help the young man along "if he inspired confidence."[16] In reply Chikhachev wrote that he was very impressed by Witte's performance and would give him a boost as soon as the opportunity arose.[17] The opportunity would soon appear. Fadeev also provided help on another front. With his assistance, Witte was appointed to the honorific post of "official on special assignment" in the chancellery of the governor-general of New Russia and Bessarabia, a post that carried no duties but provided some status.[18] Witte was now earning a comfortable salary, enabling him to live at a hotel and be free of parental supervision.

In entering the world of railroading, Witte found himself in the midst of a new and exciting environment, one of rapid economic and social change that was categorized by various names—modernization, industrialization, and capitalist development. Rapid railroad development played a central role because the country's railroad system was still in its infancy.

In 1835, when an Austrian entrepreneur proposed building a railroad network in their country, the tsar's ministers rejected the proposal, arguing that railroads would not only offer no economic benefit but would also upset the social equilibrium. Tsar Nicholas I overruled them only to the extent of authorizing construction of lines between Tsarskoe Selo and St. Petersburg; St. Petersburg and Moscow, as well as between St. Petersburg and Warsaw and between Warsaw and Vienna. When the Crimean War began, in 1853, the total mileage of Russian railroads was 650, this in the largest country in the world. None of these lines was of any use in the military operations that followed. The war, as we know, had a devastating effect, prompting a major effort to give Russia the railroad system needed to sustain the economy and restore its status as a great power.

The government planned a large network of lines, of which the Odessa Railroad was a major section. Authorization for its construction was given by the tsar in 1863, and work on it was placed in the hands of the governor-general of New Russia and Bessarabia, the Ministry of Ways and Communications, and the Ministry of Finance, with the work to be done by contractors who employed military detachments, peasants, and convicted criminals. Also, the work was to be done as cheaply as possible, on what was considered the American model, with such economies as light rails. By the time Witte entered railroading, traffic was moving on some sections of the Odessa Railroad. It was soon after his entry that the government sold the line to the Russian Steamship and Commercial Company in the expectation that this would produce a synergistic combination that would benefit from the recent opening of the Suez Canal.[19] Witte was a novice entering an enterprise in its swaddling clothes.

It was common in later years, when speaking of Witte's remarkable career, to assert that he began as a mere ticket collector. That was not the case: he began his employment as what would be called a management trainee in later years, getting a preliminary taste of various aspects of railroading, including the collection of tickets. He brought to his work exceptional intelligence, which made for the ability to learn quickly on the job as well as the capacity for hard work. In addition, he had, as he immodestly but correctly put it, "a strong and decisive character."[20] When a problem arose, he faced it energetically and acted decisively, with a penchant for practical solutions, not going by the book when circumstances warranted it. His rough manners and provincial accent might have irritated persons of refinement but were hardly a burden in the less-than-genteel world of railroading, at least to those at the lower levels.

His task was to help make the Odessa Railroad efficient and profitable. There is no evidence that at this point he gave any serious thought to the role of railroads in the larger scheme of the ongoing major reforms. That would come later. What intellectual baggage he brought with him owed its origins to the influence of Uncle Rostislav, whose views can best be described as part Pan-Slav, part Slavophile. Witte did not share all of his uncle's views, but it is evident that he accepted some of Slavophilism, namely, a belief in autocracy, with the tsar being in communion with his people; a firm belief in the Russian Orthodox faith combined with the conviction that the church needed cleansing; and the notion that the village commune was the ideal form of peasant life. In addition, he was touched by the Pan-Slav belief in the brotherhood of Slavic peoples.[21] If anything, Slavophilism, with its misty-eyed perception of what old Russia had been like, was out of alignment with the new Russia that was emerging, a Russia in which railroads would play a vital role. In time Witte would come to shed many of these views, but for the moment his chief concern was the Odessa railroad.

As already indicated, Witte quickly earned Chikhachev's confidence and after only six months on the job was appointed traffic chief of the line, replacing Fedor Shtern, an able man but—in Witte's view, and apparently in Chikhachev's—considered to be insolent, like many Jews.[22] (Witte had stereotypical views about many ethnic groups, including Russians.) Before long Chikhachev was so impressed by his new traffic chief that he considered having him appointed manager of the line, but held back at first because of Witte's youth. Also, there was the fact that Witte did not hold the degree of engineer of ways and communications, a prerequisite for approval of such an appointment by the Ministry of Ways and Communications. Later he did make a stab at it but met with a rebuff from the ministry. Nonetheless, with the passage of time the youthful Witte became manager in all but name.

Hard worker though he was, Witte found time to think and write about public affairs. The press, although far from free, was far more vocal than it had before the press reforms of Alexander II. Several of Witte's relatives, notably Madame Blavatsky, were writers, and, as will be recalled, his sister tried her hand at writing. He had opinions on various matters and the urge to express them, although he admitted later that writing did not come easily to him.

Write he did. Under the striking pseudonym of Zelenyi Popugai (Green Parrot), he contributed articles on current questions to *Pravda*, a local newspaper considered progressive by the standards of those days, one to which some fellow alumni contributed and one with which he would maintain ties for many years. Also, he wrote about the Slavs for *Novorossiiskii telegraf*, another local newspaper, testimony to his ideological leanings. These leanings were also reflected in his contributions to *Den* and *Rus*, periodicals published by I.S. Aksakov, a leading Slavophile.[23]

By the time Witte began his career, Pan-Slavism was attracting many adherents, including clergy, generals, and high government officials, among them the ambassador to Constantinople. Pan-Slavists believed that the Slavic peoples formed a distinct and separate ethnic (some said racial) branch of mankind, that Slavic peoples under Turkish and Austro-Hungarian rule should be liberated and united in a political entity such as a federation tied to Russia, and further that Constantinople should be wrested from the Turks and either become a free city or be placed under Russian rule. That the Polish subjects of the tsar might wish to be liberated was conveniently overlooked.

Uncle Fadeev turned out to be a leading exponent of Pan-Slav ideas and worked closely with Russia's ambassador to Constantinople. In 1869 Fadeev published a series of inflammatory and controversial articles entitled "Opinion Concerning the Eastern Question," which made the point that for Russia to ensure her future, she must cast her lot with her "Slavic brothers," whose help was requisite in the task of destroying the Ottoman and Austro-Hungarian empires. Such an undertaking would, of necessity, entail war with Germany. These views clashed with official foreign policy and made Fadeev persona non grata at court, but not with many in a position to affect policy.

Witte, although very much under his uncle's influence, did not, as far as we know, subscribe to all of these fantastic and dangerous views, but he was clearly in sympathy with the goal of forging links with the Balkan Slavs. So moved, he became vice chairman of the Sts. Cyril and Methodius Slavonic Benevolent Committee of Odessa, which was formed in 1870. It, like similar committees in other major cities, promoted ties with such Slavic peoples as Serbs and Bulgarians, encouraging them to send students to study in Russia, sometimes with unintended consequences, as was the case with the Bulgarian student Stefan Stambulov. A student at a theological seminary in Odessa, he also served as clerk on the committee. He would later serve as Bulgarian prime minister and follow an anti-Russian policy.[24]

In 1875 events took a dramatic turn in the Balkans, spurring the committee to begin acting in a militant manner in that area's affairs. In that year a revolt against the Turkish rulers broke out in Bosnia and Herzegovina and soon spread to Bulgaria, where the Turks acted with such brutality that it turned European, and especially Russian, public opinion against them. In Russia the plight of the rebels roused feverish support for them and hatred of the Turks, even among those cool to Pan-Slavism, a view exemplified by a character in Tolstoy's *Anna Karenina* who remarked: "I must own, up to the time of the Bulgarian atrocities, I couldn't make out why it was that all the Russians were so fond of their Slavonic brethren, while I didn't feel the slightest affection for them."[25]

In the midst of these developments, Witte's life was interrupted by a terrible tragedy that occurred in December 1875 on the Odessa Railroad at the Tiligul embankment on the line between Odessa and Balta. A trainload of recruits tumbled down the embankment on a stretch of the line where the tracks were missing and caught on fire, killing some hundred of the men. Workers had removed the track while making repairs but had failed to put up warning signs at either end of the stretch. Nor had the roadmaster in charge of the operations informed the stationmasters at either end of the line of what was afoot. And at the time of the accident the workers themselves were in a nearby hut, seeking refuge from the blizzard that was raging.[26]

The accident was appalling, the irresponsibility that caused it shocking. Dmitrii Miliutin, the war minister, in a report to the tsar, declared that half the railroad lines in Russia were in the same shape as the Odessa Railroad and that one might expect another tragedy such as had happened at Tiligul to occur at any time.[27] Public opinion, such as it was, demanded that those responsible for the tragedy be punished; blame was fixed on the roadmaster, Chikhachev, and Witte, remote though the responsibility of the last two might be. Witte believed that he and Chikhachev were punished because of what he called antipathy among "educated, liberal people" for those in high places.[28] Investigation of the accident and determination of blame went on and on, while the roadmaster went mad and Chikhachev and Witte continued at their jobs.

Witte continued his tasks at the Slavonic Benevolent Society after working hours. There the tempo picked up dramatically after Serbia went to war against the Ottoman Empire in June 1876 under command of a retired Russian general. As one would expect, sentiment in Russia was fervently pro-Serb, and when it became evident that the Serbs might be defeated, a broad campaign, in which Witte participated, was mounted to recruit volunteers to help "brother Slavs" and to provide these volunteers with the necessary transportation.

Before long, in April 1877, Russia entered the fray against Turkey. Not that the tsar wanted to—far from it—but popular opinion as well as power politics contrived to drag Russia into war. With this, Witte's role changed abruptly from providing maritime transportation to individual volunteers to providing transportation for soldiers on the Odessa Railroad, an effort in which he would play a key role. This was quite a challenge for a man still in his twenties, a challenge that gave him the opportunity to display the qualities that would make him the dominating figure in his country's government—

decisiveness, imagination, practicality, readiness to take risks, and the capacity to learn quickly.

By this time the verdict on the Tiligul disaster was in: short prison terms for Chikhachev and Witte, with the starting date left open. When Grand Duke Nicholas Nikolaevich, who was to serve as commander in chief of the forces in the Balkans, the main theater of war (the other being the Caucasus, where Alexander Witte was serving), sought to discuss with Witte the latter's duties in getting troops to the scene of action, Witte had a disingenuous reply. He would rather start serving his prison term immediately than wait till the end of the war because he might be subject to additional penalties if he failed in his duties. He obviously expected the reply he received, namely, that if Witte carried out his duties successfully, the grand duke would persuade the tsar to annul his sentence.[29] Witte gladly agreed and plunged into the task of supervising the movement of tens of thousands of troops, together with their horses and equipment, along the Odessa Railroad line that connected with a line of the friendly principality of Romania. The troops were then to proceed to the Danube and cross into Bulgaria, where they would engage the enemy, drive on to Constantinople, and force the Turks to sue for peace.

Witte was expected to proceed according to plans worked out in St. Petersburg, plans that optimistically spelled out in minute detail how the movement of trains and troops would be coordinated but failed to take into account the limitations of the real world with which Witte had to deal; these were many indeed, creating formidable challenges. Witte had grown up in a milieu where general-staff types were held in contempt. Instead of trying to conform to the unrealistic plans he received, he relied on his sound common sense and dealt decisively with the challenges he faced.

The challenges were great, for this was a major war with heavy casualties that put a heavy strain on the railroad. Was rolling stock in short supply? Without waiting for authorization, Witte ordered cavalrymen and their horses off the trains some distance from Kishinev, close to the Romanian border, and had them proceed to Kishinev and then go on by train into Romania. Facing a shortage of locomotives because of the practice of having them stand idle while the locomotive's engineer rested, Witte assigned assistants to help man the locomotives around the clock. Was movement along the single-track line slowed up by the practice of waiting for a telegraphic signal from the next station that a troop train had arrived? Well, he had these trains leave at intervals of fifteen minutes or so, without waiting for a signal. Was there a grave shortage of hospital trains to bring back the tens of thousands of wounded? Well, he had freight cars with straw for bedding do the job. He did whatever he could to help troops and equipment to reach the theater of war and the wounded to return as quickly as possible for treatment. Witte put his heart into everything he undertook. This task had a special meaning for him, with his Pan-Slav leanings. His commitment to the war effort was strengthened by the fact that his brother Alexander was in active combat, fighting with exceptional gallantry, and that Uncle Rostislav, although too old for active service, was doing his bit by acting as the representative of the Russian forces then in Montenegro.

A German general described the war as one "between the blind and the one-eyed," to highlight the grave defects on both sides. The Russian high command, inspired by the overblown reports of Turkish weakness provided by the Pan-Slavist ambassador to Constantinople, expected speedy victory. But that was not to be. The war was much longer and bloodier than expected, with the advantage shifting frequently from one side to the other. In the end Russia proved the stronger. By early January 1878 the Turkish forces in Bulgaria were collapsing and the Russians were advancing on the Caucasian front. On January 8, with the capture of Adrianople, the Russians were in a position to take Constantinople. The Turks threw in the towel, signing an armistice on January 19 and a humiliating peace treaty at San Stefano a month later, which provided for independence for Serbia, Romania, and Montenegro, autonomy for Bulgaria, and limited autonomy for Bosnia and Herzegovina, as well as some territorial gains for Russia in the Balkans and the Caucasus. The other great powers, with England in the lead, saw the treaty as one that would give Russia primacy in the Balkans and otherwise threaten their interests, and consequently used the threat of force to compel Russia to agree to a new treaty, signed in Berlin, that cut back Russian influence in the Balkans. The Treaty of Berlin, a bitter pill, increased existing animosity toward England. Nonetheless, Russia had won the war and added some territory, and Serbia, Romania, and Montenegro had won independence.

For Witte, as for so many others of his generation, this was *the* war that was stamped in his memory—victory, sacrifice, the courage and endurance of the Russian soldier, the bloody sieges of Plevna and Shipka Pass, and the feats of remarkable generals such as Loris-Melikov, who was soon to play a political role. He was also aware of the dark side of the war: that "war is hell" went without saying, but in addition to the unavoidable horrors of war, there was the miserable state of the medical and supply services, the venality of the contractors who furnished food and fodder—venality matched by that of supply officers and of Princess Dolgorukaia, the tsar's youthful mistress, who allegedly accepted gifts from contractors. And then there were the grand dukes, nearly a dozen of them, who had been given commands for which they were ill-suited. Add the fact that although the armed forces had come a long way technologically since the Crimean War, they were still behind the times, inferior in some respects to the Turks. Also, Witte would come to know how much the war had weakened his country's finances, which were still recovering from the Crimean War.

Witte received no decorations for his part in the war effort, but Grand Duke Nicholas Nikolaevich expressed his appreciation by assuring Witte that he would recommend that the tsar annul Witte's prison sentence. He kept his word. Alexander II annulled Witte's sentence as well as that of Chikhachev, who commanded the Black Sea defenses during the war. None of this prevented a fruitless investigation of Witte's unauthorized wartime actions. Nor, as will be seen, did the annulment put an end to the Tiligul case.[30]

Chapter 3

St. Petersburg and Kiev, 1879–1891

With the end of the war, Witte's career and private life took a sharp turn. That turn came as a result of the consolidation of the Odessa, Kiev-Brest, and Brest-Gaevo lines into the Southwestern Railroad, creating one of the country's major railroads. The government, with its strong commitment to railroad construction, gave the new company a guarantee of a 5 percent return on its capital, hoping that it would soon be profitable enough to make it on its own.[1] The personnel changes that followed the merger opened the way for advancement to Witte, who accepted an appointment to be chief of the railroad's operational section, a move that entailed a transfer to St. Petersburg. To be sure, he would rather have been appointed traffic chief, but that post was already spoken for. Moreover, it would have entailed moving to Kiev, which would have been embarrassing because of a scandal involving his wife-to-be.

Toward the end of the war, Witte, verging on thirty, was smitten by a very pretty young woman named Spiridonova, a Kievan. She had left her husband, a compulsive gambler, and come with her daughter, Sonia, to Odessa, pursued by a scandal. Her wastrel husband, unable to pay his debts, had persuaded her to steal some jewelry from her sister, assuming that the sister would hold her tongue. Not so. Criminal charges were brought against Spiridonova, who managed to wriggle out of them through the good offices of an amenable judge.

It was then that she made her way to Odessa, where Witte met and wooed her, prevailing on her to seek a divorce, which Eastern Orthodox canon law permitted in the case of adultery. The hapless husband, in return for a small sum of money, presumably supplied by Witte, admitted adultery, and the divorce was granted by the church, leaving Spiridonova, as the innocent party, free to remarry.[2]

Another reason for Witte's willingness to move to the capital was the invitation to participate in the work of the Commission for the Investigation of Railroad Operations, chaired by Count E. T. Baranov. It was brought into being in response to the war minister's report to the tsar, already referred to, warning that too many of the railroads, most of them privately owned, were ill-prepared to serve in the event of war. Also included in the tasks of the Baranov Commission was the study of the fitness of the railroads to serve commerce and industry. Its work was interrupted by the war and resumed once the hostilities were over.[3] For Witte participation in the work was an opportunity both to learn more about the railroad system and to make a contribution to the commission's work, with obvious benefits to his career.

So he and Spiridonova took up residence in St. Petersburg, where they were married. He adopted the daughter, but neither he nor his wife had much affection for the girl, who was left in the care of her grandmother in Kiev. What the Witte family thought of this odd marriage is not known but can easily be imagined.

The couple had barely settled in their new quarters, on Troitskii Street, when late one night a servant awakened Witte with the news that a gendarme and several policemen were outside and wished to see him. Without being offered an explanation, Witte was hauled off to a nearby police station, where he was told that he was being held on orders of General Adelson, commandant of the Winter Palace. Rather bewildered, Witte feared that his arrest had something to do with the ongoing campaign against revolutionary terrorists and that somehow he had come under suspicion for having employed as a secretary a man with ties to the revolutionaries.[4] That fear was dispelled when he was taken to the Winter Palace, where he learned that the Tiligul disaster had come back to haunt him. He was told that, by orders of the tsar, Chikhachev was under house arrest and that he, Witte, was to serve a short term at the Haymarket Guardhouse.

Soon thereafter he was given an explanation by General Annenkov, who was acting as chief administrative assistant to Baranov. He was told that at the end of the war, the minister of justice had advised the tsar that he did not have the authority to annul criminal sentences and that, moreover, public opinion demanded that those responsible for Tiligul pay a price. The tsar accepted the counsel but reduced the sentences to a few weeks. Even so, Witte got off more lightly as a result of Baranov's plea to the tsar that he needed Witte's services: it was arranged that for the duration of his sentence Witte be released from the guardhouse during the day.[5]

For the next few months Witte managed to participate in the work of the commission as well as carry out his duties with the Southwestern Railroad. The Baranov Commission was a huge body, what with including officials from the Ministry of Ways and Communications and other agencies plus subcommissions made up of railroad engineers, economists, landowners, industrialists, and merchants who had some knowledge of railroad problems. Their efforts, which dragged on for years, produced mountains of data, much of which went into a six-volume report. Much, if not most, of the commission's work was fruitless, given the vested interests of so many of the participants.[6] It did produce one substantial result, a railroad charter that, among other things, provided for a council on railroad affairs, under the Ministry of Ways and Communications, that included representatives from several government agencies as well as some from the private sector.

The charter was largely the work of Witte, who, although still a small frog in a big pond, left his mark on the commission's deliberations. In so doing he became more acquainted than he had been with the hazards one encountered in dealing with the bureaucracy. Because the proposed council would cut into the power of some bureaucrats, the proposed charter met concerted opposition in the State Council, the body that had to give or withhold its blessings before the charter reached Tsar Alexander. Witte, being the chief object of the opposition, was summoned by General Loris-Melikov, who had been entrusted by the sovereign with implementing what was called the "dictatorship of the heart," a program to deal with terrorism and other manifestations of unrest then plaguing the country. It was a friendly summons. The general, an Armenian from the Caucasus who was acquainted with the Witte family, advised the young man about the value of tact, not one of Witte's strong points. In the end, the charter became law.[7]

Witte was moving up in the world, becoming acquainted with the powers that be, both in railroading and in government operations. In the process he increased his store of knowledge about the vested interests he would have to take into account, among them those of the so-called railroad kings, notably his new boss, Jan Bloch.

Bloch, a converted Jew from Warsaw, his home base, was typical of the new breed, a self-made man who had moved from small-scale operations into railroading and banking, acquiring money, power, influence, and the airs of a grandee. From time to time he would visit St. Petersburg to deal with his railroad's business, leaving the chief burden of directing affairs to Ivan A. Vyshnegradskii, vice chairman of the board. Witte wrote that Bloch, "like most Jews," was "insolent," and Witte, unlike Vyshnegradskii, would not stoop to ingratiate himself with his boss. As might be expected, he did not win Bloch's affection, but he did win his respect. Within a year of his arrival in St. Petersburg, Witte was transferred to Kiev, center of the railroad's operations, with a mandate to make those operations profitable.[8]

Unlike Odessa, Kiev was an ancient city, almost a millennium old, but like Odessa, its inhabitants were mainly newcomers, drawn to it by its commerce and industry. A large segment of the population was Ukrainian, and the surrounding area was Ukrainian, but the city itself was Russified. (The Ukrainians were considered an inferior branch of the Russian nationality and their language nothing more than a dialect that was barred from the printed page.)[9]

A significant minority of the population was Polish, a reminder of the days when Kiev was part of the Polish realm. Although Kiev had been annexed by Russia in the seventeenth century, Poles remained a presence as landowners in both the city proper and its environs. In response to the Polish revolt of 1863 St. Petersburg dealt harshly with Poles in Kiev as well as elsewhere, striving, among other things, to eliminate them from the civil service.

And then there was a Jewish minority, concentrated in the Podol, a low-lying area close to the Dnieper River. The Jews' history in Kiev was a checkered one, running the gamut from the right of residence to total exclusion. It goes without saying that Kievan Jews endured the same official anti-Semitic treatment as Jews elsewhere in Russia.

In the course of Witte's residence in the city he had occasion to employ members of these three groups. Not that he was free of prejudice toward them, clinging to commonly held stereotypes that Ukrainians were sly, upperclass Poles given to extravagance of manner, and Jews greedy as well as insolent. Nonetheless, he believed in "careers open to talent," following the policy of using able men regardless of their ethnicity or religion and backing them up when necessary.

At the time that Witte and his wife took up residence in Kiev, the revolutionary movement was a mounting threat to the government. He, as expected, plunged into his work with his usual vigor, but it would not be too long before he would find himself embroiled in counterrevolutionary efforts. So before we deal with his work with the Southwestern Railroad it seems appropriate to note briefly the circumstances in which Witte became involved.

The revolutionary movement at this time was dominated by its terrorist wing, Narodnaia volia (the People's Will), which was led by Andrei Zheliabov, Witte's fellow alumnus. After its campaign of assassinating hated officials had failed to frighten the government into submission, it had decided to make the tsar its target. One of its many near misses came in February 1880, when dynamite it had detonated in the Winter Palace failed to kill the tsar but killed many others. The act set off a wave of panic. Grand Duke Constantine Nikolaevich wrote in his diary: "We are reliving the Terror, but with this difference: during the revolution the Parisians saw their enemy face-to-face. We neither see them nor do we know them."[10]

Reluctantly, Alexander II admitted that stronger measures than were already in effect were needed, and he established the Supreme Commission under General Loris-Melikov, which was authorized to employ whatever means were needed to eradicate what he called the *kramola* (sedition), while at the same time proposing measures to improve the ties between the sovereign and his people. This quixotic policy of the carrot and the stick was soon dubbed the "dictatorship of the heart."

The stick entailed encouraging governors, governors-general, and the like to employ even sterner measures than before to ferret out and deal with revolutionaries, while Loris-Melikov and his associates would use both the stick to direct the counterrevolutionary campaign and the carrot by proposing ameliorative reforms such as a representative body with advisory powers. In Kiev the stick was already in use.

Governor-General Michael Chertkov, a rather stupid type, had already been working assiduously to root out revolutionaries. He had his work cut out for him. On February 11, 1879, revolutionaries engaged in a rare and foolhardy action, a shootout with gendarmes sent to arrest them. They were arrested and tried by a military court, which sentenced four of them to be hanged and sixteen to long terms of exile and hard labor. The harsh sentences failed to stifle revolutionary ferment in the city, with new recruits, many of them expelled university students, joining the movement. In response, Chertkov became even more energetic in his campaign against "sedition," employing methods so egregious, even for such troubled times, that he was subjected to an investigation that ended with his replacement by Alexander von Drenteln, former chief of the political police.[11]

All this occurred shortly before Witte's arrival in Kiev. Probably under the influence of Fadeev, who was critical of many of the policies of Alexander II, Witte took a dim view of the current counterrevolutionary tactics, but he was in no position to help shape policy, at least not until the assassination of the tsar on March 1, 1881.

That evening, while Witte and his wife were attending a play, they learned of the tragic event. They hurried home from the theater, where he dashed off a letter to Uncle Rostislav, then residing in St. Petersburg, condemning the ongoing antiterrorist operations, comparing them to the use of a steam hammer to crush a grain of sand. What he proposed was a covert operation, manned by volunteers of irreproachable character, to seek out and do away with would-be regicides.[12] His was not the only proposal for a new modus operandi being considered in those days. It was some time before he received a reply, an encouraging one, informing him that his proposal had been well received and had been shown to the new tsar, Alexander III, and that he would soon be asked to come to the capital. And so it happened. Witte was received by Count Ilarion Vorontsov-Dashkov, then temporarily in charge of imperial security, a friend of the Witte family.[13] The count turned Witte over to his aide-de-camp, Count Paul (Bobby) Shuvalov, who inducted Witte into the newly formed secret Sviashchennaia druzhina (Holy Brotherhood). Shuvalov, who, it should be noted, was a morphine addict, instructed Witte in the rules, rituals, and operations of the Brotherhood.

The term *druzhina* has many shades of meaning. In this case it conjures up the image of a medieval Russian warrior, a member of a princely guard, a formidable-looking man astride an equally formidable-looking horse, ready to fight to the death to destroy his lord's enemies, with the difference that the members of the Holy Brotherhood were engaged in a clandestine struggle to defend their sovereign. The Brotherhood was a hierarchical society in which all but the top echelon was to know only the person directly above him and to know only what he was assigned to do. A member had to take an oath on the Bible to defend the tsar and fight "sedition." How many became members we do not know, but what is known is that the aristocracy was well represented, particularly at the top, and that among its members were the composer Peter Ilich Tchaikovsky and A.M. Bezobrazov, who would later become Witte's mortal enemy. Witte himself was assigned by Shuvalov to be head of the Kievan branch.[14]

The Holy Brotherhood, which was well financed, engaged in a variety of clandestine activities considered consistent with its aims. One would have expected to find elimination of terrorists at the top of the list, but from what we know there was only one planned attempt, in which Witte had an indirect role, and that one came to naught.[15] The terrorists who died during the brief span of the Brotherhood's existence did so on the gallows at the hands of official hangmen, not in some back alley at the hands of a Brotherhood member or agent.

The Brotherhood was no exception to the rule that clandestine organizations are usually unable to conceal the fact of their existence even when they conceal their operations. Soon its existence was common knowledge. Some called it "a state within a state," which was justified to the extent that it rivaled the secret police. The gathering of intelligence was a major activity, one that Witte assisted by reporting on the political mood in southern Russia.[16] In an attempt to identify revolutionary students, the Brotherhood operated a tavern in Kiev intended to attract university students, whose attitudes were monitored by its agents, while at St. Petersburg University a secret organization was installed to collect the names of students with revolutionary leanings.[17]

The Brotherhood engaged in covert diplomacy, attempting in vain to negotiate an agreement with revolutionary leaders in exile for a cease-fire to be observed until after the coronation of Alexander III in return for the promise of some political reforms.[18] Also, it ventured into the field of "black" propaganda, publishing a journal named *Volnoe slovo* (Free Word) for clandestine circulation in Russia, posing as the organ of Zemskii soiuz (Zemstvo Union). There was, of course, no such organization. Witte was one of its pseudonymous contributors.[19] In addition, he is said to have been the pseudonymous author of a counterrevolutionary pamphlet published in Berlin for clandestine dissemination in Russia.[20]

Clandestine organizations tend to be bizarre and often ridiculous by their very nature and because of the characters they attract. The Holy Brotherhood was no exception. Blessed with a solid fund of common sense, Witte soon found himself thoroughly repelled when he saw the organization turning "into a ludicrous, possibly shameful, affair," and he decided to give up his membership.[21] This he did, but under the influence of Fadeev he continued for some time to participate in the publication of "black" propaganda.

As the panicky mood in the higher circles that had served as the rationale for the Holy Brotherhood began to subside and some of its shenanigans became public, hostility toward what was being perceived as a fifth wheel began to rise in places where it counted. C.P. Pobedonostsev, the reactionary overprocurator of the Holy Synod of the Russian Orthodox Church, who had the ear of the tsar, became increasingly convinced that the organization had no place in a well-ordered state. And the newly appointed minister of interior, Count D.A. Tolstoi, advised Alexander that "a colony for young thugs is the right place for Count Bobby (P.P.) Shuvalov and Co."[22] Both Tolstoi and Pobedonostsev knew that some of the leaders supported mildly liberal and Slavophile ideas, such as strengthening the Zemstvos and freeing the Orthodox Church from state domination, and they succeeded in persuading the tsar that the Brotherhood had to go. The order to close up shop came at the end of December 1882.

By this time, reaction, as personified by Pobedonostsev and Tolstoi, was in the ascendant and the belief of Fadeev and his comrades that police methods alone would not suffice to produce calm was ignored. Instead, under the new dispensation so-called exceptional laws increased the police powers of governors-general, governors, and other administrators; censorship was made more repressive; the hold of the state over the established church was made tighter; the role of the landed nobility was enhanced at the expense of the peasantry; the position of ethnic minorities, particularly the Jews, was made more difficult; and educational policy took a marked conservative turn. Many of the restrictive measures were issued in the form of temporary legislation that was to be allowed to lapse when the country had calmed down, but "temporary" tended to become permanent. Firm control was now the order of the day, encouraging a prominent journalist to write: "Stand up gentlemen. The government is here—the government is returning."[23]

Clearly, what was happening was not to Witte's liking, as is evident from his memoirs, in which he condemns Pobedonostsev as a man incapable of positive thought and denounces him for helping set the political clock back. He also expresses anger at Tolstoi for his policies with respect to education and the peasantry. But he excuses Alexander III, whom he came to admire fulsomely, for acceding early in his reign to unwise policies.[24]

Witte remained committed for some time to the beliefs he had imbibed from Fadeev, who died in 1883. He continued to write for the Slavophile Aksakov's *Rus*, which in 1885 published an article by Witte in which he raised the fear that the development of capitalism would transform factory workers into robots.[25] But with Fadeev gone and with experience in the real world he would eventually shed most of his Slavophile and Pan-Slav views, although to the end of his days he would consider himself an "Aksakovian nationalist."[26] Before leaving the subject of the Holy Brotherhood, it should be noted that Witte's part in it helped his career by bringing him to the attention of the tsar and strengthening his ties with Vorontsov-Dashkov, who would remain an important figure at court for years to come.[27]

Witte's work with the Holy Brotherhood was a distraction that did not interfere with his work on the railroad. He was an important man in a major city as well as in the world of railroading, earned a handsome salary, was married to a pretty woman, and lived in a fashionable district with neighbors such as the estranged wife of Grand Duke Nicholas Nikolaevich. Although he maintained close ties with his friends and family in Odessa, he quickly became part of the Kievan scene. Such was his energy and capacity for hard work that he found time to enter vigorously into Kievan public discourse.

To the extent permitted by the censors he aired his views on controversial questions in *Rus*, the conservative *Moskovskie vedemosti*, and Kievan newspapers.[28] Mostly he dealt with topics concerning railroading, but he also commented on matters such as student unrest at the local university (taking the side of the students in a disciplinary case, much to the dismay of the faculty) and the growth of industrial capitalism. He even ventured into the realm of belles lettres with a feuilleton entitled "Monologue of a Locomotive."[29]

He savored the give-and-take of polemics, displaying an unusual aptitude for getting to the heart of an argument. And he was not one to flee from controversy. Finding himself under attack by a leading Kievan newspaper concerning railroad policy in general and the operations of his own railroad in particular, he established his own newspaper, *Kievskoe slovo*. And since he did not think it appropriate to be identified as publisher, he appointed A.Ia. Antonovich as his stand-in.[30] This was not as big an enterprise as one might think; most newspapers were modest, poorly financed ventures.

As so often happens, one thing led to another. In this case debate about freight rates prompted Witte to write a short work entitled *Principles of Railroad Freight Rates*, published in 1883 (about which more later). It was hardly the kind of work ripe for best-sellerdom, but it sold well enough to merit a second edition. A silent helper in the writing was S.I. Sychevskii, a Shakespearean scholar who had fallen on hard times and had been helped by

Witte with a railroad job.[31] This was to be but one of many cases in which Witte had a silent collaborator, for he was a very busy man and, as he wrote later, "I do not like to write."[32] But he did want to air his views, albeit without acknowledging help. The book both helped build his reputation and build his railroad's earnings.

The Southwestern Railroad, eighteen hundred miles long, mostly single-track, and with some thirty thousand employees, ran from the Romanian border through Kishinev, Odessa, and Kiev to Gaevo. In the process it crossed Bessarabia, "New" Russia, western Ukraine, and Belorussia, with connections to Austro-Hungarian, German, and Romanian lines. It was one of the longest lines in Russia, the bulk of its business being the hauling of agricultural products. The line was both a product of economic growth and a spur to further growth.

As I.V. Hessen, who knew Witte well, observed, this man brought luster to every position he held, rather than basking in the light cast by high position.[33] With a much larger railroad to work with and with greater authority than he had previously held, he was in a strategic position to demonstrate his extraordinary ability as well as his thirst for work and acclaim. And he was, as one associate put it, practical "from head to toe." Witte had little patience with theory not based on experience. He was practical without being mired in petty detail, as was the minister of ways and communications, who took an inordinate interest in the toilet facilities at passenger stations but not in more important railroad problems. Nor was Witte a bean counter. His passion was for major problems and the means of coping with them. In this situation the question was how to put the Southwestern Railroad on the path to profitability.

As was the case in Odessa, he surrounded himself with able men, regardless of their ethnicity, including V.V. Maksimov, a Russian; A.A. Abragamson, a Jew; E.K. Ziegler von Schaffhausen, probably a Baltic German; and B.F. Maleshevskii, a Pole. As Witte wrote, with his usual and largely justified bravado: "In whatever post I have served I have been fortunate enough to be surrounded by a galaxy of able and talented subordinates. This is . . . because I have the highly developed knack of finding the right people, of evaluating their strengths and weaknesses."[34] To men such as these he delegated considerable responsibility without loosening the reins. And then there were those such as N.A. Demchinskii, whom Witte characterized as "representative of a type of talented but unstable Russian who goes from one enthusiasm to another."[35] Demchinskii was a second-rate railroad engineer but an able writer. Witte made use of his writing skills, as he was to do with many others.

In Witte's view, the chief problem bedeviling the railroads was the chaotic and irrational system of freight rates. Privately owned railroads were free of government control over freight rates. They were not required to make their rates public, and they did not. They were free to give secret rebates to favored customers, and they did. These railroads were in private hands, but they could and did feed at the public trough in the form of governmental payments to cover shortfalls in earnings that the government had guaranteed as incentives for construction of the lines.

He was convinced that the remedy was a set of governmental rules that would require rational setting of rates and total public disclosure. He had brought the problem to the attention of the Baranov Commission, had written articles on the subject in a professional journal, and, as noted, had published a book on the subject.[36]

He followed his own recommendations in his efforts to make his line profitable, making use of his mathematical expertise. This was only part of his energetic and innovative efforts to increase earnings. He saw to the construction of feeder lines, the opening of new stations, the placing of agents at border stations, and the provision of loans to shippers. Also under his aegis, the railroad's pension system for permanent employees was rescued by Maleshevskii, a skilled mathematician and a veteran railroad man, who, by applying actuarial principles based on reliable statistics, put the system on a sound basis.[37] All in all, on Witte's watch the Southwestern Railroad became the best line in the land.

His work was recognized in company headquarters, where an effort was made to have him promoted to manager of the railroad, but such an act required confirmation by the Ministry of Ways and Communications, which at first stubbornly adhered to its policy that such a post could be filled only by a railroad engineer. But when the post became vacant in 1886, the ministry, given Witte's brilliant record, could no longer demur; it broke with precedent and confirmed the nomination of Witte to become manager.[38]

The following year, with Vyshnegradskii's appointment as minister of finance, Witte found himself in greener pastures than Kiev. The new finance minister asked him for recommendations about how to reduce the huge subsidies that the government was paying the privately owned railroads to cover their shortfalls. For some years the Ministry of Finance had been concerned over the freedom enjoyed by privately owned companies to do as they pleased about freight (and passenger) rates, including the freedom to engage in savage fare cutting to stifle competition. This state of affairs made for survival of the fittest, which did not suit the interests of the government, which sought what it considered desirable economic growth. Such competition had practical as well as political consequences. First of all, a drop in earnings for weaker companies—a drop often inflated by "creative" bookkeeping—meant an increased drain on the imperial treasury. Second, it weakened government protectionist efforts to nurture industry. For example, in the area close to the Baltic Sea, companies that served its ports sought to ensure full freight cars on return trips by offering very low rates to foreign exporters, thus giving them an advantage in the Russian market. Rate wars often induced shippers to use circuitous routes to save money. Some practices hurt regions the government was trying to develop. Freight rate anarchy disquieted not only the Ministry of Finance but also the Ministry of Ways and Communications, the Office of the State Controller, and the Ministry of State Domains. Further pressure for action came from large landowners, with their considerable political power, and merchants involved in the export of grain, which accounted for about one-third of the freight carried.[39]

Witte's response to Vyshnegradskii's request included what he had already expressed as well as ambitious recommendations for governmental action. He proposed the creation of a department of railroad affairs under the Ministry of Finance that would supervise and regulate the setting of rates on all railroads as well as financial dealings between the government and lines that benefited from government-guaranteed returns. He recommended enactment of a law requiring railroads to publish their rate schedules. Further, he proposed establishment of an interagency committee, to be headed by the chairman of the new department, to review rates already enforced as well as those proposed. It was evident from what followed that he expected to be named chairman. But, what with bureaucratic infighting, there was no assurance that the proposed department would ever see the light of day, at least not until an accident that might have killed the tsar occurred at Borki, an event that would mark a turning point in Witte's career. To learn why, we need to go back a bit.

It was the practice that when the imperial train was on the tracks of a given company, an official of that company accompanied the train to see that all went well. On one occasion before Borki when the task fell to Witte, he created a fuss over a proposed train schedule that had been sent to him by Admiral Possiet, the minister of ways and communications. He informed the admiral that the speed called for was a dangerous one, considering the weight of the train, its two locomotives, and the condition of the track, and threatened not to be on the train unless the speed was cut. This was contumacious behavior and was so construed by the tsar and his entourage, but Witte stood up for his action, insisting that the sovereign's safety was his prime concern.[40]

His concern for the tsar's safety was soon justified. On October 17, 1888, the imperial train jumped the track near Borki, on the Kursk-Kharkov-Azov line, killing twenty-two and injuring dozens more but sparing Alexander III and his immediate family, who were having lunch in the dining car. There were many who chose to believe that he was saved by providence (a church was later built in Borki to mark the event) and others who chose to believe the unfounded story that he had saved himself and his fellow diners by displaying superhuman strength in supporting the car's roof on his back while it was collapsing.[41] And then there were those who chose to believe that the wreck was the work of revolutionaries, a plausible explanation given their record, but untrue.

Witte was among the many investigators summoned to Borki to determine the cause of the accident. Much of what he found pointed the finger at Admiral Possiet. But how to present the facts? He turned to A.F. Koni, a noted jurist, who was one of the investigating team and with whom he was acquainted. He confided in him that he was expecting a major appointment and that therefore he could not afford to antagonize Admiral Possiet. If he told all he knew, the admiral would turn against him and block the appointment. The jurist advised him to tell all, for both moral and practical reasons, but he did advise Witte how best to phrase his report. In the end, Witte produced a rather circumspect report, omitting some details that might damage the admiral, but what he included was damaging enough.[42] In the end, because of what Witte and others reported, Possiet's position became untenable, and a month after Borki he was replaced by General G.E. Paucker. Possiet's fall was coupled with Witte's rise, for as a result of the Borki accident, the tsar looked with favor on the outspoken Witte, who came to regard the accident as a turning point in his career.[43] It was indeed, for with the tsar's favor he was to begin a meteoric career in government.

Evidence of this favor was quick in coming. After Witte's recommendations to Vyshnegradskii had been considered by an ad hoc committee, the tsar issued an edict establishing the Department of Railroad Affairs in the Ministry of Finance on March 8, 1889. Two days later Witte was appointed director of the department.

As Witte recalled it, he peremptorily refused the offer of the directorship when it was offered to him by Vyshnegradskii because "he had no intention of leaving an important position, with a high salary, a position that gave me independence, for a bureaucratic post, although one of high status." Witte went on to say that the finance minister informed him that there was no choice because it was the tsar's wish that he accept the post, that the tsar was so impressed by the fact that Witte had been right about the speed of the imperial train that he "had big plans for him." Witte said he agreed to accept the post while managing to extract a larger salary than the post usually carried.[44] Witte clearly tarted up the facts, as already indicated. He wanted the post even though there were costs entailed: he would suffer a drop in income and, as he noted, diminution in independence, and he would be entering the poisonous atmosphere of the St. Petersburg bureaucracy. Outweighing these costs were the opportunity to deal with the problems being experienced by the whole railroad system and the power and status that came with the post.

And what a jump in status it was. The new post carried with it the civil service rank of actual state councilor, which put Witte in the fourth rank of the Table of Ranks that Peter the Great had established. When Witte gave up his honorific position in the civil service in 1880, he had the rank of titular councilor, which put him in the ninth rank of the Table of Ranks. Had he been a full-time civil servant, it would have taken him fifteen years through automatic promotions to reach the fifth rank, in which he might have remained for the rest of his career, for promotion from that rank was at the pleasure of the tsar. Here he was in the fourth rank, having gotten the civil service equivalent of a promotion from captain to major general. Small wonder that this appointment created a sensation in bureaucratic circles and beyond.

Witte's wife was not thrilled at the thought of exchanging their comfortable way of life in Kiev for a more constricted one in the capital. To make things worse, Sonia, her unloved daughter, had finished her schooling and had come to live with them.[45] But his career was on the rise, and he had clear and bold ideas concerning what he would do in his new post. Moreover, he had ideas about the country's economy in general. He was moving away from the Slavophile bias against industrialization. He had become acquainted with the work of Friedrich List and in the very year of his new appointment published a short work entitled *Natsionalnaia ekonomiia i Fridrikh List* (The National Economy and Friedrich List), about which more later.

Toward the end of his life he would say that the happiest years of his career were spent in the south, that is, Kiev and Odessa.[46] He was leaving behind a region where he felt comfortable, had friends, and earned an excellent salary, moving to a city that was physically and spiritually colder but offered more scope for one such as he, an ambitious man with ideas.

Chapter 4

Monsieur Vite, 1889–1892

Some time after Witte had become director he was being referred to privately as Monsieur Vite (Mr. Speedy), a play on his surname, which in transliteration from the Cyrillic alphabet is Vitte.[1] This was in derision of the low speed of Russian trains, an average of twenty miles an hour—the result of the use of light rails in construction, the prevalence of single-track lines, and the practice of stopping at every station. More important, "Monsieur Vite" was a reference of sorts to Witte's rapid rise and the belief that he was power hungry. Many accused Witte of being motivated solely by the lust for power. No question that he sought power. No question that he was, as even those who held him in high esteem acknowledged, quite egocentric and power hungry.[2] Some seek power for its own sake, others to do something they think needs to be done, but there are precious few power seekers who are not egotists. Witte, like other major figures, including Bismarck and de Gaulle, was able to identify the interests of his country with his own interests.

Witte had tasted life in St. Petersburg, but not as a member of the capital's upper bureaucracy, which, like others of its kind, tended to be cumbersome, snobbish, clannish, and given to gossip that was nastier than in other capitals. Perhaps it was the miserable weather. The bureaucratic spirit discouraged initiative, encouraged the emission of mountains of paper written in a fulsome and archaic language called "chancery," and produced molehills of result. This spirit produced a studied indifference toward work in many ministries. As Baron Nicholas E. Wrangel recalls being told when he asked for work:

> You want to work? How odd! Don't you know that that a civil servant who works is a lost man? There are only two kinds of civil servants, you know. There are the needy, who do the same job day after day, and end up by being good for nothing else. Then there are the gentlemen, who don't do anything, but conserve their mental faculties and in a few years become State Councillors, and who can get anything they want, if they know how to go about it. You must choose.[3]

That answer had to be taken with more than a grain of salt, but it was the case that many civil servants, particularly in the Ministry of Foreign Affairs, managed to make careers without doing much of anything. The Ministry of Finance was more fortunate, thanks to a series of able ministers, but it was not free of deadwood.

It would take Witte, accustomed as he was to independence, hard work, and intolerance of nonsense, some time to adjust to his new world without becoming a different person. In addition to coping with the bureaucratic world, he had to deal with Vyshnegradskii, an able man but a hard taskmaster, an insomniac who kept strange hours to which he required his subordinates to conform, and someone who took such a narrow view of his duties that he was described as "a cashier rather than a minister."[4] Witte, who would later lament that assistant ministers spent much effort trying to replace their superiors, may have harbored such an ambition early on, as evidenced by the fact that he chose to speak critically of his superior at the salon of Alexandra Bogdanovich, a notorious gossip.[5] Nonetheless, he was considered Vyshnegradskii's man and did, in fact, work closely with him.

As a newcomer, he was subject to critical inspection by bureaucrats and socialites. The verdict was mixed.[6] His remarkable intelligence, his height, and his forceful personality were impressive, but his rough manners and equally rough speech raised hackles. To envision the impression he made and continued to make, one should think of a very intelligent and towering backwoodsman becoming an important member of a select club whose members had refined manners, spoke with a perfect St. Petersburg accent, and most likely were products of elite schools such as the Imperial School of Jurisprudence or the Tsarskoe Selo Lycée. The result? Witte the outsider. Witte could have adapted himself by improving his manners and speech but chose to remain a diamond in the rough, refusing to obey the old adage "When in Rome, do as the Romans do." He was the kind of outsider who regarded adaptation as a form of weakness, which is not to say that he could not seek to be ingratiating when it suited him. If his wife made any attempt to smooth the rough edges, there is no sign that she succeeded.

In organizing the new department, Witte brought in several colleagues from the Southwestern Railroad, no easy task given the bureaucracy's aversion to outsiders. Also, he enticed several already in the ministry to join him. In the process he was bold enough to bring in V.I. Kovalevskii, a very able man who was under a cloud for innocently having given shelter to the notorious revolutionary Nechaev. Always the strong leader, Witte, unlike Vyshnegradskii, continued his practice of delegating much of the work to his colleagues. As usual, he continued to grow with the job, learning more about the empire, the economy, and the railroad system.

Even as he was organizing his new domain he had to deal quickly with his first priority, that of putting the freight rate system on a rational basis. That was easier said than done, given the pressures from other ministries, including the Ministry of the Imperial Court (which was responsible for the management of the vast land holdings of the imperial family), as well as landed nobles and merchants involved in the grain trade. Small wonder that a Grain Section within the department was soon established and began holding meetings that included both government and nongovernment representatives. The ministry was seeking to increase the profitability of the railroads while at the same time seeking lower rates for grain shipments intended for export, since such shipments accounted for much of the country's export earnings.

Some two months after the creation of the department, a conference, attended by officials as well as major landowners, was held to consider grain freight rates. Then came nearly a hundred meetings on the subject. Witte's experience with the Baranov Commission had prepared him for such grinding of the governmental mill. Not a mellifluent speaker, he was, nonetheless, a persuasive one, capable of overwhelming his listeners with the force of his argument. Finally, on November 15, 1889, temporary regulations, later made permanent, lowering freight rates on grain shipments intended for export as well as for some domestic markets went into effect. Subsequently rates for other freight and for passengers were regulated.[7] It came as no surprise that the large grain-exporting landowners and merchants benefited from the new rates while the railroads benefited less despite the increase in grain freight that resulted, but the net result of regulation was favorable for both the government and the railroads.

In the course of this work, which involved dealing with many noble landowners, Witte's unfavorable impressions of the landed nobility, formed during his time with the Odessa and Southwestern Railroads, were only strengthened. Among other things, he had come to take a dim view of those Russians who had taken over estates from Polish landowners whose land had been confiscated as a result of the Polish revolt of 1863. He would refer to them as "artistes on tour," who knew less about agriculture than their peasants. As for those Polish nobles who were able to hold on to their land, he characterized them as being more solicitous of their cattle than of their peasants. He felt, too, that "many of the aristocracy are unbelievably avaricious hypocrites, scoundrels and good-for-nothings," some of them with high positions at the imperial court.[8] All in all, his experience thus far, fortified by his later experience as finance minister, left him with a low opinion of much of the landed nobility, even though he prided himself on being a hereditary noble, albeit not a landed one. Yet he had to take into account that the landed nobility formed a powerful group considered by the tsar to be his good right arm.

During his tenure as director Witte enlarged his ken of the Russian Empire. In the autumn of 1890 he accompanied Vyshnegradskii on an inspection trip to Russian Turkestan and the Russian protectorate of Bukhara.

Russian Turkestan was a vast, thinly populated, largely Muslim area. Its conquest was the work of generals stationed close to its border, who had the support of higher-ups in the foreign office, who in turn justified such expansionism as being a "civilizing mission"—comparable to what the British claimed to be doing in expanding their control in northwest India. Uncle Fadeev had expressed a similar view, that Russia had a mission in Asia, one for which she was better endowed spiritually than other powers. The drive was also supported by textile manufacturers with a mundane interest in the cotton grown there, a matter of interest as well to the Ministry of Finance.

The trip was an eye-opener. First there was a stopover in Tiflis, now accessible by railroad, and from there they went to Baku, an oil center, of interest to John D. Rockefeller and the Rothschilds, among others. From there they crossed the Caspian to the western terminus of the still-incomplete Trans-Caspian Railroad. Then it was on through an area that evoked memories of Marco Polo, Genghis Khan, and Tamerlane, of the fabled Silk Road between China and Europe, the route that brought conquerors from the East. They could not help but spend some time sightseeing, but not to the extent of neglecting their duties.

First there was the railroad, which was being constructed to speed up the pacification of Russian Turkestan as well as for use in the event of conflict with England over Afghanistan. In time, it would serve economic purposes as well. In charge of construction was General M.N. Annenkov, with whom Witte had a run-in during the war with Turkey, and among the military engineers was Prince M.I. Khilkov, who would later figure in Witte's career. Begun in 1880, the line had reached Samarkand by the time of the trip. Construction was far from easy, especially across the Kara-Kum Desert, where laying track that would not sink into the sand was an almost Sisyphean task.[9]

The Trans-Caspian did help speed up the process of pacification and did provide for the contingency of a conflict with England. But at the same time it could not help but rouse English concerns about Russian intentions in not just Central Asia but Persia, for the new line increased the opportunities for Russian intervention in that decaying land. As finance minister, Witte would take more than a passing interest in that country.

For the moment the chief interest of the voyagers was in the economic possibilities of the area, which was about twice the size of Texas and largely arid except in the land adjoining the two main rivers, which were fed by the snows of the towering mountains to the south. As indicated, the area could produce cotton, and the party did visit a cotton-growing estate that belonged to the tsar. Witte was, of course, interested in the economic potential of the area and was impressed by its "untapped resources," which, as it turned out, were not to be tapped in his lifetime.

The journey could not have failed to impress him with its evidence of Russian expansionism. By no means a rabid imperialist, he believed that whatever land had been gained by "Russian blood" should remain in Russian hands, but with due regard for the rights of its non-Russian inhabitants. And he was realist enough, at least later on, to note: "For a thousand years . . . we have been swallowing up non-Russian peoples. As a consequence the Russian Empire is a conglomerate of nationalities."[10]

While Witte was on the road so was his wife, stopping first at Kislovodsk, a spa, apparently in hopes of alleviating a kidney ailment. While she was there she received a telegram from Witte about some happy event, probably about his admission to the quasi-chivalric order of St. Vladimir, one of several orders admission to which marked the advancement of higher officials. In reply, according to Witte, she sent him congratulations and accurately predicted his future career. From Kislovodsk she went on to visit her brother in the province of Chernigov and then her mother in Kiev, where she died unexpectedly of a heart attack. Witte was left with responsibility for her daughter, Sonia, whom he had adopted, and the memory of a checkered marriage.[11]

On his return from Central Asia Witte resumed his usual activities—regulating freight rates, compiling statistics, and auditing the earnings of privately owned railroads, some of which were being acquired by the government. In addition, he took part in the work of a commission preparing a new tariff.

Tariff policy had been informed by the spirit of free trade until the 1870s, when the growth of industry prompted a shift to protectionism to cushion infant industries against foreign competition, with duties on coal, iron, and locomotives. The tariff of 1891 raised duties on these and added cotton to the list of protected items. It set basic tariff policy for the remainder of the empire's life.[12]

Protectionism favored heavy industry in particular, but it increased costs for various groups, notably the peasantry. The negative features were aggravated by the famine that broke out that year in the central provinces as a result of a poor harvest brought on by drought and compounded by a lack of reserve stocks of grain. Add to this an outbreak of cholera that was taking thousands of lives.

The famine energized liberals who had long been silent because of government repression into raising their voices, blaming the regime and in particular the Ministry of Finance for creating conditions that intensified the famine. They took Vyshnegradskii to task for vigorous encouragement of grain export, harping on his unfortunate remark: "We ourselves may not eat, but we shall export grain." True, once it became evident that there was a famine he barred grain exports, but the government dithered in sending help to the stricken provinces, permitting liberals to step in and embarrass the government by taking the initiative in relief efforts.[13]

While all this was occurring, Vyshnegradskii and A.I. Hübbenet, minister of ways and communications, were feuding. The minister of finance, supported by Witte, considered Hübbenet incompetent and was particularly disturbed by his failure to deal with the pileups of grain on the railroads. The latter, for his part, was angry over what he perceived to be the Ministry of Finance's incursion into his jurisdiction. Ill will had reached the point where one night, evidently in his cups, Hübbenet referred to Vyshnegradskii and Witte as "thieves."[14] Vyshnegradskii, enjoying the tsar's favor, held better cards. To make matters worse, Hübbenet found himself under attack by one of his own subordinates, Colonel A.A. Wendrich, a military engineer, who had gained direct access to the tsar and was being considered by the tsar as successor to the minister. Then there were the attacks on the hapless minister by the notorious and influential Prince V.P. Meshcherskii, one of the few on *tutoyer* terms with the tsar.

Once the word had spread that Hübbenet was on his way out, the intrigue over a successor began in earnest. Vyshnegradskii pushed the candidacy of Witte. Some favored other candidates, while some, including Witte, worked to ensure that Wendrich, an energetic but somewhat stupid man, be removed from the running. In the end, Alexander III appointed Witte as acting minister of ways and communications on February 15, 1892, it being the custom for a tsar to make a person acting minister and later raising him to minister.

The appointment of Witte was generally considered a victory for Vyshnegradskii. A.A. Abaza, an important official, declared that the minister of finance thought Witte would be serving him as a kind of aide.[15] But report had it that when someone said to the tsar that fusion of the two ministries would have produced the same result as Witte's appointment, the sovereign replied: "No, he is not one of those who can subordinate himself to someone else."[16] He was right, and it would not be long before Witte would be casting covetous glances at Vyshnegradskii's post.

Entry into the ministerial ranks usually came to men in their late fifties or early sixties. Witte was forty-two at the time of his appointment, a comparative stripling—the youngest man ever to reach such heights in Russia. Naturally, his ascension to such a prestigious office attracted attention and caused tongues to wag. It was acknowledged that he was very intelligent, ambitious, and an expert on railroading. Beyond that there was some gossip that he and Vyshnegradskii engaged in such activities as playing the stock market.[17] An entry in the diary of A.A. Polovtsov, imperial secretary of the State Council, with whom Witte would have to work for many a year, represents the reaction of some to Witte:

Witte, in uniform [officials wore uniforms on specified occasions], calls on me in connection with his appointment as minister of ways and communications. I explain that one appears in uniform only before superiors and that I am obviously not his superior. He is obviously very intelligent, will act with restraint, will do well in his office, but with respect to honor and conscientiousness he does not inspire any confidence.[18]

What lay behind the caveat was the fact that Witte at this time was both gauche and conceited. In time his achievements would make more of an impression than his bearing and manners.

The fact that he had arrived at a position of importance and power, with direct access to the tsar, could not help but bolster his ego. He particularly valued his weekly reports to the tsar; arrayed in dress uniform, he would journey to whichever palace the tsar was residing at (usually the one at Pavlovsk), be escorted into the palace by liveried servants, and be summoned into the tsar's study, where he would read his report. It was all rather stuffy but was valued highly by Witte as an opportunity both to help make policy and to impress the ruler.

In many ways the two were well paired. Both were big, somewhat ungainly men, strong-willed, unlikely to stand on ceremony any more than they had to. The same could not be said about their intellects. Witte was very intelligent, possibly a genius. Alexander III was neither well rounded nor especially intelligent, although he possessed a core of common sense. Had the tsar's older brother, Nicholas, heir to the throne, not died an untimely death, Alexander would have spent his years in relative obscurity, holding a military command that he could not have achieved on the basis of merit, such as inspector general of the cavalry. But here he was, "by the grace of Almighty God, the Emperor and Autocrat of All the Russias . . . Tsar of Poland . . . Grand Duke of Finland," et cetera. (Formally the ruler was referred to as emperor, informally as tsar.)

The reign of Alexander III is widely associated with the word *reactionary*. In scaling back some of the reforms of Alexander II it was reactionary, but in seeking to preserve the principle of autocracy, the powerful position of the landed nobility, and the primacy of the Russian Orthodox Church it was conservative. Its chief ideological spokesman was C.P. Pobedonostsev, the overprocurator of the Holy Synod of the Russian Orthodox Church, who declared "among the falsest of political principles is the principle of the sovereignty of the people. . . . Thence proceeds the theory of Parliamentarianism, which, up to the present day, has deluded much of the so-called intelligence [intelligentsia], and unhappily infatuated certain foolish Russians."[19] Of course Witte, too, believed in autocracy, but his view was tinged by the

Slavophile fantasy of tsar and people. And it is quite likely that the saying attributed to German ministers—"Unser Kaiser ist absolut wenn er nur unser Willen tut" (Our emperor is absolute if only he does what we will)—applied to Witte, who found power through his sovereign.

Witte, it will be recalled, had supported the spirit of reform following the assassination of Alexander II and was privately opposed to many of the policies followed under Alexander III, but he kept these thoughts to himself and was happy to serve under this tsar. On occasion these differences came to the surface, as was the case of his stand on the so-called Jewish question. In this case, as Witte relates it, the tsar asked him if, as he had heard, it was true that he was a friend of the Jews. No one had ever accused Alexander of such a thing. It is reported that the first time he saw a Jewish cemetery he said: "If all the Jews were buried there, we would have peace."[20] Witte writes that he replied by saying that if "the Jewish question" could be solved by dumping all of Russia's Jews into the Black Sea that would be that, but since such a course was not possible, the answer must be the gradual lifting of the many legal disabilities under which the Jews labored.[21] "The Jewish question" was the term used to cover the problems entailed in governmental dealings with the five million Jewish subjects of the tsar, half of the world's Jews. Before 1772, when the infamous partitions of Poland among Austria, Prussia, and Russia began, Russia had barred Jews, except for a small sect, from living within its borders. This was done for the same reason that Western European countries in medieval times had expelled Jews or confined them to ghettos: the belief that Jews were the enemies of Christendom.

With the territories Russia acquired from Poland came a considerable number of Jews that had to be accepted as subjects and the problem of how to treat them. In Poland, Jews had enjoyed a fairly favorable status: they were free of the obligation to serve in the military and were allowed some self-rule. That was not to be the case under the tsar. Considering the Jews as enemies of Christendom, the Russian government passed dozens and dozens of discriminatory laws, decrees, and regulations that put Jews in the category of second-class subjects.

Apparently, Witte had acquired the reputation of being a friend of the Jews through his association with and employment of Jews and converted Jews, the latter being considered by Alexander III and other anti-Semites as none the better for having converted. Witte had come to believe that Russia had no choice but to follow the Western European example of granting its Jewish citizens legal equality, but he was convinced that it must be done with caution, a step at a time, to prevent an explosion of mass hatred. However, he did not take the initiative in seeking to get the process started. That would have endangered his career and, what is more, would have been to no avail, as such an effort would have been shot down by the powers that be. And on at least two occasions he catered to his sovereign's prejudices.[22] Witte sought to keep in the good graces of his sovereign, a strong-willed man very conscious of his position, but, reportedly, he sometimes argued with the tsar, with both raising their voices.[23] Be that as it may, Witte did not forget that he was required by the facts of life to play the humble subject. Their relationship turned out to be a very comfortable one, with Alexander respecting and valuing Witte for his ability and for his energy, which was far greater than that of the older ministers. Witte, in turn, revered the tsar, finding in him a strong, peace-loving man who led an exemplary life and believed that had Alexander had a chance to live out his three score and ten, he would have mitigated the harsh policies associated with him.[24] It would not be long before observers would be comparing Witte to Otto von Bismarck, the "Iron Chancellor" of Germany, who was just at the end of his career as Witte was coming into prominence. Whether or not Witte was another Bismarck remains to be seen, as does the question of whether Alexander III was another William I, who had provided the chancellor with solid backing.

The tsar was both head of state and head of government. His power of appointment was very broad, covering both civilian and military posts. Ministers did not form a collective body; such a body, the Council of Ministers, existed, but only on paper. The ministers reported to the tsar, usually every week, and in theory coordinated their work. When he was faced with a problem of an interministerial nature, the tsar might summon a special conference to which he would invite the concerned ministers and perhaps a grand duke or two; he would generally preside over its meetings and decide what view or views to accept. Such an arrangement did not make for efficient government, but it kept power in the hands of the sovereign and of course encouraged ministers to fight for the tsar's goodwill. Witte was to prove successful in doing so with Alexander III.

In his new role as minister Witte had to serve ex officio as member of two of the highest institutions of the state, the Committee of Ministers and the State Council. The first consisted of the ministers, certain other high officials, and additional members the tsar chose to appoint, one being at this time the heir to the throne, Grand Duke Nicholas Aleksandrovich. The committee's chairman was Nicholas Bunge, a former minister of finance. who had been kicked upstairs to this dead-end post, one that Witte was destined to occupy.

As Witte was to put it pungently after he had served as chairman: "To it came all kinds of administrative rubbish—everything that was not clearly defined in law, as well as important bills that had encountered or might encounter opposition in the State Council."[25] At one session the committee might consider proposed charters of new corporations or lists of books suitable for public libraries, at another renewal of so-called temporary legislation such as the notoriously repressive exceptional laws or the equally notorious laws that imposed heightened restrictions on Jews.

Far more important in the scheme of things and in Witte's work as minister was the State Council, the closest thing to a legislature in the autocratic regime. It had come into being under Alexander I, who envisioned it as part of a constitutional order, an appointive upper house of the legislature supplemented by an elective State Duma. The constitutional order was aborted thanks to fierce opposition from the upper class and the tsar's infirmity of will, but the State Council survived.

It was considered to be "the highest institution in the empire." It did not initiate legislation. That was the task of the ministries. Its task was to consider and edit the proposed legislation, then send it on, with its considered recommendation, to the tsar. As the "autocratic and unlimited sovereign," he could reject the council's recommendation, and on occasion he did so. Such occasions were rare, given the fact that the council's members were appointed and almost to a man members of the hereditary nobility, usually former ministers or retired generals or admirals, for whom memberships in this body was what the empress called a "bon-bon," an honor and a generous substitute for a pension. They were for the most part older men, some of them out of touch with what was being considered, either because of ignorance or because of senility.[26]

The council met once a week, for an hour, at the Mariinskii Palace, the members in appropriate uniform. Little of substance was debated at its stuffy sessions, most of its work being done by seasoned bureaucrats in its departments, of which the Department of State Economy was the one that most affected Witte's work. From time to time, when there was debate on the floor of the council on a subject of concern to Witte, he would speak up, usually to good effect, for although he was far from being a polished orator, he could speak persuasively. His dealings were largely with A.A. Abaza, head of the Department of State Economy, about whom more later, and Polovtsov, whom we have already met. He had little to do with the aged Grand Duke Michael Nikolaevich, a cipher, a former viceroy of the Caucasus who served as chairman of the council and whom Witte had met much earlier on. As mentioned earlier, if there was opposition to proposed legislation in the council, it would most likely be shipped off to the Committee of Ministers to be transmuted into "temporary" law, which as often as not remained in effect until the end of the regime by virtue of periodic renewal.

Witte's stay in the office of minister of ways and communications, barely six months, was too brief for him to have significant impact on its operations, which were badly in need of correction.[27] However, several events in this brief interlude deserve notice.

One was the entry into Witte's life of the notorious Prince Vladimir ("Vovo" to his friends) Petrovich Meshcherskii, one of the shady characters with influence in high places and with whom he would come into contact. The prince, an impecunious member of a very aristocratic family, was a supple and unscrupulous intriguer, fond of handsome guards officers, and variously described as a "son of a bitch," "Prince Merzetskii" (a play on the word meaning "scoundrel"), and "Prince of Sodom [a reference to his homosexuality] and Citizen [*grazhdanin*] of Gomorrah."[28] *Grazhdanin* was the name of the ultraconservative daily that he both published and edited, the source of both influence and income. Its income came from a generous subsidy provided by the tsar and payments for publication of government notices. Its influence was derived from the widespread and justified belief that the prince enjoyed imperial favor and could therefore affect bureaucratic careers by what he wrote, as was the case with Witte. Meshcherskii assiduously cultivated ministers, inviting them to his weekly dinners, and did not fail to seek quid pro quo.

In the presence of his strong-willed wife, Marie Fedorovna, who despised the prince, the tsar falsely denied reading *Grazhdanin* or permitting the prince to call on him.[29] Some believed that this was the only newspaper Alexander read and that he subsidized it because he wanted an organ to support his ultraconservative views.[30] Since belief in Meshcherskii's influence was widespread, many ministers, Witte among them, sought to remain in his good graces.

It was not long after Witte had become minister that the prince called on him, asking that he keep an eye on a man named I.I. Kolyshko, one of the prince's favorites, who had been appointed to the supernumerary post of "official on special assignment" by Hübbenet. Witte obliged and became acquainted with the man, finding him to be unscrupulous but a gifted writer. Since he was on the lookout for such talent, he used Kolyshko to polish official reports and, under a pseudonym, to write newspaper articles that supported the ministry's policies.[31] He was destined to retain ties with Meshcherskii and Kolyshko for many years.

Witte soon had an occasion to do the prince another favor, by arranging for Meshcherskii's new printing press, made possible by a subsidy provided by Vyshnegradskii, to enjoy the exclusive right to do all the printing for the government-owned railroads.[32] It was a right that brought in a pretty penny. And when Nicholas II, on ascending the throne, wished to end the subsidy to *Grazhdanin*, it was Witte who dissuaded him from doing so.[33]

It was during his short tenure as minister of ways and communications that a far more important event in Witte's life occurred: his marriage to Matilda Lisanevich, a converted Jew, a lady "of dark beauty and dignified manner with an intelligent manner and a luminous smile."[34] When he first met her, she happened to be unhappily married. He was smitten and, with her approval, undertook to get Lisanevich to agree to a divorce, which meant admitting that he was guilty of adultery. In return Lisanevich asked for thirty thousand rubles and a government position paying at least three thousand rubles a year. Witte was able to arrange for the position but did not have the requested money. At this point a friend of the estranged wife, a "fixer" named Gravenhof, arranged for a banker to provide the money, presumably in the expectation that he would not go unrewarded.[35]

But Lisanevich was not the only obstacle. Although the Orthodox Church permitted divorce, albeit infrequently and at considerable expense to the plaintiff, divorce still carried a heavy stigma, one much heavier than discreet adultery did. Witte feared that the tsar would turn against him if he went through with the marriage because Matilda Lisanevich was a divorcée and of Jewish origin to boot. Witte was well aware of the case of General Chertkov, former governor-general of Kiev, who had fallen out of favor with the imperial court for marrying a converted Jewish divorcée.[36] He would be taking a risk, but, ambitious as he was, he would rather give up his career than give up Matilda. He was ready to let the tsar decide his fate by informing him of his intention to marry even if it meant leaving government service. To tip the scales in his favor he enlisted the help of two men who enjoyed the tsar's confidence, Minister of Interior Durnovo and General Richter, who held an important position at court. Thus prepared, Witte told the tsar, in the course of a regular report, of his intention to marry and of his readiness to give up his position if the tsar disapproved of the proposed marriage. Alexander replied that he would not think of parting with him.[37] The marriage took place soon thereafter.

In many respects the second marriage resembled the first. In each case the wife was good-looking; in each the husband was bought off; in each there was a daughter to be adopted. Why did his choice fall on unhappily married women? Perhaps it was because he was not much good at courting, and these women did not take much courting. There was, however, a sharp difference between the two marriages in that the second turned out well. Witte obviously drew much strength and comfort from Matilda and was devoted to her, so much so that some in high places who did not put a high value on marital fidelity were amused. Such were his feelings that he once declared that Matilda and her daughter, Vera, were the two things he valued most in life.[38]

Marital bliss came at a heavy price: ostracism of his wife and continuing nasty gossip about her. As a divorcée, she could not be received at court, which meant, among other things, being denied the coveted, albeit dubious, privilege of *baise-main*, kissing the hand of the empress on New Year's Day. Witte was so irked that after Alexander's death he asked the dowager empress to lift the ban, but to no avail.[39] Matilda was ostracized, too, by Witte's ministerial colleagues, who would not invite her to functions to which the wives of ministers were ordinarily invited.[40] As for gossip, it reached such intensity that Empress Marie Fedorovna asked the interior minister to check the reliability of what she was hearing from her ladies-in-waiting about Matilda's reputation for being "fast." Durnovo reported that "although she is a divorcée, she is a very decent woman" and went on to refer to the ladies-in-waiting as being foolish, a comment that irked the empress.[41] At one point Witte was so distressed about the way his wife's name was being taken at the home of Grand Duke Nicholas Nikolaevich that he called on him to protest.[42] Princess Cantacuzene, granddaughter of Ulysses S. Grant, who had married into the Russian nobility and was a friend of the Wittes, had this to say concerning the gossip about Matilda: "She was a lady of vague antecedents and I decided they were vague only because so many excited people told such extraordinary stories about her. She stood easily on her own merits . . . and she in her own way was acting as brilliant a rôle as her husband's."[43]

The new couple dealt with the problem of Sonia, whom, it will be recalled, Witte had adopted after his first marriage. They helped provide her with a dowry, allowing her to marry M.F. Mering, a banker and son of a prominent physician with whom Witte was well acquainted. Apparently, Witte expected that, once married, Sonia would no longer be a burden to him and his wife. Not so. Mering was a speculator who, using Witte's name for credit, ran his bank into the ground and left his wife and the country. Sonia proved to be an embarrassment, complaining loudly that she was ill-treated by her stepmother and her "papa."[44]

As indicated earlier, Witte's marriage did not hurt his standing with the tsar. When cholera swept the Volga region in the spring of 1892, Alexander picked Witte to inspect the area and report on what was being done and what needed to be done, saying that he chose him because he was the youngest of his ministers. It was hardly a choice assignment, considering the danger of infection and the calamitous sights, but it carried considerable responsibility.[45]

Witte's work on this assignment as well as his general performance increased the tsar's confidence in him at a time when Vyshnegradskii's stock was falling, apparently because of the minister's lukewarm interest in two of Alexander's pet projects—building a railroad across Siberia and the establishment of a government monopoly of liquor sales.[46] The finance minister's declining health, the result of a series of what appear to have been transient ischemic attacks (ministrokes), further undermined his position. In April 1892 a colleague described Vyshnegradskii's mental condition as "hopeless." The following month the tsar confided in Durnovo that he was thinking of replacing the minister with Witte.[47] Apparently, Witte sought to make sure that the tsar was aware of Vyshnegradskii's diminished powers. On one occasion, when he had the opportunity, he informed the tsar of Vyshnegradskii's diminished mental capacity in an alleged effort to keep Alexander from being shocked, but one can not help thinking that his motive was less than pure.[48]

For his part, the finance minister tried to cling to his position despite his inability to perform adequately by proposing to turn over some responsibilities to his thickheaded assistant minister, F.G. Thörner, a man in his early sixties, while retaining his policy-making powers. Alexander would have none of this, seeing in the proposal an effort to infringe on the autocrat's power.[49] On August 30, 1892, he appointed Witte acting finance minister, and a few months later raised him to the rank of minister. Vyshnegradskii took his removal with poor grace.[50] For Witte the most important chapter in his life, the one in which he would make his greatest mark, was opening.

Chapter 5

Minister of Finance, 1892–1894

Witte's tenure as minister of finance would stir the country up in a manner rarely seen in its history and would bring him international renown. He had become chief of a powerful and influential ministry, with the capacity "to set the tone of the entire economic life" of the country.[1] Its functions were equivalent to the combined functions of the American Treasury Department, Office of Management and Budget, Commerce Department, Government Printing Office, Bureau of Standards, Internal Revenue Service, and a land-based equivalent of the Coast Guard, namely, the Border Guard, the chief task of which was to stop contraband. The ministry minted and printed money, collected customs duties, set the state budget with the help of the State Council, exercised powers in railroad affairs, encouraged and often subsidized commercial and industrial ventures, lent money to landed nobles and peasants, negotiated commercial treaties, and was represented abroad by financial agents, who in some countries (such as Korea and Persia) wielded considerable influence. Moreover, the minister had the power to shift money to other ministries or withhold it, giving him the ability to reward, punish, and earn goodwill.[2] Obviously, the ministry had broad responsibility, which Witte would extend. In addition, Witte would soon be able to influence the operations of the Ministry of Ways and Communications when Prince M.I. Khilkov, a rather docile type, became its head. And within a few years Witte would have a role in the making of Far Eastern policy. How much power he could expect to exercise was another matter, depending on the disposition of the tsar, Witte's energy and talent, the support and ability of his subordinates, the attitude of the Department of State Economy of the State Council, and the influence of nongovernmental power groups, particularly the landed nobility.

He did not begin work with a minutely detailed program, but he did bring with him ideas that would characterize his tenure as finance minister. His 1889 pamphlet about Friedrich List's *The National System of Political Economy* provides a look at these ideas. True, it was not an explicit statement of his own views. It was, rather, an attempt to acquaint the public with those of List, whose book had not yet been translated into Russian. In the course of so doing, Witte associated himself with certain key positions that were to characterize his work as finance minister.

The title of List's work provides the key to his message. List argues that prevailing economic theory, exemplified by the teachings of Adam Smith, was mistaken in the sense of being motivated by the idea of serving all humanity, whereas it should serve national interests until such distant time as humanity had reached the stage where a cosmopolitan approach was viable.[3] Witte agreed, arguing that Russian interests were being ill served by Russian economists, who were following "the recipes of cosmopolitan economics."[4] Witte accepted List's view that for a nation to reach its full potential it should develop manufacturing and commerce, quoting List's words: "History presents examples of the downfall of many nations because they were unable to carry out at a favorable time the great task of safeguarding their moral, economic, and political independence by the establishment of manufacturing and the creation of a strong class of manufacturers and merchants."[5] This was a far cry from his condemnation of industrial capitalism four years earlier. In accepting List's call for industrialization, Witte also accepted the German's arguments in favor of protectionism and a significant role for the state in the encouragement of industry and commerce. It will be recalled that Witte had a hand in the framing of the protectionist tariff of 1891. It is evident that Witte began his tenure with the clear aim of overcoming his country's backwardness by pushing industrialization and commerce at a pace required to ensure Russia's survival as a great power.

The three preceding finance ministers, Reutern, Bunge, and Vyshnegradskii, recognized their country's backwardness and sought to overcome it. They recognized the need for an adequate banking system, a stable currency, and large-scale foreign investment in industry as long as native investors could not provide the necessary capital, but their achievements fell far short of their goals. With Witte a new day began. As we already know, he brought immense energy, an iron will, the ability to grow on the job, a broad vision, and, last but not least, the tsar's support. Early on in his tenure, in a proposal for enlarging the staff of the Department of Commerce and Manufacture, he made his objectives clear. Noting recent growth in industry, he argued that the country was still at an early stage in the process of developing from a purely agrarian country into an agrarian-industrial one. The West, he argued, had made the transition gradually and naturally, but Russia would have to leapfrog some stages, with governmental help.[6]

At a time when advanced countries had adopted the gold standard, Russia was still relying on paper money technically redeemable in silver, but that had been a fiction since the Crimean War, with its heavy costs. Without the backing of silver, the ruble fluctuated below its face value, and the fluctuations were enhanced by speculation. All of this produced a chilling effect on foreign investors. This state of affairs prompted agitation for the adoption of the gold standard, but that was easier said than done without substantial growth of the economy.

Witte, a greenhorn in finance, turned for advice and help to A.Ia. Antonovich, professor of economics at Kiev University, who, it will be recalled, had served as publisher of record for Witte's newspaper in Kiev. Witte was impressed by the professor's writing on monetary policy, particularly by his support of a metallic standard. When A.S. Ermolov, one of his two assistant ministers, left to become minister of state domains in March 1893, Witte, who was glad to see him go, succeeded in having Antonovich replace him. Disillusionment with the new man soon set in as Witte noted that Antonovich was weak, sly, and too easily influenced by opponents of monetary reform. In time Witte would turn to A.S. Rothstein for advice and assistance with respect to monetary reforms and international financial operations.[7] We will encounter Rothstein subsequently. Meanwhile, Witte had to deal with other issues, some made pressing by the tsar's wishes, others rendered so by ongoing events.

One of the tsar's wishes was to create a government liquor monopoly as a means of fighting alcoholism, particularly rampant among the peasantry, which, as Witte observed, "does not drink much, but it gets drunk more often than do other people."[8] Vyshnegradskii had been interested in a liquor monopoly because it would be a better source of revenue than the existing excise taxes, but he had taken only small, preliminary steps. Witte was more obliging.

In February 1893 he suggested to the tsar that the monopoly first be introduced, as a trial, in four relatively remote provinces. Preparations for the trial went so well that Alexander ordered preparations for the rapid extension of the monopoly to the twenty-five provinces to which Jews, with a few exceptions, were restricted. Most of these provinces had once been under the rule of Poland, where the nobility enjoyed a monopoly over liquor production and sale, the exploitation of which they farmed out to Jews. Witte responded to the order with a report in which he said that "the government liquor monopoly will create an opportunity for the local Christian population to be freed of dependence on the Jews."[9] The tsar agreed. Witte was obviously catering to the tsar's belief that Jews exploited Christians.

Actual introduction of the monopoly had to wait until after Alexander's death, when Nicholas II ordered speedy action in the twenty-five provinces noted above.[10] By 1901 the monopoly was in effect in all of European Russia, except for the northern Caucasus. Subsequently, the monopoly was introduced into Asiatic Russia. The process did not go without a hitch. Thus, when the turn of the city and province of St. Petersburg came, there were dire predictions that the local distillers and liquor dealers would riot at the prospect of losing their livelihoods, but the change came off peacefully.[11]

Witte worked vigorously at this task, making inspection trips to provinces in which the monopoly had recently been introduced. On one such trip his contempt for parliamentary regimes was reinforced by the remarks of a French official accompanying him, who, in praising the monopoly, remarked that "it would be beneficial for France if she were ruled by a strong, unlimited monarch." Apropos of this remark, Witte noted in his memoirs, "Under parliamentary regimes, particularly republican ones, such a reform would be unthinkable because it hurts the interests of highly placed and well-to-do persons," adding that such persons were well represented in the French Chamber of Deputies.[12]

As noted, the monopoly was intended to curb alcoholism and incidentally raise revenues. To curb the heavy drinking common on Sundays and holidays, sales on these days were prohibited. In addition, Witte launched a vigorous campaign to discourage heavy drinking with the creation of temperance committees at the provincial and district levels, with members drawn from the civil service, clergy, and other bodies. Indicative of the importance attached to these committees, governors presided over the provincial ones and district marshals of the nobility over the district committees. It is difficult to believe that all those involved took the fight against alcoholism seriously, but quite evidently many of them did, notably Witte. He even sought the aid of Leo Tolstoy, whose moral influence was great and whose abhorrence of alcohol was well known. Unfortunately, Witte's effort, through an intermediary, came to naught, for the novelist would support only one remedy, prohibition.[13] In any event, the temperance committees succeeded in opening thousands of tearooms, reading rooms, and centers for popular entertainment, which were intended to provide a nonalcoholic and uplifting atmosphere. Undoubtedly, such efforts were not without effect, but they were not enough to eliminate alcoholism.

Another of the tsar's major interests that would occupy Witte was construction of a railroad across Siberia to the Pacific, an interest that the minister had no difficulty embracing. Talk of constructing such a line went back several decades, with various schemes being floated, one of them by an English engineer proposing the use of horsepower![14] Serious consideration of possible routes began in the 1860s, to the accompaniment of hot debate within the government and the press. At one point General Annenkov offered to finance and direct construction of such a railroad. Debate about feasibility as well as financing dragged on through the 1870s and 1880s, with the weight of opinion being that the country could not afford the cost. The arguments in favor were economic, political, and strategic. Siberia, it was argued, was a region of vast, untapped resources. Catherine the Great had called it "our India, Mexico or Peru."[15] Proponents also underscored the need of fusing the region with the rest of the empire by settling Russians there, thereby not only Russifying Siberia but also relieving population pressure in European Russia. Finally, there was the expressed need to defend the easternmost part as well as to strengthen Russia's presence in the Far East.

In 1882, convinced by the yea-sayers, Alexander gave the go-ahead, but successive finance ministers, notably Vyshnegradskii, continued to argue that the proposed undertaking would be too costly. This view was more than balanced by renewed pressure from the governor-general of the Amur region, who put in powerful terms the need for adequate communications between his bailiwick and the distant capital as well as the need for strengthened defense of the region. Early in 1891, the tsar held a special conference with top officials, who recommended that the railroad be constructed. It appeared that work would be started immediately. With this expectation, Grand Duke Nicholas Aleksandrovich, heir to the throne, who was rounding out his education with a grand tour, turned over the first spade of earth in a groundbreaking ceremony in Vladivostok. As it turned out, the ceremony was premature, since Vyshnegradskii budgeted so picayune an appropriation for construction that rapid and sustained work was unlikely in the near future. The replacement of Vyshnegradskii radically changed the scenario.

Already acquainted with some aspects of the proposed line, Witte jumped into the enterprise with both feet. Railroading, after all, was his specialty, but the Trans-Siberian Railroad presented new challenges aside from its size. First, he would have to consider the development of Siberia. Second, he would have to give thought to the impact of the line on Russia's role in the Far East, an area in which he had shown little interest in the past.

No sooner had he taken over the helm at the Ministry of Finance than he was asked by the tsar for advice on how to finance construction. Witte's reply was to recommend that Alexander devote a special conference to the subject. Apparently Witte was seeking support from colleagues. Shortly thereafter he presented a memorandum to Alexander detailing the benefits that the Trans-Siberian would confer. In short order the tsar summoned a special conference at which the finance minister's ideas were presented and debated.

Witte declared that construction could be financed without foreign help, and proceeded to paint a glowing picture of the benefits that a trans-Siberian railroad would confer. It would rank near the top of all the great undertakings of the current century. It would produce enormous economic benefits by opening Siberia's vast resources to exploitation and at the same time provide land for Russia's poorest peasants and greatly reduce transit time between east and west. Moreover, the line would enhance Russia's status as a great power and improve her reputation. In addition, the line would assist China in her rivalry with England in the tea market and gain Chinese support for Russia vis-à-vis England. And "in passing" he noted the likelihood of constructing branch lines into China, including one to the Yellow Sea, which would provide an ice-free port, a great plus given the fact that the railroad's terminus, Vladivostok, was closed by ice during part of the year.[16] Witte's views were approved, and the grandiose project was under way.

Grandiose is the proper term for the undertaking to build the world's longest railroad, five thousand miles from end to end. Not only the longest, but also one of the most difficult to construct, with long stretches over land that was permanently frozen and other long stretches where the earth did not thaw until July, revealing insect-infested swamps. There were formidable mountains to circumvent or tunnel through, and there was Lake Baikal, ten times the size of Rhode Island, to bypass. The work was to be done on the run and as cheaply as possible: a single-track line, lightweight rails, and in many places wooden bridges. The task was made more difficult by the great distances from supply sources and labor pools.[17] To deal with one of these problems Witte proposed establishment of rail-manufacturing mills at convenient locations. To speed up deliveries Witte encouraged use of the northern sea route, weather permitting, to the mouth of the mighty Enisei River and then upriver to the railhead at Krasnoiarsk. Construction was to be carried out in three stages: the first, starting simultaneously from both the eastern and western terminuses, was to be completed by 1900; the second, in Eastern Siberia, by 1902; and the third, around Lake Baikal and the northern shore of the Amur River, thereafter. As will be seen, there was already some thought of an alternative route in the third stage, one that would go south of the Amur through Manchuria and on to the eastern terminus, Vladivostok.

To circumvent bureaucratic hurdles Witte successfully proposed creation of an interministerial body, the Siberian Railroad Committee, which would have decision-making power over construction. For the chairmanship of the body he astutely proposed Grand Duke Nicholas Aleksandrovich in the expectation that he would identify himself with the project. The tsar agreed reluctantly, noting that his son was still very callow.[18] In January 1893, Nicholas was named to the post, but the dominant voice in the committee was Witte's, and his was the guiding spirit in the construction of the line, with the donkeywork of supervising construction falling on the shoulders of Prince Khilkov, minister of ways and communications.

Construction was rapid, with some of the labor performed under the aegis of the Ministry of Ways and Communications, but most of it farmed out to contractors. Labor, some of it voluntary and some of it drafted—peasants, Cossacks, soldiers, prisoners, and exiles—came chiefly from local sources. When necessary, chiefly for skilled work, laborers were brought in from European Russia and the West. By the time of Alexander's death, in October 1894, 875 miles of line had been laid.[19] The Trans-Siberian Railroad, or the

Great Siberian Mainline, as the Russians called it, was off to a fast start at the beginning of a turbulent time in the Far East, a time when Japan, which regarded the line as "a dagger aimed at our heart," was going to war with China.

Even before that war began, and shortly after the start of construction, Witte became entangled in Russia's Far Eastern politics by lending misguided support to a harebrained scheme hatched by a self-styled doctor of Tibetan medicine named P.A. Badmaev. Nothing would come of the scheme except embarrassment and evidence of the unintended consequences that could come with the Trans-Siberian Railroad.

Badmaev, a Russified Buriat Mongol, a recent convert to Russian Orthodoxy, whose godfather was none other than the tsar, sought to influence Russia's China policy and line his own pockets. Toward that end he managed to reach Witte through the good offices of Prince E.E. Ukhtomskii, who had served as a tutor during the tsarevich's trip abroad. In February 1893, Badmaev put a lengthy memorandum in Witte's hand for transmittal to the tsar. This Witte did, together with his own commentary.

The essence of Badmaev's missive was a fantastic proposal for acts that were intended to lead to the overthrow of the Manchu rulers of China and the subsequent voluntary submission of China and Tibet to Russian rule. The scheme, which would require covert Russian aid, called for a lengthy branch line from the Trans-Siberian Railroad to the city of Lanchow in Hansu Province. That line would confer enormous commercial benefits on Russia, and Lanchow would provide a jumping-off site for a revolt against the Manchu Dynasty led by Badmaev and his cohorts. The uprising would spread eastward, the dynasty would collapse, and a popular cry would arise for the tsar to assume dominion over China and Tibet.[20] It was the kind of scheme that might have been hatched in a later era by the CIA.

Strange though it seems, Witte endorsed Badmaev's proposal. In his commentary he repeated the Slavophile argument about Russian uniqueness as well as his uncle Fadeev's views about Russia's role in Asia. In so doing he asserted that whereas the West had used Christianity to exploit China, Russia had employed its faith for the purpose of enlightenment, and it was this difference that had produced antagonism between Russia and the West. That antagonism, according to Witte, explained efforts by the West to prevent Russia from reaping benefits from the new railroad, efforts that might include inciting China against Russia. If the Badmaev scheme was successfully carried out, Russia would become dominant in Asiatic as well as European affairs. He recommended that Badmaev be given some covert assistance, noting that the record showed that major undertakings had been carried out under private auspices and then taken over by the government.[21]

The tsar's reaction to the Badmaev scheme was short and sensible: "All this is so novel, so unusual and fantastic that it is difficult to believe in the possibility of success."[22] Even if success had been possible, it is difficult to believe that a great power such as England would have countenanced Russian dominion over China.

Why Witte gave his endorsement to this scheme is a puzzlement. It may be that he thought his sovereign would favor it, and Witte sought to please him. It may be that he was still naive about the Far East and accepted Badmaev's claim to vast knowledge of that part of the world. In any case, his endorsement was out of keeping with his aversion to anything that smacked of adventurism. The Badmaev scheme joined the archival dust heap, and Witte soon became disenchanted with the mendacious Badmaev. But the episode at least had the merit of calling attention to the decay of the Chinese Empire, which would embroil Russia very soon.

Russia was already involved in commercial conflict nearer home, with Germany, providing Witte with an opportunity to show his mettle and thus strengthen his position with the tsar. Germany, Russia's major trading partner, had begun, under heavy pressure from Prussian landowners, to set high tariff rates on imports of Russian grain, while Russia, in turn, had adopted a protectionist tariff in 1891, already referred to. The atmosphere grew tenser in 1892 with the creation of the secret Franco-Russian alliance and Germany's conclusion of most-favored-nation commercial treaties with several countries other than Russia.

Witte entered the controversy with both arms swinging by proposing the establishment of minimum and maximum tariff rates, the former being those of the 1891 tariff, the latter to be applied against Germany at his discretion. Nervous members of the State Council saw the proposed action as a dangerous provocation, but that body finally gave its approval. What followed was a tariff war, with much trading of blows—all this in the midst of sputtering efforts to negotiate a commercial treaty with Germany. The tariff war soon raised fears both in official circles and among the literate public that the minister of finance was engaging in what would be called brinkmanship in later days. Soon he began to feel as if he had been sent to Coventry, but he retained the full support of the tsar.

In the end Germany threw in her hand, agreeing to a conference in Berlin to negotiate a commercial treaty that would put commercial relations on an amicable footing. V.I. Timiriazev, an official in the Ministry of Finance, headed the Russian delegation, its directives coming from Witte. The bargaining at the conference, which opened in October 1893, was hard and lengthy. Three months later, the treaty, subject to renegotiation in ten years, was signed and soon thereafter ratified. In it Germany registered some gains, but Russia was clearly the winner, with Germany cutting tariff rates on grain and lumber and granting Russia most-favored-nation status. There were additional benefits for Russia, with the treaty providing a model for commercial treaties with other countries and a slight improvement in Russo-German relations. Also, the traditional "special relationship" between the Romanov and Hohenzollern dynasties was preserved, at least pro forma. Witte was widely praised, even by Bismarck, who was now in forced retirement. Witte emerged a celebrity, not at all averse to promoting himself. More to the point, his position with the tsar was further solidified.[23]

Not unexpectedly, his hubris could only grow. Earlier that year, the publisher Suvorin wrote in his diary:

> Witte has become unrecognizable. When he delivers a report [to the tsar?] his eyes are turned up to the sky, as if he were dreaming of things not of this world or of the eminence of his calling. When one speaks to him, he barely answers. It is said the tsar is pleased with his authoritative manner.[24]

Three months after ratification of the treaty, the tsar once more displayed his confidence in his finance minister by sending him on an important inspection mission to the Murman coast, north of the Arctic Circle, with two objectives in mind. The first was to study the merits and demerits of a railroad line to Murmansk, a city located on the edge of the White Sea; the second was to study the desirability of a major naval base at Murmansk or another harbor along the Murman coast.

Both Alexander and Witte were interested in the economic development of northern European Russia, hitherto a neglected area. To that end a commission had met in December 1893 to consider which of three proposed railroad lines to the north was the most desirable. All three had been found to be worthwhile, but the one to Murmansk had come in third and had been dropped from further consideration. Both the tsar and Witte thought otherwise, apparently because of the ongoing debate over the idea of a naval base on the Murman coast, this at a time when construction of a major naval base at Libau, on the Baltic Sea, had begun.

The major impulse for the Libau base had come from General N.N. Obruchev, army chief of staff, who was engaged in revising war plans. He was supported by major figures in the army and navy, most notably by Grand Duke General-Admiral Alexis Aleksandrovich, head of the navy, a bachelor noted for his interest in fast women and good food. Behind the push for this base was the growth of the German navy under the recently enthroned William II and the ongoing construction of the Kiel Canal, which would allow German warships to move swiftly between the North and Baltic Seas. There were, however, high-ranking officers who, while agreeing that there was a need for a new ice-free naval base to counter Germany, argued that Libau could be easily blockaded, while a base on the Murman coast, north of the Arctic Circle, where the Gulf Stream provided ice-free conditions, would have the advantage of facing the open sea and was therefore easier to defend. The tsar was sufficiently moved to have this alternative investigated.

So in June 1894, Witte set forth with an entourage that included experts from the Ministry of the Navy, among them a protégé of Grand Duke Alexander' Mikhailovich, son-in-law of the tsar, whose ambition it was to replace the general-admiral. Also in the entourage was a journalist, testimony to Witte's keen awareness of the power of the press, and a young artist to render memorable sights, of which there were many.[25] In accepting the assignment, Witte would be stepping on the toes of important admirals and generals, but this would be offset by the tsar's support.

Most of the trip was made via the northern rivers and the White Sea, with various stopovers, one of them at Solovetskii Island with its famous (notorious in the Soviet era) monastery, which made a deep impression on Witte. From there it was on to the Murman coast and Murmansk, with the party returning home by way of nearby Norway and Sweden.

On his return he prepared a lengthy report, which he read to an eager tsar.[26] He dwelt at length on the economic importance of the far northern part of European Russia as well as on the question of a naval base, noting that Ekaterinskaia, on the Murman coast, had a magnificent harbor, even more so than Vladivostok, and making much of the fact that it was ice-free and was on the open sea. And, for the benefit of the cost-conscious tsar, he stressed that a base on the Murman coast would be less expensive than the base under construction at Libau and that his ministry could find the funds for the northern site. Witte asserts that had Alexander lived, he would have chosen that site, but that was not to be.

This was the last time Witte would see the tsar alive. Alexander III died in his Yalta residence in October 1894. With his passing the happiest chapter in Witte's governmental career came to an end, but the most memorable achievements of his career lay ahead.

Chapter 6

A New Reign, an Old Course, 1894–1896

When Witte was asked for his assessment of the new tsar, Nicholas II, he replied that on the basis of what little he knew of him, he was of the opinion that the new ruler was "well bred, well intentioned and likable" but inexperienced and that within ten years he would be doing well. I.N. Durnovo, the minister of interior, told Witte that he was better informed and that one could expect "misfortune" under the new ruler. And there were some who saw some resemblance between Nicholas and the abnormal and somewhat despotic Tsar Paul I.[1]

The new tsar was twenty-six. He had received a "home tutoring" education that, on paper at least, was the equivalent of that provided by a university and the General Staff Academy. He had been lectured at, but not challenged, by ministers, eminent professors, generals, and clergymen. He appears to have been bored most of the time—as well he might, given the setting. In April 1890 he noted in his diary: "Today, at last and forever, I ended my studies."[2] Then there had followed four years of practical training: attendance at meetings of the State Council, the Committee of Ministers, and the Siberian Railroad Committee, and service in the Hussar and Preobrazhenskii Guards, leading to nominal command of a battalion in the latter. But, as before, he had not been challenged, nor is there any indication that he had sought to be challenged. And there was many an indication of immaturity.

"Like father, like son" did not apply to Alexander III and Nicholas II in many respects. Taking after his mother, Nicholas was of slight build, at least a head shorter than his father as well as other male members of the imperial family. Where his father was decisive and plainspoken, the new tsar lacked backbone, had excellent manners, was a "charmeur," and did not use strong language (eyebrows were raised if he uttered as much as a "damn"). Where his father inspired awe and sometimes fear, he inspired condescension during the first years of his reign and was seen as being tied to his mother's apron strings. Witte would often have occasion to bemoan Alexander's passing.

Among Witte's many regrets over Alexander's death was the fact that his successor lacked the strength to keep a tight rein over other members of the imperial family. This was quickly sensed by the grand dukes, particularly the uncles, who held high positions in the army and navy. An early instance involved Grand Duke Alexis Aleksandrovich, who, upon learning that his nephew was inclined, thanks to Witte, to support a naval base on the Murman coast, threatened to resign his post as general-admiral unless Nicholas gave up the idea. The grand duke won. Some time later the young tsar had an illuminating run-in with his uncle Grand Duke Vladimir Aleksandrovich, commander of the Imperial Guard and the St. Petersburg Military District, who repeatedly ignored the tsar's wishes about appointments. Nicholas finally exploded in a letter to his uncle: "My *kindness* is responsible for this whole incident—yes, I insist on this—my stupid kindness. I have constantly given in to avoid quarreling and disturbing family relationships . . . a blockhead, without will or character. Now, I do not merely ask, I command you to carry out my *previously expressed will*" (emphasis in original).[3]

His ministers could not take such liberties as the older grand dukes allowed themselves, but many, notably Witte, although obsequious in words, adopted a didactic and domineering manner toward their young sovereign, something Nicholas chafed at but endured, although we find him some dozen years later reminding Witte that he was a grown man.[4] This huge, rough-hewn man made the tsar uncomfortable, yet Nicholas backed his finance minister. He was committed to continuing his father's policies, and he was aware of the esteem in which both parents held Witte. He and Witte were a mismatch, yet they were destined to be linked, uneasily, for a dozen years.

The finance minister would continue on the course he had been following, but an unexpected event, the Sino-Japanese War, which had begun in August 1894, dragged him into the domain of foreign affairs, adding to the heavy burden of work he was already engaged in. As will be seen, he became involved because of the Trans-Siberian Railroad. The war put Russia on a path that would lead to bloody conflict with Japan.

At issue in the Sino-Japanese War was Korea, which China considered to be its tributary and on which Japan, less than a generation into the process of modernization, had designs. The crushing Japanese victory shocked most of the great powers, particularly Russia, and they sought to assure themselves that their interests would not be harmed by the peace terms. China, for her part, sought all the help she could get to avoid harsh terms, while Japan attempted to buy goodwill from the great powers by offering favors at China's expense. In the background was the larger issue of the continued existence of the Chinese empire, which was being ravaged by internal weakness and the external pressure of European imperialism—and now Japanese imperialism as well.

In January 1895, as Japan began peace negotiations with China without publicly revealing what terms she would demand, the tsar began to give mind to what position Russia should take. Nicholas and some of his ministers favored taking a friendly position toward Japan in return for her support of Russian efforts to acquire a port in southern Korea, a port that, being ice-free, would make the Russian naval squadron based in the often icebound harbor of Vladivostok more mobile. Witte—and he was not alone—opposed appeasing Japan, especially after terms became known in March: Chinese cession of the south Manchurian Liaotung Peninsula, Formosa (present-day Taiwan), and the Pescadores Islands, as well as recognition of Korea as an independent country and payment of a huge indemnity.

At a special conference, summoned by the tsar and presided over by Grand Duke Alexis Aleksandrovich, held on March 30, the views of the ruler were presented, leading to a heated discussion. Witte, his right to participate based on his role in the Trans-Siberian Railroad, spoke vigorously in opposition. In his view, Japan was a threat. If she was permitted to annex the Liaotung Peninsula, she would have a foothold on the Chinese mainland, allowing her to expand her grasp on Chinese territory and ultimately to take Peking (present-day Beijing) and install the mikado on the Chinese throne. In his view, the Japanese attack on China was a preemptive move intended to anticipate the completion of the Trans-Siberian Railroad, which would sharply curb Japanese ambitions. Once the Japanese were on the mainland, he argued, Russia would have to employ tens of thousands of troops to rein them in, and that would entail expenditures large enough to undermine the fiscal stability that had been established.

Since conflict with Japan was inevitable, he continued, it was better to risk war while Russia enjoyed military superiority than to wait. His proposal: an ultimatum to Japan to forgo annexation on the Chinese mainland or else. Such action, he continued, would bring the dividend of Chinese goodwill, which needed to be cultivated so that at a later date Peking could be persuaded to cede some land south of the Amur River. This would make completion of the Trans-Siberian Railroad easier. And, he continued, once that line was completed, Russia would be in a position to fulfill her ambitions in the Far East. Witte's call for an anti-Japanese position was shared by a majority of those present, a rare show of disagreement with the tsar.

Nicholas dealt with this challenge by meeting with Witte and the heads of the war, navy, and foreign affairs ministries, who succeeded in winning him over to the anti-Japanese view. The following day, April 5, China and Japan signed a treaty of peace at Shimonoseki, embodying all the terms that Tokyo had presented. Accordingly, Russia, acting in concert with France and Germany, demanded that Japan retrocede the Liaotung Peninsula. In the face of such an array, Japan had no choice but to yield without forgetting.[5] Russia, which had been relatively inactive in Far Eastern politics for some time, was now deeply enmeshed in the imperialistic rivalries there, with Witte as one of the actors in that drama.

Seeking to nurture China's assumed goodwill, his eye on rerouting the Trans-Siberian Railroad through Manchuria, he undertook to help China obtain the money with which to pay Japan the first half of the indemnity, which would soon be due. But there was a hurdle in that Russia was herself a borrower, not a lender, and the Chinese naturally first turned to Western bankers for help. They were ready, on the condition that China accept international control over her finances, as the Ottoman Empire had, to guarantee repayment, but China found the condition unacceptable—this when Witte was secretly offering to put up the money without international control.[6]

What followed was typical of his boldness, brass, and ambitious goals. He obviously expected the help of French bankers to produce the money, and as luck would have it, several of them who had been trying, with unsatisfactory results, to arrange a loan to China turned to Witte, offering to bring him into an arrangement that would not require Russia to put up much of the money. More than willing, he invited several leading French bankers to St. Petersburg, where he arranged an audience with the tsar that was followed by a meeting on June 24 at the foreign office at which the Chinese minister, in the presence of Witte and Prince A.B. Lobanov-Rostovskii, the recently appointed acting minister of foreign affairs, signed a declaration stipulating the conditions under which his country accepted the loan. Russia guaranteed repayment of the loan, most of which was provided by French bankers, the rest by Russian ones.[7]

Witte, who was proving to be as adroit as the bankers, then took them by surprise in proposing the creation of a quasi-private bank, chartered by the Russian government and to be named the Russo-Chinese Bank, to do business in China. Five-eighths of its capital was to be provided by French bankers, the rest by Russian ones. When it came to the governing board, the ratios were reversed, with the Russians getting five of the eight seats. The French were unhappy with the proposal but not enough to prevent acceptance. It was soon evident, if evidence were needed, that the bank would be a Russian tool wielded by Witte, what with Prince E.E. Ukhtomskii, his close ally, serving as director and A.Iu. Rothstein, head of the St. Petersburg International Bank, who had been instrumental in the negotiations with the French bankers, a member of the bank's board.[8]

The bank's charter permitted it to engage in a broad range of activities in

China. It could issue money and lend money for all kinds of activities, including railroads—and that included the hoped-for line through Manchuria. In a report to the tsar, Witte stated that his aim was "the strengthening of Russian economic influence in China to counteract" that of England, which he considered to be Russia's chief enemy.[9]

Witte was now ready to approach China for permission to route the Trans-Siberian Railroad through northern Manchuria. Motivating this effort was the recently gained knowledge that the route north of the Amur presented unexpected difficulties. The Manchurian route would be less expensive and shorter. Given the growing intensity of the international power struggle in China, he was anxious to complete the entire line as quickly as possible, and this meant losing no time in routing it through Manchuria.

This meant getting the tsar to approve the attempt to wheedle China into agreement. Even before the French had signed the contract for the new bank, Witte went to work. As soon as word went out about what he was up to, several high officials went on the attack, but Witte was persuasive enough to win permission from the tsar for him and Lobanov-Rostovskii to negotiate with the Chinese.

Already apprehensive about Russian intentions, with good reason, the Chinese became even more edgy and dug in their heels against granting a railroad concession to the Russian government, but there were a few high officials who were willing to entertain the thought of a concession to a Russian-backed private company. This opened the way for negotiations, but, as it turned out, not conclusive ones. When Witte learned that Li Hung-chang, China's chief minister, a friend of Russia's, was scheduled to represent his country at the tsar's coronation, scheduled for May 1896, and that he would be armed with plenipotentiary powers, Witte went to work to have exclusive access to him until an agreement could be achieved. To begin with, he was able to succeed in having Li come directly to Russia, rather than first visiting Western Europe, as planned, and to do so without contact with the press, the object being the maintenance of secrecy until an agreement was reached. Accordingly, Prince Ukhtomskii was commissioned to pick Li up at Alexandria and escort him as discreetly as possible to St. Petersburg, where Witte, Prince Lobanov-Rostovskii, Prince Ukhtomskii, and Rothstein would employ their powers of persuasion on the emissary. Ukhtomskii and his charge arrived in St. Petersburg three weeks before the coronation, providing ample time for negotiations.[10]

The going was rough. Li was aware that Russia was not the only shark trying to swim in Manchurian waters. He was also aware that he would have to pay dearly on his return home if it appeared that he had not adequately protected his country's interests. His government, justifiably suspicious of Russia, proved very difficult about granting economic concessions in the dynasty's homeland, Manchuria. To make a concession palatable, Witte, with authority granted by the tsar, offered China a defensive alliance against Japan coupled with the assurance that the proposed railroad would enhance Russia's ability to rush assistance to its ally. And, to make Li as amenable as possible, Witte was authorized to offer him a "gift" of three million rubles, one-third of which was to be paid when an agreement was signed. "Gifts" such as this one were not uncommon in dealings with the Chinese. They did not buy assent but were expected to smooth negotiations.[11] Witte arranged an audience with the tsar as an additional inducement.

In any event, Li proved to be a hard bargainer, immovable on many points but willing to give on some and to accept face-saving compromises on others. He held fast to his refusal to accept a railroad concession to the Russian government or to agree to Russian construction of the line, but he did agree to make the concession to the Russo-Chinese Bank, which would have Chinese representation on its board.

There were other points of contention as well. With the coronation approaching, negotiations were moved to Moscow, scene of the event. Finally, on May 24, 1896, Lobanov-Rostovskii (who played second fiddle in the negotiations), Witte, and Li signed a secret treaty of alliance.[12] Under its terms, an attack by Japan upon China, Korea, or Russia's Far Eastern territory would be considered a *casus foederis*. In addition, China agreed to the construction of a railroad in northern Manchuria by the Russo-Chinese Bank.

Three months later, on August 27, a contract was signed by Rothstein and Ukhtomskii for construction of a line connecting Chita on the Trans-Siberian line in the west to run through northern Manchuria and connect with the Trans-Siberian line in the east. To save face for the Chinese, it was to be called the Chinese Eastern Railroad, financed by the Russo-Chinese Bank, and constructed by a company to be called the Chinese Eastern Railroad Company. That the line would, in fact, be Russian was demonstrated by the decision to make it a broad-gauge line, to conform to the gauge used in Russia, rather than standard gauge, which the Chinese preferred.[13]

Among the many face-saving requirements that China insisted on was one that called for sale of shares in the new company to be public. Witte scuttled this restriction by having notice of the sale published in the official newspaper, which appeared the morning of the sale, with the sale hour scheduled too early for any self-respecting businessman to attend. The ruse worked, permitting his government to purchase a quarter of the shares and obtain options on the rest.[14] In short, despite provisions in the contract that assigned

China a prominent role in the company, its real master was the Russian government, with Witte acting as steward.

Moreover, the power of the Chinese Eastern Railroad was broad indeed. It was given possession of an extensive right of way, which it could administer and protect. Protection brought with it installation of units from the Ministry of Finance's Corps of Border Guards, units that came to known as "Matilda's Guards," after Witte's wife.[15] The Chinese Eastern Railroad would bring with it growing Russian influence in northern Manchuria and with it the tendency to speak of "Witte's empire."

Witte would later be accused of contributing to a critical turn in Russian Far Eastern policies. For the moment let it suffice to say that with or without Witte, Russia would have been flexing her muscle in the Far East in the wake of the Sino-Japanese War. To this must be added the fact that Witte was acquiring a strong voice in the determination of Russia's Far Eastern policy, sometimes stronger than that of the foreign affairs minister.[16] In fact, he created a quasi-Far Eastern foreign office of his own, using personnel of his own chancellery, the Chinese Eastern Railroad, the Russo-Chinese Bank, and the ministry's Far Eastern financial agents to provide him with information on which to base his views.[17] Although he disavowed the title of diplomat, he had entered the world of Far Eastern diplomacy, his chief interest the search for economic benefits, confident that this could be done without the risk of war.

Economic benefits were not enough. Recognition of Russian economic growth was also necessary. What better way than a major exposition to show off advances in Russian industry and technology, timed to open on May 28, 1896, just a few days after the close of the coronation ceremonies in Moscow, making it convenient for the tsar and dignitaries such as Li Hung-chang to visit and be impressed? Witte counted, too, on this event, located on two square miles of grounds, to attract masses of ordinary Russians and win their admiration. He was, of course, too busy to handle the preparations and first put them in the hands of a man who turned out not to be equal to the task, and then in those of one of his ablest associates, V.I. Kovalevskii.

At the opening of the exposition, in Nizhnii Novgorod, Witte delivered the welcoming remarks, declaring, among other things: "Our task is to show Russia and the entire world the spiritual and economic results which our fatherland has achieved since the Moscow Exposition of 1882." He went on to refer to "the extraordinary growth" of the country during those years, linking it to the country's protective tariff.[18] That rosy view was not shared by all.

In August, while the exposition was still in progress, a congress on industry and commerce, initiated by Witte, was held in Nizhnii Novgorod. He expected that this gathering of invited guests from government, business, and academe would provide a favorable chorus for his work. Instead, he encountered considerable criticism of the 1891 tariff, which, it was claimed, had driven up the cost of agricultural machinery, imposing a heavy burden on agriculture. Representatives from industry defended the tariff, but they were outnumbered by the naysayers. Witte did not blink, replying to criticism by declaring that the government was amenable only to "reasoned" counsel and that what he was hearing from the opposition did not so qualify.[19] What he was hearing was a sample of what he would encounter in establishing the gold standard, a process that he had already begun.

Chapter 7

The Witte System in Operation, 1892–1899

"The establishment of the gold standard was my greatest achievement as minister of finance. . . . It was I who carried out this tremendous reform, which will be regarded by history as one of the bright spots in the reign of Emperor Nicholas II."[1] Such was Witte's verdict, a bit immodest but not far from the mark. The gold standard was a pivotal part of his massive effort to create an environment that would nourish the growth of industrial capitalism. In the process of introducing the gold standard he would demonstrate once more his iron will, his ability to ride roughshod over opposition, and his dependence on the goodwill of the autocrat.

In March 1895, at a time when his ministry had accumulated a comfortable gold reserve, and believing that the time was ripe, Witte presented his case to the Finance Committee, an interagency body that dealt with matters affecting the country's credit and over which he exercised considerable influence. The committee's response was favorable, and the tsar concurred.

The next step was to win approval from the State Council's Department of State Economy for the necessary legislation. There many questions of a delaying nature were raised. Was there any need for a change in the status quo? If so, should Russia adopt a gold standard, a silver standard, or a bimetallic standard? If a metallic standard was adopted, what should the conversion rate for the paper ruble be?[2]

The bureaucratic wheels ground slowly, and it was not until March 1896 that Witte could address the moot questions at sessions of the Finance Committee, where he argued for a gold standard and against either a bimetallic standard or a silver standard, insisting that those who favored either were mistaken in the belief that silver, which had fallen in value, would soon rebound. As for the conversion rate, he favored making the gold ruble worth one and a half paper rubles. His views were supported by the committee and approved by the sovereign.[3] Next stop was the State Council, and that is where Witte encountered real trouble. Some of the opposition was the product of personal animosity, but more important was the hostility expressed by the many members of that body who were landowners and who, like others of their class, tended to believe that the depreciated paper ruble worked to their advantage.[4]

Once details of the Witte plan became public, it met with widespread hostility. As the minister of finance put it: "Virtually all educated Russians opposed [it.] . . . [They] had become accustomed to paper money, just as one becomes accustomed to chronic sickness, however debilitating such a sickness may be."[5] Even the venerable Free Economic Society spoke out in opposition. Established in 1765, one of the first of Russia's learned societies, it had a distinguished membership and enjoyed considerable support among the educated.

Witte courted public opinion, such as it was in autocratic Russia, but he was not swayed by it. What concerned him was keeping the tsar on course. Nicholas was contemptuous of what passed for public opinion, but he was susceptible to what those around him had to say and, so Witte thought, to what foreign dignitaries might have to say about an issue such as the gold standard. Accordingly, he sought, with mixed results, the support of experts and notables such as William E. Gladstone, the former British prime minister, and Felix-Jules Méline, the French premier. But he need not have worried. The tsar remained steadfast in his support. Meanwhile, time was slipping away.

Under these circumstances Witte decided to ignore the State Council and go through the Finance Committee, a procedure that he condemned in principle but was willing to employ when he saw no alternative way to accomplish what he considered of overriding importance. On January 2, 1897, with the tsar presiding, the Finance Committee approved the necessary legislation, and on the following day the monarch issued a decree calling for the minting of gold coins, with each gold ruble to be worth one and a half paper rubles. Russia was now on the gold standard, although not all the i's had been dotted and the t's crossed. This was done through decrees issued during the next two years.[6]

The January 3 decree aroused sharp anger among some State Council members, with one privately declaring it an act worthy of Paul I, whose name was commonly invoked in regard to any imperial act that seemed outrageous or bizarre.[7] But the State Council was not about to rebel and subsequently approved a statute encapsulating the gold standard decrees.

The shift to the gold standard indeed proved to be a major event in Russia's economic life. It greatly improved Russian credit abroad, helped by official publicity and the bribing of French journalists (handled with a "skill bordering on genius" by Witte).[8] A good credit rating encouraged foreign investment in Russian industry, enhancing a process already in operation. Monetary reform came at a propitious time, enabling the ruble to weather many a storm, including the war with Japan and the Revolution of 1905. By improving the country's credit, Witte was able to improve the terms under which foreign loans, an important item, could be made. Moreover, the reform went off smoothly, without disturbing prices, as had been feared. Its success owed much to the good counsel provided by Adolph Rothstein (who had helped install the gold standard in Austria-Hungary), the firm support of the tsar, and, above all, Witte's skill and iron will.

But the gold standard exacted a price. To maintain it, it was necessary to continue a protectionist policy and heavy taxation, especially burdensome to the peasantry. And while the reform enhanced Witte's reputation abroad and, to a limited degree, at home, it did not sit well with some elements at home and met with some derision, such as the dubbing of new bank notes, redeemable in gold at par, as "Witte's notes" and of new gold coins as "Matildory" (based on the given name of Witte's wife) or "Wittekindery" (Witte's children).[9]

The gold standard helped accelerate the implementation of what has been called the "Witte system," his well-articulated and impressively ambitious design for turning Russia into an industrial power. It is time to consider that system in operation. In his eyes, as it was in the eyes of others, the mainspring of industrialization was the railroad. Railroad construction increased the demand for iron and coal. To expand mining it was necessary to build more access lines. To meet the demand for rolling stock and rails by domestic production it was necessary to enlarge the capacity for iron and steel production and the manufacture of locomotives, freight cars, and the like.

In all this, his ministry's Department of Railroad Affairs, headed first by V.V. Maksimov, who had succeeded him in the post and later had to leave because of a scandal and was replaced by E.K. Ziegler von Schaffhausen, both with railroad experience under Witte, played a major role under the minister's guidance. Also involved was the Ministry of Ways and Communications, indirectly controlled by Witte. The government planned new lines, bought up some privately owned lines including the Southwestern Railroad, encouraged the merger of several privately owned lines, provided financial incentives for private construction of new lines, and assumed the task of construction of lines spurned by investors. All this in addition to construction of the Trans-Siberian and Chinese Eastern Railroads.[10]

Contributing to and benefiting from a burgeoning economy in the nineties, railroad construction was the second highest in the world, with eleven thousand miles of track, exceeded only by the United States. This gave the country a total of thirty thousand miles, again the second highest in the world. To be sure, the Russian railroad system had to serve a much larger area than those of the advanced industrial states, which had completed their railroad networks decades earlier, but what was accomplished was striking and significant.

The new lines intensified economic and social influences already at work. Heavy industry, mining, and grain export were the leading beneficiaries of growth, but the railroad age affected virtually everyone to a greater or lesser degree. Consider passenger traffic. In 1897, the railroads carried some seventy-one million passengers, traveling an average of seventy miles.[11] The economic, psychological, and social effects can easily be imagined. Moreover, the railroads provided over four hundred thousand permanent and seasonal jobs. Not to be overlooked was the military importance of many of the lines, what with the assumption in war plans of possible conflict in the Far East with one of several powers and that the enemies in the West would be Germany and her allies.

Much of the responsibility for boosting the economy lay with the ministry's Department of Commerce and Manufacture, the status of which was elevated in 1900 when its operations were placed under the aegis of an assistant minister. The department's jurisdiction was very broad, ranging from stock exchanges to weights and measures. When Witte became minister of finance, the director of the department was the lackluster A.B. Bähr, who conveniently died within a few months, which enabled Witte to replace him with V.I. Kovalevskii, who for a decade provided able and energetic leadership, cut short in 1902 by scandal brought on by Kovalevskii's mistress. Although Kovalevskii himself was free of guilt, Witte protected his own skin by easing Kovalevskii out of office and replacing him with the less talented but experienced V.I. Timiriazev.[12]

Witte's efforts were directed toward enhancing the environment in which industry and commerce could flourish as well as providing direct aid, an undertaking reminiscent of the days of Peter the Great. His efforts at improving the economic environment were awe-inspiring. He sought to reduce to the minimum the bureaucratic obstacles to the establishment of limited liability joint-stock companies (that is, corporations) but ran into a thicket of opposition. He was successful, however, in getting legislation that removed obstacles to the obtaining of patents and the registration of trademarks.[13] Then there was the problem of Russia's idiosyncratic system of weights and measures. Here he had the support of D.I. Mendeleev, the noted chemist, head of the ministry's Board of Weights and Measures, who, like Witte, favored the introduction of the metric system. This effort was foiled by bureaucratic obstacles, but the minister was able to improve the existing system.[14] Illustrative of roadblocks was that created by Pobedonostsev in preventing the attempt to shift from the Gregorian calendar, then in use in Russia and twelve days behind the Julian calendar used in the West: he successfully denounced it as a concession to Roman Catholic influence.[15] Once, on hearing

Witte speak of a working class in Russia, Pobedonostsev, still a powerful figure, exploded:

> Workers? A working class? I know of no such class in Russia. And I do not understand, Sergei Iulevich, what you are talking about. There are peasants, who constitute 90 percent of the population. And among them is a comparatively small number who work in mills and factories, but who, nonetheless, remain peasants. You are seeking artificially to create some sort of new class, some sort of new social relations, all completely alien to Russia. In this respect you, Sergei Iulevich, are a dangerous socialist.[16]

Needless to say, Witte was not perturbed by such outbursts, considering its author the last of the Mohicans. He simply continued with his program, which gave high priority to the training of skilled personnel for industry and commerce. This entailed having his ministry enter the field of education. In 1894 the ministry was given jurisdiction over new commercial schools, this at a time when there were only eight such institutions in all of Russia. Within the next few years, over 140 such institutions were established. This was only a small part of his achievements in the educational field. He succeeded in establishing polytechnic institutes in St. Petersburg, Moscow, and Warsaw, of which the first was his pride and joy. But these were not all: there were trade schools for peasants (where machine repairing was one of the subjects), commercial schools for women, merchant marine schools, and drafting and design schools. Needless to say, his efforts received the moral and sometimes financial support of businessmen. Some of them financed privately owned commercial and trade schools, one of which was named after Witte by the Brewers Association.[17]

In addition, Witte recognized the business world's need for information, more than provided by the ministry's weekly *Vestnik finansov* (Financial News). He established the daily *Torgovo-promyshlennaia gazeta* (Commercial-Industrial News) in 1893, which grew to become a robust publication. As if this were not enough, he established *Russkoe ekonomicheskoe obozrenie* (the Russian Economic Review), which dealt with general and governmental economic questions. It was the first scholarly economics journal in the country. And, using his discretionary powers, he made it possible to hold the first full-scale census in Russia's history.[18] Subsequently, he created a telegraphic agency to disseminate commercial news.

But that was not all. As suggested earlier, his system included giving direct aid to industry on an even larger scale than before. First, it provided a market (and a large one at that) for rails and other railroad equipment and for sundry needs of the armed forces, and it paid above-market prices. For example, in the late 1890s rails were bought at some 40 percent above market price.[19] If this were not enough, the government provided direct financial aid in the form of loans. Early in the reign of Nicholas II, the charter of the State Bank was revised on Witte's initiative to extend its powers to make loans for both industrial and commercial undertakings that the government considered worthy of help.[20] In practice, the State Bank often liberally interpreted restrictions on the granting of loans. And then there was the 1891 tariff, which insulated much of industry from foreign competition. Finally, it should be noted that industry benefited from preferential freight rates.

Witte's massive efforts came at a time when industry and commerce were on the upswing, and he helped accelerate their growth. During the 1890s the major cities became boomtowns. Existing industrial establishments enlarged their facilities, and new industries were coming in. Tens of thousands of peasants were flocking to the cities to supplement their meager incomes, some to work during the agricultural off-season, and others for year-round work, leaving care of their plots to their families. Some, from the poorest stratum, simply abandoned their meager rural holdings. St. Petersburg, for example, grew by one-third in the decade, reaching a population of one and a quarter million, with much of the growth resulting from immigration from the countryside.[21]

What were the consequences of Witte's efforts to speed up industrial growth? The year 1900 provides a good vantage point for assessment, for, as will be seen, it saw the beginning of a slump that affected not just Russia alone and would continue throughout the rest of his tenure as minister of finance (though the economy would make a strong recovery).

The picture is impressive. During the preceding decade the number of factory workers and miners had nearly doubled, as had industrial output. In some categories production was equal to that of already industrialized nations. In the production of oil, for which there was a growing demand, Russia led the world until 1900, when the United States began to take the lead. Some economic historians argue that Russia was ready to experience a true industrial revolution. Blackwell, for example, argues that "Russia was undergoing in the 1890's the fundamental economic change or 'take-off' that is associated with an industrial revolution."[22]

Witte wrote that on his watch "a Russian national industrial system had been established," and went on to note, "This was made possible by the system of protectionism and by attracting foreign capital."[23] Such was the case. Protectionism has already been referred to. As for foreign capital, the figures are impressive: in the five-year period from 1894 to 1899, 226 foreign-owned companies were established in Russia, in contrast to the 68 foreign-owned companies created during the preceding forty-three years.[24]

Witte does not speak of an industrial revolution, and rightly so. Some regions, such as the eastern Ukraine, could truly be said to have experienced an industrial revolution, but others, like the Urals, which had once been in the forefront in metallurgy, were still marching in the rear. Moreover, not only was Russia still overwhelmingly agricultural, but, despite some change, the countryside was still living in an earlier age. Add the fact that industry was still heavily dependent on foreign capital and that the country was yet to develop a substantial capitalist class. And although a substantial working class was forming, a considerable part of it, as noted earlier, had close ties with the rural world. Add too the fact that, in contrast with the already industrialized countries, the market for consumer goods was quite small, with much of the demand for manufactured products coming from heavy industry and the railroads. As Roger Portal put it, Russia might be said to be experiencing an industrial revolution, "but it was an incomplete revolution, incapable of effecting fundamental and rapid changes at the same time, except in certain limited geographic and economic sectors."[25] Nonetheless, Russian industry now had a momentum that it had not had before.

Another way of assessing the state of Russia's economy is to consider how far it had come in meeting Witte's stated goal, that of bringing his country's economic strength up to a level commensurate with her status as a great power. Witte was proud, very proud, of how far Russian industrialization had come, yet deeply conscious of the distance left to go.

In February 1900, in his report that accompanied the proposed state budget, he subjected the tsar to a report on the state of the economy. We can picture him, standing, in dress uniform, reading his report to a tsar who had grown somewhat wearied by his minister's didactic manner yet was far from indifferent to the substance of what he heard and would undoubtedly later read.

There was good news and bad news. The good news was that Russian industry and mining had grown at an astonishing rate in the past few years, a rate much more rapid than that experienced by the developed nations. But, Witte continued, Russia had a long way to go before she could stand on her own feet economically, to be able to meet foreign competition not only in the domestic market but also in the Asiatic markets in which she already had a foothold as well as in those she hoped to penetrate. To make his point, he cited many striking figures, such as the fact that per capita production of pig iron in Great Britain was thirteen times as great as in Russia, in the United States nine times as great, in Belgium nearly nine times as great, in Germany almost eight times as great, and in France almost four times as great. The comparative figures for the cotton textile industry that he cited were even more unfavorable. As for commerce, the figures were yet lower.

In short, Witte argued, there was a long way to go, a journey for which the country had the necessary psychic strength and the physical resources. What was necessary was the determination not to waver, for if the pace was not maintained, Russia would become a second-rate power.[26]

But he did not concern himself greatly with the collateral consequences of what may fairly be called modernization. Would autocracy survive? Would the outdated legal class system established by Catherine the Great be dismantled? Would the preeminence enjoyed by the landed nobility endure? Would the structure of peasant life be maintained? Would the growth of industry bring with it the kind of labor unrest already experienced by the developed countries? Witte was not much given to speculation. Ever the practical man, he was consumed by the task at hand rather than by the distant consequences of its implementation. But he did give some scattered indications of what collateral changes there might or might not be. Autocracy, he was convinced, would endure. He did not foresee any change in its structure but cautioned that the tsar must retain the age-old link with his people. With respect to class, he believed that within fifty years industrialists and bankers would displace the landed nobility in preeminence (see page 89). What effect this would have on political structure he left in the air.

Yet it should have been obvious even then that the growth of the bourgeoisie would lead to demands that it share in power. And a growing middle class and a growing working class could make waves. He convinced himself that Russia need not experience labor unrest. In a Pollyannaish statement in 1895 issued to his factory inspectors he declared: "In Russia there exists no working class in the same sense as in Western Europe, and hence no labor question. There is not and cannot be any ground for its growth, if together with the solicitude of the manufacturers you make every effort to strengthen the sense of legality and moral duty among the workers."[27] He appears to have believed that the workers, by virtue of their peasant ties, were more docile than their Western counterparts. And when labor unrest did begin in earnest in 1903 he put the blame on the Ministry of Interior for its labor policies. With respect to the peasantry, Witte held, as did List, that the rising tide of industrialization would lift that class in the long run. For the time being, the peasantry would have to endure the heavy burden of taxation that industrialization entailed, but its position would improve if the legal burdens under which it suffered were removed.

As a new century dawned, Witte's future seemed bright. He was the most powerful of the tsar's ministers, blessed with the visible signs of bureaucratic grace: the second highest rank in the civil service, that of actual privy councilor, the civilian equivalent of full general (no one held the highest civilian rank then or later); the position of state secretary to His Majesty, the civilian equivalent of general-adjutant; member of the highest orders of the empire.[28] He was an international celebrity, and his doings were closely followed by the domestic and foreign press.

Yet there were signs that neither he nor his system was secure. As will be seen, the tsar was beginning to waver in his support, and the economy was already feeling the effects of a European recession.

Chapter 8

Questions of War and Peace, 1896–1899

Like preceding ministers of finance, Witte dreaded war, with its unproductive drain on scarce resources. This is not say that he opposed economic and political imperialism as long as, in his opinion, it did not entail the risk of war. Increasingly, he found himself involved in the making of policies regarding matters of war and peace. Reference has already been made to his role in Far Eastern policy making. Even as he was dealing with China in 1896, he found himself having a voice in Near Eastern matters, specifically, a very risky proposal to seize the Bosporus, a part of the Turkish inland waterway, known as the Straits, that connects the Black and Mediterranean Seas.

The occasion was a series of massacres of Armenians in the Ottoman Empire in October 1895 that roused the great powers to employ what amounted to gunboat diplomacy to induce necessary reforms. As usual with crises suffered by the Ottoman Empire, this one impinged on the Eastern Question, as the congeries of problems growing out of the empire's continuing decline was called. For Russia, the use of gunboat diplomacy touched on a vital interest, that of the Straits.

An international convention, to which Russia was an unwilling signatory, closed the Straits to foreign warships when Turkey (the Ottoman Empire) was at peace unless the Turks chose to permit passage. This gave them a stranglehold on the Russian Black Sea fleet and gave Russia a mighty incentive to break out of the stranglehold one way or the other. In this instance, a foolhardy scheme was vigorously pushed by A.I. Nelidov, Russia's hawkish ambassador in Constantinople, to use the crisis as an opportunity for seizing the Bosporus. This would be a first step toward the ultimate goal, control of the Straits. Five battleships and an expeditionary force of thirty thousand men were to be used in the undertaking, which would be launched when Nelidov sent a coded signal that the time was ripe.[1]

The need for appropriations for the procurement of the shipping required for the expedition provided Witte with a voice in the special conferences that the tsar summoned to consider the scheme, which was soon scaled down to seizure of the upper Bosporus. From the first, he objected to the diversion of scarce financial resources to the undertaking and then to the undertaking itself, risking the displeasure of the tsar, who was inclined to support it. At the same time the tsar was under pressure, particularly from the French, to agree to some form of international effort to get the Turks to reform.[2] Months passed, in the course of which he submitted a memorandum to the tsar concerning the current difficulties with the Ottoman Empire.

In his opinion, that empire still had some life to it. It was in Russia's interest to help maintain its integrity. If joint European diplomatic pressure failed to result in necessary reforms, the task should be taken up by an international conference. Under no circumstances, he continued, should Russia resort to unilateral force. As for a long-term solution to the Eastern Question, that would not be possible without a large-scale war.[3] (As it turned out, World War I solved at least part of the question by destroying the Ottoman Empire.)

Evidently, Nicholas was not impressed by the argument and continued to consider going through with the action. At a special conference Witte spoke up vigorously, declaring that "this undertaking would lead in the end to a European war that would undermine the excellent political and financial situation in which Emperor Alexander III had placed the Russian Empire."[4] Seeing that Nicholas was still on the side of action, Witte subsequently sought the aid of Grand Duke Vladimir Aleksandrovich and Pobedonostsev, with whom he was on friendly terms despite their ideological differences. Soon the tsar reversed himself. The Nelidov scheme was dead, but Russian ambitions with respect to the Straits remained on the agenda. Witte attributed the reversal either to the influence of the aforementioned two or to that of God.[5] In fact, it was due to the opposition of the French, who had gotten wind of what was afoot.

In his memorandum about the Nelidov scheme Witte gave a hint of an idea that was developing in his mind, a European coalition (*soiuz*). It was probably inspired by his opposition to a proposal for a continental coalition directed against England that was being touted by the recently appointed foreign minister, Count M.N. Muravev, and General N.N Obruchev, chief of staff. In Witte's eyes England, which neither he nor the English considered to be part of Europe, was less of a potential threat than some developing nations overseas. In his view, Europe must protect her power by means of a coalition, at the core of which would be Russia, France, and Germany. Such a coalition would save Europe from internecine conflict, reduce expenditures for armaments, and give her the strength to face the rest of the world.[6]

The state visit to Russia of Emperor William II in July 1897, in the course of which he bestowed flattering attention on Witte, provided the latter with an opportunity to present his vision. This he did, eliciting a polite but noncommittal response of "interesting" from the German ruler.[7] Although nothing came of Witte's idea, he clung to it and would later assert that if it had been implemented, the 1914 war would have been averted.

Nonetheless, the Kaiser's visit had indirect practical consequences for Witte. William, eager to enhance his country's status, had decided to play a role in the Far East, which would require a naval presence there, and that would entail acquiring a naval base. The German eye fell on the Chinese port of Tsingtao, in the Kiaochow district, a port that Russia had used to berth warships from Vladivostok during the winter.

During his visit, when the two were alone, William asked Nicholas if he had any objection to a German base in Kiaochow. Apparently caught off guard, the tsar answered equivocally, enough for the reply to be transmuted by William into assent. Next followed German efforts to ensure assent from other powers. This done, it was necessary to wait for a pretext for action. Reputedly, Bismarck had said in 1890, when Germany took over protection of German Catholics abroad from the French, "The next time a German is killed, we will present the bill."[8] That time came in November 1897, when two German missionaries were murdered not far from Kiaochow. The bill that was presented and paid under duress was the lease of the Kiaochow district. In return for their assent to the German action, several powers sought "compensation," that is, leases from China! Russia pretended to be supporting China's futile resistance but would soon seek "compensation," too.[9]

The driving force in this effort was Count M.N. Muravev. Although a lazy type, he was ambitious and, unlike his predecessor, favored a vigorous policy in the Far East. Moreover, he was a bit of a schemer. Witte despised him, referring to him as "a son of Ivan Aleksandrovich Khlestakov," Gogol's fictional con man.[10] Swiftly on the heels of the German action, Muravev, in a memorandum to the tsar, argued that the time had come to acquire an ice-free port, namely, Talienwan, located at the tip of the Liaotung Peninsula on the Yellow Sea, adding that since China had asked for help against Germany, the Russian act could be justified as a response to that plea. Nicholas was won over and called a special conference for November 14, to which Witte was invited.

The session was a heated one, with the minister of war and the director of the naval ministry disagreeing and Witte objecting heatedly. It was the minister of finance's position that the German action, if countenanced, would endanger the peace and should therefore be reversed by seeking to persuade Berlin to choose some compensation for the deaths of the missionaries other than land. And if Muravev's proposal was implemented, he argued, it would only add fuel to the fire, antagonizing England, China, and Japan. Yes, Russia should win access to the Yellow Sea, but not before completion of the Chinese Eastern and then only by peaceful means. As he had done on earlier occasions, Witte spoke of Russia as following a good-neighbor policy in the Far East, in contrast to the predatory policies of European powers. In so doing, he was straining the facts, but there is no doubt that he opposed the use of force. In the end, the conferees recommended tabling the Muravev proposal, and the tsar, with obvious reluctance, acquiesced.[11]

Within days of this conference Witte was able to employ his own policy of peaceful penetration when Li Hung-chang sought Russian support for a loan with which to pay the second half of his country's indemnity to Japan. In response, Witte made support conditional on Chinese permission for the Chinese Eastern Railroad to construct a branch line to the Yellow Sea, something that had been asked for previously and was presumably tied to the completion of the railroad. In addition, the minister of finance asked for what amounted to a sphere of influence in Manchuria and Mongolia. Li Hung-chang balked and sought help elsewhere.[12]

Meanwhile, the tsar was under increasing pressure to change his mind about taking Talienwan. Witte writes that it was Muravev who engineered the reversal by waving the danger of a British landing at Port Arthur, near Talienwan, before Nicholas. There is no documentation for this assertion, but it seems valid.[13] In any event, early in December, in the course of his weekly report to the tsar, he was appalled to be told of a change of heart: the order had been given for His Imperial Majesty's warships to enter the harbors of Port Arthur and Talienwan. Witte could barely contain himself. On encountering Grand Duke Alexander Mikhailovich as he left the tsar, he said to him: "Remember this day, Your Highness: it is one that will be remembered for the terrible consequences it will have for Russia."[14]

Distraught though he was, Witte did not despair of preventing the proposed action. Earlier on, he had taken it upon himself to call on the German ambassador to advise that Berlin seek some other form of satisfaction from the Chinese other than land. Now, after seeing the tsar, he went to the German embassy to avail himself of the Kaiser's permission to communicate directly with him. At the embassy he asked that a telegram be sent to William giving him the same advice he had given the ambassador.

In so acting, he was taking a great deal of liberty with some risk to himself, knowing, as he did, that the Russian foreign office was able to decode telegrams sent from the German and other embassies. At a subsequent report to the tsar, he noted that the sovereign's manner was frigid. At the close of the report, the tsar said: "Sergei Iulevich, I advise you to be more careful in your conversations with foreign ambassadors." Witte pretended that he did not know what conversation was being referred to, assuring the tsar that he had never said anything ill-advised. He was convinced that it was Muravev who had tattled on him and that the incident accounted for the sovereign's subsequent icy attitude toward him. His suspicion about Muravev was later confirmed when Lamsdorff, Muravev's successor, showed him a decoded telegram from Prince Radolin, the German ambassador, to William II concerning Witte's advice about Kiaochow.[15]

Meanwhile, the decision to acquire Port Arthur as a naval base was being slowly implemented. Early in December, Russian warships dropped anchor in Port Arthur and nearby Talienwan, without landing any troops. Russia professed that this was a gesture to show support for China. A few days later, British warships put into Port Arthur with the explanation that they were going to winter there. This gave rise to an amusing, possibly fictitious exchange between the publisher Suvorin and an unnamed questioner, who asked why the tsar had endured such an insult. Suvorin replied: "He is only a colonel." (Upon ascending the throne, Nicholas, as a gesture of filial piety, had chosen to remain at the rank his father had appointed him to, that of colonel, a gesture that did not go over well.) To which the questioner replied: "Let him promote himself to general and not swallow such insults."[16]

What with indecision in St. Petersburg and strong British and Japanese opposition to the extension of Russian power, some two months passed in dithering. Once Britain had been appeased, Russia was ready to act firmly about the fate of Port Arthur and Talienwan. On February 28, 1898, a special conference considered what would be requested from China. By this time appetites had swelled. The majority, consisting of top brass, favored leasing not only Port Arthur and Talienwan but also the territory in which they were located, Kwantung, an area of about one thousand square miles at the tip of Liaotung Peninsula. In addition, they called for the right of the Chinese Eastern Railroad to build a branch line to the tip of the peninsula. Witte was in the minority, while the tsar enthusiastically approved of the majority opinion.[17]

At the first opportunity, Witte, apparently wishing to be assured that he still enjoyed the tsar's favor, asked if it might not be appropriate for him to be relieved of his duties, given his opposition to the adopted policy. Nicholas replied that he still valued Witte's services as minister of finance. Thereupon, Witte sought to buttress his standing, as well as to ensure that force would not be used to win Chinese agreement to Russian wishes, by resorting to the time-honored practice of bribing the appropriate officials.[18]

Bribes helped, but not enough to overcome initial Chinese reluctance to accept what amounted to demands disguised as requests motivated by Russian friendship. St. Petersburg kept pressing without threatening. Failing to find support for resistance from the other great powers, Peking finally yielded, and on March 15, 1898, Russia and China signed a convention that granted Russia what had been called for at the February 28 special conference. Russia was given a twenty-five-year lease, renewable by mutual consent, of the Kwantung Territory. Port Arthur would be a naval base, its harbor closed to all but Russian and Chinese warships. Talienwan would be a commercial port and terminus of a Chinese Eastern Railroad branch line. In the text of the convention was disingenuous, face-saving, and oleaginous language alleging that none of the provisions impinged on Chinese sovereignty and that the convention was intended to strengthen Russia's military and naval ability to protect China's northern seacoast.[19] Nicholas was so pleased with the outcome that on the following New Year's Day he bestowed signs of his favor on several of those, Witte among them, who had participated in making the convention possible.

As the minister of finance feared, the Russian action hastened the erosion of the Chinese empire. Other powers staked out spheres of influence and claimed other privileges that undermined Chinese sovereignty, while Japan, indignant at the fact that Russia was occupying land that Russia had helped deny to her, was rapidly building up her armed forces.[20]

China, for her part, felt betrayed by Russia as it became evident that, far from supporting China against the seizure of Kiaochow, Russia had supported Germany. As a result, the Sino-Russian alliance of 1896, always a bit of a fiction, became attenuated to the point of extinction. All this for a naval base for which there was no urgent need, one that was not the first choice of the armed forces.[21]

Witte deserves credit for seeking to prevent a risky action, but he was not without sin given the effect of his policy of economic penetration of Manchuria. In fact, there were allegations that his work in routing the Trans-Siberian Railroad through northern Manchuria was responsible for Russia's action in the Kwantung Territory. To such allegations he responded by saying on occasion: "Suppose that I had taken some guests of mine to the Aquarium [a cabaret] and there they had become drunk and then found their way to a brothel, where they created a scene, would I have been held responsible?"[22] The obvious answer is that in such a case he would have borne some responsibility, but there is no question that had he been successful in his efforts to restrain Germany and Russia in 1898, subsequent events would probably have taken a better turn.

Even as negotiations for the Kwantung lease were coming to an end, attention was shifting to Europe. Late in February 1898, minister of war A.N. Kuropatkin, who would play a part in the next stage of Witte's career, alerted the tsar to the fact that France and Germany were acquiring rapid-firing field artillery, a luxury that Russia could not afford—a point that Witte had already made in opposing further increases in military expenditures.[23] The general proposed that Russia and Austria-Hungary, which had not yet adopted the advanced weaponry, sign a ten-year moratorium on new weaponry. If the proposal succeeded, he argued, it might encourage a halt to the arms race, save the world vast amounts of money, and bestow the "aureole" of peace-maker on the tsar. Even if the proposal failed, the tsar would earn good press.

Nicholas was more than a little receptive. He authorized Kuropatkin to proceed, in partnership with Muravev.[24] Before long the proposal became the basis for a plan to have the tsar summon an international conference to consider a halt to the arms race. The foreign minister was certain that such an initiative would earn praise abroad and assure other powers that, despite her recent actions in the Far East, Russia was committed to preserving the peace in Europe.[25]

During the preparations for the conference Kuropatkin shared with the tsar a picture of what an enduring peace would require. As he saw it, Russia's chief goal in the coming century was to seize control of the Bosporus and thus dominate the Straits. Such an act would rouse the Slavs to actions that would hasten the "inevitable" disintegration of the Austro-Hungarian Empire. Russia would form a confederation with Serbia and Bulgaria, while Germany would be permitted to annex the Germanic parts of the defunct empire, an act that would make her somewhat amenable to returning Alsace-Lorraine to France but not quite ready to actually do so. The odds for a successful joint attack by Russia and France to force Germany were no more than even, in his opinion, but when the "inevitable" war between Germany on one side and England and the United States on the other over markets and colonies broke out, it would be possible to compel Germany to return the two provinces. That done, Russia could be satisfied with the status quo in Europe. As for the Far East, Russia had a "historical mission" there, about which more later. Such were the musings of a man called "a clever and brave general" with "the soul of a staff clerk."[26]

Nearly six months passed between the birth of the idea of a conference and the issuance of the invitation to attend it—months of meetings and planning, of calming those who feared that the goal was disarmament rather than arms limitation and those in the French military that recovery of Alsace-Lorraine was in peril.[27] During that time, Witte, when asked by Muravev for his thoughts about the conference, repeated the views about the dire consequences of the arms race he had expressed to the kaiser a year earlier. In addition, he noted that Great Britain and the United States were employing the advantage of geography to maintain small armies while adding to their respective navies, which gave the two an increasing voice in world affairs. Hence he argued that limiting further naval buildup would increase the advantage that the two enjoyed while "limiting the ability of several powers to safeguard their extra-European rights and interests."[28] Although he played a minor role in preparing the conference, his views were well represented in the tsar's invitation to the conference, which became known as the First Hague Peace Conference.

Meeting in the Hague from May to July 1899, it produced little to show for all its length and its unending series of solemn and long-winded speeches. It did not realize its chief purpose, a halt to the arms race, though this could have been expected given the extensive opposition to any limitation among the powers. But the conference took several steps, such as prohibiting the use of poison gas, otherwise limiting the hellishness of war, and maintaining the peace through means such as establishing a permanent court of arbitration. The court was not quite the kind of body Witte sought for the settlement of international disputes, but it was a step forward. And Russia did receive good press, given the fact that motherhood and the language of peace are sure to win applause.

Chapter 9

Decline and Fall, 1899–1903

The abrupt and unexpected removal of Witte from the office of minister of finance in August 1903 gave rise to a spate of conflicting accounts, some hair-raising, of the circumstances of his departure. One lurid account is by A.A. Lopukhin, director of the Department of Police of the Ministry of Interior at the time of Witte's departure. He claims that Witte was toppled for engaging in a conspiracy, using trumped-up evidence, to replace his hated rival, V.K. Plehve, as minister of interior; the latter was informed of the effort and passed on the information to the tsar, who summarily sacked the minister of finance. This version, published two decades after the event, does not seem credible.[1]

More credible, but only part of the story, is the explanation offered by Kuropatkin, entered in his diary less than two weeks after the event. He spoke of three mines exploding simultaneously under the minister of finance: the first, set by Grand Duke Alexander Mikhailovich, who persuaded the tsar, if persuasion were necessary, that Witte had amassed too much power; the second set by A.M. Bezobrazov, whom we shall soon meet, who put it to the tsar that Witte's views on Far Eastern policy were harming the country; the third set by Plehve, who was getting Nicholas to believe that the minister of finance was disloyal, that he was encouraging dissident elements among the Armenians, Finns, Jews, and students.[2] The general's interpretation has to be considered against a background that includes the state of the economy.

But be it noted that although Witte began experiencing difficulties in 1899, he was able to register some victories for a few years. First was the replacement of minister of interior I.L. Goremykin, a colorless bureaucrat, by D.S. Sipiagin. Witte and Goremykin crossed swords in 1898 over police brutality toward students who were boisterously celebrating the anniversary of the founding of St. Petersburg University. Goremykin defended the police, who treated the high jinks as a political act, while Witte and others defended the students and condemned the police. Subsequent investigation affirmed Witte's view.[3]

A more serious difference between Witte and Goremykin arose in the same year, when the minister of interior proposed extending the institution of zemstvos to the western provinces, which had been denied the privilege because of their part in the Polish revolt of 1863. Zemstvos were local elective bodies that had been established during the reform period. Goremykin considered them to be useful bodies that were compatible with the autocratic principle. Witte, on the other hand, believed that zemstvos and autocracy were at odds, that not only should they not be extended to the western provinces but also that zemstvos should be subject to corrective measures. In the course of polemics with Goremykin over the proposal he submitted a very lengthy, quasi-scholarly disquisition, reputedly prepared for him by a law professor, in which he presented his arguments, concluding with his affirmation that he concurred with the view that constitutionalism was "the great lie of our times."[4] The document appears to have been a shot aimed at Goremykin and his proposal. At the same time, it served to reaffirm in the eyes of the tsar that Witte was a true believer in autocracy. In any event, Goremykin was replaced and his proposal was shelved, but we have not seen the last of the man or the proposal. Goremykin would turn out to be the tortoise and Witte the hare.

For Witte the tsar's choice of Sipiagin to be head of the powerful Ministry of Interior was a happy one. The new minister was married into the upper nobility and well thought of at court, and therefore in a position to counter the hostility toward Witte that prevailed there. The two ministers were an odd pair. Sipiagin was deeply concerned over the welfare of the landed nobility, while Witte pursued policies much resented among that class. Sipiagin believed that the sovereign was free to act however he pleased, no matter what the law said. Witte, on the other hand, while believing that the autocrat was free to change the law, argued he was bound to observe existing law and that to think otherwise was equivalent to believing in papal infallibility.[5] Sipiagin was a perfect gentleman in appearance and demeanor, Witte quite the contrary. Yet they got along famously, with Sipiagin helping the minister of finance win approval for his proposals and Witte being generous in approving funds for remodeling the minister of interior's official residence.

Of even more value was the appointment, in 1900, following Count Muravev's unexpected death, of Count Lamsdorff as minister of foreign affairs. Unlike his predecessor, Lamsdorff believed in a cautious foreign policy. We will find him working in tandem with Witte in the formulation of Far Eastern policy. Doubtless, Witte expected this when he responded to the tsar's request for the name of a suitable person to head the Ministry of Foreign Affairs by recommending the count. The fact that Nicholas waited a month before making the appointment suggests that he was not enthusiastic about the candidate, whom he reportedly referred to as "madam" because of the count's homosexuality.[6] For Witte the appointment was a godsend, what with Far Eastern affairs coming to a boil.

Then, on the first day of 1903, came the tenth anniversary of his being raised from the post of acting minister of finance to that of minister. By this time he was the only one of the ministers Nicholas had taken over from Alexander III still in office. He managed to make the most of the occasion, and the tsar made it sweeter by sending Witte a rescript (letter of commendation) warmly congratulating him on the occasion, thanking him for his valuable services, and expressing his continuing confidence in the minister. In addition, the tsar thanked Witte for providing instruction in economics to the heir to the throne, Grand Duke Michael Aleksandrovich.[7] That, far from feeling kindly toward Witte, Nicholas was actually ready to part with him is a possibility that will be dealt with later.

Despite appearances, Witte's position was, as indicated earlier, being eroded. His major troubles began with an economic depression that started in 1899 and impinged on Russia as well as the rest of Europe. It opened with the tightening of the money markets in western Europe, with a consequent rise in interest rates. The fact that many Russian industrial and railroad firms were involved in banking operations made them vulnerable to developments in the West. Two such major firms, Mamontov and von Derviz, went bankrupt in August of that year. Russia, like the rest of the Europe, had its taste of depression. Orders and prices fell, workers were laid off, more firms went bankrupt.

As could have been expected, management's efforts to maintain profits at the expense of labor led to widespread strikes. The most serious of these was a railroad strike in 1902 in southern Russia. This strike spread quickly and was marked by political as well as the usual economic characteristics, a harbinger of things to come.

Witte used what resources were available to him to help ailing and failing enterprises, while at the same time putting as good a face as he could on the state of the economy.[8] An ailing economy could not help but shake the tsar's confidence in Witte's exhortations against wavering in pursuing the goal of industrialization. Even before the onset of economic depression, criticism of Witte's policies was voiced in high places. In 1898 Nicholas was subject to advice from some close to him that it was necessary to limit the influx of foreign capital. Witte got wind of this and met the challenge head-on by asking the tsar to summon a special conference. The minister carried the day at the meeting, but this did not silence the voices of those in a position of influence who insinuated that there was something sinister as well as dangerous in the policy of attracting foreign capital.[9]

Another source of trouble for Witte came from the countryside, particularly the landed nobility. Illustrative was the report that the nobility of Orlov province had declared that if Ermolov, the minister of agriculture, and Witte exchanged posts, all would be well with the Russian economy.[10] The point of this flippant suggestion was that Ermolov, being a passive type, would follow a do-nothing policy and that Witte would apply his overwhelming energy to dealing with the needs of the countryside, particularly those of the landed nobility.

First, a word or two about terms. The landed nobility, landowners whose holdings were large enough to provide them with a substantial income, were part of the nobility, the first estate in the system of estates established by Catherine the Great. In 1885, Alexander III reaffirmed the preeminence of the nobility in a document declaring that estate to be his good right arm and that it should enjoy "preponderance in the army, local administration and in the courts."[11] The nobility as a whole enjoyed some privileges, but it was the landed nobility, well represented at court, in the officer corps and the State Council, that sought and received the most attention. Thus, 1885 saw the creation of the Nobles Land Bank, which was intended to provide credit on easy terms to the landed nobility as "a means of preserving their estates for their posterity."[12]

But the prospects of the landed nobility were dimming, as had been the case ever since the emancipation of the serfs, and had become even dimmer during Witte's tenure as minister of finance. Increasingly, its members were either mortgaging their land to the Nobles Land Bank or selling some or all of their land to municipalities, merchants, or peasants. Falling grain prices, brought on by foreign competition, contributed to their troubles. Landed nobles tended to see Witte as a major source of their difficulties. In their view, his protectionist policies, which favored industry, had raised the cost of agricultural tools and machinery. And then there was the gold standard, which they saw as the cause of much of their hardship. Among the more conservative of them, what might fairly be called the lunatic fringe, were those who saw the gold standard as a tool of an international Jewish conspiracy. Their spokesman was S.F. Sharapov, a journalist who once worked for Witte. In one of his diatribes about the gold standard he wrote:

> The closely woven web of international Jewry . . . is concerned that the present situation should be maintained at all costs, whereby the international usurers increase their wealth, the productive classes are destroyed and the old Christian structure of Europe collapses.[13]

Not unexpectedly, Sharapov saw Witte as the ally of Jewry and wrote to the tsar urging the minister's removal and even recommending possible successors.[14]

Witte gave as good as he got. In his scheme of things the landed nobility was seen as a moribund breed. At a Special Conference on the Needs of the

Nobility that opened in 1897 he spoke at length about the future of the landed nobility. He predicted that within fifty years Russia would be in the same position as western Europe was then, dominated by industrialists and bankers, and advised landed nobles that if they sought a secure future, they should pay less attention to shoring up their position as landowners and move into industry and banking.[15] These were not words that would make friends.

As he saw it, the majority of landed nobles were "degenerates" who looked to the government for sustenance.[16] In his opinion what was worse was the fact that successive ministers of agriculture and ministers of interior catered to the landed nobility.

The condition of agriculture had not received much attention from Witte, but with the passage of time and the growing cry that the country was faced with a threatening agrarian question, he had no choice but to become involved in attempts to deal with it and in so doing clarify and express his views. He was given such an opportunity when he was invited to participate ex officio in the 1897 Special Conference on the Needs of the Nobility. As already seen, he was not shy about expressing his views. At one of the early sessions he argued that since the well-being of the landed nobility was closely linked with that of the peasantry, the conference should give primary attention to the latter. The suggestion died aborning, though the conference sputtered on until 1901, accomplishing little of importance.[17] But it should noted that at this conference Witte came to verbal blows with V.K. Plehve, who aligned himself with the landed nobility and would contribute mightily to the minister of finance's downfall.

The Committee of Ministers' proposal, in 1898, for holding a conference on the problems of the peasantry gave Witte an opportunity to share his thoughts on the subject with the tsar. He had little knowledge, direct or indirect, of the countryside, but, as usual, he had learned on the job, processing what he had learned from the point of view of the needs of Russia as a great power. In October 1898, he sent a lengthy, impassioned letter to the tsar, then vacationing in the Crimea, about the rationale for consideration of the needs of the peasantry. He argued that "the most pressing question facing Russia is that of the peasantry."

The heart of the matter, in his opinion, was that the peasants had been robbed of initiative, that half of them merely "vegetated" because of the legal restrictions that hobbled them, because of the defects of the village commune, because of their lack of proper education. In describing the state of the peasantry he showed compassion, but his emphasis was on what in later years would be called the bottom line. In his view: "The destiny of Russia requires ever increasing expenditures. These are small considering the size of our population. That they seem excessive arises not from poverty but from disorganization." In short, from his point of view, it was urgent to address the peasant question with the aim of increasing their taxpaying capacity.[18]

He assumed that the tsar would follow the recommendation of the Committee of Ministers for the summoning of a conference on the peasant question and ventured to suggest D.M. Solskii, chairman of the State Council's Department of State Economy and a close acquaintance of Witte's, to chair the conference. Witte was mistaken. Such a conference was not to be, but early in January 1902, after a bad harvest, the tsar directed Sipiagin to review existing peasant legislation. Not long thereafter Nicholas decreed the formation of a Special Conference on the Needs of Agricultural Industry, with Witte as chairman. This was not a burden that he sought, but it was one he could not avoid, being told by the tsar that he was the only person who could handle the responsibility.[19]

The chairmanship was a liability as well as a responsibility. There was many an important toe he could step on, not to speak of the landed nobles already arrayed against him. One major subject that had to be dealt with using extreme caution was the village commune, which the powers that be considered sacrosanct. Not all village communes were cut from the same cloth, but they shared some basic features. Almost all peasant land was part of a village commune. The land was divided into noncontiguous strips, with each peasant family entitled to several strips, the number depending on the family's size. The village commune decided what and when to plant and when to let some of the land lie fallow. Individual initiative was not encouraged, and productivity was low. In theory a peasant could withdraw his land from the commune, consolidate strips, and farm as he wished, but in practice he could not. In his Slavophile days Witte had extolled the village commune as one of the key institutions that made Russia superior to the West. By this time his faith in the village commune was gone, yet he had to avoid raising the subject of its viability.[20]

Early on, the conference came under the shadow of two events. The first, in March 1902, was a series of peasant riots in Kherson and Poltava provinces, in the course of which landed nobles were driven from their homes, some of which were set afire, all this accompanied by looting. Did this spur the tsar to engage in serious thought about the agrarian question? Not at all. His response was to assure the local landed nobility that it was his "constant concern" to strengthen the nobility, which he considered the "traditional bastion of order and of the moral strength of Russia." His message to the local peasantry was that they set aside any expectation of land redistribution and that they obey the powers that be.[21] The implicit message to Witte and his conference was not to challenge the status quo.

That message was underlined by the tsar's choice of a successor to Sipiagin, who was assassinated by a revolutionary student on April 12, 1902, this at a time of widespread labor strikes. The man he selected, much to Witte's dismay, was Plehve, who became ex officio a member of the conference. The new minister of interior supported the landed nobility, loathed Witte, and sought to undermine the minister of finance and the conference. Plehve was not the only cross Witte had to bear in those days. Nonetheless, he threw himself into the work of the conference with his usual energy.

The conference, essentially an ad hoc committee consisting of Witte, other ministers, key members of the State Council, and the head of the Moscow Agricultural Society, took a fairly bold step by creating provincial and district (county) committees to collect information and make recommendations about rural needs. These committees enlisted the services of local officials, zemstvo members, agricultural specialists, and a *few* peasants. Although the committees hardly ever ventured into politically dangerous territory, it was enough to ring alarm bells in the Ministry of Interior and lead to some arrests.

The committees worked diligently, collecting vast amounts of information and recommendations about such matters as rural education, the legal status of the peasantry, the operations of the village commune, local administration, and the local judiciary. The work went fairly quickly, with the provincial committees collating and editing the material supplied by the district committees. Final distillation was left to the Special Conference personnel. The end product was contained in several dozen volumes. But the conference had yet to agree on the recommendations that it would transmit to the tsar when the sovereign summarily decreed the end of the conference early in 1905 without showing Witte the courtesy of advance notification. This affront was a clear sign that Nicholas had been influenced by those who had long been insinuating that the conference was somehow subversive, a sign reinforced by his choice of Goremykin to chair a commission to consider the peasant question.[22]

Witte's troubles were compounded by setbacks relating to Far Eastern policy, setbacks that involved three Bs: Bezobrazov, the Boxer Rebellion, and Briner. The principal issues impinging on the minister of finance's future were whether he would continue to have a major voice in the shaping of Far Eastern policy—a policy of peaceful penetration of China and the pretense of being China's friend, of avoiding risks, especially the risk of provoking Japan, all of which required the maintenance of the tsar's confidence. To be sure, Witte had already suffered a setback in the decision to lease the Liaotung Peninsula and to construct a naval base at Port Arthur. But he was in a strong position, with support from General A.N. Kuropatkin, the minister of war, and from Lamsdorff, once Muravev was gone.

The Briner story begins in 1896, when a Russian merchant named I.I. Briner received a concession from the Korean ruler giving him the exclusive right to cut timber in an area, slightly smaller than Delaware, that bordered on Manchuria and was close to Russia's Maritime Province, with waterways of strategic importance to both Japan and Russia. One condition of the concession was that Briner begin operations within five years. Being short of capital, he used a stay in St. Petersburg to seek support for the enterprise, but he met with no success until he was put in touch with V.M. Vonliarliarskii.

Vonliarliarskii, a former Chevalier Guards officer with good connections at court and an eye for the easy ruble, saw the possibility of using the concession as a base for creating a major company that would do business not only in Korea but in other parts of the Far East as well. After failing to rouse the interest of Witte's "right-hand man" in banking affairs, Rothstein, he turned to A.M. Bezobrazov, who had also served in the Chevalier Guards, and was even better connected at court than he.[23]

Bezobrazov had served in the Holy Brotherhood (see page 25), working closely under Count I.I. Vorontsov-Dashkov, the minister of the imperial court, and had subsequently held a series of minor positions in that ministry. Although Vorontsov-Dashkov, a grandee, was no longer minister, he retained access to the tsar and made it possible for Bezobrazov to submit the idea of the government's taking over the Briner concession to the tsar.[24]

Bezobrazov, a man in his forties, had obviously not had a distinguished career, but he was now in a position to make a mark. A man of strong opinions on a variety of subjects, opinions not necessarily buttressed by knowledge, he was thought by some to be a genius and by others no more than a gasbag who could talk the ears off a deaf donkey.[25] He shared the view that Witte's economic policies were a disaster and that the minister of finance was working hand in hand with the Jews. More to the point, he attacked Witte's Far Eastern policy as being too timid because of its reliance on Chinese friendship (a weak reed, in his opinion) and his fear of provoking Japan. Bezobrazov believed that Russia should act vigorously and that Japan would not dare to attack her.

Bezobrazov was convinced that the Briner concession, if used properly, would permit Russia to control northern Korea and use it as a staging area for operations in Manchuria. He envisioned the stationing of twenty thousand reservists and veterans disguised as lumberjacks for possible use. In a memorandum that he and Vonliarliarskii prepared that was transmitted to the tsar by Vorontsov-Dashkov in late February 1898, it was proposed that an allegedly private commercial company, under government aegis, would be able to gain virtual control over all of Korea. The tsar, who by this time was anxious to assert himself and, it seems, was not immune to dreams of Russian expansion in East Asia, authorized the purchase, with imperial funds, of the Briner concession in the name of an imperial court official. He delegated authority over this secret operation to Grand Duke Alexander Mikhailovich and Count Vorontsov-Dashkov, with day-to-day supervision to be in the hands of Bezobrazov and Vonliarliarskii.[26] Bezobrazov soon proved to be the senior figure in what is usually called the Yalu concession, so named for the river that was its border. All this at a time when Russia was concluding the Nissi-Rosen Convention recognizing Japanese interests in Korea!

What may be called the Bezobrazov proposal was sheer fantasy, perhaps not as fantastic as the Badmaev proposal (see pages 55–56), but fantasy nonetheless. Witte had been taken in by Badmaev, while Alexander III had not. Now, roles were reversed. More important, we see the beginning of what Vorontsov-Dashkov would justify in a letter to Witte: a two-track Far Eastern policy, with the tsar having an official policy with one set of personnel and an unofficial policy with another set.[27] Work on implementing the Yalu concession was begun and would continue for several years without concrete results, but it was not without some significance. It marked the beginning of a two-track policy, the declining influence of Witte and Lamsdorff, and the corresponding growth of the influence of Bezobrazov at a critical time in the Far East, namely, the outbreak of the Boxer Rebellion.

"Boxers" was the English name given to a populist xenophobic group whose Chinese name translates as "Fists of Righteous Harmony." The group's aim was to forcibly relieve the white man of his "burden" of dominating, exploiting, and converting the Chinese. This they undertook to do in late 1899, soon receiving covert, and sometimes open, support from the Chinese government, which was being pushed to the wall by imperialistic pressure. The rebellion opened with attacks on missionaries and converts, followed by attacks on foreign-owned property in and around Peking, culminating in the besieging of the legations in the capital. In this the rebels were aided by Chinese troops.

The foreign powers affected by the rebellion were of no mind to tolerate attacks on persons or property and undertook to overcome force with force, see to it that the guilty were punished, exact reparations, and demand new privileges. That was also the sentiment in St. Petersburg, but there dissenting voices were heard. Witte, supported by Lamsdorff, counseled restraint so as to retain Chinese goodwill and would support action only if Russian interests in Manchuria were threatened. The two quickly found themselves in collision with Kuropatkin on the question of using force, while the tsar vacillated between the two sides. Before long, the decision was made to have a Russian force participate in a joint expedition to relieve the legations in Peking. And when it became evident that the Ministry of Finance's Border Guards were not equal to protecting the Chinese Eastern Railroad, Witte reluctantly asked for regular troops to be sent to Manchuria.[28] The question now on the table was what use, if any, would be made of the presence of Russian troops in Manchuria? Would they depart without further ado once order was restored, or would they remain until some advantages could be squeezed out of the Chinese government?

In December 1900, in a letter to Lamsdorff, Kuropatkin declared that he was not in favor of annexing Manchuria but was in favor of retaining some regular troops there even after order was restored, to help protect the Chinese Eastern Railroad.[29] Witte, as could have been predicted, wanted all regular troops withdrawn as soon as order was restored, and to bring that day closer he provided help to the governors of the three provinces that constituted Manchuria.

Over Witte's and Lamsdorff's objections, regular troops remained even after order was restored, acting as an occupying force. This raised the question among foreign powers of what Russia's intentions toward Manchuria were. Annexation? Exclusion of other powers from any economic activities? Use of it as a staging area for penetration of Korea? England and Japan were especially sensitive to the possibilities, as was, it goes without saying, China, its government barely functioning. So things dragged on during 1901.

Japan's major aim was to solidify its predominant position in Korea, and Russia seemed to be the major obstacle to achieving that aim. Also fanning Japanese fears of Russia was the prospect of having Manchuria completely closed to it. The closer the Trans-Siberian and Chinese Eastern lines came to completion, the more uneasy the Japanese became, and although there were still gaps in the lines, Russia had just shown that it could transport troops overland to China. And although the paperwork on the Yalu concession was being kept secret, the existence of the bombastic Bezobrazov was visible. Those in Japan favoring war against Russia were quite vocal, but there were also those in high places who preferred negotiation with Russia as the means to solidify the Japanese position in Korea. It was under these circumstances that Marquis Ito arrived in St. Petersburg in December 1901.

At the time he held no office, having recently been replaced as prime minister, but he was a member of the Genro, the group of elder statesmen who wielded great power in Japanese policy making, and he was speaking unofficially for his government. What he asked for was Russian recognition that Korea was Japan's exclusive sphere of influence in return for some token concessions.

Had Ito's proposal been accepted, the forces for peaceful negotiation in Japan would have been strengthened, something that Witte, Lamsdorff, and Kuropatkin favored, but they were not prepared to give Ito as free a hand as he asked for, and they wanted quid pro quo. Lamsdorff, in consultation with the ministers of finance and war, prepared a counterproposal, approved by the tsar, that put some limitations on Japanese exclusive rights in Korea and that called for Japanese recognition of the Chinese areas bordering Russia as Russian spheres of influence.[30]

Witte attributes the failure of the Ito mission to the influence of Bezobrazov and his coterie, but that is obviously not the case. Despite the fact that he did not consider Korea a vital interest and did not deem Japanese annexation of that peninsula a casus belli, together with Lamsdorff and Kuropatkin he apparently thought of Korea as a bargaining chip.

The Japanese, however, were in no mood for bargaining at this time because they were moving ahead toward an alliance with Great Britain and saw no reason to give an inch. It is easy to imagine the shock produced when the alliance was announced in February 1902. Although not specifically directed against Russia, it was clear that such was the case. Great Britain obligated herself to observe benevolent neutrality if Japan should find herself at war in defense of her "special interests" in Korea and to go to her aid if a third power entered the fray.

The alliance was but one blow to the Russian position in the Far East. The United States, which had recently become a Pacific power, unofficially aligned itself with British policy toward Russia. China was stiffening its spine against Russian pressure, helped by the fact that other powers were evacuating the troops they had sent in to cope with the Boxer Rebellion. Russia was becoming isolated in a hostile environment, and Witte and Lamsdorff were sharing the blame for Russian setbacks.[31]

For many, especially in the military, the Russian evacuation agreement, signed in March 1902, was such a setback, an unjustified concession to outside pressure. The agreement obliged Russia to remove her troops from Manchuria in three stages within eighteen months.[32] How faithfully she fulfilled the obligation would tip the balance toward war or peace.

Of course Witte was pleased by the agreement, but he was increasingly weighed down by the weakening of his own position and by the general state of affairs. First there was the growing influence of Bezobrazov as the tsar grew disenchanted with what might be called the Witte-Lamsdorff-Kuropatkin line, that the risk of war with Japan, a war that could only promote domestic unrest, must be avoided.[33] As early as July 1901 we find Witte complaining to Sipiagin that Bezobrazov was getting to see the tsar twice a week for long chats, in the course of which he was proposing all sorts of harebrained schemes and trying to undermine the minister of finance's position.[34] And equally disturbing was the fact that Plehve, the new minister of interior, was allying himself with Bezobrazov.

Plehve quickly proved to be Witte's most dangerous enemy, inspired by ideology and to a greater degree by ambition. His new position gave him considerable power to undermine his rival. He had the opportunity to see the tsar to report on what he deemed to be the state of the country and in so doing to bring to the sovereign's attention letters addressed to the minister denouncing Witte, as well as copies of similar letters a unit of the post office obtained through what it called "perlustration."[35] What is more, Nicholas found Plehve more to his liking as a person than he did Witte.

A few days after Plehve's appointment Suvorin, the publisher, called on Witte and afterward noted in his diary: "I have never seen him so depressed, so weepy. He says that if he could find a proper way to get out, he would ask to be relieved of his position."[36] Plehve was not Witte's only concern, but he was the most formidable one. The two had squared off earlier on many issues, chief among them the physiognomy of Russia. Witte envisioned a Russia in which autocracy coexisted with industrial capitalism, Plehve a Russia in which the old regime lived on, with the landed nobility holding the place of honor, a regime that had no place for Jews, whom he considered a cancer on the body politic.[37] Witte, although far from being the friend of the Jews, as charged by his enemies, believed, as has been seen, in the ultimate assimilation of the Jews.

Among the many issues between them was the employment of Russification policies towards the minorities. Despite the fact that he upheld the doctrine of "Russia, one and indivisible," Witte opposed Russification. Thus, he clashed with Plehve over the latter's ongoing role in seeking to destroy the autonomy of Finland, in which the fires of opposition were raging out of control. Also, they were at odds over Russification policies being imposed, at great political cost, on Armenians in the Caucasus, a region toward which Witte had an almost proprietary feeling.[38]

For good measure the two disagreed on Far Eastern policy. On becoming minister, Plehve chose to support Bezobrazov, a move that would please the tsar. In return the sovereign would include the minister of interior in the small group that would help decide Far Eastern policy.

The fact that Witte and Plehve disagreed on many important matters did not necessarily spell enmity. Witte disagreed with Sipiagin on some matters and with Pobedonostsev on many more, but he respected both. In his book, both were straight arrows, men foreign to subterfuge and intrigue, but he saw in Plehve a chameleon, a scoundrel. For the record, Plehve said that although he disagreed with Witte on some matters, he thought highly of the minister of finance's accomplishments. Off the record, in an egregious understatement he admitted that he was not one of Witte's admirers.[39]

As already noted, a lesser enemy, but one who carried considerable weight, was Grand Duke Alexander Mikhailovich, the tsar's brother-in-law. The grand duke, an ambitious but limited naval officer, having failed to displace the head of the naval ministry, set his sights on the merchant marine. In 1901 Witte agreed to having the grand duke become a member of the Merchant Marine Council of the Ministry of Finance. They soon were at odds, leading the grand duke to inform his brother-in-law that it was impossible to work with Witte.[40] One of the grand duke's ambitions was to turn a section of the Ministry of Finance into a new body, the Ministry of the Merchant Marine, but he was frustrated in this by the combined efforts of Witte and the head of the Ministry of the Navy.[41] Having failed in this effort, he succeeded in persuading the tsar to agree to the creation, in July 1902, of the Chief Administration of the Merchant Marine, an independent agency, with the grand duke as its chief and Bezobrazov's cousin, A.M. Abaza, a naval officer, as the grand duke's deputy.[42] This was one in the loss column for Witte.

Meanwhile, he was being buffeted during the ongoing depression for several of his economic policies. In 1902 he was beset by attacks on the record of the Trans-Siberian and Chinese Eastern railroads. He had predicted a very rosy future for the Trans-Siberian. In 1902, a decade after work on the line had been started and at a time when damage done to the Chinese Eastern Railroad by the Boxers was being assessed and repaired, Witte was being charged with failing to deliver on his predictions. The benefits promised had yet to materialize, while the cost of construction and maintenance had been far greater than anticipated.[43]

Never one to run away from a fight, Witte won permission from the tsar to visit Manchuria to check on the state of the Chinese Eastern Railroad. He left in the late summer of 1902, including in his itinerary the naval bases in Vladivostok and Port Arthur. On his return he hand-delivered his report to Nicholas, then vacationing in the Crimea. The minister of finance used the document not only to deal with the railroad but also to paint a glowing picture of what he had accomplished in the Far East and a somber picture of what would eventuate from failing to complete the evacuation of troops from Manchuria, from meddling in Korea, and from failing to come to terms with Japan.

The effort was self-defeating. The tsar, most likely put off by Witte's self-promotion and counsel, was evidently listening to Bezobrazov, who had returned to favor after a brief period out of it.[44] Significantly, as the year was drawing to a close, Nicholas authorized Bezobrazov to journey to Manchuria to expedite work on the Yalu concession, about which more later.

Toward the end of the year Witte's stock seemed down, far down. In November A. Boutiron, the chargé d'affaires of the French embassy, wrote home that Witte's position was shaky, that most of his colleagues were hostile toward him, that his absence in Manchuria had been exploited for intrigue against him, and that Plehve seemed to be the mastermind.[45] A month later we find Suvorin writing in his diary that Witte was barely holding his own.[46]

The year 1903 had started off on a favorable note for Witte, with the imperial rescript honoring him on the anniversary of his becoming minister of finance. But the document masked the tsar's real feelings about the man. It is evident that he was prepared to part with Witte both because he was trying to assert his authority and because he was coming to accept the view that his minister of finance was on the wrong track. But he was still not up to the challenge of what would be a traumatic step. As the atmosphere in the Far East grew more ominous and the debates more acrimonious, with Witte opposed to positions taken by the tsar, the tsar's resolve to part with the man evidently became firmer.

Evacuation of Russian troops from Manchuria continued to be the focus of attention, but not to the exclusion of the Yalu concession. What policy should be followed: Bezobrazov's, one of boldness, or Witte's, one of caution? The tsar wavered, but he was clearly leaning toward the former. Debates over policy sometimes resulted in compromise, but the tsar was quite evidently moving toward the Bezobrazov line.

Evacuation was the most pressing question. The first stage was completed on schedule, but even before it was completed it was decided, with Witte and Lamsdorff agreeing, to make the next stage conditional on Chinese acknowledgment that Manchuria was a Russian sphere of influence. When China categorically refused, the decision was made to delay further evacuation.[47] This was clearly a provocative act, but Witte (supported by Lamsdorff) believed, as was shown in the Ito episode, that the Russian stake in Manchuria had to be made secure. At the same time they favored complete evacuation as soon as possible.

In the meantime Bezobrazov was in Manchuria, riding high, moving about extensively, talking in grandiose terms, as if he were speaking for the tsar, to Russian top officers and officials of the Chinese Eastern Railroad and setting up various enterprises with government money while giving some attention to the Yalu concession. Back home his supporters were hard at work, trying with some success, according to Kuropatkin, to influence the tsar with visions of expanding the empire without risk of war.[48]

It was evidently under the influence of Bezobrazov's coterie that Nicholas summoned a special conference, with himself in the chair, for March 26, 1903, to consider the use of the Yalu concession as a buffer zone against the Japanese. Very little had been done thus far to develop the concession.

The very idea of such a conference was the antithesis of what Witte had been urging and would continue to urge, the reaching of a modus vivendi with the Japanese. The tsar's choice of the man to present the proposal they would consider, A.M. Abaza, recently promoted to rear admiral, a member of Bezobrazov's camp, showed which way the wind was blowing. That Plehve was among those invited to attend was another indication.

It was clear that the tsar, who opened the conference by expressing his approval of the idea of a timber company on both the Korean and Chinese sides of the Yalu, was well acquainted with the proposal. In it Abaza argued that there was a pressing need to establish a buffer zone in northern Korea against a likely Japanese attack from there aimed at Port Arthur. He went on to urge the acquisition of a timber concession on the Chinese side of the Yalu and the operation of the concessions on both sides of the Yalu by a strong company, modeled on English chartered companies, headed by a man who would hold the rank of state secretary of His Imperial Majesty. Army reservists, in the role of lumberjacks, would be employed in the concessions. Also proposed was the consolidation of Russian Far Eastern operations under one agency.

What the Abaza proposal amounted to was a "new course" in the Far East, based on the premise that the country's interests would best be served by a firm, no-nonsense policy based on strengthening Russia's position, one that would challenge Japan's pretensions in Korea. The "new course" was indication that Nicholas was taking Bezobrazov's advice rather than Witte's.

Not unexpectedly, Witte reacted to the Abaza proposal heatedly and at length, arguing that Russia must avoid provocative acts and must seek a modus vivendi with Japan. However, in an apparent effort not to be too contrarian, he expressed support for a timber company of a purely commercial nature with as few governmental ties as possible. Lamsdorff supported Witte, as did Kuropatkin for the most part, being particularly concerned about the use of reservists as lumberjacks. As a result of such objections, the conference recommended that the proposed timber company be placed under the jurisdiction of the head of the Kwantung District, Admiral E.I. Alekseev, rather than a state secretary, and made no mention of consolidating the Russian Far Eastern operations.[49] This represented a compromise that would not last long.

As spring progressed, it was clear that the idea of a "new course" was gaining ground, particularly among the military, and that the Japanese were becoming more and more edgy. Witte was alarmed and at the same time aware that the tsar was not paying heed to his cautionary advice. So Witte turned to Prince Meshcherskii, who was still on *tutoyer* terms with the tsar, for assistance. In a letter to the tsar, the prince warned about the pitfalls of listening to Bezobrazov. He received a sharp reply, dated May 1: "It would be absurd, to say the least, if you believed that I would carry out all your wishes. I, too, have my own opinion, my own will, of which you will soon be convinced."[50]

Soon meant May 6, the tsar's thirty-fifth birthday, which, so he informed Meshcherskii, he approached "in good spirits and with an unshakable belief in God." On that day there appeared the announcement that Nicholas was bestowing the title of state secretary on Bezobrazov and that of general *à la suite* on Bezobrazov's close associate, Colonel K.I. Vogak, military agent for China and Japan. This amounted to the tsar's thumbing his nose at the naysayers. It was an imperious gesture. As noted earlier, the title of state secretary, an honor usually bestowed on a handful of ministers and other high officials, was the civilian equivalent of general-adjutant. And Vogak's new title put him in the rank below that of general-adjutant in the imperial suite. These appointments made a strong statement about whose stars were in the ascendant.

The special conference that Nicholas called for the following evening made an even stronger statement, what with Bezobrazov, Vogak, Abaza, and Plehve being among those invited to attend. Bezobrazov, who was the most vocal, presented his well-known views on what course the country should follow in the Far East, being supported by the tsar, who was more outspoken and decisive than was his wont on such occasions.

One of Bezobrazov's arguments was for enhancing the military element in the Yalu concession. In this he was supported by the tsar, and it was decreed that a timber company with close governmental ties be created. With regard to Manchuria, the majority held that Russian interests there required bolstering of the military already in place and the maintenance of a "closed door" policy. Nicholas directed Bezobrazov to write up the minutes of the conference. And when he did, Witte and Lamsdorff refused to sign, on the ground that the minutes misrepresented what was said.[51]

The conference left Witte deeply depressed. Bezobrazov noted that at the conference Witte was far from being his usual vocal and aggressive self and made "a truly pitiful impression."[52] An acquaintance, meeting the minister of finance a few weeks later, found him looking so anguished that he was virtually unrecognizable.[53] As for Lamsdorff, he soon asked to be relieved of his duties, but was persuaded to stay on. (Tsarist ministers were not permitted to resign.)

The "new course" unfolded swiftly, with the formation of the Russian Timber Company. It was given broad authority and was closely connected to the government, with shares made available to several personages with ties at court and provision made for the employment of military personnel in civilian clothes. Next came the dispatch of Bezobrazov to Manchuria to confer with Kuropatkin (on tour there) and Alekseev. Bezobrazov traveled in grand style, accompanied by a large suite, on a special train. In late June, he met with Kuropatkin and Alekseev and local officers and officials in Port Arthur, where they concluded that the Russian position in Manchuria must be strengthened in several ways, chiefly by eviscerating the 1902 evacuation convention while paying lip service to it.[54]

In the spirit of the "new course," the tsar decided to carry out still another Abaza recommendation, the concentration of authority in the Russian Far East in the hands of Admiral Alekseev, reputedly the bastard son of Alexander II and certainly a man whose ability was inversely proportional to his amour propre. The decision was reached without the participation or knowledge of Witte, Lamsdorff, or Kuropatkin. On July 30, the official government newspaper published a decree announcing that all Russian territory east of Lake Baikal plus the Kwantung leased territory and the Chinese Eastern Railroad zone would form a new administrative entity, the Far Eastern Viceroyalty, with Alekseev as viceroy, who would have the authority to conduct diplomatic relations with China and Japan. The tsar made a compensatory gesture to Witte, Lamsdorff, and Kuropatkin, who were referred to as "the lousy trio" by the Bezobrazov clique, by including them in the newly created Special Committee for Far Eastern Affairs, of which he would be chairman and Plehve vice chairman. The committee proved to be a paper organization that would disappear in a diplomatic swamp.[55]

The viceroyalty was doomed to a short life, but its initial impact was dramatic. Japan, which was about to initiate negotiations with Russia, had no choice but to regard the July 30 edict as an sign of intransigence, while Witte, Lamsdorff, and Kuropatkin could not help but see themselves as relegated to back seats.

Ironically, only a few days before the edict, Lamsdorff had asked the tsar for permission to meet with Witte and Kuropatkin for a discussion of Far Eastern policy. Nicholas agreed but with a proviso that Bezobrazov participate, clearly in an attempt to tip the scales; as it turned out, the latter was unable to attend. At their meeting the three recommended a moderate course with respect to Korea and Manchuria, a recommendation with which the tsar disagreed but to which he gave partial approval, though only on paper.[56]

Obviously the three were, to varying degrees, at odds with the tsar on Far Eastern policy, but the tsar chose to dismiss only one of these, Witte. This was the case because Witte's opposition to the "new course" was but one part of the case against the minister of finance that had built up in the mind and heart of the sovereign. He had been of a mind to get rid of Witte for some time and was obviously trying to steel himself to act. Not long before he acted he reassured Bezobrazov, who was complaining about Witte, that the minister of finance would soon be gone.[57] But there was still a rough road for the weak-willed tsar between intending to act and facing this huge and intimidating man as well as his sharp-tongued mother.

It appears that he was waiting impatiently for his mother to make one of her frequent visits to Denmark, but when it appeared that she would not be going soon, he forced himself to be strong.[58] He later told Kuropatkin that if he had been a horse, he would have bolted under the stress he had felt in preparing to face Witte.[59] The decision to act came to him during a religious service.[60] He would deliver the blow on August 16, when Witte was scheduled to give his weekly report. He would get rid of him by the device of kicking him "upstairs" to the vacant chairmanship of the Committee of Ministers, a dodge that had been used on earlier occasions.

The day before the report, Nicholas sent Witte a note asking him to bring E.D. Pleske, the director of the State Bank, along with him, a request that befuddled the minister of finance. On the appointed day the two sailed to Peterhof, the tsar's summer residence. The tsar summoned Witte first, receiving him as if nothing unusual were afoot. He listened politely to the minister's report and granted his request for permission to inspect a region where the liquor monopoly was being introduced. Then, as Witte was about to leave, Nicholas asked him for his opinion of Pleske. Witte responded favorably. The tsar then said: "I am asking you to take the post of chairman of the Committee of Ministers and wish to appoint Pleske as minister of finance." Witte's shocked expression caused the tsar to ask: "Are you dissatisfied with the appointment? Don't you know that the position of chairman of the Committee of Ministers is the highest in the Empire?"

Witte was both shocked and angry, very angry, but replied in a suitably deferential manner. He would not mind, he replied, if he did not see the action as a sign of disfavor, then went on to remind his sovereign that he had been earning sixty thousand rubles a year before entering government service. Life in St. Petersburg was difficult enough, made all the more so by the ostracism of his wife and daughter. He suggested that he would be willing to accept a post that was outside the capital and carried more responsibility, but permitted himself to be persuaded to accept the offer.[61]

On returning to his office, Witte, facing an icon, told S.M. Propper, a prominent newspaper publisher: "I swear in the name of those I hold dearest in the world, my wife and my daughter, that I shall never forget what he has done."[62] When he returned home to tell his wife the sad news, she was as bitter as he, declaring that not even the tsar's lackeys received such scurvy treatment.[63]

What was on the tsar's mind that August 16 is not easy to discern for lack of direct evidence except for an entry in his diary: "Now I rule."[64] He would no longer feel himself under the thumb of this imperious man, no longer chafe at being talked down to. Indirect evidence indicates that he no longer saw Witte as a kind of economic wizard, that he was put off by the minister of finance's views on Far Eastern policy, and that he accepted the opinion that Witte was too well disposed toward troublesome minorities such as the Finns, the Armenians, and particularly the Jews. Whether or not he already accepted the canard, popular among some conservative nobles, of a Jewish-Masonic conspiracy involving Witte is not clear, but within the year he would be labeling Witte a Mason. And it seems that he was already determined to make the chairmanship a cul-de-sac, as it had been for preceding chairmen. At the same time, he sought to purchase Witte's goodwill by a gift of four hundred thousand rubles and some other acts of kindness.[65]

Goodwill was not obtained that easily. His professions of affection for the tsar to the contrary, Witte was embittered by the treatment he had received. This feeling, coupled with contempt for the tsar, might have impelled him, had he been another type of person, to wash his hands of government service and accept a lucrative position in the banking world. A probable explanation of his decision to stay on was his drive for power and his self-confidence, which led him to believe that the time would soon come when circumstances would force Nicholas to summon him back to a major position.[66]

Chapter 10

A Mere Spectator, 1903–1904

Suddenly, Witte found himself facing a new life in things both great and small. He was no longer the master of a small empire. There were no longer the weekly reports to the emperor, to which he had looked forward so eagerly. He no longer participated in policy making. He was now, as he put it, a mere spectator, but it was soon evident that he had no intention of slipping into the slough of oblivion.

Even if he had chosen to retire to the sidelines he would have been sought out, for he had dominated the scene for so long. A century earlier Count Michael Speranskii, with whom Witte was often compared, was exiled after falling from favor, but this was another century and the tsar had to endure his former minister of finance's presence in St. Petersburg, an occasion for gossip, intrigue, and speculation.

But, first, each could enjoy a few months of respite, as both tsars and ministers were wont to do in summer and early fall. Witte and his wife chose to head for Vichy, for the cure, with stopovers in Berlin and Paris. In Berlin he had an opportunity to gossip with his banker friend Mendelssohn-Bartholdy. Paris proved a disquieting experience. First of all, he noticed that he was being shadowed by Russian plainclothesmen, who, he learned, were acting on Plehve's orders. A visit with Baron Alphonse Rothschild, another banker friend, added to his disquiet, as the baron expressed concern over "occult forces" at the Russian court. This was a reference to the faith healer Philippe of Lyons, who had won the confidence of the tsar and his wife. Witte, too, was concerned. Witte was also upset by the fact that Nelidov, the Russian ambassador, was proclaiming that Russia's current Far Eastern policy would ensure peace. He was equally disturbed by what he learned from Baron Freedericksz, minister of the imperial court, who was visiting Paris at the time, namely, that Lamsdorff was being kept in ignorance about his country's Far Eastern diplomacy, which was in the hands of Admiral Alekseev. He was indeed glad to leave Paris for Vichy.[1]

In the fall he and his wife returned to St. Petersburg to begin the new chapter in his life. First, there was their new home—a three-story residence on Kamenno-Ostrovskii Prospekt. Then, there was his new office, chairman of the Committee of Ministers, the nature of which has already been described. In his memoirs Witte referred to the business that came before the

committee as "administrative rubbish" and noted, "Like some of my predecessors I tried to shift as much of the distasteful business that came to the
committee to other bodies so as not to have a hand in it."[2]

He was still chairman of the Special Conference on the Needs of Rural
Industry, which was continuing its work despite hindrances emanating largely
from Plehve. In addition to taking police action against some local committees, which he accused of going beyond their mandates, he mounted a rival
operation within his own ministry. Moreover, Witte had to endure some opposition, both overt and covert, from some conservative conference members.

Despite being cut out of policy making, he remained deeply concerned
with affairs of state and the state of the nation, not to speak of the state of his
own reputation, and when he had the chance he would seek to exert an influence on the course of events. First, a few words about his reputation, which
he fiercely defended. As always, he courted the press and press lords. Strik-
ingly significant of this concern was his association with Joseph Dillon, the
Russian correspondent of the London *Daily Telegraph* since 1887, a remarkable man.

Dillon, a very well-educated man who had studied in Russian and other
universities, had "gone native," marrying a Russian woman, teaching for a
time in a Russian university, briefly editing an Odessa newspaper, and getting Witte's help when in trouble with the censorship.[3] The circumstances of
the beginning of their close association, which endured from 1903 until the
outbreak of World War I, are not known. Probably Witte, who already used
the services of journalists, saw in Dillon a man exceptionally able to blow
the horn for him. After Witte's death Dillon described himself as "private
adviser [a euphemism for public relations man] to Count Witte, 1903–1914."[4]
Whether or not Dillon was in Witte's pay, as has been alleged, is moot, but it
is evident that Witte made considerable use of Dillon's services without openly
acknowledging the fact.[5]

When he was concerned with the state of the country and its operations
he turned to Kuropatkin, Lamsdorff, former associates in the Ministry of
Finance, and the like. Growing unrest at home and increasing tensions in
Russo-Japanese relations were high among his worries.

He was, of course, aware that there was growing unrest: within "society"
(that is, the educated), among workers, and within various classes of the national minorities. But he underestimated, as did so many in the government,
the severity of unrest and he misunderstood its causes. He tended to put the
blame on the weakness of the tsar and inadequacy of most of the ministers,
particularly Plehve for his repressive policies and his flirtation with the
government-inspired labor organizations. As for the responsibility of the tsar,
Witte still clung to the Slavophile belief that autocracy rested on the close tie

between the sovereign and the people, a tie that in his view no longer existed.[6] For the time being, Witte focused his attention on the worsening relations with Japan. In the spring of 1903, the Japanese powers that be became convinced that the time was drawing nigh when they must either reach a settlement about outstanding issues or fight. They were alarmed by Russian failure to carry out the second stage of the promised evacuation of Manchuria and by the buildup of Russian forces in Manchuria and northern Korea. And they were convinced that if they waited much longer, the balance of strength would shift in favor of Russia. Consequently, Japan began to seek assurance from Great Britain of support in the coming confrontation. In July Japan took the first step to determine whether or not Russia was prepared to negotiate in good faith.

Japan took that step by offering an agreement couched in the usual diplomatic finery. In essence what Japan proposed was that she recognize Russia's existing rights in Manchuria and that in return Russia withdraw her troops from Manchuria, recognize the rights of other powers to trade and invest in that region, and also recognize the exclusive right of Japan to intervene in Korea if the need arose.

St. Petersburg agreed to negotiate but did so at a snail's pace, partly because of lack of will to come to terms, partly because of bureaucratic problems. The tsar, while sincere in his profession that he did not want war, felt little urgency, being confident that time was on his side and that Japan would not dare to go to war. As the weeks and months passed, talk of war increased, and Witte became more anxious.

Although he professed to be a mere "spectator," Witte took as active a hand as he could in efforts to influence policy. It was natural that he would focus his attention on Lamsdorff and Kuropatkin, his former cohorts. In particular, he sought to get the minister of foreign affairs to stiffen his spine in relations with the tsar. And, as he had done in 1896, he also turned to Pobedonostsev, providing him with documentary material to show how fraught with danger the present course was. The overprocurator did not have much influence with the tsar anymore, but he did have access. However, he proved more sympathetic than helpful.[7]

Witte, though out of power, was sought out. Thus, late in the negotiations, toward the end of December 1903, Viscount S. Kurino, the Japanese minister to St. Petersburg, called on Witte for advice. Witte, remembering earlier experiences, asked Kurino not to report their conversation by telegraph, since the foreign office was able to decipher telegrams. Kurino agreed.

Witte was blunt. He stated that his and Lamsdorff's views had failed to prevail and that he was now "a spectator." He asserted that Russian assurances, be they in the form of treaties or whatever, were good only as long as circumstances did not change, that time was on Russia's side, and that when Russia felt the time to be ripe, she would do as she pleased.

He advised that Japan should make "a final effort" to come to terms with Russia. If that failed, Japan should assert that she stood by existing treaties and that if Japanese rights under these treaties were breached, Japan would have the right to take whatever steps she deemed appropriate.[8] Did he have in mind such a step as annexation of Korea? We do not know. To say the least, his advice was indiscreet, the words of an angry, overwrought man rather than those of a loyal subject trying to put as good a face as he could on his country's diplomacy.

Of course the English were informed of the meeting. Cecil Spring-Rice, secretary of their embassy, prepared the memorandum about the meeting that was sent on to London. It was probably the knowledge gained from this experience that prompted him to write to President Theodore Roosevelt that Witte fought neither for God nor for Satan but only for himself.

In the meantime Tokyo was coming closer to a decision to go to war, while in St. Petersburg preparations were being made for the opening of the social season. On New Year's Day 1904 the social season began with a reception for the diplomatic corps. The tsar sought out Kurino and talked sternly to him, telling him that Russia did not have unlimited patience.[9] On that same day St. Petersburg received new proposals from Tokyo.

As usual, Nicholas let time slip by despite urgent requests from Kurino for a quick reply. His confidence that Japan would not dare to attack was illustrated in a telegram that he sent to the German emperor, which said in part: "All the alarming news about war preparations in the Far East emanate from [a] certain origin, whose interest it is to keep up this agitation."[10]

It was only on the fifteenth that a conference was held to prepare counterproposals, to be followed by a lapse of a few days before Nicholas gave approval. Meanwhile the social season was in full swing, with a round of balls, galas, and parties.

It was at the Grand Ball, held on the nineteenth, that Witte, who had been alerted by Kurino, expressed his deep concern about the imminence of war to Kuropatkin. He felt that the situation was so grave that he should be recalled to his former post while being permitted to retain his current position.[11] Of course, that did not happen.

The war that Witte feared drew nearer. Transmission of Russian counterproposals proceeded at what amounted to a snail's pace, perhaps because of Japanese design. On January 24, already poised for war, Japan broke off negotiations and recalled Kurino, a fairly clear signal of what was to come.

In his diary entry for the twenty-fifth the tsar noted that there was nothing new from the Far East. On the morning of the twenty-sixth he held a conference in which the commitment not to be the first to attack was reiterated. Somehow that day found him and those around him in an "elated mood." In the evening he attended a performance of *Rusalka*, which he enjoyed. On his return home he found a telegram from his uncle General-Admiral Grand Duke Alexis informing him of the Japanese attack on Russian warships in the outer harbor of Port Arthur without a declaration of war.[12] Ironically, it was Witte who was the first to receive details of the attack, from the Ministry of Finance's agent in Peking, which Witte transmitted to General Kuropatkin and Admiral Avelan, director of the Ministry of the Navy.[13]

Witte writes: "Thus a terrible period began, with the most unfortunate of wars leading to a revolution for which the police-cum-nobility regime, or rather police-cum-court camarilla regime had paved the way."[14] He tells us that shortly after the outbreak of the war, when Kuropatkin took Plehve to task for helping lead the country into war, Plehve replied: "Alexis Nikolaevich, you do not know Russia's internal situation: we need a little, victorious war to stem [the tide of] revolution."[15] This is the most quoted of all the passages from Witte's memoirs, having even provided the title of a book. Alas, like so many quotes, it does not stand up to scrutiny. A search of Kuropatkin's diary for the period does not corroborate Witte's account. It shows Plehve being certain that if war came, Russia would win without paying a cost in domestic unrest.[16] The diary does show that in December of the preceding year Lamsdorff expressed concern that Plehve was not worried about the prospect of war, "hoping that war will distract the attention of the masses from political questions." Kuropatkin noted that after hearing this he saw Plehve and succeeded in convincing him that if war did not go well, there would be serious unrest. But he does note that Plehve did say that "Russia had come out victorious from all difficulties."[17] What is possible is that Kuropatkin, knowing Witte's flaming hatred for Plehve, was playing up to Witte, who considered the minister of interior to be one of the chief instigators of the war.

As for his own responsibility, Witte wanted to make certain to dissociate himself from any blame. This was typified by Witte's reply to the suggestion that his drive to construct the Chinese Eastern Railroad led to the seizure of Port Arthur, which Witte considered a major step on the road to war. (See page 80) Sensitivity to criticism may explain his letter to Count S.D. Sheremetev, a member of the Witte conference on agriculture. In this letter, dated May 20, 1904, he wrote that he rarely left the house and was averse to meeting most of his St. Petersburg acquaintances, who criticized him behind his back.[18] In the meantime he was preparing a kind of "white book" of documents intended to present his version of the events that led to the war—not to be published, of course, since publication would mean the end of his career, but to be distributed to a narrow circle. We will hear about this collection later.

Witte's hopes of being recalled to the office he had left had risen when his successor, Pleske, died in February, but were dashed when, after an interval of several weeks, V.N. Kokovtsev was given the office. Witte, who did not consider anyone but himself capable of being minister of finance, had no choice but to continue to be a "mere spectator," disingenuously claiming that he sought nothing for himself.[19]

The war tested Witte's work in the Far East, particularly the Trans-Siberian and Chinese Eastern Railroads. Remarkable though they were, they fell short of meeting the needs of the army because of the sacrifice of quality on the altar of speedy and inexpensive construction. Shortly before the outbreak of hostilities Kuropatkin had warned that these single-track railroads could not bear the traffic necessary to give Russia numerical superiority over the enemy in the short run.[20] No question that the railroads could not carry as many troops as desired, but they did transport tens of thousands of men in a much shorter time than it would have taken by sea.

Witte shared the widespread assumption that time was on Russia's side and that victory was certain, given proper leadership, but he had no confidence in Admiral Alekseev, the commander-in chief of the land and sea forces in the Far East. In February Kuropatkin was appointed commander of the land forces, to serve under Alekseev. It was a popular choice, given Kuropatkin's reputation as a courageous and successful officer. True, Witte had reservations about the man, remembering the prediction that A.A. Abaza had made about him. Abaza had predicted that Kuropatkin would rise high but that in the end everyone would be "disappointed in him because although he is a clever and brave general, he has the soul of a staff clerk."[21]

Nonetheless, Witte believed early on that Kuropatkin would bring victory, but only if Alekseev were out of the way. Shortly before the general's departure for Mukden, Alekseev's headquarters, he advised the general that as soon as he arrived there he should place the commander in chief under arrest, ship him back to St. Petersburg, and throw himself on the tsar's mercy for his action. Kuropatkin took the advice as a joke, laughed heartily, and said, "You are right."[22] Witte continued to advise and inform Kuropatkin. On April 19, he wrote: "Dear Alexis Nikolaevich, I beg you not to forget that Kuropatkin is not only a famous general but also a statesman [*gosudarstvennyi muzh*]."[23] He urged Kuropatkin not to forget what he had written on an earlier occasion to the tsar, that Russia's vital interest was in the Near East. Witte was anxious lest victory lead to annexations that would be dangerous for Russia. In the same letter he displayed a combination of joy and snobbery: "Yesterday was a joyous day for me: [my daughter]

Vera married Naryshkin, nephew of Count Vorontsov, and, moreover, his sister is married to the count's son."

Witte, in describing Kuropatkin's departure for Manchuria, writes: "General Kuropatkin left for Manchuria, with great pomp, as if he were certain of victory. It would have been more prudent if he had departed quietly and saved the pomp for a victorious return. Unfortunately, there was to be no victory to celebrate."[24] It was Kuropatkin's plan to take up a position near Harbin, the chief city on the Chinese Eastern Railroad line, and wait for troops arriving from Russia and troops then in Manchuria to retreat to Harbin; then, when he had sufficient numbers (he had thought a ratio of two Russian soldiers to three Japanese would do), he would mount an offensive that would drive the enemy into the sea and make peace in Tokyo.[25] (Early on, Admiral Alekseev thought that the Japanese would sue for peace within three months but feared that if it were granted then, the enemy would get off too lightly.)[26]

But things went miserably for Russia. Port Arthur was soon completely encircled and placed under relentless siege. Attempts to break out by the ships in the harbor met with humiliating and severe failure. Attempts by Russian warships stationed in Vladivostok to go to the aid of Port Arthur would also end in failure. Witte would write to Kuropatkin in August that to all intents and purposes Russia might still have ships and brave sailors in the Pacific, but it had no fleet there, and he doubted that the plan to send a squadron from the Baltic Fleet to the Pacific would be of any use.[27]

Witte watched with alarm as the initial patriotic mood that had prevailed at the beginning of the conflict soon waned as it became evident that this would not be "a short, victorious war," despite the rosy picture painted by the press. True, upper-class women rolled bandages or served as nurses, and patriotic rallies were held, but the general mood became one of disengagement from this distant war that did not appear to threaten Russia.[28] But for some time Witte remained convinced that "in the end" Russia would be victorious.

But what kind of peace would he like to see imposed? A conversation he had with Sir Charles Hardinge, the British ambassador, early in June, is revealing. When asked if he had any idea of what terms Russia would impose in the event of victory, he spoke out of school by saying that if Lamsdorff were still in office at the time, "the views and rights of other powers would be honestly laid before the Emperor, but that if that moment a new minister had been installed he would probably, with the view of maintaining his position, follow the example of other ministers who only advise the Emperor in the sense that they think will be most pleasing to His Majesty."[29] He added that much depended upon whether the war would end quickly with a "succession of victories" or be drawn out. He preferred the latter because if the former occurred, his country would seek and get territory that would only redound to Russia's disadvantage. He felt that if victory came after a drawn-out war, his government would be more moderate in its terms. For himself he shared the view of those that a defeated Japan should be deprived of the right to maintain a fleet and that Russia should enjoy supremacy in the Yellow Sea by receiving ports "at the mouth of the Yalu and on the South East coast of Corea [sic]), so as to control the country traversed by the Yalu and to command the Corean straits." What he proposed bore similarities to Bezobrazov's plan for protecting Russian interests in Manchuria by creating a buffer zone in north Korea. But against whom? Was he assuming that a defeated Japan, deprived of naval power, would still be capable of using Korea as a staging area? He did not say.

As the war dragged on, Witte found himself increasingly engaged in negotiations to renew the commercial treaty with Germany he had hammered out in 1894. The treaty was for a term of ten years and would soon expire. Both sides had a stake in renewal, what with one-third of Russian exports going to Germany and one-quarter of Russian exports being of German origin.[30] Of late there had been difficulties, with Berlin raising tariffs on some Russian imports and St. Petersburg increasing tariffs on goods arriving by land, which struck at imports from Germany. Russia wanted the terms of the 1894 treaty maintained; the Germans did not. Witte had begun negotiating in 1902 and was permitted to continue with the task after he left the Ministry of Finance. The negotiations, carried on at long distance, went slowly until Emperor William II wrote to the tsar, one of those famous Willy-Nicky letters, late in March, advising his cousin to act firmly by sending a man of importance to Berlin to settle the matter.[31]

The tempo picked up. Talks began about sending Witte to Berlin, evidently with the tsar's assent. The German chancellor, von Bülow, writes in his memoirs that he had Mendelssohn-Bartholdy get in touch with Witte to ask if he would be willing to go to Berlin and that Witte gave an affirmative answer.[32]

At the tsar's behest a special interagency conference was held, with Witte presiding, on May 1. At issue were two questions: whether to proceed with dispatch and whether to stand up to German demands. The fact that Russia's ability to bargain was weakened by the war, all the more so by the Kaiser's assurance to the tsar that Russia need have no fear about an attack on her western border, leaving her free to withdraw troops from her western provinces to use in the Far East. Grand Duke Alexander Mikhailovich, one of the participants, appeared to reflect the tsar's views in arguing for dispatch and moderation. Most agreed with him, while Witte opposed haste and favored a strong stand, finding himself in the minority.[33] Apparently Witte did not put much faith in the German emperor, for we find him soon writing to

Kuropatkin: "Indeed, if the Germans were to think now of going into action they would reach a line running from Smolensk to Kiev and Nikolaev within a month and a half."[34]

The tempo may have picked up, but not greatly. More than two weeks after the conference, Nicholas said in a letter to William:

> In your last letter you mentioned that our treaty of Commerce has come to a deadlock. That is quite true. I have the matter reconsidered by some of the ministers and I have given Witte direction to meet the German proposals as far as possible.[35]

It was not until the end of June that Witte, accompanied by several officials of the Ministry of Finance left for Germany. Since it was summer, negotiations were held on the island of Nordeney, just off the German coast. The talks were lengthy, two weeks of give-and-take. Much of the specifics were hammered out between Witte and Posadowski, the state secretary for internal affairs, but Witte managed to spend most of his free time with von Bülow, discussing general matters.[36]

In accordance with his instructions, Witte yielded to most German wishes, which included higher tariffs on Russian agricultural products, but through hard and stubborn bargaining was able to win on a few items. In the course of the negotiations he was able to avoid a diplomatic pitfall.

The German foreign office desired the resurrection of the Three Emperors' League, which had lapsed in 1887. Von Richthofen, the state secretary for foreign affairs, hoped to use the occasion of Witte's presence in Nordeney for talks on the subject, but Witte's refusal to meet with him aborted the German effort.[37]

As the talks drew to a close, Witte suggested that the signing ceremonies be moved to Berlin, while insisting that the German money market be opened to Russia. Von Bülow agreed to the former but balked at the latter, citing the kaiser as having declared that the German money market was for Germans. Witte refused to sign until the German chancellor provided a signed assurance that Russia would be permitted to seek a loan. On July 15 (28) the convention between the two countries was signed, to go into force a year after ratification and remain in force until 1917.[38] Under the circumstances under which Witte had to negotiate, he did quite well, but there were naysayers, particularly among the large landowners, who felt that their interests had been hurt. And the tsar did not seem elated, given his suspicions about Witte, who wrote that on his return the tsar received him coldly.[39]

During his stay in Nordeney Witte spoke at length and freely with von Bülow about the war as well as about his country's domestic affairs. He noted that the war was vastly unpopular and that the general sentiment was for a speedy peace without annexations. As for himself, he believed that, given enough time, Kuropatkin would prevail, adding in confidence that as a "patriot," he had to find joy in Russian victories, but that as a "statesman," he feared that "speedy and splendid victories would move leading circles in St. Petersburg" to make excessive and dangerous demands.[40]

Fortuitously, Witte's presence in Germany provided the opportunity for a negotiated peace. Baron Tadasu Hayashi, the Japanese minister to Great Britain, with the approval of his government, sought a meeting with Witte to discuss such a peace. He communicated his desire to the Ministry of Finance's agent in London through an unofficial intermediary, apparently to avoid the appearance of a formal peace effort. The agent, in turn, informed both Count Alexander Benckendorff, the Russian ambassador to Great Britain, and Witte of Hayashi's quest. Witte quickly got in touch with St. Petersburg for permission to meet Hayashi, while Benckendorff signaled his support of such an effort.

There was nothing but silence from St. Petersburg, and that was that. Why? On his return to Russia, Witte came to the conclusion from what he learned that his request and Benckendorff's approval had been taken by those around the tsar as acts of stupidity verging on treason.[41]

Writing several years later, Witte argued:

> Had I been authorized to negotiate at the time, we would have been forced to give up the Kwantung region, including Port Arthur, as we had to later, but we would have been able to retain the southern branch of the Chinese Eastern Railroad and all of Sakhalin Island. Most important of all, we would have been spared the shame of Liaoyang, Mukden, and Tsushima.[42]

Obviously, Witte had lost confidence in the likelihood of Russia's ability to win so decisively as to be able to dictate the terms of peace, while the tsar and those around still believed in a triumphant end. Moreover, Witte was becoming alarmed at the baneful effects of the war at home.

He shared his concerns with von Bülow about the way in which the "unfortunate" war was fueling domestic unrest. He characterized his country's domestic policies directed against Jews, Finns, Catholics, Armenians, students, and the press as "false and stupid." These policies, in his view, were more reactionary than those of Alexander III, this at a time when the country had changed to such a degree that dire consequences were in the offing. He did not foresee a Western-type revolution but did predict a wave of assassinations and attempts at assassination like those that had characterized the last years of Alexander II's reign. He did not blame Plehve and the tsar for these policies, but blame was implied in his talks with the German chancellor.

What was the way out of this explosive situation? Witte confided to von Bülow that a "weak character" (Nicholas II) was likely to swing from one extreme to the other, and that if the response to a series of assassinations should be the granting of a constitution providing for a parliament and universal suffrage, it would mean "the end of Russia." In his opinion what was needed to nip the growing opposition in the bud was a program of "greater toleration of non-Russian nationalities and religious minorities, less brutalization of the educated youth, some press freedom, and with respect to administration to replace sweeping bureaucratic tutelage with limited self-government."[43] The last was clearly a retreat from the position he had taken earlier on with respect to a proposal to broaden the powers of the zemstvos. He was still holding fast to the Slavophile belief that Western constitutionalism was not for Russia. And, like his colleagues, he greatly underestimated how explosive the situation in his country was.

But his prediction about assassinations came to pass all too soon. On the very day that the Russo-German Commercial and Navigation Convention was signed in Berlin, Plehve and his coachman were blown to bits by a bomb thrown by a young revolutionary student. Witte learned of the event while "walking on Unter den Linden," presumably from a newsboy.[44] How he reacted to this event is recorded in several sources and they are worth noting. Von Bülow writes that as he was riding in the Tiergarten he passed Witte, who called out to him: "Good news: Plehve has just been murdered."[45] Shortly after his return to Russia, Witte was visited by the publisher A.S. Suvorin, who noted in his diary that Witte spoke furiously about Plehve, screaming, "Why do they write about him. Why don't they write about the coachman? And Plehve died in a disgusting manner. Sipiagin was a limited man, but he died honorably."[46]

Some weeks later he wrote to Kuropatkin:

> What happened to Mr. von Plehve is what he deserved and it is remarkable that nowhere has this crime elicited condolence. All that one hears is a sigh of relief and curses directed at his memory. As is always the case, after a person's death, the tongues of these near to him, of his associates, are loosened. . . . But what should be of interest to you is that it is clear that Mr. von Plehve was the soul of the band of adventurers who led us into this unfortunate war.[47]

There was at least one who shed tears for Plehve, and that was the tsar. In his diary he noted that the assassination had robbed him of "a friend and of an irreplaceable minister of interior."[48] Whom would he select to replace Plehve, and what would it mean?

Chapter 11

Political Spring, July–December 1904

On July 19, the tsar received N.V. Muravev, minister of justice, who took it upon himself to speak frankly about the critical situation in which the country found itself and the role Plehve had played in bringing it about. He went on to speak of the need to regain the support of "society," which had been alienated by Plehve. He then went into specifics about methods of achieving that aim. The tsar reportedly replied in a sarcastic tone: "Do you expect me to establish a cabinet with Witte as its head?" Muravev: "Not a cabinet, but you have a council of ministers which does not meet." Tsar: "Does that mean that it's my fault? How can I preside over trivia?" Muravev: "Your Majesty could appoint someone in your place." Tsar: "Do you expect me to rule with the aid of a Petrunkevich. He is a criminal who should be sent into exile." Muravev: "As long as he is not in exile, one could govern with his aid." When Muravev next reported to the tsar, Nicholas made no reference to their earlier conversation.[1]

The allusion to I.I. Petrunkevich was an apt one, for his career told much about the alienation of "society" from the government, "society"(*obshchestvo*) being taken to mean the educated classes. Petrunkevich, a member of the nobility, had come of age during the period of the great reforms of Alexander II. Early on, he became active in zemstvo affairs, seeing in the zemstvos, as did so many others, an institution of self-government that, modest though it was at the time, would help the lot of the common folk as well as give the educated class a voice in government. As the years passed, he continued to be active in zemstvo affairs while coming to the conviction, as did many other liberals, that the tsarist government was the obstacle to progress. In 1901 he helped establish *Osvobozhdenie* (Liberation), a newspaper that was printed abroad and smuggled into Russia and that sought to disseminate leftist liberal ideas. He was chosen chairman of the Union of Liberation, a clandestine organization that was established in January 1904 and soon become the rallying point of the burgeoning left wing of the liberal movement.

The right wing of the liberal movement, conveniently referred to as zemstvo liberals, was by no means negligible, but it was losing ground to the left. Far from homogeneous, its membership ranged from those described as Slavophile to those described as constitutionalist. But the common thread was a belief that change could be effected within the system, by legal means. The leading figure among the zemstvo liberals was Dmitrii Shipov, with whom Witte would be dealing in October 1905. In his view, it was not the tsarist government that was the obstacle to progress but the tsar, because he had lost touch with his people. The task, therefore, was to convince Nicholas of the need for change and to do so by legal means.

The liberal movement—that is, those who considered a change in the political structure of Russia imperative, a change that would bring with it freedom of speech, press, religion, and assembly, and some form of representative government—was growing rapidly in number and becoming more impatient. True, there was a wing of the educated classes that supported autocracy as it was then and was beginning to organize into what came to be known pejoratively as the Black Hundreds, but it was easily overshadowed by the liberal movement, which was moving to the left. Of course, there were many who had not given voice to their feelings, but the perception that "society" was becoming alienated from the government seemed justified.

Those in a position to influence the tsar were divided between persons who favored a successor to Plehve who would seek to accommodate "society" as a way of restoring calm and the ones who favored a man cut from the same cloth as Plehve to make sure that the government kept a firm hold on the reins.[2] Rumors about possible candidates abounded.

Many thought that Witte, who was said to want the post and to have a program, would be the man, as witnessed by the many ministers who trooped out to welcome him home.[3] They were mistaken. First, there was the fact that the tsar was relieved at being freed of Witte's tutelage. Then there was the fact that Plehve had worked hard to poison the sovereign's mind against the former minister of finance. As if that were not enough, an incident occurred in July that could only intensify the tsar's hostility toward Witte.

In that month there appeared in the London-based *Quarterly Review* an anonymous article entitled "The Tsar," purportedly written by "a Russian official of high rank." The author, claiming to be a supporter of a strong monarchy, painted a devastating picture of Nicholas II, describing him as a vacillating tyrant who listened to bad advice and was surrounded by men, Witte excepted, who brought out the worst in him. As for Witte, "if the one-eyed man is necessarily the leader in the kingdom of the blind, M. de Witte deserved to be the head of the government in contemporary Russia."[4]

As can be imagined, the article made a sensation, so much so that the German foreign office ordered thirty copies of the journal.[5] The tsar, needless to say, was upset by the article, which he suspected had been written by Witte. Reportedly, he was so anxious to learn the identity of the author that he sent an agent to London to investigate.[6] In fact, the author was none other than Joseph Dillon, something that the tsar was unable to discover.[7] In addition to sending an agent to London, the tsar ordered Admiral Abaza to have Lopukhin, head of the Department of Police, get his hands on a pamphlet allegedly prepared by Witte concerning the events leading to the war. The tsar wished to see if passages in the pamphlet were comparable to those in the article. When Witte heard about the effort, he made a joke of it, saying the tsar could have saved time by asking him directly for a copy. The pamphlet was a documentary collection prepared by the Ministry of Finance concerning the ministry's part in Far Eastern affairs between 1898 and 1900. Witte writes that the pamphlet was ready for distribution when war was close, leading him to have all but a few copies destroyed, the remaining copies to be kept by him.[8]

What part, if any, Witte played in the preparation of the Dillon article is a mystery, as is his reaction to the appearance of the article. If he had any part in it, he was playing a dangerous game, letting his spleen rather than his head guide him. Undoubtedly his opinions about the tsar and those who surrounded him were echoed in the article, but that is understandable given the fact that Dillon was by now well acquainted with Witte's views and agreed with him. In any case, the article could only strengthen the tsar's antipathy toward and distrust of Witte.

Reference has already been made to Plehve's role in nurturing that distrust. After his death, an examination of his papers revealed copies of letters alleging that Witte was linked to "kikish-Masonic" organizations, copies that had been shown to the tsar. That Nicholas would now turn to Witte was most improbable.[9]

Nonetheless, rumor had it that such a choice would come to pass and that Witte was actively seeking the post.[10] Given the fact that Witte chose to go off to his summer home in faraway Sochi, in the Caucasus, it seems unlikely that he entertained any hope of being tapped for the post. Not that he was reconciled to being out of power.

Weeks passed as the tsar was beset by conflicting advice about what policies to pursue and whom to choose to carry out these policies. He also had two other major preoccupations, with his wife's coming to term and giving birth to their first son and with the war, which was approaching a critical point. On July 30, to the great joy of Nicholas and Alexandra, their son was born. Many days passed before his baptism. Meanwhile Kuropatkin was about to begin his long-promised offensive against the Japanese, at Liaoyang. In the midst of this the tsar went on the road for a few days, to review troops bound for the fray and to hand out icons to them, as he had been doing on other occasions, acts that had encouraged General Dragomirov to offer a widely repeated observation that Russia was replying to Japanese bullets with icons.[11] The battle at Liaoyang went badly, prompting Suvorin to note sadly in his diary on August 21 that the day marked the anniversary of the disastrous Battle of Sedan, in which the French were surrounded by the Prussians, and that Russia was now suffering her own Sedan.[12] Of course he was exaggerating. The Russians were in retreat, not surrounded, but the battle dashed the widely held hope that Russia was about to gain the upper hand.

On August 25 the tsar finally filled Plehve's shoes by offering the post to Prince V.D. Sviatopolk-Mirskii. At first Nicholas had been inclined to appoint someone who would continue Plehve's policies, but at the strong urging of his mother he finally decided on the prince, who was known to have been opposed to Plehve and to have gained the reputation of somewhat of a moderate in his capacity as the Vilna governor-general. The prince had been reluctant to take the position but yielded to the pleas of the dowager empress, who was sharply critical of Plehve's policies. So, on August 25, the prince, still reluctant, accepted the offer, but not without sharing with the tsar the program he wished to follow. He told Nicholas that he had disagreed with the policies of both Sipiagin and Plehve, adding that the government and the country seemed to be at war, that the government had to come to terms with the country or face the prospect of a land divided between "those under surveillance and those conducting surveillance." Punishment should be meted out only to criminals. Then, referring to the policy of Russification in Finland, Russian Poland, and the Caucasus, he said that a new policy was needed. Also, he favored increasing the rights of the press. The tsar expressed agreement. The prince also expressed the view that representatives of the people should be invited to the capital to discuss the country's needs. The tsar seemed to agree. At the end Nicholas embraced him and told him to see the dowager empress, which he did. She expressed joy at his acceptance of the position and embraced him. The prince emerged from the encounter thinking that all would be well.[13]

Witte's views about what was needed were very close to those of Sviatopolk-Mirskii, and he indicated as much in replying to a telegram in which the prince declared that Witte should have succeeded Plehve.[14] On his return to St. Petersburg, in October, Witte established close ties with the new minister of interior, giving him both support and advice. Many in the higher circles chose to believe that the prince was Witte's "protégé."[15] Such a belief is understandable given the fact that the prince was not in good health and not a strong personality, while Witte was what he always was, a dynamo, and St. Petersburg was what it always was, a hotbed of malicious gossip. But this belief is not credible. Both took roughly the same view of the urgency of change. And both underestimated the momentum of crises such as the one facing Russia.

Sviatopolk-Mirskii's program was twofold: first, to restore confidence in the government on the part of what he called "thinking Russia," by a series of steps that would indicate that the government trusted the public and that it would refrain from arbitrary use of power; second, that the government would enact necessary reforms, something that would take a little time.

He moved swiftly to show the government's commitment to change by dissociating himself from the Plehve heritage through easing out the late minister's lieutenants, by relaxing controls on the newspapers and the zemstvos, and by his public statements.

The effect was immediate. Newspapers, for the most part, expressed enthusiasm for the new course while speaking freely of the need for reform. Even publishers such as Prince Meshcherskii and Suvorin, known for their conservatism, were caught up in the spirit of optimistic expectation. Suvorin, and not he alone, spoke of a spring-like new era. This mood was shared widely by the educated, some ready to let the new minister of interior set the pace, others eager to use the expanding freedom to press for change that would transform the autocratic regime into a constitutional monarchy, still others now talking of getting rid of autocracy and replacing it with a democratic regime. There were, of course, those on the far right who would not hear of any change in the autocratic regime. As for the tsar, he was now reluctantly committed to change but not to any infringement of his autocratic power.

Once he had taken those initial steps that roused expectations, Sviatopolk-Mirskii found himself moving more slowly than he had anticipated. Early in October, he told Suvorin, "I find myself in the position of someone who has signed a promissory note for a sum he cannot pay."[16] That was so partly because he was a weak administrator trying to cope with a less than friendly bureaucracy.[17] Witte was supportive but was not in a position to be of much help. Another reason for the plight in which the prince found himself was that events were fast outrunning his own expectations.

First was the fact that the left wing of the liberal movement was gaining more and more strength in that movement, about which more later. Second was the fact that the left wing had begun to make common cause with the revolutionaries, as was dramatically demonstrated by a conference held in Paris beginning at the end of September. There the Union of Liberation together with assorted Russian and minority socialist and liberal parties and leagues hammered out a common platform that called for the overthrow of autocracy and its replacement by a democratic regime, for the restoration of Finnish rights, for the end of restrictions on national minorities, and for the recognition of the right of national self-determination.[18] The participants were, moreover, defeatists, believing that their cause would benefit from Japanese victory, some going so far as to accept covert aid from the enemy.

Prince Sviatopolk-Mirskii placed much of his hope for reconciliation of government and society in the zemstvos, which he expected to be moderate in their aspirations, but this was not to be. Shortly after the prince's appointment, the zemstvo organizational bureau, located in Moscow and led by Shipov, decided to hold a congress to consider zemstvo problems, one of which was how to shake off the fetters placed on them by Plehve. But "the appetite grew with the eating": Union of Liberation elements, which had become dominant, insisted that the congress be a forum for proclaiming very liberal demands, which would amount to throwing down the gauntlet, something that Shipov and the prince sought to avoid. Witte advised Sviatopolk-Mirskii not to permit the proposed congress to meet, in the conviction that it would adopt demands that would only exacerbate relations between government and society.[19] The minister of interior, however, chose to go ahead, negotiating with both Shipov and the tsar, whose suspicions of the zemstvos had been sharpened by Witte's memorandum on the subject some years earlier. In the end the prince worked out a scheme that would ease tensions: the congress would meet in St. Petersburg rather than in Moscow as originally proposed, the latter city being regarded as a hotbed of radicalism. Furthermore, it would meet in private homes rather than in a public hall, thus avoiding any violation of existing rules about public assembly.

Despite the efforts of Shipov and several of his associates to ensure a spirit of moderation, the congress, which opened on November 6, kicked over the traces. A sign of what was to come was provided by the Saratov delegation, which marched to the railroad station from which they were to embark singing the French revolutionary hymn, "La Marseillaise."[20] Despite Shipov's efforts, the congress adopted eleven theses, chief among them those calling for legal equality of all subjects (which would mean, for example, elimination of all laws restricting the rights of Jews), for representative government, and for the guarantee of freedom of speech, press, religion, association, and assembly.[21]

Witte was no longer an idle bystander. He was seeking to become acquainted with the leading figures at the congress and to do so in a friendly manner, even going so far as to say that if he were certain that the next tsar would be a wise man, he would not object to the idea of representative government, a somewhat vapid remark considering that Nicholas was only thirty-six years old and his heir but three months of age.[22] Such language may be behind the prince's remark to his wife that Witte might be giving him contradictory advice, urging the prince to remain firm in his opposition to the demand for representative government while taking a different position with others. Also, he complained that Witte tattled everything, even what was spoken in confidence.[23]

The zemstvo congress marked the explosive radicalization of the liberal movement and the beginning of the end of the prince's tenure. Within the imperial family, at court, among the upper bureaucracy, and in "society," antipathy toward the prince was high. Grand Duke Sergei Aleksandrovich, who was close to the tsar, spoke bitterly about Sviatopolk-Mirskii, on occasion referring to him as "Sviatopolk the Accursed," a rather absurd reference to the Kievan grand prince responsible for the murder of his own brothers. True, the prince had supporters in high places, notably the dowager empress, who threatened to return to her native Denmark if he were "touched." Nonetheless, Sviatopolk-Mirskii, who did not have much staying power, began to worry lest the tsar be influenced by those hostile to him. Toward the end of November, he broached the subject of leaving his post, even suggesting Witte as his replacement. To this suggestion the tsar replied that he had no confidence in the man and that, moreover, he was believed to be a Mason, a serious charge given that Masonry was prohibited, that being a Mason meant automatic excommunication, and that the Masons were alleged to be working with international Jewry to overthrow the monarchy. In any case he would not hear of the prince's leaving at a time when Grand Duke Sergei Aleksandrovich, governor-general of Moscow, and N.V. Muravev, minister of justice, wished to give up their posts.[24]

The prince then continued with the preparation of a draft of an imperial decree that would embody the reforms he had in mind, warning his sovereign that if mildly liberal reforms were not enacted, revolution would follow. The tsar replied that he hated the word *liberal* and did not foresee the dire consequences about which Sviatopolk-Mirskii was warning, promising that if he was mistaken, he would admit his error.[25] The prince continued his preparations amidst the storm that followed the adoption of the Eleven Theses, which had quickly become public knowledge. It seemed that all but a small minority of the educated were clamoring for change, with voices ranging from mild to strident, the more militant holding political banquets reminiscent of the early days of the French Revolution of 1848. At several of these banquets there were some who called for a constituent assembly to decide the political fate of Russia.

The tsar continued to believe that these voices did not represent the true voice of Russia, and the prince continued to believe that the reforms he had in mind would quiet the storm. Before long he submitted his draft to the tsar. What followed is difficult to reconstruct because of lack of a record of the proceedings, forcing one to rely on diaries and self-serving memoirs alone.

According to the most reliable evidence, the tsar agreed on November 18 to hold a conference to consider the prince's proposal, which was still in preparation. Two weeks passed before the tsar summoned ministers and a few others for a conference on December 2 over which he would preside. When Sviatopolk-Mirskii noted that Witte's name was not on the list of those invited, the tsar repeated the charge that Witte was a Mason, adding that Witte would not have anything useful to say, but agreed to invite him.[26] The prince, as expected, counted on Witte to support him, despite his misgivings about the man.

In his opening remarks at the December 2 session the tsar posed a rhetorical question: did they want to take measures to quiet unrest or did they want to resume the policies of Sipiagin and Plehve? Obviously they were there to consider Sviatopolk-Mirskii's proposals, of which the one calling for enlarging the State Council by the addition of elected "responsible public men," that is, men elected by the zemstvos and municipal dumas, was the most important and controversial.

Concerning the question raised by the tsar, Witte spoke strongly of the need for positive change, as did most of the others. The proposal to add elected members produced heated debate, with Witte, Kokovtsev, and Pobedonostsev, an odd trio, opposing it. The tsar said he agreed with the majority and charged Witte and Baron E.Iu. Nolde, chief administrative assistant of the Committee of Ministers, with drafting a decree embodying the majority view.

Several days passed, with Sviatopolk-Mirskii growing more worried about the tsar's intentions as well as Witte's. During that time Witte helped edit the document. Finally the tsar called a conference for December 8, this time also inviting three of his uncles and his brother. This time, as before, there was heated debate over adding elected members to the State Council. Witte, as before, argued against the elective principle, preferring that the additional members be appointed. In the end, at the suggestion of Count D.M. Solskii, Article Three of the proposed decree was changed to provide that elected representatives would meet as a separate body.[27] As Witte tells it, at the conclusion of the session, Count Solskii made such a moving expression of gratitude to the tsar for leading the country in "a new direction" that several ministers wept.[28]

Witte was not one of them. The next day he told Suvorin that the forthcoming decree might have done some good in placating "society" three months earlier, that is, shortly after the death of Plehve, but that now it was too late to be effective.[29]

For the tsar, the very idea of the proposed decree was galling, and the third article, providing for elected representatives participating in the legislative process, was especially so. In this he was strongly supported by Grand

Duke Sergei Aleksandrovich, who was visiting him. At the same time Nicholas felt committed to sign the decree. Perhaps because he believed that Witte would give him the advice he wanted to hear, he summoned his former minister of finance to see him on December 11.

Witte dutifully informed Sviatopolk-Mirskii of the summons. When he was ushered in to see the tsar, he found Grand Duke Sergei Aleksandrovich already there. Nicholas told Witte that he had changed Article Three to provide for appointment rather than election and wanted Witte's opinion.

Witte hedged, replying that he approved of the decree as it stood but felt it necessary to point out that participation of representatives, be they elected or appointed, was a first step, sure to be followed by others, toward constitutional government, an end "for which all civilized countries were instinctively striving." He went on to say that if the tsar felt that he must swim with the tide of history, he should retain the article in question, but if he felt that he could not reconcile himself to the idea of representative government, he should delete it. The tsar chose to delete it.[30] The next day he signed the Imperial Decree to the Governing Senate, December 12, 1904, Concerning Plans for the Improvement of the Social Order.[31]

Written in the ornate and antiquated style characteristic of imperial documents, the decree expressed the hope that it would have the support of people of goodwill. After giving pride of place to the need to improve the peasants' lot, it proceeded to address other pressing problems that Sviatopolk-Mirskii and Witte as well as liberal leaders believed to be in need of attention, but on a more limited scale than liberal leaders demanded. The decree called for careful observance of the rule of law, for broadening the jurisdiction of zemstvos and municipal dumas, for equality before the law through ensuring the independence of the judiciary, and for adequate protection of factory workers.

Also, the decree called for review, but not elimination, of the law on exceptional measures, enacted in 1881 following the assassination of Alexander II. It will be recalled that the law invested governors-general, governors, and police officials with extraordinary repressive powers in localities deemed seditious. Enacted as an emergency measure for three years, it had been renewed without interruption and had come to be applied in most of the country. To the opposition the law represented the sorest of sore points, the almost despotic power of the government. In the eyes of the opposition its elimination was of as much importance as the institution of representative government.

Additionally, the decree dealt with a matter of particular concern to ethnic and religious minorities: the discriminatory legislation they had to endure. It promised review of such legislation with the aim of removing those features it found to be without merit. In the same cautious spirit, the decree promised to "remove unnecessary limitations" from the legislation governing the press.

Responsibility for preparing the legislation necessary for implementing the decree was placed on the Committee of Ministers, which would report to the tsar. This obviously meant that Witte now had some work he could dig his teeth into and that he would have more access to the tsar than he had had for nearly a year and a half.

On the whole, there was little in the decree that would give Witte pause. True, he did not believe that the decree would satisfy "society." It is also true that, as far as we know, he had no broad ideas of what else needed to be done to dispel the rising voice of discontent. But he did have some suggestions for improving governmental efficiency, such as coordinating the work of the ministries, which implied the formation of something like a cabinet.[32] He had become increasingly aware of the need for changes in the peasants' way of life, as expressed in the memorandum about the peasantry he had recently sent to the tsar.[33] He was still firmly committed to the autocratic principle and could in good conscience work on implementing the decree in the belief that it would help promote necessary changes even though they would not be enough to mollify the opposition. What kind of outcome he expected we do not know. Perhaps he thought that what he considered to be the voice of reason would prevail among the members of "society."

Witte's new responsibility drew considerable comment from those who were speculating about if and when he would return to power. Thus, the British ambassador Sir Charles Hardinge wrote home late in December: "The success he has achieved in once more imposing his services upon the Emperor, to whom it is known that he is personally distasteful, is an interesting instance of his energy and ability, but it is not probable that his services will be long retained when order and calm have once more been restored."[34]

Elsewhere in his report, Sir Charles stated that Witte told him that he would support some reforms he did not believe in only because they would have a calming effect. Witte also told him that while his heart told him that autocracy was "the only form of government suitable to Russia," his mind told him that sooner or later Russia would have some form of representative government, a refrain that he would repeat many a time.

As the year drew to an end, so did the political "spring." A few saw the December 12 decree as a harbinger of good things to come. Kuropatkin was one such. He wrote Witte an enthusiastic letter, recalling that they had spoken of precisely the same reforms called for in the decree and assuring him that the tsar would certainly avail himself of a "strong, historic figure" such as Witte.[35] The general response was hostile. As for Sviatopolk-Mirskii, nothing was left for him but to leave his post, as he made clear to the tsar on the day after the signing of the decree. When he mentioned Witte's name, the tsar replied that he would have no qualms about appointing him if he could be certain that the man was not a Mason.[36] By now the tsar was prepared to part with the prince but said it would take another month before he could find an adequate replacement.

Meanwhile, the war news could only add to discontent. Early in October, Admiral Rozhdestvenskii's ships, en route from the Baltic to Port Arthur, had fired on British fishing trawlers in the Dogger Bank of the North Sea under the illusion that Japanese torpedo boats were in the vicinity. For a few days Britain was seized by war fever, which, fortunately, subsided. The admiral had reached Madagascar in time to receive the news that Port Arthur had surrendered on December 19. With Port Arthur gone, new plans had to be formulated before the admiral could resume his journey.

At home the capitulation of Port Arthur wrought further damage to the government's prestige. Although the government had instructed the press to prepare its readers for such an outcome, the public reaction was one of deep outrage.[37] Even among the indifferent there had been widespread admiration for the garrison, which had endured thousands and thousands of casualties. Nonetheless, the last weeks of December saw a superficial calm produced by preparations for the Christmas holiday, which included recesses for university students and factory workers. But there were ominous exceptions to that superficial calm. In the Caucasus there were pockets of open revolt. Finland, where virtually the entire population was in opposition to the Russification policies that Plehve had supported and where that opposition had been capped by the assassination of Governor-General Bobrikov, was far from calm. In the Polish border provinces the Polish Socialist Party was carrying out a terror campaign following an incident in which troops had fired upon an antiwar demonstration, the first Russo-Polish clash in forty years. And in Baku some fifty thousand striking workers introduced a new element in the labor movement, voicing political demands for a constituent assembly and civil rights as well as the usual economic demands for fewer hours and higher pay.

More ominous was a little-noticed group in the capital, the Assembly of St. Petersburg Factory Workers, led by Father George Gapon, who had sought and received police permission to form this group. Its stated aim was to provide a means for workers to come together in an organization of loyal Russian Orthodox men that would create a sober environment for socializing and for voicing concerns about their working conditions through legitimate channels. Its unstated aim was to insulate workers from revolutionary influence.

Nonetheless, revolutionary influence was beginning to creep in, and many of the workers were becoming militant. During the Christmas recess, after four workers at the Putilov Ironworks had been dismissed for belonging to the Assembly, a group of workers presented management with strong demands, the first step toward a strike that would provide the kind of revolution Witte had said could not occur in Russia.

Witte had become aware early on of efforts to form legal labor organizations with police authorization in St. Petersburg. Thus we find him sending a top-secret letter of inquiry to Plehve early in January 1903 asking for information about such efforts for the benefit of his own ministry's factory inspectors.[38] Undoubtedly he would have used his power as minister of finance to help scuttle the Gapon organization when it began its operations early in 1904, but by then his influence had become quite limited. He was, after all, all too well acquainted with the fiasco produced by a similar effort in Moscow that had had to be aborted in 1903.

Chapter 12

In the Wake of Bloody Sunday, January–June 1905

Toward the end of 1904, Witte, when asked by a grand duke about Russia's future, replied that the country was like a patient for whom a remedy could be prescribed but that the outcome was in God's hands. He regarded the December 12 decree as no more than a small part of the remedy, but he was eager to get to work.

Among his colleagues as well as at court there were those who believed that Witte valued his own career above the interests of the motherland. And at court and elsewhere there were those who saw in him a shameless hypocrite who, while professing to be a devout believer in autocracy, was conspiring with revolutionaries, mainly Jewish, of course, to create crisis conditions that would permit him to step in as the country's savior and proclaim a republic with himself as president. V.A. Gringmut, editor of the highly conservative *Moskovskie vedomosti*, a stalwart in the ranks of Witte's enemies, complained that those at court who felt that Witte must be stopped did nothing beyond uttering words.[1] Witte was not a shameless and disloyal hypocrite. He was a shameless egoist and a loyal subject.

It was the case at this time that he was in touch with a number of moderate liberals, several of whom he invited to participate in dealing with relevant aspects of the work on the December 12 decree. In so doing he was displaying his characteristic ability to learn on the job. Not that he was turning into a liberal. What he was doing was enlisting the help of those he presumed capable of influencing "society." At the same time he was learning more about the liberal mind-set.

He set to work immediately and would continue to work on his new project with his usual energy, but a tragedy that no one foresaw clouded his efforts and gravely reduced whatever impact implementation of the decree might have had. The tragedy was Bloody Sunday.

The strike, which had begun in late December 1904, spread throughout the capital, acquiring political overtones in the process. In this spirit Father Gapon and his associates proposed to stage a peaceful march to the Winter Palace on Sunday, January 9, and there to present a "humble" petition to the tsar, who would, they assumed, be there to receive them. The language of the petition was reasonably humble, but its points, among them a call to end the war, were far from humble and could well have come from a left-wing liberal organization.[2]

The strike and the planned march caught the government by surprise and unsure about how to react. Witte was excluded from the deliberations about the tactics to be pursued in dealing with the proposed march. On the eve of the march a ten-man delegation, largely liberal in composition, called on Witte in hopes that he could persuade the powers that be to permit the march so as to avoid bloodshed. When he told them that it was not in his power to help, they departed angrily in a vain effort to see the minister of interior, whom Witte informed of their visit. It was that night that Sviatopolk-Mirskii and his colleagues made the firm decision to stop the march, by command if possible, by force if necessary.[3]

As planned, Gapon and his followers marched in columns toward the Winter Palace from several starting points on that wintry Sunday, carrying church banners and icons, giving the impression of a religious procession. As they neared their destination they were confronted by massed troops and police, from whose ranks came orders to disperse. The orders were ignored, as were warning shots and cavalry charges. Then came the deadly volleys, which had the intended effect of dispersing the marchers. Witte was able to see one of the columns from the balcony of his house, to hear the shots and see terror-stricken men, women, and children fleeing, some carrying off dead and wounded.[4] But that was not the end of that day's carnage: nervous senior officers ordered curious crowds that had gathered near the Winter Palace to be dispersed by deadly fire. The official count was 96 dead and 333 wounded (of whom 34 died subsequently).The unofficial count, made by journalists, was over four thousand victims.

The impact of Bloody Sunday, as that day came to be called, was volcanic. The spirit of the response to that event was captured by an editorial in *Osvobozhdenie* that declared, "Tsar Nicholas has revealed himself as the enemy and butcher of the people," and proclaimed, "It is impossible to live thus any longer."[5] Revolution had come to Russia, enveloping industrial workers and most of the educated class and, somewhat later, leaving its mark on the peasantry and the armed forces.

Witte blamed the tsar, Sviatopolk-Mirskii, and others in high positions for the carnage and quickly, as one would expect from him, sought to dissociate himself from any responsibility for Bloody Sunday. He granted a brief interview to a correspondent of a French newspaper, in the course of which he asserted that he had not been consulted at all before the event. The same newspaper also carried an account, attributed to "a former minister," not named but evidently Witte, who asserted that the tragedy could have been averted if the tsar had followed his counsel. The "former minister" said that "only a fool or an adventurer" would accept the position of minister of interior under current circumstances, and that he would not accept the rank of chancellor, if it were offered, unless he were given full power to carry out his program.[6] Chancellor was the highest rank in the bureaucracy, one that no one had held since 1882. Witte was obviously daydreaming of a triumphant return to power.

He believed that the chief cause of the unrest that had been gripping the country and that was now ballooning into what he later called "the so-called revolution" was the war. With that thought in mind he suggested to the lame-duck Sviatopolk-Mirskii that the tsar summon a *zemskii sobor* (Assembly of the Land) representing all social levels to advise him about the question of peace.[7] This was a remnant of his Slavophile belief in a rosy past in which the tsar and his people were united by means of the Assembly of the Land. Although he still retained some Slavophile ideas, Witte pooh-poohed the idea of reviving the institution on a permanent basis, but obviously thought of it as a temporary palliative.[8] Nothing came of it, but his conviction that peace must be made quickly persisted.

That conviction was vividly demonstrated in a lengthy and impassioned letter to Kuropatkin, dated January 19, which he had hand-delivered by Prince Trubetskoi. In it he underlined his conviction that the war was the chief cause of the convulsion that Russia was experiencing, indicating, as expected, that he bore no responsibility for the conflict. A secondary cause of current troubles was the mistaken policies toward the non-Russian 44 percent of the population—Jews, Finns, Poles, Armenians, and others—who had become enemies of the regime. He sought to convince the general that even if his army took the offensive and drove the Japanese back to the Korean border, and even if Admiral Rozhdestvenskii managed to reach Vladivostok with his ships, continuation of the war would only make matters worse at home.

In the same letter he wrote that "now anarchists, revolutionaries and constitutionalists have begun their propaganda with all their might and main," and added that "the government has grown less and less significant. Previously the ministers were loathed. Now they are despised. Previously people did not love the government but they accepted it, but now they laugh at it maliciously and want to do away with it." He went on to say that the zemstvos and the nobility were now arrayed against the tsar. As for the masses, while they were still loyal to their sovereign, they wanted nothing more than to have the land still under private ownership turned over to them. He asserted that Russia had not been in such a parlous state since the time of Peter the Great.

What was to be done? he asked. The current state of affairs, he assured Kuropatkin, was the result not of historical circumstances but of the inadequacy of the men who served the tsar. Given existing conditions and given the caliber of the men in power, the solution was in the hands of Providence, which could do its work if only the war were brought to a speedy conclusion. If it were not, he predicted, all Russia would lose its mental balance, and then anything could happen.

What use would the December 12 decree be at this time? he asked. He had argued for its essential points ten years earlier, but no one listened, he wrote. If they had, the regime would have had ten good years. Now it was unlikely that the decree would do much good, but it was necessary to implement it and see what God would grant.[9]

In referring to the "caliber" of the men serving the tsar he was probably referring not only to those already in harness but also to those just taking up new and important positions, namely, General Dmitrii F. Trepov and Alexander G. Bulygin, both of whom would be of more than a little importance in Witte's life during the near future.

In the days following Bloody Sunday, Nicholas saw the imperative need to restore order while at the same time repairing the damage done to his prestige by that terrible day. To restore order he established the temporary office of governor-general of the province and city of St. Petersburg, with authority over the government of the area and the military forces there, and appointed Trepov to that office.

The general had served as Moscow's police superintendent under Grand Duke Sergei Aleksandrovich. He had left that office the preceding December in tandem with the grand duke and, like him, was hostile to Sviatopolk-Mirskii, whom the tsar was committed to replace.

In Witte's memoirs Trepov receives much the same hateful treatment accorded to Bezobrazov and Plehve. He quotes with approval Prince Urusov's characterization of Trepov as "a sergeant major by training and a pogrom-maker by conviction"—a man with the mentality and knowledge of a drill sergeant, a man incapable of dealing with complex problems, yet confident of his capacity to do so.[10] Trepov was a man much to the liking of the tsar and enjoyed his sovereign's confidence to the end of his days, which turned out to be little more than a year.

Obviously, the general did not inspire the same confidence in Witte. Oddly enough, Trepov thought enough of the former minister of finance to take the trouble to call on him and even to tell the tsar that Witte was the only man capable of bringing "society" and government together, a view shared by many but not by Nicholas.[11] This was in the first months of Trepov's tenure. Subsequently he would turn against Witte.

Witte thought more highly of Bulygin, who succeeded Sviatopolk-Mirskii, than he did of Trepov. He writes: "Bulygin is a very decent man, far from stupid, a man with a broad knowledge of statecraft, but a placid personality who dislikes unpleasant situations of any kind."[12] This was a widely shared view. Unlike his predecessor, Bulygin did not bring with him any kind of program. That fact, plus his lack of drive, were hardly the kind of credentials required for those critical times, but they obviously suited the tsar more so than those of Witte, whom Sviatopolk-Mirskii had again recommended after Bloody Sunday.[13]

Thus Witte remained in a secondary and therefore hateful role, but a busy one for now. In addition to the routine duties of the Committee of Ministers and of the Special Conference on the Needs of Rural Industry, he was not only concerned with implementing the December 12 decree but soon found himself involved in dealing with the dire consequences of Bloody Sunday: strikes and demonstrations in the major cities, most of "society" in a furor of denunciations, as well as demands for immediate and major reforms. Students and faculty in the universities were in such a hostile state that the institutions were closed down.

The priorities as seen at the top were, in addition to the restoration of order, steps to reassure workers that their tsar was still the benevolent "Little Father" of his people. It was in this spirit that Nicholas received Witte and Kokovtsev five days after Bloody Sunday to talk about the "workers question."[14] The outcome of this talk would be a do-nothing commission, but the tsar was not alarmed enough to think of bold efforts to deal with the psychological blow to his prestige that Bloody Sunday had inflicted.

An alarm call came from an unlikely source: A.S. Ermolov, minister of agriculture, a gentle soul to whom Witte referred as "ladybug."[15] On January 17, during the course of a regular report to the tsar, the minister took his courage in his hands and spoke frankly and passionately to Nicholas, placing some of the blame for Bloody Sunday on the government, warning of the spread of revolution, and dwelling on the need for the tsar to address his people. According to Ermolov's account, Nicholas was so moved that he ordered him to convey immediately to Witte his wish that he summon a meeting of the ministers and chairmen of the departments of the State Council to consider recent events as well as further reforms relevant to the December 12 decree.[16]

Witte complied immediately. The following day the meeting was held. According to the incomplete record, the hasty notes of a participant, the conferees concentrated on refurbishing the tsar's image. As Witte put it, the people thought that the tsar knew nothing of what had occurred; therefore he must address the people lest revolutionaries seize leadership, in which case "the aureole of the ruler will be destroyed."[17] The majority was of the same opinion, voting for an imperial manifesto. The tsar chose instead to receive a carefully chosen delegation of St. Petersburg workers, whom he chided for listening to allegedly false prophets, at the same time assuring them of his concern for their needs.

The pace of events, with unrest spreading and deepening, clearly meant that the government would have to go beyond the December 12 decree, but while the need for further concessions was being recognized, work on giving flesh to the decree continued. This in the midst of mounting unrest, of heightened police and military presence in the capital, of discouraging news from the war front. Witte, with his usual drive and energy, devoted himself to the task, bringing in experts from the government and outside, among them several liberals, supervising the collection of relevant material, holding meeting after meeting. In addition, Witte took the singular step of publicizing decisions and later of publishing the minutes of these meetings.[18] This in an effort to show the public that something was being done.

What did the Committee of Ministers accomplish? Witte puts it succinctly:

> I, of course, hoped that speedy enactment of reforms would reduce discontent, but, as might be expected, I encountered obstacles from the beginning: First, there was apathy in high places, then intrigue and hostility, particularly after the departure of Mirskii, finally, lack of faith on the part of the Emperor in the promised reforms.

> Consequently, our accomplishments were to be limited to partial extension of religious toleration, and partial lifting of the ban on publication in the Little Russian [Ukrainian] language and on instruction in non-Russian languages in the western provinces and the Kingdom of Poland. All the other proposals for reform were put on the shelf, under the influence of succeeding events. However, some of the work that we did that had no immediate results was to prove useful to me later, when I became premier.[19]

As Witte notes, he achieved some success in advancing religious toleration, but in doing so he brought down on himself the wrath of Pobedonostsev, the fearsome overprocurator of the Holy Synod, whom even the tsar was afraid to cross. Trouble between Witte and him arose because Witte tried to go beyond the mandate given him by point six of the December 12 decree, which required the Committee of Ministers "to review the legislation concerning the rights of schismatics [Old Believers] and of persons belonging to unorthodox and heterodox faiths, and, independently of this, to take immediate administrative action for the issuance of measures to free religious life from all restrictions not prescribed by law."[20]

Consideration of the condition of the Russian Orthodox Church was not the business before the Committee of Ministers. Its task was to implement all the points in the December 12 decree, among them point six. Nonetheless, Witte as well as Antonii, metropolitan of St. Petersburg, believed that implementation of point six would give Old Believers and sectarians the advantage of being free of government control while leaving the established church still shackled. It was this belief that led to conflict with Pobedonostsev, who opposed any change that, in his opinion, would harm autocracy and the church.

The overprocurator, because of illness and pique, missed most of the sessions dealing with point six. At one of these sessions, Metropolitan Antonii, there at Witte's invitation, expressed his views about the need for church reform. Witte expanded on these views in a memorandum to the tsar. When Pobedonostsev learned of what was afoot he sent vigorous rebuttals to both Nicholas and Witte. The latter, not one to flee from a dispute, answered with equal vigor. Soon the exchange became public knowledge, at home as well as abroad. In the end, Pobedonostsev won a temporary victory by persuading the tsar to inform Witte that the matter of church reform was solely the business of the Holy Synod.[21] Later that year, when Witte became premier, he would turn again to church reform, something close to his heart.

Witte returned to the business at hand, point six. After many a meeting, the Committee of Ministers sent its recommendations to the tsar, who accepted them and signed a decree issued on April 17. Under its terms, many of the onerous restrictions on Old Believers and sectarians were lifted. Among its terms, the decree permitted members of the established church to leave and join other faiths, a provision that permitted several hundred thousand persons, among them Old Believers and sectarians, who had been members of the established church in name only, to declare their true faith openly.

As Witte notes, the only other direct consequences of the work on the December 12 decree were chiefly in the field of language rights for some non-Russians, and that was because of his influence. During the course of lengthy discussions of existing restrictions on the Poles, he showed sympathy for lightening those restrictions.[22] The result, meager to be sure, was a series of measures chiefly concerned with the use of Polish and Lithuanian for instructional purposes.[23]

It was Witte's intervention that provided a modest step forward for Ukrainian language rights. What was at issue was a request to the Holy Synod and the Academy of Sciences for permission to publish a Ukrainian translation of the Gospels, something hitherto forbidden on the specious ground that Ukrainian was no more than a Russian dialect. The request had been approved by Prince Sviatopolk-Mirskii and the academy but denied by the Holy Synod. Witte, who was on friendly terms with Grand Duke Constantine Konstantinovich, president of the academy, somehow managed to get approval from the tsar for lifting of the ban.[24]

When it came to the question of what to do about the heavy burden of legal disabilities borne by the Jews, Witte and his committee fudged. Their task was to review legislation affecting Jews and other minorities and to recommend retention only of legislation that served the state and the people. The committee did the reviewing and came to the conclusion that the task was too complex to be dealt with in the time at their disposal.[25] Of course, it would have taken but a few minutes to decide that all laws discriminating against Jews should be dumped in the wastebasket. This was the demand of Jews of all classes and of the opposition movement in general. But such a recommendation had absolutely no chance of being accepted by the tsar, as Witte well knew. He believed then, as he had long believed, that the Jewish question could be solved only "by the gradual elimination of all discriminatory laws against the Jews."[26] But he obviously found that it was impolitic to propose starting the process then.

Witte held to this position consistently and did so at the meetings about the December 12 decree. But any action to ease the burdens on the Jews was controversial and certain to be approached with caution by the bureaucracy. Moreover, the rationale for the legislation had changed over time. To deal with the Jewish question in a brief span of time was clearly impractical as well as impolitic. So the task was left for future consideration.

It is ironic that while Witte and his cohorts were working on implementing the December 12 decree, the point dropped from the draft of the decree, about elected representatives, was reemerging, in a slightly different form. The feeling of crisis within the government was so great after Bloody Sunday, with each day witnessing mounting opposition, that the tsar's advisers were able to convince him that some concession to the demands for representative government must be made.

Nicholas entrusted the preliminary work to his recently appointed minister of interior, Bulygin. After his group had done its work, the task was shifted to Count D.M. Solskii, whom he had just appointed chairman pro tem of the Council of Ministers. Much debate followed about the power and method of election to the proposed representative body. Finally, after some progress had been achieved, the tsar chaired a meeting of the council on February 3. After considerable discussion, the tsar entrusted Baron Nolde with drafting a directive, to Bulygin, instructing him to draft the necessary legislation.

Nolde went to work quickly, but it took over two weeks and three sessions of the council before the directive received its final form, on February 18. The document promised an elected body representing the people that would have a consultative role in the preparation of legislation. The new body would be far less than generally demanded and far more than the tsar had previously considered tolerable. Because, as far as is known, there is no written record of the sessions leading to the rescript, little can be said about the specifics of the discussions at these meetings. One source claims that at one of the meetings, probably the one on February 11, Witte, General P.L. Lobko, the state controller, and Grand Duke Vladimir Aleksandrovich spoke out against the notion of elected representatives.[27] Such a position was consistent with Witte's previously expressed views. In any case, Witte accepted the fait accompli that there would be an elective body with some role in the preparation of legislation, but with the mental reservation that such a body would be the first step toward a constitution. That reservation would be expressed in the course of the deliberations on the creation of the new body.

Witte's role in these deliberations would be decidedly minor, one sign of his fading fortunes. According to hearsay, various persons, Trepov allegedly among them, were seeking to undercut Witte. And the tsar, evidently, was easy to persuade that Witte was again becoming too powerful. On the other hand, many Witte watchers could not keep from wondering if Witte might not be the man of the hour. Thus M. Bompard, the French ambassador, wrote home early in February that events were moving toward a responsible ministry and that the only man capable of heading such a ministry was Witte but that the tsar was still unable to overcome his distaste for the man.[28] Such turned out to be the case, with Nicholas moving to deprive his former minister of finance of any substantial power.

The first sign came with the publication of an imperial decree on February 18 granting subjects the right to send to the tsar proposals "for improving the public well-being," which the tsar would turn over to the Council of Ministers. This meant that Count Solskii, not Witte, would have the responsibility. Also, the decree in effect marked finis to an effort begun a month earlier by Witte to meld the Committee of Ministers and the Council of Ministers under the name of the latter body.[29] That effort was the product of the conference that Nicholas had placed under Witte's direction to consider means of coordinating the activities of the government. Many ministers saw the need for coordination, given the existing system, under which the ruler provided some form of coordination but which had proved inadequate in the past and proved even more so in current crisis conditions. Witte's proposal had occasioned much debate and several counterproposals, all impinging on the authority of the autocrat. Nothing had come of all this. The February 18 decree simply meant that the government would continue to limp along much as before, with Solskii saddled with more duties but no more power and Witte with less.

Another, striking sign of disfavor came on March 30 when *Pravitelstvennyi vestnik*, the official government newspaper, published an imperial decree ending the operation of Witte's Special Conference on the Needs of Rural Industry. The news came as a complete surprise and an obvious slap in the face that was made even more painful by the tsar's establishment of the Special Conference on Measures to Strengthen Peasant Landholding, to be chaired by I.L. Goremykin, one of Witte's many enemies.

The Witte special conference had produced many volumes of information that would be used for subsequent agrarian reform. It had done preliminary work on legislative recommendations and had produced some minor changes, but it still had many major tasks to complete when the end came. Witte argues that if the conference had been permitted to finish its work, much of the subsequent turbulence in the countryside would have been averted.[30] That is doubtful, given the time required to carry out reforms.

In the course of this special conference's work, Witte learned much about the problems facing the countryside and became more sensitive to the nature and importance of peasant discontent than he had been while minister of finance. An example of his growing awareness was shown in a report to the tsar, dated March 14, in which he warned of a dangerous movement among the peasantry.[31] He was obviously referring to the spread of revolutionary propaganda among the peasants.

Why the special conference was closed is the subject of much speculation. Witte himself insists that a major source of hostility toward the body came from the mistaken notion that it favored abolition of the village commune, an institution dear to conservatives.[32] That may not be the case, but it is interesting that not long afterward, Sharapov, long a journalistic spokesman for the anti-Witte camp, accused his foe of being an inveterate enemy of the village commune and stated that the Jewish press was echoing his views.[33] Interesting too is the report of the French ambassador that the proximate cause of the tsar's action came from an allegation to him by one of Witte's foes that the former minister of finance favored division of the land.[34]

In any case, Witte was furious, as one can gather from his comments in his memoirs about the closing of the conference:

> Those who are absolute rulers "by the grace of God" must accept whatever responsibility they bear for such consequences.
>
> Unfortunately, our Emperor says that he is answerable only to God when it comes to making decisions, but when it comes to answering to mortals, he responded that this one had deceived him, that one had undermined

him and so forth. If an unlimited monarch wishes to hold his servants responsible for their official actions, he should be bound by their counsel and opinions. Otherwise he should consider himself responsible for his actions and hold his servants responsible only for carrying out his orders exactly.[35]

Witte's repugnance for the tsar was, of course, more than reciprocated—hardly a good sign for his future.

Two weeks after the closing of the conference on the needs of rural industry came the closing of Witte's conference on reform of administration. This was virtually an act of redundancy, since the conference had been left without an agenda. There was still the Committee of Ministers with its usual "vermicelli" plus the task of implementing the December 12 decree. Sensing the mood at court, Witte speeded up the work on the decree, then turned the protocols and proposals over to the tsar, who gave his approval on June 25.[36]

Bulygin's work in preparing legislation based on the February 18 decree went slowly, with no role in it for Witte. The weeks went on, with much give-and-take in an effort to create a body that would please "society" without eroding autocratic power. Finally, on May 17, the minister of interior turned over to the tsar a draft of a law establishing an elected, consultative duma (assembly). The draft was to be considered by the Council of Ministers before it would become law. At last Witte would have a voice, albeit a minor one, in the process of creating Russia's first elected national assembly.

The deliberations of the Council of Ministers took place against a background of tumultuous unrest at home and shameful defeat on land and sea that fanned domestic unrest. At the Manchurian front, near Mukden, in the middle of February, the two largest forces ever assembled engaged in a bloody eight-day battle that cost the Russians some one hundred thousand casualties. This was to have been the beginning of the long-promised Russian offensive. Instead, Kuropatkin, still confident of ultimate victory, was forced to retreat to a new defensive position. A month later, Russia suffered the worst and most humiliating defeat in her history when Rozhdestvenskii's ships were ambushed by the Japanese in the Tsushima Straits. As can be imagined, the blow to the government's prestige at home and abroad was fearful.

The need of speed in completing the preparatory work for the Bulygin Duma was great. The liberal movement was becoming even more vocal and demanding. The mass strike movement was picking up more strength. The revolutionary movement was stronger, more influential, with some of the revolutionaries armed, some of the arms amassed with covert Japanese help. The government was feebly attempting to cope through a combination of coercion and persuasion. Trepov became the personification of the former with his appointment in May to the post of assistant minister of interior in charge of the considerable security apparatus that helped to keep autocracy in power, while retaining his post of governor-general of St. Petersburg. The Bulygin Duma represented the chief hope of retaining the support of those willing to work with the government. Nonetheless, work on the duma proceeded with maddening slowness.

Witte played a minor role at the sessions of the Council of Ministers devoted to work on the draft dealing with the Bulygin Duma. But he did speak up firmly from time to time. He objected to the exclusion of most workers from the franchise, warning that it would be at a considerable political cost. He urged that the peasantry be given a major voice in the proposed body under the proposed system of indirect voting. Also, supported by Kokovtsev and others, he argued against exclusion of Jews from the right to serve as deputies in the duma, as proposed by Bulygin. The argument, appealing to expediency rather than equity, set off lengthy debate. The issue of Jewish exclusion had not yet been settled by the time a change in Witte's fortunes took him to America. It was so important to him for dealing with American Jewish leaders that he asked Kokovtsev to inform him of the outcome, which turned out to be favorable.[37]

Chapter 13

Peace with Honor?

As has been seen, Witte had been in favor of a negotiated peace for some time. Before Mukden he favored an early peace even if Russia was able to drive the Japanese out of Manchuria. After Mukden he became more than ever convinced that the war must end. The human cost was staggering. Public support for the war, far from great to start with, was eroding. The financial cost was equally staggering: prewar estimates of what an eighteen-month war with Japan would cost quickly proved far too low, raising the question of how to finance the fighting without leaving the gold standard. Witte, in close touch with Kokovtsev, as well as being a member of the interagency Finance Committee, could not help but be concerned with the country's financial state.[1]

To pay for the war it was necessary to borrow money, and to borrow money it was imperative to maintain the country's credit, which was badly battered by revolution at home and defeat abroad. French investors, who held most of Russia's bonds, were particularly jittery. And the French government could not help but be concerned about the reliability of Russia as an ally in the event of conflict with Germany. In February, before the battle of Mukden, Edouard Noetzlin, head of the banking group that dealt with Russian loans, came to Russia, where he shared with Kokovtsev the concerns of the French investing public. The minister of finance arranged for a meeting with Witte that was far from fruitful, but an audience with the tsar left Noetzlin feeling optimistic, a feeling that did not last long.[2]

The Russian defeat at Mukden improved the prospect of a negotiated peace. First of all, the Japanese, even before Mukden, felt that they lacked the resources to carry on the war much longer. They had been sending out secret peace feelers, to no avail, and were now more willing to try, with the United States as mediator. President Theodore Roosevelt, although sympathetic to the Japanese cause, did not regard continuation of the war to be in America's interest. Other powers, Germany excepted, also sought an end to the conflict.

Witte, being close to Lamsdorff, was privy to some of what was going on in the diplomatic field. He was also acutely aware of the cost of the defeat at Mukden. On February 28 he wrote an impassioned letter to the tsar, imploring him to move immediately to seek peace and to make sure the directive of

February 18 to Bulygin was implemented as soon as possible, as a way of calming public opinion. He assured the tsar that he was not distraught but was writing as a most loyal subject.[3] Nicholas did not respond, but one can imagine that he was irritated by such unsolicited advice.

The tsar was determined to save his country's honor, but the pressure to accept mediation was increasing, and Witte took it upon himself to facilitate the process after Theodore Roosevelt's announcement early in March of his plan for mediation. In the middle of that month he spoke to Sir Charles Hardinge, the British ambassador, about his country's need for peace and the danger of revolution if the war continued much longer. On his own, evidently expecting that Sir Charles would pass on what he said to the Japanese, he outlined the terms that would be acceptable to his country, terms that would turn out to be realistic. These included recognition of Korea as a Japanese sphere of influence, transfer of the Port Arthur and Liaotung lease to Japan, and cession of the South Manchurian Railroad, but excluded any form of indemnity. Several weeks later he sought to impress on the ambassador that prolongation of the war would harm the interests of all European powers except for Germany.[4] Soon thereafter he repeated his stricture to Cecil Spring-Rice, secretary of the embassy, not neglecting to emphasize how he had opposed the policies that had led to the war.[5] It is possible that although he was acting without authorization, he was acting with Lamsdorff's knowledge, but that is pure speculation.

Then came the Tsushima disaster, intensifying the pressure for a negotiated peace. On May 18 Japan asked the United States to mediate. The tsar was not quite ready. At the very least he wanted to win a major battle. Reinforcements were pouring into Manchuria, promising a decisive numerical advantage over the Japanese. Many generals, among them Kuropatkin, now demoted to chief of staff, believed that the enemy could still be defeated on land.

Beset by conflicting advice, Nicholas held a military conference on May 24, to which he had invited the minister of war and other ranking generals, including Grand Duke Vladimir Aleksandrovich, commander of the St. Petersburg Military District, and Grand Duke Alexis Aleksandrovich, head of the navy. The question put before them by the tsar was this: given recent losses on land and sea, and given the domestic situation (which had grown more critical as a result of Tsushima), should Russia fight on, at the risk of losing Sakhalin Island, the Amur region, and Kamchatka, thus making the achievement of peace more difficult, or should the country seek peace immediately? Opinion was divided. The minister of war, supported by several of the other generals, favored fighting on long enough to win a decisive victory. Grand Duke Vladimir, supported by some generals, favored an immediate effort to end the war. One of the moot points at the conference was whether or not the people could be roused to support the war with the enthusiasm shown by the Japanese for their side. No decision was reached on the matter under discussion.[6]

Two days later President Roosevelt invited the warring parties to a peace conference. It required two days for the Japanese to signal their acceptance and four days for the Russians to do the same. But there was no armistice.

Apparently Witte was not informed immediately about the decision to negotiate and feared that General Linevich, the new commander in Manchuria, would undertake offensive action. Early in June he wrote to Count P.A. Heyden, chief of the tsar's Field Chancellery, warning that such an action would only serve to make the peace terms Russia would have to agree to even more onerous than before. In the letter, which he apparently expected would be shown to the tsar, he did not fail to mention how he had favored negotiation earlier on.[7] In his memoirs Witte writes that he received a sharp answer from the count, to which he replied with equal sharpness.[8] The episode could only have heightened the tsar's distaste for his former minister of finance.

In late June, in an emotional reply to a letter from Kuropatkin, stating the need to continue the war, Witte revealed his views about what needed to be done to ensure Russia's future. He strongly rejected the notion that the country had anything to gain from continuing the war. He argued that as a result of the war Russia had become a second-rate power, and that Russia was in "the first phase of revolution" and desperately needed "a speedy and enduring peace" to deal with unrest and regain her strength. Further, he argued, the country must accept the fact that for some time to come she could not play the part of a great power and must give up what she had gained in the preceding decade. What Russia desperately needed, he insisted, was twenty to twenty-five years of peace, during which she would have to forgo the role of a great power in order to reestablish stability and rebuild her armed forces, for defensive, not offensive, purposes. In response to Kuropatkin's plea that patriotism required continuation of the war, Witte replied that he knew the general to be a "true patriot" but he too loved his country and that, because he did, he wanted peace for his "poor, poor, dear and sweet Rus!"[9]

Less than a week after writing this letter Witte would be appointed first plenipotentiary of Russia's peace delegation, this after nearly three weeks of the tsar's resistance to the idea. The process of selection began on June 11, when Lamsdorff proposed that A.I. Nelidov, ambassador to France, be given the post and that Witte be a member of the delegation. The tsar's note on the proposal: "anyone but Witte." When Nelidov was informed of the possible assignment he begged off, citing age and lack of expertise.[10]

Lamsdorff continued to push Witte's candidacy, emphasizing his expertise in Far Eastern affairs, but Nicholas preferred to look elsewhere, as would be expected. But he did not hurry: despite the lack of an armistice, the Manchurian front was quiet aside from a few skirmishes. He was preoccupied, among other things, with the mutiny on the cruiser *Potemkin* of the Black Sea fleet.

In casting about for candidates, his thoughts turned to A.P. Izvolskii, his minister to Denmark. Unlike Nelidov, Izvolskii had some knowledge of Far Eastern affairs, having served as minister to Japan. As Izvolskii tells it, without knowing what was afoot, he wrote to the tsar recommending Witte, noting that he was highly respected in the Far East.[11] The tsar, however, decided on his ambassador to Rome, N.V. Muravev, one of Witte's bitterest rivals and a protégé of the late Grand Duke Sergei Aleksandrovich. Muravev agreed to serve and was summoned to the capital. On June 27 he was received by the tsar. As it appears, the ambassador quickly had second thoughts, apparently arising from his recognition of the pitfalls he might encounter if he accepted. As Witte tells it, he was informed by Lamsdorff on the twenty-eighth that the tsar had decided to appoint him first plenipotentiary, to which he replied that he would accept only if the ruler personally made him the offer. This was done on the following day.[12] He was once more in the limelight, but he, too, was aware of the pitfalls of his new position, saying to Kokovtsev: "When a sewer has to be cleaned, they send Witte; but as soon as work of a cleaner and nicer kind appears, plenty of other candidates spring up."[13] He, too, might have begged off, but, it appears that he was moved to accept because he was certain that peace was imperative, that he was the man for the task, and that he would be once more on center stage.

News of the appointment drew mixed reactions. Abroad, the reaction was quite favorable, based on the perception that here was a man of sufficient stature to do what was required. At home there was applause from those who thought it was time to end the war and catcalls from those who believed the war should go on and those who believed that his only interest was in self-advancement.[14]

Next came the question of the composition of Witte's entourage. The tsar proposed that Izvolskii be the second plenipotentiary, but Witte's preference, which won out, was for Baron Roman von Rosen, a Baltic German, who had served as minister to Japan and had only recently been appointed ambassador to the United States.[15] Professor F.F. Martens was included for his widely known expertise in international law. Witte "shocked" the good professor by declaring that he "didn't think it necessary to be guided by the norms of international law or by diplomatic precedents but rather by common sense and circumstance."[16] The mission also included several men with recent experience in Manchuria, as well as two secretaries, one of whom, I.Ia.

Korostovets, was detailed to maintain a diary covering the conference. In addition, Joseph Dillon, whom we have met before, was associated with the group; his task was to deal with public relations.[17]

Witte used Dillon in a vain effort to make sure that Marquis Ito, with whom he had dealt before and with whom he saw eye to eye on many questions, would replace Baron Komura, who had already been appointed chief of the Japanese delegation. To this end he had the journalist speak to Hayashi, the Japanese minister to London. Witte fancied that the knowledge of his own appointment would convince the Japanese that a man of Ito's stature would be more suitable for negotiating with a man of his own stature. In fact, Ito had been the first choice but had declined in favor of Komura, the foreign minister.[18]

The site of the conference was Portsmouth, New Hampshire. Witte preferred a location near the scene of battle, but it was not his to choose. In any case, it is not likely that he looked forward to a sea voyage. As von Bülow once noted, Witte, like many Russians, lacked "sea legs."[19] In the days that followed his appointment the first plenipotentiary was, predictably, a very busy man. With the tsar's authorization he acquainted himself with the military and naval situation, one that could only strengthen his conviction that Russia must have peace.[20] It was a conviction that he concealed then and later, since it was his task to act as if he held good cards. On July 6, together with his wife and infant grandson, upon whom he doted, he left St. Petersburg.

En route he stopped in Paris, chiefly for the purpose of talking to President Loubet and Premier Rouvier about a major loan of which Russia was in desperate need. In fact, it was his country's parlous fiscal state that had helped sway the tsar toward a negotiated peace.

Both Loubet and Rouvier impressed on Witte that Russia must make peace as soon as possible. Rouvier went further and told Witte that while France would support a loan once peace was achieved—a loan that would include provision for payment of an indemnity—there would be no loan for continuation of the fighting. Witte bridled at the mention of an indemnity, insisting, as his instructions required, that Russia would not pay a sou.[21]

The advice he received was given by declared friends of Russia, but the general attitude he found in Paris ranged from indifference to hostility, in sharp contrast to the mood that prevailed when the Franco-Russian alliance had been signed. In the face of this mood Witte kept his head high, letting it be known that, if need be, Russia was ready to resume active fighting. While in Paris he learned of a meeting between Nicholas and the German emperor at Björkö, which Lamsdorff took as a sign of recovery of Russian prestige.[22]

Nonetheless, he was in a depressed mood when he departed from

Cherbourg, leaving his family behind. The ship was the *Kaiser Wilhelm der Grosse*, considered to be very speedy and seaworthy, something he appreciated. Also aboard were many of his entourage, as well as many eminent journalists, for the coming conference was world news. Some were pessimistic about the outcome, an example being Sir Donald Mackenzie Wallace, Russian correspondent for the London *Times*, who was also advising King Edward VII. Dillon was the most visible in his efforts to ensure Witte good press.

As his ship sped over the ocean, with an occasional pitch and roll that brought on a bout of seasickness, Witte mapped out the tactics that he would follow. He would act as though the tsar were seeking peace only out of deference to world opinion; he "would act in a manner befitting the representative of the greatest of empires, an empire that had suffered no more than a minor unpleasantness." Also, in view of the importance of the press in the United States, he would be very accessible to journalists, and he "would act in an unaffected and democratic manner so as to win over the American public, which is very democratic." Finally, he would not show any animus toward Jews, given "their considerable influence in New York and in the American press."[23]

Witte started employing these tactics aboard ship and continued to do so throughout his stay in America, being very accessible, speaking as freely as protocol would permit to the many reporters who followed him, shaking hands all around, signing autographs. Among the reporters to whom he gave interviews was a cousin by marriage, the husband of a niece of the notorious Madame Blavatsky.

His ship arrived in Hoboken in the late afternoon of July 20/August 2. He and his party were then ferried to New York, where they were housed in the posh St. Regis Hotel. He found its rates exorbitant and its food "vile"— typical, in his opinion, of American food, which he considered to be "dangerous" as well.

He was scheduled to meet President Roosevelt two days later and made some use of his free time to visit the Lower East Side, home to most of the city's Jews. Accompanied by the plainclothesmen assigned to protect him, he spoke in Russian with a few of the Jews he met, finding some friendly, others less so.[24] On one occasion during his New York stay, Baron Rosen dismissed the plainclothesmen and he and Witte went off for two hours. To see a dentist? Visit the Tenderloin?

Also, Witte used his time to visit the New York Stock Exchange, where he received an ovation. The visit gave him the opportunity to speak to several financiers, among them George Perkins, reputedly J.P. Morgan's "right-hand man."[25] After all, Witte had to keep the need for a loan in mind. In addition, he had agreed to talk to the president about tariff difficulties being experienced with America, a subject he put off until after the peace negotiations. Such obligations required that he keep in touch with Kokovtsev, whom he asked to keep him informed of developments at home since he did not trust other sources of information.

On July 22/August 4 Witte and his party attended services at a Russian Orthodox church about a mile from his hotel in honor of the name day of the dowager empress. Shortly thereafter he and Baron Rosen journeyed to Oyster Bay to have lunch with the president at Sagamore Hill, the "summer White House." Witte looked down his nose at what he considered to be the president's "bourgeois" tastes.[26] Other than that, his first impression of Roosevelt was quite favorable. About the president's impression the French chargé wrote home: "In a country where physical development is universally admired, the height and broad shoulders of Witte have won not only the sympathies of the crowd but also, it appears, of the President, who is said to have stated after their first meeting at Oyster Bay: 'He is a splendid fellow.'"[27] Witte was taller than Roosevelt and towered over the Japanese. It would turn out that the president's lasting impression was one of ambivalence.

For two and a half hours, before and after lunch, Witte, in the company of Rosen, spoke to the president about the work ahead. Witte presented the Russian position emphatically, mincing no words. Briefly, what he asserted was that Russia was not defeated and would discuss only the terms consistent with the advantages the Japanese had gained rather than what advantages further fighting might bring them. Russia would not accept any terms that would bring dishonor upon her, and that included payment of an indemnity. He assured Roosevelt that Russia's internal situation was far less black than it was painted in the non-Russian press. The president tried to persuade Witte to be prepared to be more flexible, but with no visible success. He conceded that the negotiations might come to naught and offered his help if it should turn out that a second round of negotiations would be sought. Clearly, the prospects for success were not bright.[28]

Upon the return of Witte and Rosen to the city, George Perkins and Frank Vanderlip, vice president of the National City Bank, called on the first plenipotentiary to talk about floating a loan. They made it clear that a loan would be possible only if peace was achieved.[29]

The following day was devoted to the meeting of the Russian and Japanese plenipotentiaries and their departure for Portsmouth by sea. This was done with a great deal of pomp.

Witte, having had more than enough of the sea and not averse to being less than a model guest, had let it be known that he preferred staying on land. This created a minor diplomatic tempest of the kind that Herbert Pierce, assistant secretary of state, who had several years of service in St. Petersburg under his belt, had to deal with as well as other details of the conference. The decision was made to maintain the fiction that he was traveling by sea, this by having him depart with the rest of the Russian delegation on the *May-flower*, debark at Newport, and continue by train to Portsmouth. This he did, with an overnight stop in Boston that permitted him to visit Harvard University. Once in Portsmouth he was taken out to the *Mayflower*, from which he and his delegation debarked. The ship carrying the Japanese arrived at about the same time. Once the delegates were ashore they received a tumultuous welcome and were then taken to the Wentworth Hotel, their home for the next four weeks.[30]

Witte and Komura made a starkly contrasting pair, one huge, combative, overbearing, the other slight, soft-spoken, polite, but tough as nails. At Witte's request the conferees got to work quickly, at the Portsmouth naval armory. At Japanese insistence, negotiations were to be secret, with terse statements agreed to by both parties to be released every day. Early on, Witte skirted the restriction in the belief that the more the public knew, the greater its sympathy for the Russian position.

Once initial formalities were out of the way, negotiations began, with the Japanese, the first to take the floor, presenting their demands. Witte had anticipated some of the demands but, despite considerable effort, had failed to learn all of them beforehand.

Several of these demands dealt with the familiar subjects of Korea and Manchuria. Russia was required to recognize the former as an exclusively Japanese sphere of influence, to evacuate all troops from Manchuria, to transfer the lease of Port Arthur, Dalny, and the Kwantung Peninsula to Japan, to turn over the South Manchurian Railroad to the victor, to limit the use of the Chinese Eastern Railroad to commercial and industrial use (that is, not carry troops over that line), and to recognize the right of all countries to do business in Manchuria. Also, the Japanese demanded limitation of Russian naval power in the Far East and the yielding up of Russian warships interned in neutral ports. In addition, the Japanese demanded fishing rights along Russia's Pacific coast and the cession of Sakhalin Island, which Russia had annexed a generation ago and which had been occupied by the Japanese a few weeks earlier. Finally, the Japanese demanded reimbursement for their war expenditures but, at Roosevelt's suggestion, avoided the use of the word *indemnity*.[31] Quite a list!

In preparing a reply, Witte was bound by the instructions he had received. These stipulated Russia's position with respect to demands that might be raised by the enemy. Some demands, such as an indemnity, cession of Russian territory, cession of the Chinese Eastern Railroad, limitations on

Russian naval power in the Pacific, and demilitarization of Vladivostok, were unacceptable. However, Japan might be offered some revenue-producing benefits in lieu of an indemnity. According to the instructions, some demands, such as recognition of Korea as a Japanese sphere of interest, transfer of the lease of Port Arthur and others, and cession of the South Manchurian Railroad, were negotiable.[32]

These instructions did not leave Witte much room for maneuver, which will ultimately require an answer to the question of what credit he is due for the final results of the peace conference. As we know, opening demands are bargaining chips and are not inscribed in stone. Although the war party was strong in Japan, the country was not capable of resuming large-scale operations. And there were other factors to be taken into account, such as the influence America and Japan's ally Great Britain might exert on both the victor and the defeated. Thus, although an impasse could easily result if neither side budged from initial positions, the possibility of accommodation existed, and it was Witte's task to make use of the possibilities. His first reaction, as indicated in a telegram to Lamsdorff, was highly pessimistic. He informed the foreign minister that he feared Russia was doomed to seeing the war prolonged at a heavy cost that would demand foreign loans, and to secure loans in the midst of war it was necessary to change many minds.[33]

Witte wasted no time in drafting a reply to demands he found more onerous than he had feared. In the discussion with his colleagues, which he dominated, eight of the twelve Japanese demands were found acceptable, with some reservations. The rest were rejected: payment of an indemnity, cession of Sakhalin, limitation of naval power in the Pacific, and yielding up of interned warships.[34] The reply was handed to the Japanese, and what turned out to be a drawn-out task of bargaining began. Witte hoped that an effort to win the Japanese over to some kind of postwar alliance would make them more tractable, but he received little support from his colleagues and none from the tsar.[35]

The first plenipotentiary continued to court public opinion, relying largely on the efforts of Dillon and I.I. Korostovets, his chief secretary. He was also aided by Jeremiah Curtin, one of the first American Slavists. He overestimated the results of their efforts, but he himself received good press.[36]

As part of his effort to win over American Jews, he met early on with a group of leading figures from the Jewish community. It was an uphill battle, given Jewish antipathy toward Russia for its anti-Semitic policies. Jacob Schiff, the banker, who had helped Japan float a loan, was especially hostile. Nonetheless, Witte unjustifiably believed he had scored some points. He would meet with the group again. He was assuming that Jewish American opinion would be assuaged by the fact that Jews would not be denied the right to be elected to the forthcoming Bulygin Duma.[37]

Meanwhile, he was feverishly at work in the negotiations with the Japanese. His aim was to get them to compromise on the negotiable demands and to yield on the nonnegotiable ones in return for token concessions. Fortunately for him, he had already submitted his reply to the Japanese demands before receiving new instructions from home that cession of the South Manchurian Railroad and the granting of fishing rights were nonnegotiable. His response included a pessimistic forecast.[38]

In conducting negotiations Witte had much to learn about the specifics of the moot questions as well as about some of the fine points of diplomacy, even though he had professed earlier that good old common sense was enough to see him through. With the help of his entourage he filled in gaps in his knowledge and, as always, learned quickly. At Portsmouth he proved himself a master negotiator. As usual, his delivery was powerful, his self-confidence overwhelming, his nerves taut. Not that his opponents were easily swayed, but they could be persuaded by an argument that called for a concession that was not too costly and was at the time face-saving.

Take the demand for cession of the full length of the South Manchurian Railroad, which joined the Chinese Eastern Railroad at Harbin, its headquarters. Witte, sticking to his argument that the Japanese should not seek anything they had not already gained, was able to argue successfully that they should content themselves with that part of the railroad over which their military had gained control.

The "nonnegotiable" demands, as one would expect, were the stumbling blocks to peace. The first to be argued over was Sakhalin. Predictably, the heated and lengthy give-and-take changed no minds, and the conference could have ended then and there, but neither side was ready to call it quits. It was agreed to go on to another demand and return to this issue later.

Witte informed St. Petersburg of the impasse over Sakhalin, asking if there would be any new instructions from the tsar on this issue, implying that it was negotiable. His rationale, it appeared from his later dispatches, was that foreign opinion considered the island one of the legitimate spoils of war. He did not receive new instructions, and it became clear that Nicholas was holding tenaciously to the policy of not one kopek of indemnity to be given and not one square inch of Russian territory to be ceded.[39]

Witte's efforts to win Komura over to the idea of a postwar alliance were based on the belief that acceptance of the idea would lead Japan to soften her demands. The effort failed, and he so informed Lamsdorff.[40] The road ahead was foreboding.

That proved to be the case when the indemnity question was on the table on August 4/17. Witte, as instructed, gave no ground. Komura, apparently on the advice of Roosevelt, employed a more moderate tone but gave no ground either. Toward the very end of the day's meetings, Witte proposed that following the next day's sessions, which would deal with the last of the Japanese demands, there be a break, to be followed by meetings on August 8/21, which would be the last day of negotiations. Komura agreed. Witte was engaging in bluster and bluff and succeeded, at least with respect to Komura.

Witte's telegrams to St. Petersburg indicating the gravity of the situation and suggesting a compromise about Sakhalin produced no new instructions, but on August 5/18 Komura showed an inclination to bargain. He informed the Russians that Japan was willing to drop the demands for the transfer of interned Russian warships and for limitation of Russian naval power in the Pacific if Russia showed flexibility with respect to the indemnity and Sakhalin issues. Acting on his own authority, he asked Komura if he would agree to excuse the secretaries from the room and hold a "private" meeting of the first and second plenipotentiaries of both sides. It was so agreed, and when the four were alone Witte proposed a bargain: cession of the southern half of Sakhalin. Komura was agreeable if Russia would recompense Japan. The sum he mentioned was equal to the sum Japan wanted as an indemnity, a sum that Witte regarded as nothing more than a sugar-coated indemnity and therefore unacceptable.[41] Nonetheless, the discussion provided a way to prevent the breakup of the peace conference and put the proposal for division of Sakhalin on the bargaining table.

Even before he was informed of the proposal to divide Sakhalin, Roosevelt took a hand in an effort to keep the talks going. He sent a message to Witte asking him to send an emissary to Sagamore Hill. Baron Rosen was chosen for the task, made the trip, and learned of the president's proposal: that Russia cede Sakhalin and agree to submit the indemnity question to nonbinding arbitration. Witte, who along with his colleagues resented what they considered to be the president's interference, informed the tsar of the proposal, as did Roosevelt. The president also instructed his ambassador to Russia, Meyer, to talk to the tsar about the proposal. The ambassador had to wait until August 10/23 for an appointment to do so.

Meanwhile, on August 9/22, Nicholas directed Witte to end negotiations if the Japanese showed no signs of yielding. The first plenipotentiary asked for enough time for the tsar to respond to Roosevelt's proposal. The following day, Meyer, by this time aware of Komura's agreement to divide Sakhalin, succeeded in bringing Nicholas over to the idea of division but not to the idea of reimbursing the Japanese. Nor would he yield on the indemnity question, but it was now possible to continue the negotiations.[42]

During the next few days there was little for the negotiators to do, since all of the Japanese demands had been discussed. But there was a great deal of activity, what with telegrams between St. Petersburg and Portsmouth, between Tokyo and Portsmouth, and strenuous efforts by Roosevelt to move things along, with much emphasis on persuading Tokyo to be flexible on the indemnity question. Tension grew, with both Russia and Japan considering renewal of action in Manchuria. Witte, who had begun negotiations while ill, was showing signs of the strain under which he was working. His colleagues were restless, chafing at their isolation as well as the intrusiveness of the reporters.

In Tokyo the oligarchy was making peace with the evidence that their army was incapable of achieving a major victory over the Russians. Still unaware that the tsar had agreed to the division of Sakhalin, they sent instructions to Komura to withdraw the demands for the island and the indemnity. Shortly thereafter, on learning of the tsar's agreement to divide the island, they instructed Komura to agree to division. This was on August 15/28. On the same day Witte received instructions from Nicholas to break off negotiations rather than wait on signs of Japan's goodwill. Again the first plenipotentiary demurred, wiring back that the onus for ending the conference should fall on the Japanese, assuming that the following day's session would provide evidence that Japanese intransigence would put the finishing touch on the negotiations. He was aware that Komura was waiting for new instructions but had no inkling, other than rumors, of what they would be. In his memoirs he poignantly writes that he "spent a restless, nightmarish night" agonizing over what he would face on the morrow.[43]

The next morning, the plenipotentiaries met for an hour and a half. Emerging from the meeting, his face beaming, Witte loudly said to his waiting colleagues: "Well, gentlemen, peace, the Japanese have yielded on everything."[44] The next step was to sign an armistice and work out the wording of the peace treaty. Reporters rushed to file the story. Witte immediately wired the good news to the tsar, assuring him that Russia remained a major power in the Far East.[45] The news caught Nicholas by surprise, since he had not expected the conference to succeed: he felt confused that day, but the following day he was able to "to cope with the idea that peace would be concluded and that this was for the best because it was necessary."[46]

Nonetheless, the tsar was ambivalent, finding it difficult to believe that his army could not have won and reluctantly accepting the notion that there

PEACE WITH HONOR? 153

had been no choice. Congratulations from foreign dignitaries poured in on him, as well as support from many around him, including his mother, who told a trusted English journalist, off the record, that "he [Witte] has done wonderfully. There is nothing he cannot do. . . . Witte is so clever. It is almost as if he were a devil, he is so clever." But there were others around the tsar, his wife reportedly among them, who were bitter about the peace and about Witte. There were even those who alleged that the first plenipotentiary had tricked his sovereign. These battling influences were reflected in the remarks the tsar made to the same journalist, again off the record: "Yes, he is a very clever man, not very sympathetic, but a clever man."[47]

The task of translating what had been agreed to into a finished form was turned over to two three-man teams, the Russian team being headed by Professor Martens with Baron Rosen providing whatever help was required. For Witte the interlude meant a brief respite, which he badly needed, given the pressure under which he had been working for the past weeks and his poor state of health. But he was not completely idle and clearly far from relaxed. He worried, and with good reason, about what was being said about him at court.[48] He was concerned about arranging a loan. And, needless to say, he was thinking about what the future held for him. Also, he had to keep abreast of developments at home.

By August 20/September 2 the final draft was ready. The plenipotentiaries read the document and made preparations for the signing of the treaty three days later. J.P. Morgan, taking Witte under his wing, sent his private train to take Witte back to New York, from which the first plenipotentiary planned to set sail on August 30/September 12.[49]

In midafternoon on August 23/September 5, the four plenipotentiaries signed the treaty of peace that ended the eighteen-month bloody and financially burdensome war. Its chief terms were Russian recognition of Japan's paramount interest in Korea; simultaneous evacuation of Japanese and Russian troops from Manchuria, except for the Kwantung leased territory, the lease of which would be transferred to Japan; cession of that part of the South Manchurian Railroad running from Port Arthur to Changchungfu and Kuangchangtsu; cession of the southern half of Sakhalin Island; and granting of fishing rights to Japan along Russia's Pacific coast.[50]

The treaty marked a reduction in Russian power in the Far East and the emergence of Japan as a power in that region, but it was a far better settlement than could have been expected, as the sorrow and anger felt by the Japanese attest. Had Izvolskii, Muravev, or Nelidov been the first plenipotentiary, it was likely that peace would have been achieved at a much later time and under more onerous terms, and Russia desperately needed peace.

Witte's role in making the conference a success was great, but others, notably Roosevelt, shared in the credit.

After the treaty was signed, a nineteen-gun salute was fired and church bells were rung throughout the area. The occasion was celebrated at Christ Church with participation by a large contingent of Russian Orthodox priests and choristers from New York. It was a highly emotional service, which the Japanese, although invited, did not attend.

The next day, Witte and his entourage left for New York on Morgan's train. The following days were packed with dinners honoring him, a trip to West Point on Morgan's yacht (on which he ate the only food he found decent in America), a visit to Columbia University, which bestowed honorary LL.D.'s on him and Komura, a trip to Washington, D.C., and Mt. Vernon, another session with Jewish leaders, several talks with Morgan, and dinner at Sagamore Hill. He also found time to sample the joys of riding the subway. And he experienced a slight brush with American law enforcement when mounted police gave chase to the car in which he was riding in Central Park but gave up when plainclothesmen accompanying him showed their badges.[51]

His most important task in New York was to lay the groundwork for a major loan to make up for the drain that the war had imposed on his country's financial resources. That, plus the desire to reduce Jewish hostility toward Russia, was behind his talks with Jewish leaders, an effort that failed. His main hope was J.P. Morgan, who had shown him much attention. On August 26/September 8 he had his first extended talk with the financier, who gave Witte good grounds for hope. In an optimistic telegram to Kokovtsev, Witte expressed confidence that, with Morgan's help, American investors would provide a good market for Russian loans. That confidence would prove to be misplaced.[52]

The day after his meeting with Morgan, Witte and Baron Rosen dined at Sagamore Hill. Witte gave the president a message from the tsar declaring the abolition of discriminatory tariffs on imports from the United States. A few days after the dinner, Roosevelt expressed his opinion of Witte in a letter to the noted historian Sir George Otto Trevelyan. He thought Witte to be "the best man Russia could have at the head of affairs and probably too good a man for the grand dukes to stand him. He interested me. I cannot say that I liked him for I thought his bragging and bluster not only foolish but shockingly vulgar . . . moreover he struck me as a very selfish man without high ideals."[53]

In his memoirs, Witte is fairly kind toward Roosevelt. Pairing him with William II, he wrote: "They are both young, original, *restless*, rash, yet able to keep their own counsel." But he faulted the president for being naive about international relations, like other Americans who favored the demise of the Ottoman Empire and wanted to see the resurrection of an independent Poland.[54] Roosevelt's belief that Witte should be "head of affairs" proved to be prescient.

Witte talked as if such a future was not what he sought or expected. He told his associates that his plan was to return to St. Petersburg, report to the tsar, take a few months' rest, and then ask for permission to leave government service.[55] He was probably being a bit disingenuous, but he certainly wanted and needed a long rest. He was feeling very poorly and was seeking relief in soothing cocaine massages and diet to help him overcome the effects of American food.[56]

Chapter 14

Return Home

On September 5/18, Witte arrived in Cherbourg, where his wife was waiting for him. Unlike Komura, who had to be smuggled into Tokyo, he had the aura of success. He had not snatched victory from defeat, but he had achieved better terms of peace than had been expected. Now he sought permission from the tsar to spend a few weeks in Brussels, where his son-in-law served in the Russian legation, to see his daughter and grandson. Lamsdorff informed Witte that he was not submitting the request because the tsar wanted him in St. Petersburg.[1] Something was clearly afoot. Bompard, the French ambassador to Russia, indicated what it was in a dispatch to Premier Rouvier. He wrote that "the Tsar has decided to receive him [Witte] in a most gracious fashion." Further, that it "is heard that Madame Witte, to whom the doors of the court had been closed until now, will be presented to the Empress. It is expected that the presidency [chairmanship] of the Council of Ministers will be offered to M. Witte." Bompard went on to say that Witte would probably accept and that if he did, there would be conflict between the two men.[2] Bompard was referring here to the ongoing effort that had begun earlier in the year to transform the Council of Ministers into something like a cabinet that would coordinate the multitude of ministries and chief administrations (see page 137).

Many important persons shared Bompard's belief that Witte's star was in the ascendant, that he would be able to influence policy. Accordingly, he was much sought out, notably by King Edward VII and Kaiser William II, both of whom invited him to call on them. He declined, explaining that he first had to report to his sovereign, but when he received word that the tsar wished him to stop en route home to call on the kaiser at his hunting lodge in Rominten, he, of course, replied that he would.

But first, while he was still in Paris, he had to do what he could to arrange for a loan. It will be recalled that Rouvier had made a loan conditional on the end of the war with Japan. Now there was a new obstacle, acute friction between France and Germany over Morocco, which had created a war scare. There could be no talk of a loan, said the premier, until the "Moroccan nightmare" was over. As Witte tells it, the premier asked for his help. Witte advised holding an international conference to deal with the Moroccan question.

In trying to help, it is evident that Witte sought to persuade the Germans that he was friendly toward them and hostile toward the English and that in so doing he would incline the Germans to be accommodating in the Moroccan dispute, thus hastening the time when it would be possible to secure the vitally necessary loan. At the same time he tried to assure the English that he was not hostile toward them. Thus, when Poklewski-Kozell, secretary of the Russian embassy in London, came to see him in an effort to persuade .him to accept King Edward's invitation, saying that the king wanted rapprochement with Russia, Witte replied that he "favored good relations with England." And then he went on to say that if there was talk of an Anglo-Russian entente he would oppose it because it would incite Germany to demand a similar commitment, which would harm Russia's efforts to regain great-power status, and that required remaining free of entangling commitments that might entail the danger of war, this at a time when Russia required a generation of peace.[3]

To help Rouvier he called on Prince Radolin, the German ambassador to France, whom he knew from the days when the prince had been ambassador to Russia. During the course of a two-hour talk he urged that Germany be conciliatory toward France, while buttering up the prince by dwelling on the danger posed by English ambitions and what he had done to thwart "perfidious Albion." And he argued for a continental bloc aimed at containing the British. Here, he was reverting to an idea he had suggested to the kaiser a decade earlier. Radolin quickly informed von Bülow of his conversation with Witte.[4]

Two days later, while stopping over in Berlin, en route to Rominten, Witte had a two-hour conversation with von Bülow, in the course of which he repeated the views he had expressed to Prince Radolin. In addition, he asked the chancellor to convey his wish that the kaiser suggest to the tsar that Witte be given an opportunity to express his views about the international situation. The chancellor immediately informed the kaiser about his conversation.[5] He did not mention the fear he had expressed two months earlier that once peace was concluded, Witte and Lamsdorff would try to arrange an Anglo-Franco-Russian entente, an eventuality that could be avoided by "engaging" the tsar.[6] The tsar was already "engaged," as Witte would learn at Rominten, where he was due to arrive on the day after seeing von Bülow.

Witte's reception at the imperial hunting lodge was very flattering indeed. Soon after his arrival at the lodge, he was ushered in to see the kaiser, with whom he had a lengthy talk that was continued later in the day. The conversation ranged over many subjects, with emphasis on the terms and implications of the Treaty of Björkö. Also, William bestowed on Witte the Order of the Red Eagle, one of the highest orders he could bestow, and further gave him a signed, gold-framed photograph of himself, inscribed "Portsmouth-Björkö-Rominten." The point of the remarkable attention that Witte received was based on the assumption that he would play an important role in policy making and therefore be in a position to support the treaty and its consequences for Russo-German relations. Further evidence of the importance that the kaiser attached to Witte was provided when Prince Philipp Eulenberg, a member of what Witte called "the court camarilla," informed Witte that if he wished to write to William, the prince would serve as the conduit.

In Witte's memoirs the treaty and its undoing have a prominent place as an example of the tsar's weakness and Witte's ability to compensate for that trait. The treaty goes back to the aftermath of the Dogger Bank incident, when the kaiser proposed an alliance to the tsar. The proposal came to naught after Witte and Lamsdorff objected that it would be incompatible with the Franco-Russian alliance. Hostility between Britain and Germany over the latter's breach of neutrality by aiding Russia to fuel her ships bound for the Far East led to a temporary Russo-German mutual aid agreement. The kaiser remained determined to achieve an alliance with Russia, believing in his ability to sweet-talk the tsar when the two were alone.

He had that opportunity when his yacht and that of the tsar rendezvoused off Björkö when Witte was still in Paris en route to America. William had brought with him a draft of a treaty that obliged each country to come to the aid of the other if either were attacked by a European power. It also called for Russia to inform France of the treaty and to seek French adherence to this alliance.[7] Without consulting or informing his foreign minister, Nicholas had signed the treaty. The document was secret, not only from the public but also for some time from the tsar's ministers. When he authorized Witte to call on the kaiser, he also gave William permission to inform Witte of the terms of the treaty.

In informing von Bülow of his conversation with Witte, the kaiser related that Witte had waxed eloquent on the need for forming a Franco-Russo-German entente that would isolate England. He then told of how, when he informed Witte of the terms of the Treaty of Björkö, the Russian was overcome with such joy that he came to tears and thanked God.[8]

Subsequently, Witte alleged that William had not shown him the text of the treaty, giving him only a sketchy outline of the terms, so he did not realize what an unacceptable commitment the tsar had made until he was later informed by Lamsdorff of the actual terms. Some critics claim that even if Witte did not see text of the treaty, he was given a clear idea of its terms.[9]

Whichever view one accepts, it is unlikely that he was pleased by what he heard, and it is likely that he was expressing pleasure that the kaiser was accepting his argument that Germany and France should draw closer, particularly with respect to the Moroccan dispute. Also, it seems very likely that he was keenly aware that remaining in the good graces of the kaiser would aid his career. Undoubtedly it did, for William quickly wrote Nicholas a letter extolling Witte, stressing his fitness for high office.[10]

Witte returned to St. Petersburg on September 15, to a mixed reception. Those who had favored peace were pleased that it had been achieved, but, given the widespread hostility toward the government, little public enthusiasm was shown toward the man who had played so large a role in ending the war. Those who had favored continuation of the war were hostile, some to the point of claiming that he had tricked the tsar into approving the peace treaty.

Nicholas himself was quite pleased. As predicted, he received Witte graciously. The tsar was then aboard his yacht off Björkö. He informed Witte that, in recognition of the great service he had rendered, he was conferring the title of count on him. In a letter to his mother, the sovereign reported that Witte "went quite stiff with emotion and then three times tried to kiss my hand."[11]

Although Witte professed to be indifferent toward honors, he was, in fact, no less touched by them than most other humans. In this case the title not only warmed his amour propre but also conferred practical benefits: the ostracism from which he and his wife suffered was lifted, permitting her and their daughter to be received at court and opening many doors in the social world that had hitherto been closed to them.

The tsar's turnabout from saying "anyone but Witte" to conferring a significant honor on him was striking. Witte writes in his memoirs that he asked Nicholas: "Your Majesty, do you still have any doubts about my loyalty to you and do you believe those who have tried to persuade you that I am a revolutionary?" And he notes that Nicholas replied: "I trust you completely and have never believed those slanders."[12] The tsar, who was known as a *charmeur*, was not being candid. Apparently he was swayed by his mother and others who now thought of Witte as a genius, or at least a near-genius, who had served his country well and could be relied on to cope with the great problems still facing her.

Reportedly, in the course of his conversation with the tsar Witte asked permission to go abroad for three months' rest and was told that he was needed at home.[13] Witte was badly in need of a rest, but, as we know, he was driven by ambition as well as concern for his country. Also, as has been noted, he was aware that the chairmanship of the Council of Ministers might be his soon. His wife, observing anxiously what was unfolding, was fearful about his physical and psychic health. The way out, she reasoned, was for her husband to replace the aged ambassador to Paris, Nelidov, the rationale offered being that he would be more capable than the incumbent in persuading France to join the alliance created at Björkö. It was in that spirit that she wrote to their friend Ernest von Mendelssohn-Bartholdy, asking him to use his good offices to persuade the kaiser to suggest that her husband would be a good choice to replace Nelidov, adding that "within a few weeks all sorts of positions would be offered" to her husband and that, given the state of his health and the state of Russian domestic affairs, it would be best for him to be out of the country.[14]

One can imagine that Witte was not enthused at his wife's effort, but he did participate in it. Taking advantage of what Prince Eulenberg had told him at Rominten, he wrote to the prince, pointing out that to implement the Björkö treaty it was necessary to bring France into the projected alliance, and to achieve that would require the right sort of ambassador in Paris. Evidently, von Bülow was shown the letter, for we find him writing to the prince, urging him to keep up his ties with Witte but to keep them secret while being sure "to spin the thread out skillfully and carefully, because it is of the greatest importance that it not be broken." Eulenberg informed Witte that he had shown his letter to the kaiser and expressed regret that, given Russia's domestic situation, it was not possible for Witte to be sent to Paris, although in his opinion Witte as ambassador to France would be "the right man in the right place."[15] That was that. Whether Witte was disappointed by the outcome we do not know, but it is obvious that he now had no choice but to remain in the midst of swiftly unfolding events. Had the charade continued, Witte would have found himself in a most embarrassing position, for he was quickly enlisted by Lamsdorff in an effort to have the Björkö treaty annulled because it was incompatible with the Franco-Russian alliance.

"The state of domestic affairs" to which Mme. Witte referred was far from good. True, General Trepov was able to provide an air of calm in public places by the use of police, gendarmes, and soldiers, but it was only an air. The opposition was growing stronger, and the government was slowly retreating. The tsar and his ministers hoped that the reforms initiated earlier, capped by the proposed State Duma, would satisfy much of the opposition and that stern measures would silence the rest.

On August 6, legislation establishing a State Duma had been enacted, accompanied by legislation concerning elections to that body, the first elected imperial legislative body in the country's history. It would have the right to consider legislation proposed by the State Council and other matters such as the state budget, but it could not initiate legislation and no bill could become law without the tsar's approval. The franchise, and thereby representation, was denied to the residents of Siberia and most of the non-Russian borderlands unless they resided in such cities as Tiflis and Warsaw. In the areas entitled to representation the franchise was restricted to males twenty-five and older who met stipulated property restrictions. Voting for deputies to the State Duma was indirect, with the votes weighted according to class and in some cases nationality. In short, the new body would have the right to speak but not to act, its deputies predominantly Russian and rural. The date for elections had not yet been announced, but the date for the opening of the State Duma was set for the beginning of the next year.

As would have been expected, the opposition was divided in its response to the news. And it was an opposition that was continuously growing, becoming more demanding and impatient. The right-wing liberals accepted what was still being called the Bulygin Duma as an acceptable reform, one that would enable the public to use a legal channel for making itself heard and, so it was hoped, listened to. The left-wing liberals remained committed to the creation of a constituent assembly that would determine what kind of government Russia would have and consequently called for boycott of the forthcoming election. The socialists took the same position.

Meanwhile, the government was at work on reforming the Council of Ministers in an effort to enable it to provide unified and effective leadership. Witte had begun that work earlier in the year, but, as will be recalled, it had been cut short by the tsar. The creation of the Bulygin Duma provided impetus for rapid work on reforming the council because there was fear that the duma might take the bit into its teeth and transform itself into a real parliament. Accordingly, Nicholas added to the heavy burden of work that Count Solskii was already bearing by having his special conference work on fleshing out the law on the Bulygin Duma and also dealing with reform of the Council of Ministers. This was toward the end of August. When Witte returned to Russia he was invited at the count's suggestion to participate, and participate he did, amid wide speculation that Witte would be made chairman of the reformed council. Thus, on September 27, Spring-Rice, whom we have already met, wrote to Mrs. Theodore Roosevelt that Witte expected to get the appointment, noting that he would have a difficult time because he was disliked at court and mistrusted by the liberals, adding: "He is foolish to take the job but he fears if he doesn't the chance may not recur."[16] Not long after his return Witte told one of his colleagues that he had planned to spend the winter in Sicily but as a result of the warm reception he had received he had decided to remain. The colleague surmised, as did many others, that Witte was aiming to be chairman of a reformed council of ministers, despite his poor health.[17]

In dealing with the Council of Ministers the conference was trying to reform the cumbersome and highly inefficient current system under which the tsar was both head of state and head of government. What was being proposed was something like the cabinet system in Western and other countries, but a cabinet responsible to the tsar, not to an elective legislature. And it would still be called the Council of Ministers.

The council would be headed by a chairman, appointed by the tsar. He would preside over its meetings unless the tsar chose to do so. The chairman would in effect be head of government, his position being equivalent to that of premier or prime minister. As noted, Witte took a vigorous part in the discussions at the Solskii conference. On September 21, six days after his return home, he provided a forceful exposition of his position, declaring that the forces of revolution were growing stronger and bolder, that Russia was in a position comparable to that of France following the convening of the Estates General, and that the government had no plan for coping with the demon of revolution. What was needed, he argued, was a strong Council of Ministers, consisting of like-minded members nominated by a powerful chairman. He proposed too that as a means of giving credibility to the State Council, half its members should be elected by the nobility, clergy, merchant, and industrialist classes and by the higher educational institutions, with the rest appointed by the tsar. He was obviously making peace with the dread idea that Russia was in the process of becoming a constitutional monarchy.

Witte's ideas about reforming the Council of Ministers were, for the most part, in harmony with those already on the table, though he sought more power for the chairman than did most of his colleagues. But there was a minority that wanted little or no tinkering with the existing council, among them Kokovtsev, A.S. Stishinskii, with whom he had had a run-in over the agrarian question, and Count A.P. Ignatev. The count was a formidable opponent; a former commander of the Horse Guards and thus a member of the Horse Guards old-boys club that included General Trepov and Baron Freedericksz, the minister of the Imperial Court. Ignatev had some influence at court and was believed to be at the center of intrigue there to prevent Witte from becoming chairman.[18] He had already helped undermine Witte's work on the December 12 decree in his capacity as chairman of two special conferences to implement the decree.

On October 12 the last formal session dealing with the Council of Ministers was held at the Mariinskii Palace, home of the State Council. This session, like earlier ones, was marked by controversy, this time provided by General P.L. Lobko, the state controller. He argued that he should not be in the Council of Ministers, subordinate to the chairman. Witte responded with a strong rebuttal.[19]

By now the country was in the midst of a general strike, and the need for a strong, unified council of ministers was greater than ever. But first it is necessary to pick up the account of the growth of opposition since Witte's departure for the United States.

At the time, right-wing liberals were waiting hopefully for the promised Bulygin Duma, while left-wing liberals, growing in strength, continued to demand a constituent assembly. In May, fourteen left-wing liberal unions, devoted to political change, formed the Union of Unions to coordinate their work. Nine were associations of professionals. Two, the Union of Clerks and Bookkeepers and the Union of Railroad Workers and Employees, advanced economic as well as political demands. Two were devoted to specific goals, in one case the ending of laws that discriminated against Jews, in the other the granting of equal rights to women. Last but far from least was the Union of Liberation, whose fiery leader, Paul Miliukov, was elected president of the Union of Unions.

The fact that the Union of Unions had quickly become the embodiment of the liberation movement was an ominous sign of how deep the estrangement between government and "society" had become since Sviatopolk-Mirskii had begun his effort to heal the breach. During the summer and the early fall the liberal movement seemed to embrace all of "society." To be sure, there was still the minority that was organizing in support of autocracy as well as a silent minority, but to the naked eye it appeared as if liberals spoke directly for most of "society" and, implicitly, for the rest of the country. In ever-increasing numbers they defied the law by holding unauthorized meetings, conferences, and congresses, to which the police turned a blind eye. A favorite meeting place in St. Petersburg was at the building of the venerable Free Economic Society, and in Moscow, center of the liberal movement, several prominent nobles opened their homes to such meetings. Providing the liberal movement with much of its visibility and foot soldiers were the students of the institutions of higher learning who had gone on strike in the aftermath of Bloody Sunday.

Adding to the ongoing ferment was the issuance of a decree restoring the autonomy of higher schools that had been lost in 1884, a time of reaction. It was issued on General Trepov's initiative. While using stern measures to maintain order he was, at the same time, urging the tsar to agree to modest reforms calculated to appease moderate elements. In this case he assumed that restoration of autonomy would have a calming effect on students and faculty.

The reverse turned out to be the consequence. Students, now free to hold meetings on campus, off-limits to the police, ended their strike while using their freedom to carry out and encourage antigovernmental agitation. The decree was issued in August, before Witte's return. In his memoirs, he vividly described the scene that ensued: "As I soon learned, the effect of the decree was to open the higher schools to ceaseless revolutionary meetings, attended not only by students, but also by workers (some genuine, some bogus), teachers, enlisted men and non-commissioned men in uniform, *kursistki* [female students], and even ladies from high society, who went to see these astonishing goings-on, to find the kind of thrills there that one could get from champagne, bullfights and risqué entertainment." He concludes that the decree "opened the first crack through which the developing revolution could break through to the open."[20]

Revolution was indeed developing, particularly on the labor front. The labor movement had become a formidable force since Bloody Sunday. Mass strikes were a common occurrence, fed by hostility toward the government and by small successes in lowering hours and raising wages. And although the trade union movement was still in swaddling clothes, trade unions had been organized in major cities, in defiance of legal prohibitions.

The socialists, whom Witte habitually referred to as anarchists, predictably sought to gain control of the labor movement, with mixed success. Some talked of leading the workers in an armed uprising, but that was just blustering talk. Some sought to rouse the peasantry. And there were many socialists who engaged in terroristic acts such as assassination and sabotage as means of toppling the government.

The trade union with the greatest capacity for making its power felt was the Union of Railroad Employees and Workers (usually referred to as the Union of Railroad Workers), for obvious reasons. The Central Bureau of the union followed the line laid down by the Union of Unions, but in several localities, notably Moscow, socialist influence was strong.

Although Witte was disturbed by the rising tide of unrest among workers, he was more concerned about reports from the countryside. There had been a few cases of agrarian unrest following Bloody Sunday, but, on the whole, the countryside remained what urbanites condescendingly called "deaf," that is, inert. But the impact of revolutionary events in the cities was gradually being felt as a result of the influence of peasants who worked seasonally in the cities, of various types of propagandists from the cities carrying the message of revolution, of some elements from local zemstvo organizations, and even of students from local theological seminaries. The more sophisticated propagandists tried, with little success, to convince the peasantry that economic benefits could be achieved only through political change.

One success in this effort was the creation of the Peasants Union, in which educated professionals played no small part. Its leaders for the most part identified themselves with the Union of Unions and accordingly favored the use of peaceful, albeit not necessarily legal, methods for achieving their ends.

However, peaceful methods were not the choice of large numbers of peasants and agricultural laborers who were speaking up. Two regions, remote from each other, were the centers of extreme violence. One was in Courland, where Baltic Germans owned the land and Lettish peasants and agricultural laborers tilled it. There an uprising, marked by killing of landlords and officials, as well as burning and looting, soon spread into other Baltic provinces, inspiring understandable alarm in St. Petersburg, particularly among Baltic German officials there. The other was in Georgia, in the Caucasus, where Witte was born and with which he identified himself. There agrarian violence was so intense that a punitive force of ten thousand men sent in achieved only temporary success. The general feeling was that the Caucasus was out of control. Violence was rarer in the heartland of Russia, but it was spreading, and lawlessness, such as strikes and the cutting of landlord-owned timber and the stealing of grain and hay from landlord-owned land, was increasingly common.[21] The news from the countryside prompted Witte to assert late in September that student and labor unrest were "negligible in comparison with the coming Pugachevshchina."[22] He was referring to the mass uprising of serfs, Cossacks, and others during the reign of Catherine II that was suppressed only with great difficulty.

Obviously, Witte was deeply troubled by unfolding events, doubly so because he evidently felt that he would be the one called upon to deal with the crisis. In his thinking he was faced with a dilemma. On one hand, as has been noted, he was coming to accept the most unappetizing idea that to satisfy the country the tsar must grant some sort of a constitution, a set of irretractable fundamental laws that would grant basic civil and political rights. On the other hand, he was not certain that a constitution would be enough to bring the country to heel. On October 1, he told A.A. Polovtov, a colleague, that the only hope was in the appointment of a dictator, who, presumably, would use force to restore order. But where could one find a man suitable for the task? he asked rhetorically.[23] Yet on the following day, he asked M.O. Menshikov, a journalist, whom he happened to meet, to provide him with a draft of what should be in a constitution.[24]

At this point he was assuming that the government could still act from a position of considerable strength. To be sure, there was talk of a general strike, or even of an armed uprising, but such talk seemed without substance, and many assumed that the situation was under control. Thus on September 25 the British ambassador wrote home: "The unhealthy season [a reference to the climate] is just beginning, most of my colleagues have already left, and as I do not foresee any urgent questions arising that would require my presence here, I should be glad of a rest."[25]

Chapter 15

Out of the Frying Pan, into the Fire

Had there been no general strike in October, the plans for reconstitution of the Council of Ministers and the State Council and for setting the date for elections to the new State Duma would have proceeded at a measured pace. In due time Witte would have been named chairman of the council. Then there might have followed a lengthy if bumpy period of adjustment to the new order. That, of course, was what the tsar and his officials hoped for.

The British ambassador did "not foresee any urgent questions arising." Indeed, no one foresaw any major crisis arising in the near future, but the country was like a huge plain dotted by many grass fires, with many more erupting every day. Danger spots were numerous. There was the huge mass of troops in Manchuria, kept there until ratification of the peace treaty, waiting restlessly for the return home. There was the navy, particularly the Black Sea fleet, where mutinous sentiments were rife. A congress of student representatives vowed to carry on a revolutionary struggle for a constituent assembly. Left-wing liberals and socialists committed themselves to a boycott of the coming elections. Witte had a plateful, but he was counting on the support of moderate liberals for his efforts to restore stability and evidently believed that he would be given time to do his work.

The maxim that "men make history but under conditions not of their own choosing" began to be demonstrated on September 19, with a strike by printers at the Sytin press, in Moscow. The next day the other printers in the city were called out on strike by their union. During the following days workers from other trades in the city followed suit. These were no simple economic strikes. Strikers put forth political demands, marched through the streets singing the forbidden "La Marseillaise," and holding boisterous meetings at the university, all the while receiving support from the students. Then, on October 2, several of the unions formed a soviet (council) to coordinate strike activities. As the days passed with no concessions to the strikers and 110 strikers killed or wounded, the will to carry on grew fainter, but as Moscow grew calmer the strike fever spread to St. Petersburg.

Witte had been following the growing revolutionary unrest as best he could. In fact, he did not have to go far afield to see evidence of it. In the early days of October, Prince S.N. Trubetskoi, a very popular liberal who had recently been elected rector of Moscow University, died unexpectedly while on a visit to the capital. The cortege escorting his body to a railroad station for its return to Moscow for burial was turned into a major political demonstration. Then, returning from the station, the participants stopped briefly in Palace Square, scene of Bloody Sunday and not far from Witte's home, where they knelt and bared their heads in remembrance of January 9.

At Count Solskii's suggestion Witte, on October 6, asked for an audience with the tsar to impress on him the gravity of the crisis facing Russia.[1] Nicholas, then still in Peterhof, his summer residence, could not see him until the eighth because he had previously arranged to go hunting on the seventh, which turned out to be a cold, snowy day. He bagged thirty-five birds and beasts, duly recording the fact in his diary.[2]

Peterhof, twenty-five miles from the capital, with its palaces, cascades, fountains, and liveried servants, was a world apart from the turmoil enveloping the country. True, Nicholas was receiving regular reports from General Trepov about the strikes, demonstrations, acts of violence, and illegal organizations, but these reports had yet to register on the tsar's mind that the country was being gripped by a revolutionary fever. He wasn't stupid, but he was so isolated from reality and so conditioned that he could not believe that his subjects, except for a malevolent minority, were turning against his regime.

Witte arrived for his audience armed with a memorandum based on a document prepared at his request by V.D. Kuzmin-Karavaev, a retired general and an eminently respectable right-wing liberal, the kind on whom Witte based his hopes.[3] Witte had slowly and reluctantly come to accept the need for systemic change if Russia was to regain domestic tranquility. The memorandum was consistent with the liberal Eleven Theses adopted in November 1904 by the First Zemstvo. By the time of the audience the Moscow-Kazan Railroad line was on strike, the signal of what was coming: a general strike.

As was the custom in reports to the tsar, Witte read from his memorandum. What he had to say had to come as a shock to Nicholas, who at the beginning of his reign had characterized hopes for representative government as "senseless dreams." Employing rather flowery language, Witte argued that Russia had outgrown its age-old political structure and had to change to conform to the needs of the times. Specifically, he argued for the granting of a constitution that would guarantee civil liberty, that is, freedom of press, conscience, assembly, and association, and he urged that the government abide by the rule of law, which would mean an end to the law on exceptional measures. Also, he suggested what amounted to universal manhood suffrage in the election of deputies to the coming State Duma. As for the State Council, he repeated the proposal he had made at the Solskii conference. He argued, as well, for measures to ameliorate the conditions of workers and peasants. And to direct the government, he added, it was necessary to have a unified council of ministers. Implementation of this program, he argued, would satisfy the moderate elements of society and make possible the reestablishment of order. He assured the tsar that monarchical power would be safeguarded by the retention of veto power.

Nicholas heard Witte out without comment but did arrange for an audience on the following day. During the interval Witte worked with N.I. Vuich, one of his assistants on the Committee of Ministers, on editing the memorandum. When he was ushered in the next day to see the tsar, Witte was taken aback to see Tsarina Alexandra there but no grand dukes. Usually when the tsar had to deal with a major question he summoned some of his uncles to participate in the discussion, but at this time he was not on the best of terms with several of them, and the one he would soon call on, Grand Duke Nicholas Nikolaevich, was away hunting. The presence of Alexandra was a sign of her influence, which appears to have grown after the discovery that their son had hemophilia.[4] It should be noted that the dowager empress had but recently gone to Copenhagen at the suggestion of her sister, the queen of England, who was worried about the troubles in Russia.[5]

At this audience Witte went over the same ground he had covered the preceding day and made the point that the sovereign had only two choices: he could choose the course outlined and favored by Witte and give the man chosen to implement this course, presumably Witte, the authority to carry it out, or he could choose to use force, entrusting the task to someone equal to that task. With less than genuine conviction he admitted that he might be mistaken but argued that while the latter course might restore order, the cost in blood would be great and the relief only temporary. The tsar listened, again without comment, but it was obvious that he had found Witte's argument convincing when, at the end of the audience, he suggested that it might be well to issue an imperial manifesto embodying the memorandum.[6]

There had been critical moments before in the history of Russia, such as Alexander II's decision to free the serfs. This was such a moment. It was as overwhelming for Witte as it was for Nicholas, except that Witte had been moving reluctantly toward the acceptance of constitutionalism for months. What a contrast between his memorandum on zemstvos and autocracy, presented six years earlier, and the one he had just presented! But although he was certain that there was no other viable course open to the tsar, he remained ambivalent, saying on many occasions later that while his head told him constitutionalism, his heart told him autocracy.[7] But be it noted that constitutions come in all kinds of guises. Witte and many others in high places tended to think of the Prussian constitution of 1849 when they were thinking of a constitution for Russia. That constitution, granted after the revolution of 1848 had been suppressed, gave little power to the elected legislature and retained considerable power for the monarch. Also be it noted that Nicholas and his ministers would never admit publicly that Russia had a constitution.

More than a week would pass before the tsar granted a constitution in the form of the October Manifesto. It was a time when all hell seemed to be breaking loose. On October 19, in a letter to his mother describing current events, he said: "It makes me sick to read the news! Nothing but new strikes in schools and factories, murdered policemen, Cossacks and soldiers, riots, disorder, mutinies. But the ministers, instead of acting with quick decision, only assemble in council like a lot of frightened hens and cackle about providing united ministerial action."[8]

What was happening was a general strike, the kind that revolutionaries dreamt about but hardly expected to see. After a brief lull, Moscow became the hotbed of the strike movement and the railroad men the driving force. The strike on the Moscow-Kazan line, already referred to, began on October 6 and soon spread to other lines emanating from Moscow. On October 10 a delegation from a congress to deal with railroad pensions called on Witte asking him to declare himself in favor of a constituent assembly as well as for some economic concessions. He declined to do so, saying that there could be no talk of reform while the strike was in progress. His reply, coupled with a negative response from Prince Khilkov, the minister of ways and communications, prompted the leaders of the congress to call for the broadening of the strike, which was done, giving the strikers a stranglehold on the country. Even the line between St. Petersburg and Peterhof was closed down, forcing the use of naval vessels to link the two.[9]

The first important strike was among Moscow printers, but it was the railroad strikes that roused the mood of insurgency that gripped the major cities, producing widespread strikes that paralyzed urban life. Militancy was the rule. Boisterous meetings where speakers ranging from liberal to anarchist harangued the crowds were commonplace. Speakers denounced the government, calling for immediate and fundamental change. Some called for an armed uprising.

While the strikes were spreading, Nicholas was mulling over Witte's recommendations, obviously hesitant to say yea or nay. But he was made aware of the need for quick action to deal with what he and others called the *kramola* (sedition) and especially the railroad strike. So, acting as if Witte were already chairman of the Council of Ministers, he instructed Witte, in consultation with concerned ministers and Trepov, to propose appropriate measures. On October 12 Witte reported that he and his colleagues felt that to deal with the strikes it was necessary to deal with the revolutionary movement as a whole, and such an effort would be aided by the formation of a unified government. He pointed out that there were too few troops available to safeguard the entire railroad system, but he did suggest the use of troops for this purpose at a few key points.[10] Probably this report was what lay behind the tsar's caustic comment about his ministers in the aforementioned letter to his mother.

It was on the twelfth that the railroad strike hit close to home, on the line from the capital to Peterhof, prompting the tsar to make note in his diary for the first time of the spreading rail shutdown. On the same day he met with Goremykin, Witte's enemy, presumably to talk about the proposed constitution. And the next day he met with Baron A.A. Budberg, who had played an important role in the operations of the imperial court.[11] If the baron was no enemy of Witte's, he was certainly not one of his admirers, and would soon become a bitter opponent.

Witte had given the tsar a choice between granting a constitution or appointing a dictator to use force. On the thirteenth, Nicholas had an opportunity to choose the latter course. At a meeting in which Witte had participated, Admiral Chikhachev, Witte's first employer, had declared himself in favor of the use of force, prompting Witte to suggest to the tsar that he see the admiral. This was a not very subtle effort to spur Nicholas to make a decision. When he saw the admiral on the thirteenth, the tsar said nothing about the use of force but did say he was almost ready to grant a constitution.[12]

He was almost ready, but not quite. As the tsar saw it, the first order of business was to reestablish order—an understandable position for those in positions of power, and a common one. Witte also would have preferred to act in such a fashion, but he had already indicated to his sovereign the impracticability of such thinking. This may explain his reaction to the telegram he received on the thirteenth. In it the tsar directed Witte to coordinate the efforts of the ministers to reestablish order.[13] This made Witte de facto chairman of the Council of Ministers, but it did not address the question of a constitution. The next day Witte was granted an audience, during which he spent several hours with the sovereign discussing various measures to be taken, at the same time emphasizing the centrality of a constitution. Also he used the occasion to argue that it would be wiser to proclaim the new order by publication of a brief version of the memorandum he had submitted on the eighth than by publication of an imperial manifesto, as the tsar had suggested on the ninth.[14]

The next three days, while governmental authority was steadily eroding, saw a complex contest of wills between Nicholas and Witte unfolding, a contest with a large cast of characters onstage. It was a contest over content and wording of the documents that would herald the beginning of a new era, with Nicholas wavering and Witte with his heels dug in. In some ways the action could have been a comedy of manners if not for the setting of revolution. Participating in various capacities on behalf of the tsar were Trepov, who enjoyed the sovereign's complete confidence, Budberg, Goremykin, Grand Duke Nicholas Nikolaevich, and Baron V.B. Freedericksz, who was a bit of a cipher, as well as some lesser personages. Assisting Witte were Vuich, whom we have already met, and Prince Alexis D. Obolenskii, who deserves a few words.

The prince, who had had a distinguished career in government, had worked with Witte on numerous occasions and, in fact, had been taken under his wing. Witte valued the prince's knowledge of rural affairs and through him had become acquainted with some of the liberals in the countryside. True, Witte, and he was not alone, considered the prince a bit flighty in his thinking, referring to him as a Dobchinskii, a well-known character in Gogol's *Inspector General*. At this time he found Obolenskii's assistance invaluable. An added attraction was the fact that the prince's brother was an important official in the imperial court, one of the few admirers of Witte in that exalted venue and a valuable contact.[15]

The action began to accelerate on the fourteenth. During the evening Witte received a telephone call from Prince V.N. Orlov, assistant head of the Imperial Military-Field Chancellery, rumored to be the biological father of the heir to the throne.[16] His message: the tsar was ordering Witte to prepare a draft of an imperial manifesto that he would present the following day at a conference at Peterhof chaired by the sovereign. The prince explained that a manifesto was required so that reforms would be seen as "moving from Imperial promises to the realm of Imperial deeds."[17]

Witte suspected that behind the wording of the order was an effort of some at court "to use my ideas and then dispense with me."[18] His suspicions were undoubtedly exaggerated but not without some basis in fact. Panic was rife at court. There was even talk that the tsar might have to take refuge in a safe haven.[19] At the same time many felt that concessions to the opposition were imperative for the preservation of the regime but feared putting power in the hands of Witte, some willing to believe that he was in league with the Jews to create a republic with him as president. What Witte learned later was that the tsar had summoned Budberg and Goremykin to see him after he had met with Witte, to obtain their opinions about Witte's draft.

Following Orlov's call, Witte, who was not feeling well, asked Prince A.D. Obolenskii, who happened to be visiting him, to prepare a draft manifesto and to accompany him and Vuich to Peterhof the following morning. Aboard ship Witte listened to a reading of the manifesto, made a number of suggestions, then asked the prince to edit the draft while he was with the tsar.

At the appointed hour Witte, Baron Freedericksz, Grand Duke Nicholas Nikolaevich, and General-Adjutant Richter were ushered in to see the tsar. It was obvious that the tsar had invited the grand duke, Freedericksz, and Richter because he had confidence in them and their judgment. It is noteworthy that the three were military men: the grand duke was about to assume command of the St. Petersburg Military District, and the baron was, in addition to being minister of the imperial court, chief of imperial [military] headquarters, a position previously occupied by the seventy-five-year-old Richter. Noteworthy, too, is the fact that Nicholas had not invited the minister of war, General Rödiger, to participate, although he was scheduled to report to him after the meeting. Rödiger was not a member of what Witte liked to call "the court camarilla."

According to General A.A. Mosolov, chief of the Chancellery of the Imperial Court, who had the story from Freedericksz, the baron took the opportunity before the meeting to tell the grand duke that many at court hoped he would agree to become military dictator and restore order before there could be any talk of basic reform. To this, the choleric grand duke allegedly replied in a hysterical fashion, displaying a revolver he had with him, exclaiming that rather than agreeing to such a course he would shoot himself, that it was necessary to "support Witte."[20] Because the account is secondhand and because it raises some questions about timing, it cannot be accepted in toto, but it does say something about the atmosphere at court and about the grand duke.

In any event, the meeting started at 11 A.M., adjourned for lunch, and resumed at 3 P.M. During the morning session the tsar asked Witte to read the memorandum he had presented to him many days earlier. The grand duke had a number of questions. Then Witte asserted that, given the blows dealt by the war and ongoing events, there was no assurance that the constitutional course would produce immediate calm, but that the results would be more effective and enduring than the results from purely military measures. When they asked if Witte had brought the draft of a manifesto with him, Witte replied that it was being readied. He restated his position that publication of his memorandum alone would be preferable.

During the break Witte went over the draft with his colleagues, then returned for the afternoon session, during which he read the draft, which aroused lively discussion, as was to be expected. The grand duke had some reservations but agreed that the constitutional course was the correct one, as did General Richter. It was late in the afternoon that the tsar ended the meeting, telling Witte that if he agreed with him, he would inform him the next day.[21]

The next day and the day after came and went without a word from the tsar. Nicholas was still loath to bite the bullet, to agree to take the leap from autocracy to constitutionalism, displaying his ambivalence by procrastination.

He turned to people he trusted, conferring with Freedericksz, Budberg, and Goremykin, working with the last two on editing Witte's draft.[22] Also, through Freedericksz he asked Trepov for his reaction to that draft and received a positive reply.

It should be noted that Budberg, who had spoken to the tsar on the thirteenth, had then prepared his own draft of a manifesto. Budberg had sounded a loud alarm about the danger confronting the regime, suggesting that the tsar steal the opposition's thunder by timely reforms. In that spirit the baron prepared a draft manifesto that went further than Witte's, including such items as amnesty for political offenses and abolition of the death penalty. During the session on the fifteenth this draft was read to the tsar, but it remained a dead letter, and Witte later tried in vain to lay his hands on a copy.[23]

Word that the tsar had been editing Witte's draft with the help of Budberg and Goremykin made Witte's "blood boil." He quickly telephoned Freedericksz with what amounted to an ultimatum: if his draft was changed, the task of coping with the current crisis should be entrusted to someone else, but if the tsar should insist on giving him the task, he should at least be shown the edited draft. The baron assured him that only minor editorial changes had been made, an assurance that did not mollify Witte.[24] He was deeply embittered by the tsar's decision to have his draft edited, especially so because he despised Budberg and Goremykin. He considered Budberg "a Baltic [German] chancellery type" and shared the general view of Goremykin as one who was eager to hold high office but too lazy to do anything significant. Both were his enemies. And shortly after October 17, Budberg, who believed Witte to be a traitor, organized a group of guards officers to place Witte under surveillance.[25]

The sixteenth was rife with rumors in high places that the Witte draft was being scrapped and that some at court were trying to prevent Witte's appointment. It is easy to imagine Witte's mood and that of his wife. Very late that night, after calling ahead, Freedericksz and Mosolov came to see Witte, apologizing for the late visit by saying that they had just been to see Trepov, who supported the Witte program. The baron then showed Witte the edited manifesto, admitting that the changes in it were more than minor. In fact, the differences were stylistic rather than substantive. Nonetheless, Witte was furious, arguing that the changes were unacceptable, that in any case he remained of the opinion that it was unwise to issue an imperial manifesto. After being told that the tsar's mind could not be changed, he assumed a Uriah Heep pose, declaring that "since it was evident that the sovereign lacked faith in him, it would be better to have Budberg or Goremykin serve as first minister, while Witte was ready to serve in a lesser position such as governor."[26]

Early the following morning Freedericksz reported to the tsar, who was now committed to a quick decision. He summoned both Grand Duke Nicholas Nikolaevich and Witte to Peterhof. The grand duke, who arrived earlier, advised his nephew to accept Witte's draft manifesto and memorandum and be guided by them.[27] The tsar by now had come to what he found to be a devastating conclusion, based on the circumstances and on what he had been advised "by almost everybody" he had consulted, to grant a constitution and to appoint Witte chairman of the Council of Ministers.[28] Nicholas ordered that Witte's version of the manifesto be transcribed for his signature. Then came a wait for Witte's arrival. At 5 P.M., after crossing himself, the tsar signed the historic manifesto and confirmed the Witte memorandum. The following day he would sign the law reforming the Council of Ministers and appoint Witte as its chairman.

On the return trip from Peterhof the grand duke noted that this day marked the seventeenth anniversary of the near-death of Alexander III and his family in the accident at Borki, making this the second time that the imperial family had been spared. Witte's mood was mixed. He told Vuich that if the government could "hold out until the convening of the State Duma all would be saved, but that if it turned out that it was impossible to hold elections he could guarantee nothing."[29] As soon as his ship docked in St. Petersburg, Witte arranged for the publication and dissemination of the two historic documents.

The first, which quickly became known as the October Manifesto, proclaimed in effect, but not in so many words, that Russia was being transformed from an autocracy into a constitutional monarchy. In the manifesto the tsar granted his subjects "civic freedom on the basis of genuine personal inviolability, freedom of conscience, speech, assembly and association." In addition, Nicholas called for extending the right to vote for deputies to the State Duma as widely as was possible in the time left before scheduled elections, at the same time accepting the principle of universal manhood suffrage, which would be implemented later. Also, he declared that it would be an "inviolable rule that no law may go into force without the consent of the State Duma and that the representatives of the people must be guaranteed the opportunity of effective participation in the supervision of the legality of the actions performed by Our appointed officials." The October Manifesto immediately assumed the character of a Magna Carta of a new age.

The second document was an abbreviated version of Witte's earlier memorandum to the tsar on the state of the country and what needed to be done. What needs to be noted here is that this document is more cautionary than the manifesto, making the point that the process of implementing the promised freedoms would of necessity be a gradual one, a caution that was generally ignored by those who greeted the manifesto with cheers. It was the need for caution that lay behind Witte's objections to a manifesto. In keeping with the spirit of caution, Witte proclaimed on the eighteenth that all existing laws remained in effect.

The same types who had accused Witte of forcing the Portsmouth Treaty on the tsar would soon be accusing him of forcing the October Manifesto on the sovereign. We have seen that Witte did not want a manifesto, but he did issue an ultimatum about proposed changes in the manifesto that he considered unacceptable. However, the tsar could easily have treated the ultimatum with scorn if he had received support for a refusal.

In any event, the die was cast. Witte warned the tsar that they were in for a stormy and risky voyage.[30] Sadly, subsequent events would prove him right.

Chapter 16

Honeymoon? The First Ten Days

On October 18 the tsar appointed Witte chairman of the Council of Ministers, as was long expected, and on the following day signed the long-gestating decree reorganizing the council. The council in fact, but not name, became a cabinet, and its chairman in fact became its premier. The aim of the decree, as can be surmised, was to unify the government to make it more effective in dealing with the problems facing it, problems that had grown more menacing than anticipated. The premier was given considerable power, including the power to submit to the tsar names of candidates for membership in the cabinet—men who, it was assumed, shared his views and would thus personify the government's commitment to the spirit and letter of the October Manifesto. In earlier drafts, the ministers of war, navy, and the imperial court were excluded from the roster of those the premier could nominate, but that provision was dropped. Nonetheless, in practice these three were excluded and reported directly to the tsar.

A frazzled and exhausted Witte, aided by Prince Obolenskii and bolstered by his worried wife, began his Sisyphean labor with a clear set of assumptions and aims expressed in his memorandum of October 8. "The roots of unrest," he wrote, ". . . are to be found in the disparity between the high-minded aspirations of Russian intellectual society and the framework within which it exists." "Russia," he declared, "has outgrown her political framework and is striving for a legal order based on civil liberty." He went on to say: "Therefore, the framework of Russian political life must be changed to conform to the ideas that animate the moderate majority of society." He concluded his memorandum by asserting:

> It is obvious that the aforementioned tasks can be carried out only through extensive and active cooperation with society and under conditions of calm that will permit concentration on fruitful work. We must have faith in the political sense of Russian society and believe that it does not want anarchy, with its attendant threat of the horrors of strife and political disintegration.[1]

His assumption that the moderate liberals would exercise a calming effect would prove mistaken. To start with, it was as if he were trying to set up a tent in the midst of a howling wind and heavy hail.

Obviously, high among Witte's immediate tasks was to replace incompatible cabinet members, other than the three noted, with competent men holding views similar to his. The manifesto and a cabinet reflecting "the new order" were expected to have an immediate effect on the mood of the country, the tsar's expectations being more sanguine than Witte's. The country was still in the grip of the general strike. To be sure, the grip was less than a few days earlier, when virtually all stores were closed and only one newspaper in all of Russia, the conservative *Kievlianin*, was being printed. Nonetheless, urban Russia was still at a virtual standstill, what with the railroad system motionless, most workers still on strike, the higher schools still venues for antigovernmental meetings, and professionals, for the most part, not discharging their duties.

Even if the strike ended quickly, the spirit behind it was bound to persist and be embodied in organized form, undermining the power of what Witte called the "police-*cum*-court camarilla regime."[2] Preceding months and the period of the general strike saw the formation of the Union of Unions, trade unions, strike committees, self-appointed committees of public safety, and, most recently, soviets and a new party, the Constitutional Democratic Party, usually referred to as the Kadets. All of these were part of the growing opposition.

The name *soviet* was used in several cities, notably St. Petersburg and Moscow, by strike committees seeking to act as quasi-governmental bodies. Witte's first encounter with such a body would be with the St. Petersburg Soviet, which made its headquarters in the Free Economic Society building. Although this soviet was not affiliated with the Union of Unions, it had close ties to it as well as to the socialists.

The Constitutional Democratic Party, which was holding its founding congress at the very time that the October Manifesto was gestating and published, represented the dominant left wing of liberalism. It was an outgrowth of the Union of Liberation and would soon become the largest and most influential party in the country. Its mood was caught by the remark its leading figure, Paul Miliukov, allegedly made when he learned of the October Manifesto: "Nothing has changed, the struggle goes on." He later wrote that those might not have been his exact words, but that they represented his thought at the time.[3] The Kadet Party, as well as the socialist parties established earlier on, had to be taken into account in assessing the response to the October Manifesto.

Thanks to the St. Petersburg Telegraph Agency, which Witte had helped establish, the contents of the manifesto became known throughout the cities of Russia within hours of its signing. Because of poor communications and, occasionally, interference by local officials, the news reached the countryside belatedly. In the cities jubilation reigned as if the enemy had admitted defeat. Huge crowds marched through the streets, with much display of red banners and singing of the forbidden "La Marseillaise," reminders of the French Revolution of 1789. In some cities demonstrators marched to the residences of governors or other officials to present demands, most often for the release of political prisoners. Officialdom was generally either confused or cowed, reluctant or unable to attempt to restore order. In some cities the so-called Black Hundreds organized counterdemonstrations to show support for the tsar and to show hostility toward the perceived enemies of the regime, notably Jews and students. Occasionally there were casualties, as was the case in Moscow, where a revolutionary named Nicholas Bauman, who had been released from prison at the demand of demonstrators, was killed by members of the Black Hundreds. In response, a public funeral, permitted by the frightened governor-general, was held, with a hundred thousand mourners and spectators filling the streets of Moscow for some eight hours. In some cities, Odessa, chief among them, counterdemonstrations turned into bloody pogroms in which Jews were the chief victims, actions that many officials, and the tsar, regarded sympathetically.[4]

It would soon become evident that while jubilation over the manifesto was widespread, there was a broad spectrum of reactions to the document. That was to be expected, but there appeared some shadings and shifts that were not in that category. For instance, right-wing liberals, represented by their leading figure, Dmitrii Shipov, although ready to accept the manifesto as a fait accompli, were less than certain that the government was fully committed to its implementation. And suspicion of the government meant groundless suspicion of Witte.

The left wing of the liberal movement quickly came to mean the Kadets, who regarded the manifesto as a way station on the road to a democratic regime. Their program contained provisions that went far beyond what could be achieved under the existing regime. For instance, it called for woman suffrage, the eight-hour day, radical agrarian reform, cultural self-determination for ethnic minorities, and restoration of the Kingdom of Poland as an autonomous entity.[5]

Those who rallied around the Kadets represented a considerable part of "society," which Witte, like Sviatopolk-Mirskii before him, hoped to win over. He admired the leaders of the party but regretted its extremism, especially its readiness to make common cause with the socialists.[6]

Among the socialists, the Russian Social-Democratic Party, riven by a factional dispute between Bolsheviks and Mensheviks over dogma and tactics, and the Russian Socialist Revolutionary Party were most important. They regarded the manifesto as an opportunity to push the revolution on, be it by an armed uprising, general strike, and/or terrorist attacks, until the tsarist regime was replaced by a democratic republic, which in turn would lead to a socialist society. The Bolsheviks believed that it might be possible to move more quickly into the socialist phase than did the Mensheviks.

We move now to the right of the liberals and find groupings still amorphous for the most part, divided between those who accepted the October Manifesto but did not wish to go beyond it, particularly with respect to national minorities and agrarian reform and, at the extreme right, those who would be generically known in the political arena as nationalists. They considered the manifesto to be a mistake, hearkening to the traditional belief in "autocracy, orthodoxy and nationality." To a man they abominated Witte. Although they resembled the emerging Black Hundreds in their beliefs, they were not rabble-rousers, preferring to exert influence through the political process.

The day after the signing of the manifesto, Witte found himself trying to navigate the "stormy seas" he had predicted would be encountered. St. Petersburg was jubilant, but the crowds were in no mood to bow to the authorities, least of all to Trepov, governor-general of the capital and thereby responsible for the maintenance of order. "A sergeant-major by training," as one critic would call him, he had added to the odium in which he was widely held by issuing an order to the troops patrolling the city: "no blank cartridge volleys and don't spare the bullets."[7] The order was bluster. There were no major incidents aside from one outside the Technological Institute, in which soldiers, claiming that a bomb had been thrown at them, fired at the crowd gathered there and inflicted casualties. That incident and the order provided ammunition to the opposition, resulting in sentiments that echoed an earlier statement by Lenin, the Bolshevik leader: "Both Witte and Trepov are necessary: Witte to beguile some, Trepov to suppress others; Witte—for promises, Trepov—for deeds."[8]

That Witte was a front for Trepov was widely believed, leading to the demand that he remove Trepov from his post and order the withdrawal of troops from the city as proof of good faith. The premier was in no position to remove the governor-general, who enjoyed the tsar's unbounded confidence, nor had he any desire to see troops removed, for he considered them necessary to guard against violence and sabotage. At the same time, he did not wish the presence of troops to be provocative. Accordingly, he asked Trepov to keep the military out of sight as much as possible.[9] He would soon find out what a liability both Trepov and the troops were.

As part of his effort to rally support for the new course, he quickly invited the editors of thirty-three local newspapers and periodicals to meet with him at his home on the morning of October 18. Lack of space made it a standing-room-only affair. His hope for a friendly gathering in which he would seek and be given assurance that the press would cooperate in winning public support for the government's efforts quickly turned to dust. The meeting turned out to be a confrontational one. Witte asked for trust and forbearance, for time in which to begin carrying out the promises without being pressured by the press. He was told that while the press might trust him, the masses did not, that consequently there would be no grace period, that it was imperative to grant political amnesty, end press censorship, and withdraw troops from the capital. There was also a call for Trepov's removal.

Witte defended Trepov as well as the presence of the military and assured his audience that the tsar was committed to serving his people. He indicated that political amnesty was under consideration and concluded the session by asking the press to refrain from ignoring censorship rules, promising that he would quickly ask the censors to use discretion in interpreting the rules, a promise that he carried out. He acted quickly, too, in meeting the demand for political amnesty, although he was not entirely confident about what the consequences would be. In any event, he met with his colleagues and drafted a decree granting full or partial amnesty for political prisoners, which the tsar approved.

Witte was particularly upset by the silence at the session of the editors of the conservative press, who gave assent by their silence. True, M.A. Suvorin, editor of the ultrapatriotic *Novoe vremia*, spoke up, but it was to say that political amnesty was imperative to ensure calm.[10] Clearly, the session was a failure, an inauspicious start to his campaign to win public support.

At the same time that he courted the press, he began his campaign to form a cabinet that would inspire public confidence in the government and that would help him carry through the promised reforms. The premise from which he worked was expressed in the last paragraph of his memorandum to the tsar, approved on October 17, which was cited earlier on.[11] The key phrase was "in the political sense of Russian society," and he assumed that he could depend on the right-wing liberals to cooperate in the task of government and expected that left-wing liberals would realize that they were courting anarchy by cooperating with the socialists, who would presumably cease to be of any consequence. In short, he was making the same assumption that Prince Sviatopolk-Mirskii had made about the role of society, but under far riskier circumstances.

Reform of the cabinet, long in the making, became law on October 19. That body included not only ministers but also the state controller and heads of chief administrations such as the ones dealing with the merchant marine, headed by Grand Duke Alexander Mikhailovich, and the one dealing with agriculture, headed by P.K. Schwanebach. Neither the grand duke nor

Schwanebach was kindly disposed to the premier, nor he toward them. The grand duke obliged by quickly giving up his post. Parting with Schwanebach would come later. Witte was content with S.S. Manukhin, the liberal-minded minister of justice, and was resigned, for the time being, to having Kokovtsev, toward whom he had become antagonistic, stay on. His first priority was to replace Bulygin, Pobedonostsev, and General V.G. Glazov, minister of education, all three symbols of the repressive regime by virtue of their offices. On Witte's recommendation, Prince A.D. Obolenskii was appointed successor to the aged and frail Pobedonostsev, toward whom Witte behaved very humanely.[12] The prince was certain to support the premier's efforts at church and other reforms. Replacement of Bulygin and Glazov proved to be more difficult.

As can be surmised, Witte wanted men in his cabinet who would sit well with "society." This meant that, insofar as possible, he would seek out what were called public men, a clumsy translation of the Russian *obshchestvennye deiateli*, to the key posts of interior and education. The term was applied to members of "society" who were active in public life in such popular institutions as zemstvos and municipal dumas, men who were not tainted by having served in the bureaucracy. The use of the term reflected a deep-seated liberal suspicion of and aversion toward the government as well as the conviction that zemstvos and municipal dumas were not part of the government as they defined government.

Witte was up to his ears in work, what with meetings with the incumbent cabinet, taking ameliorative measures, receiving importunate and (more often than not) confrontational deputations, and dealing with Trepov. All this while seeking to infuse new blood into the cabinet, apparently with some advice from Prince Obolenskii.

The most eminent public man was Dmitrii Shipov, leader of the right-wing liberals. With him on board, Witte could count on enrolling other like-minded public men. Accordingly, one of his first acts was to wire Shipov to come from Moscow to meet with him.

Meanwhile, he tried to get N.S. Tagantsev, a law professor at St. Petersburg University, to accept the post of minister of education and A.S. Posnikov, of the St. Petersburg Polytechnic Institute, to become assistant minister. Neither was a public man, but both had reasonably liberal views and were presumably respected in academe. Moreover, Posnikov had, at one time, worked in the zemstvos. Also, Witte had some ties with Posnikov, who had taught at Witte's alma mater and was now a major figure at the Polytechnic Institute, which owed its existence to the premier. After some consideration, both declined, largely because of uncertainty about the direction in which Witte was going. At that point he decided to consider Prince E.N. Trubetskoi, a noted law professor and a liberal associated with the zemstvo movement, for the post that Tagantsev had turned down.[13]

As early as the eighteenth, a member of a delegation from the Union of Unions told the new premier that if he counted on the intelligentsia (a somewhat more restrictive term than *public men*) to support his program, he was mistaken; the intelligentsia "at the moment was as powerless as the government." He added that one must look for support to the masses, which were demanding political rights for themselves immediately, meaning universal and equal suffrage, direct election, and the secret ballot. Witte professed to agree about the franchise but, as is obvious, continued to place his hopes on the public men.[14]

When Shipov arrived on the nineteenth, Witte told him what importance he attached to the participation of public men in the cabinet, especially that of Shipov because of the prestige he enjoyed. He proceeded to offer Shipov the post of state controller, to replace the terminally ill incumbent, the archconservative General Lobko, who was then on leave. The premier argued that with a man such as Shipov in the post, the public would be assured that government expenditures would be monitored properly. Shipov was willing, provided that persons to the left of him were also in the cabinet to assure the public that the promise of "a new state order" implied in the October Manifesto would be fulfilled. He based his argument on the fact that his views were then shared only by a minority in the opposition. Moreover, other public men brought into the cabinet should be in charge of such ministries as those of education, interior, and justice. Witte found the proposal acceptable provided that such men be fully committed to their tasks, implying that they not use their posts as pulpits, and that they accept the notion that the government had to represent authority and had to reestablish order.

Shipov then suggested some candidates. Witte was not acquainted with them, asked for information about them, and agreed that they be invited to meet with him. Looking back, it is clear that Witte and Shipov had different and conflicting objectives.[15] Witte wanted public men who would inspire public confidence and work with him on his vision of change, while Shipov wanted a cabinet firmly committed to the creation of a new order as the public men envisioned it. Witte believed that only minor reforms should be enacted while order was being restored and that the major work should be done by the State Duma. Public men tended to believe that a prerequisite for order was the government's demonstration of good faith by the quick implementation of the October Manifesto.

Subsequent deliberations, which continued until they came to a fruitless end on the twenty-sixth, foundered because of the intractability of some of the public men involved as well as differences between Witte and the public men on a suitable person to head the Ministry of Interior.

During the course of his meeting with Shipov, Witte asked that he wire F.A. Golovin in Moscow to send a delegation from the Bureau of the Congress of Zemstvo and Municipal Duma Public Men to meet with him. Shipov anticipated that the delegation would consist of men to his left but nonetheless willing to negotiate. As it turned out, the delegation, which arrived on the twenty-first, was in a hostile mood. They demanded immediate implementation of the rights promised in the manifesto and the election of a constituent assembly to decide on the basic laws of the empire. The result was an impasse that led Witte to summon Shipov to St. Petersburg once more.

During the twenty-second and twenty-third, Shipov conferred with Witte, with Obolenskii participating. Present, too, were M.A. Stakhovich, with whom Witte was already acquainted, and A.I. Guchkov, the dashing son of a Moscow industrialist. Shipov, Stakhovich, and Guchkov shared right-wing liberal views and thus were of a mind to negotiate rather than demand.[16]

Witte was anxious to complete the task of assembling a suitable cabinet not only to win public support but also to retain support of the tsar, who was keeping a sharp eye on his performance. Thus he enlisted what help he and Obolenskii could find. He asked I.I. Petrunkevich, the very man whom the tsar had called a criminal, to help convince Guchkov to accept a ministerial post only to find that the two men did not share the same political views.[17] Another effort to get help in persuading Prince Trubetskoi to become minister of education also failed.[18]

The prince arrived in St. Petersburg on the twenty-fourth and joined the continuing meetings with Witte and Obolenskii. He soon made it clear that he would not accept a ministerial post. By now it was evident that, as Shipov notes, the Kadets and other left-wing liberals would not join the cabinet if asked, making the prospect of a cabinet in which public men could play a significant role very dim indeed.[19] Nonetheless, Shipov and Guchkov were still willing to join the government if an acceptable person was to be named minister of interior.

Writing about these negotiations in his memoirs, Witte said that all of the accounts he had read were incorrect, that only those who took part in the meetings could provide accurate accounts, but he did not expect to live long enough to read them.[20] He was correct in predicting that he would not survive until then, but he did live long enough to engage in a newspaper polemic with Guchkov about an important phase of the negotiations.[21] The many memoirs, particularly Shipov's and Witte's, are helpful but not completely reliable, as is to be expected with memoirs, and corroboration is, in many cases, not available. But the basic facts concerning the matter of the minister of interior seem clear, although Witte's rationale for fixing on P.N. Durnovo remains a matter of unresolved speculation.

For both Witte and the public men, the choice of a minister of interior was crucial. The Ministry of Interior wielded immense power over the lives of Russian subjects and was widely seen, especially by the opposition, as the tsar's chief instrument of repression. While Witte was keenly aware of the ministry's record, he was also very conscious of the importance of the ministry in restoring and maintaining order.

In the final days of negotiation with the public men, Witte indicated that one of the very few men suitable for the post was Durnovo, then an assistant minister of interior, to which the public men present responded by declaring that none of them would serve if he became minister. Witte countered by saying that it was essential to choose a man with secret-police experience, and Durnovo had at one time been the head of the ministry's Department of Police. He argued, moreover, that Durnovo had shown himself to be more liberal in his views than most bureaucrats. However, Witte had been convinced by Prince Obolenskii that Prince S.D. Urusov, an experienced bureaucrat sympathetic to the opposition, might be a suitable candidate. The premier, who was not acquainted with the man, invited him for a talk. As Witte tells it, once he had had a chance to talk to the prince he was convinced that Urusov was not qualified to be minister and informed the public men that he was settling on Durnovo.[22] In Shipov's version, Witte came to agree to having Urusov as minister and Durnovo as assistant minister but the next day reversed the order, infuriating the public men and leading Shipov to declare that, the question of Durnovo aside, no further negotiations were possible.[23] In any event, Witte's effort to attract public men ended on the twenty-sixth. Durnovo was named acting minister, and Urusov was appointed an assistant minister.

Speculation about Witte's rationale in fixing on Durnovo has been fruitless in the sense of not being supported by documentation. Thus, the supposition that Durnovo possessed incriminating documents that Witte feared might be used against him is no more than speculation.[24] Witte's explanation for the choice has been challenged, and rightly so, because he was aware of its political cost, but for lack of evidence one must accept the belief that he felt that the restoration of order was so pressing that he was ready to accept the cost whatever it might be.

A few days after the collapse of his efforts to recruit public men, Witte invited Miliukov, by now the leader of the Kadet party, to talk about the reasons for the collapse. Each respected the other: Witte considered Miliukov to have one of the best minds in Russia, while Miliukov rated Witte as standing head and shoulders above his governmental colleagues, a man of solid sense who was capable of quickly getting to the heart of problems.

Witte's effort had collapsed, said Miliukov, for several reasons. One was that although he was ready to bring public men into his cabinet, he would not accept their programs, and these men felt that they would lose what influence they had if their programs were not accepted. Additionally, said the Kadet leader, Witte was not trusted because he was identified with a repressive regime whose ruler did not inspire trust, making it more than possible that public men would be used solely to dress mutton up as lamb.

In response to the question of what should be done to gain public support, Miliukov advised the premier to choose officials who had not been "discredited" to form a "transitional" cabinet and then proceed quickly with carrying out reforms. Witte thereupon jumped up and shook Miliukov's hand, saying: "This is the first sensible word I have heard. I have certainly decided to heed it."[25] When Miliukov asked Witte why he did not use the word *constitution*, he replied: "I can't because the tsar doesn't wish it."[26] That Russia had not acquired a constitution in the form of the October Manifesto was a fiction that was to be maintained in public, although the tsar used the dread word in private.

By the time he talked to Miliukov, Witte had already begun the process of recruiting officials who were not "discredited" and who appeared to be ready to work with him in the spirit of the October Manifesto. Durnovo, a womanizer, had that blot on his record, to be sure, but, in Witte's eyes, he had a good record as a bureaucrat. Several had served in the Ministry of Finance under Witte and could be counted on to serve faithfully. One such was I.P. Shipov, cousin to D.N. Shipov, who was chosen to replace Kokovtsev when the latter asked to be relieved of his duties.

Kokovtsev's departure deserves a few words. He and Witte had enjoyed reasonably good relations in the past, but by October Witte had become hostile toward the minister of finance, partly because the two had differed over pending reforms, partly because he felt that Kokovtsev had belittled him. With Witte chosen to be premier, Kokovtsev asked to be relieved of his duties. Nicholas agreed but sought to compensate Kokovtsev by appointing him chairman of the Department of State Economy of the State Council, a position that would bring him into close contact with Witte and many of his fellow ministers. The premier was furious, making so bold as to inform his sovereign that such an appointment was unacceptable, so much so that he and his colleagues would not attend meetings of a department headed by Kokovtsev and would send their deputies. The tsar backed down, withdrawing the appointment, but not without jotting down his reaction: "I shall never forget this insolence."[27]

Witte was able to find two ministers who, although not public men, did not belong to St. Petersburg officialdom and who enjoyed popularity in their circles. One was K.S. Nemeshaev, who succeeded Prince Khilkov as minister of ways and communications. At the time of his appointment, the new minister was head of the Southwestern Railroad, on which Witte had made his reputation. Nemeshaev was well thought of, was popular with railroad men (a major plus in those troubled times), and had come to the favorable notice of the tsar.[28]

The other was Count I.I. Tolstoi, vice president of the Academy of Arts, who took up the post of minister of education. As Witte put it: "To fill the position of minister of education I now looked for a man whose record would disturb neither society nor the court, a man who was competent, had a university education, some knowledge of the educational system, and the courage to accept the responsibility."[29] Tolstoi filled the bill.

It should be noted that Witte's life was made easier by the voluntary departure of Schwanebach and Grand Duke Alexander Mikhailovich from their posts. To replace the former he nominated N.N. Kutler, who had served under him. Kutler turned out to be quite liberal, later joining the Kadets. Witte took the grand duke's agency, combined it with several units from the Ministry of Finance to create the Ministry of Commerce and Industry, and nominated V.I. Timiriazev to be its chief. By the twenty-eighth, reorganization of the cabinet was complete.

Just as Witte was completing reorganization of the cabinet, Trepov asked the tsar to relieve him of his duties as governor-general and assistant minister of interior. Nicholas regretfully agreed and swiftly appointed Trepov palace commandant. The change was a mixed blessing for Witte. On one hand, it removed a major symbol of the old regime from public view. On the other hand, it provided Trepov, with whom Witte had fallen out, daily access to a tsar who was becoming disenchanted with his premier. This was evident in Nicholas's letter of October 27 to his mother, in which he wrote, among other things: "It is strange that such a clever man should be wrong in his forecast of an easy pacification. I do not quite like his way of getting into touch with various extremists, especially as all these talks appear in the press next day, and as often as not are distorted."[30]

Witte had not promised an easy pacification, but it was certainly the case that the going was rougher than he had anticipated. The many deputations and individuals who called on him in the first weeks of his tenure underlined the breadth and depth of the problems that had to be dealt with in coping with the unrest that still prevailed.

There was, for example, the case of Finland, where the governor-general had been so frightened by the general strike that he had fled to the naval fortress of Sveaborg. When he was approached by moderate leaders with the draft of a manifesto restoring the autonomy that the grand duchy had enjoyed, he gave it his support. After Professor Leo Mechelin, one of the moderate leaders, had called on the premier, assuring him that calm would return once autonomy was restored, the premier supported the idea and, indeed, on October 22, an imperial manifesto was issued in that spirit.[31]

Witte had opposed the Russification measures of Bobrikov and Plehve. He felt that, given the fact that Finland was so close to St. Petersburg, plus the fact that Finland had not been won by Russian blood, it deserved to have its rights respected. He did not want to see the grand duchy become, as Bunge had put it, "another Poland, a country which is inimical to us and which we may hold onto only by relying on our army."[32]

Witte's attitude with respect to Russian Poland was another matter. In his view, it was an integral part of the Russian empire, having forfeited whatever claim to autonomy it had once possessed. Nonetheless, he had opposed and continued to oppose the excesses of Russification there, which in his opinion had only succeeded in hardening Polish hostility toward the government. As has been seen, he had been instrumental in undoing some aspects of Russification there, but now the area was almost out of control, what with strikes, peasant unrest, and acts of terrorism. Accordingly, he supported the proposal to declare martial law in Russian Poland, and it was declared on October 29, an act that alienated both the Polish and Russian opposition.[33]

Then there was the sensitive Jewish question to contend with. In his memorandum of October 8, which had been published together with the manifesto, Witte stated that "normal legislative procedure" should be used for making "Your Imperial Majesty's subjects equal before the law for all, irrespective of religion or nationality." Jewish leaders assumed that equal rights for their brethren should be granted at once, but Witte was quick to inform them that, given the current hostility toward Jews, such a grant would be premature. In this he took the same position that Trepov had taken in his comments about the draft of the memorandum.[34] But Witte displayed a kindlier view of Jews, still feeling that equal rights for them were both desirable and inevitable. Nonetheless, Jewish leaders at the time concluded that it was useless to make further attempts to deal with the premier.[35]

Restoration of order, clearly, would not be easy even though the general strike was over. Opposition forces were celebrating what came to be known as "the days of freedom," ignoring censorship rules and limitations on assembly and association. The St. Petersburg and Moscow soviets were very much alive, as were similar organizations in other major cities. Socialists were gaining strength in these organizations and in trade unions. The liberal opposition remained militant. Matters were worse from the government's point of view in such borderlands as the Baltic provinces, Russian Poland, and the Caucasus. Peasant unrest was on the increase. The bureaucracy, including the police, was demoralized, uncertain of what to expect. And then, with the war over, there was the overwhelming need to return the troops from Manchuria and to demobilize reservists among both the returning troops and those in the rear. Morale among the men who had served in Manchuria and were waiting to return home was extremely low. Morale in the navy was even worse, as a brief mutiny at the Kronstadt naval base demonstrated.

Naturally, the premier had to be conscious of the mood of the tsar, whose unhappiness over the turn of events had barely diminished. In Nicholas's October 27 letter to his mother, referred to earlier, he wrote: "I am receiving letters from everywhere with touching gratitude for the liberties conceded, but also many indicating that they want autocracy to be preserved. Why were they silent before, the good people?" In his view "nine tenths of the trouble-makers are Jews," augmented by educated Russians such as engineers and lawyers.[36] This was the view embraced by the extreme right, about whom more will be said later.

We can imagine that there were times when Witte regretted that he was not in Paris, representing his country, instead of being in the midst of a storm that took an increasing toll on his nerves and body. Yet he was determined to push on with his punishing workload, which, in addition to his tasks of turning the promises made on October 17 into reality, included the obligation of creating the conditions that would guarantee a generation of peace. That meant, in his view, a huge foreign loan and the establishment of amicable relations with England and Japan. He was faced, too, with the fact that he lacked support from the public and could look for little support from the tsar, not to speak of the rest of the court.

Typical of the tsar's attitude was his reply to his mother's exhortation: "it is essential for you to show him [Witte] all your confidence now, and to let him act according to his programme." Nicholas, in a letter dated November 10, assured his mother: "I am doing my very best to ease his very difficult position—and he knows it." At the same time he expressed disappointment in the man, writing that, out of keeping with his reputation as "a very energetic and even despotic man," he was failing to show sufficient energy and determination in the restoration of order.[37]

Witte and the tsar agreed on the need for the restoration of order, but Nicholas had little sympathy for or understanding of Witte's aim to use as little force as possible while seeking to gain the confidence in the new order as the road to tranquility. True, Witte's first efforts had fizzled, but he was not ready to call it quits. Witte suspected that Trepov, with easy access to the sovereign, was reinforcing the tsar's critical view; accordingly, he was coming to hate the man.

Chapter 17

Keeping the Promise of October 17

With the State Duma scheduled to open on December 10, there was clearly insufficient time to implement all the commitments made in the October Manifesto. It was Witte's strategy to enact temporary laws to deal with such matters as civil rights, leaving the task of enacting permanent legislation to the State Duma and the State Council. But before these bodies could meet it was imperative to provide rules governing elections, structure, and operation. The obstacles to constructive work were formidable.

First, there was the continuing revolutionary and counterrevolutionary fever, which made Witte's work a nightmare. This problem will be considered in the next chapter. Then there was the all-important question of the tsar's support. It will be recalled that at the time he bestowed the title of count on Witte he assured him that he had not believed the calumnies that had been spread about. That was not quite true, but it is likely that Nicholas was able to suppress his suspicions about the man. But as the hoped-for sense of normalcy continued to be no more than a light at the end of the tunnel, the cry at court and elsewhere that Witte was a traitor grew stronger. The tsar would hear advice such as that given him by Baron A.A. Budberg: "The sooner you get rid of him [Witte] the better."[1] Nicholas, although increasingly disappointed in his premier, remained committed to supporting him.

That did not mean giving Witte his head. Take his November 10 letter to his mother in which he writes, among other things:

> I hold a meeting of the Council of Ministers every week. . . . They talk a lot, but do little. Everybody is afraid of taking courageous action: I keep on trying to force them—even Witte himself—to behave more energetically. With us nobody is accustomed to shouldering responsibility: all expect to be given orders, which, however, they disobey as often as not.[2]

Nicholas was obviously trying to impress his mother with his own importance. Witte was, as usual, energetic, but unable to force the pace as much as his sovereign desired.

Not only was the tsar able to preside over the cabinet when he wished, but he also continued to receive weekly oral reports from the ministers, something Witte had unsuccessfully tried to avoid. However, ministers were required to acquaint the premier with the content of their reports.

Still another obstacle Witte encountered was in the person of Trepov.[3] The responsibility of the palace commandant was to ensure the security of the monarch and his family. That meant close contact with the tsar and frequently the ability to exert some influence on him. Trepov, as it quickly turned out, achieved more than his predecessors, becoming in effect the tsar's confidential secretary. This was vividly described in a letter to the tsar's mother:

> Trepoff is absolutely indispensable to me: he is acting in a kind of secretarial capacity. He is experienced and clever and cautious in his advice. I give him Witte's bulky memoranda to read, then he reports on them quickly and concisely. This is of course a secret to everybody but ourselves.[4]

It was no secret to Witte, who quickly surmised what was afoot and who attributed many of his difficulties with the tsar to Trepov.[5]

The premier, no novice at using the press, sought to use it not only to sway public opinion, but also to persuade the tsar that Witte had the support of the conservative press. To these ends he took the unprecedented step of employing a press secretary, A.A. Spasskii-Odynets, an official in the Ministry of Finance. Among the secretary's many duties was that of planting items in newspapers that the tsar read with approval. He was not always successful, as was the case with Suvorin, publisher of the widely read and ultraconservative *Novoe vremia*, who did not believe that Witte would succeed and insisted that the source be identified.[6]

Witte lost no time in getting started. He held the first session of his cabinet late on the eighteenth in the quarters of General Trepov and on the next two days in the Marie Palace. The next day saw a change of venue, at the suggestion of the security police, to the guest quarters of the Winter Palace. For the duration of his premiership these quarters were the site of his residence as well as the site of cabinet meetings and staff operations.[7] The arrangements were decidedly temporary and—considering that Witte was now the head of government, with a considerable staff—cramped.

The cabinet ordinarily met in a large room so dark that lights had to be kept on during the day. On occasion, when there were meetings of the soon-to-be-abolished Committee of Ministers, that committee and the cabinet met in the Marie Palace. And when the tsar chose to preside, the cabinet would meet at his residence in Tsarskoe Selo, his usual abode for most of the year. Witte made it clear from the beginning that civilian members should come to meetings in business clothes rather than the uniforms appropriate for their civil service ranks. Like the tsar, he was punctual, but unlike his sovereign, he could be testy, the combined result of arrogance and stress. In the event of disagreement his "soft and tired voice" could rise to a screech, and he was likely to say, "Only idiots could think this way," or "Please shut up and listen while I speak."[8] When the tsar presided, meetings would be held during the day, but when Witte took the chair, the session would begin in the evening and might go on until the wee hours of the morning.

Much has been made of the fact that on one occasion Witte said that he spat on the constitution.[9] It is true that he believed that if Alexander III had lived out his three score and ten, there would have been no war and no revolution, and autocracy would still have been viable. It is also true that he recognized that the historical tide was against autocracy but convinced himself that with Alexander III still on the throne the tide could have been held back. In any event, he resigned himself to the fact that Nicholas II held the scepter and that the tide had come in. Now he was faced with the imperatives of history, and he wanted to have a place in history. As one colleague put it, he was determined to do a thorough job of transforming Russia from an absolute monarchy to one based on the rule of law and, in so doing, leave for himself "a monument not of human creation."[10] Witte was very concerned with his place in history. Shortly before October 17 he told a newspaper publisher that he would be remembered "not only as the creator of the gold standard, the man behind the Trans-Siberian Railroad, and the author of the Portsmouth Peace Treaty but also as the creator of the State Duma."[11] And shortly before his death, he expressed the hope that his gravestone would bear the inscription "Count Witte, October 17, 1905."[12]

At the top of his agenda, in addition to the restoration of order, were revision of the electoral law and of the law establishing the State Duma. The October Manifesto had promised revision in time to be effective for the election, which was set for December 10. He was uncertain about what changes should be made in the electoral law, but, as he had indicated to the public men, he felt bound to use the existing law as his framework. As for the final shape of the law, that, as the October Manifesto had stated, was a matter for the coming State Duma. Basically, he wished for a body that the people would see as their spokesman but not one that would turn into a constituent assembly, one that would have a clear voice but little muscle. As for the State Council, his position had already been staked out: that its membership should be doubled by adding elected members chosen by the educated minority and that it should serve as the upper legislative house.

Witte wasted no time in revising the Bulygin electoral law. On his first day in office he summoned S.E. Kryzhanovskii, who had played a key role in drafting the Bulygin law, and asked him to prepare a new version that would extend the franchise as widely as possible while retaining the law's basic framework. Then he carried out his pledge to D.N. Shipov that public men would be invited to participate in the preparation of a new electoral law. It took some time before Shipov and his colleagues delivered their draft, thus making it difficult to hold an election on the set date.

On November 19 and 20 the cabinet, with the participation of Shipov, other liberals, and several members of the State Council, considered the drafts prepared by Kryzhanovskii and the public men. Kryzhanovskii offered two drafts that differed in a few details. Both extended the franchise to classes and areas that had been denied the vote by the Bulygin law while retaining the framework of indirect election and the weighted vote. The liberal draft called for universal and equal manhood suffrage with direct election of deputies in the cities and indirect election elsewhere.

As would be expected, the discussion was spirited, the liberals defending their proposal, which was referred to as Project Two, and most of the cabinet arguing for the Kryzhanovskii proposal, known as Project One. But the cabinet was not entirely of one mind. A few were sympathetic to the liberals, and one, Durnovo, proved to be quite conservative, very often disagreeing with Witte. When I.I. Tolstoi joined the cabinet, Durnovo told him that he would find himself in the company of "dreamers" and expressed the hope that Tolstoi would support him, which did not take place. In the end, the cabinet rejected Project Two on the ground that the only parties well organized at that time were the revolutionary ones, which stood to benefit greatly from its provisions.[13] In the days that followed, the cabinet continued to discuss moot points in the proposed legislation. On November 30 Witte recommended to the tsar the summoning of a special conference to deal with proposed electoral legislation, to which would be invited the cabinet, several members of the State Council, Shipov and three other public men, and several others; the tsar would preside.

Simultaneously, Count Solskii, who had been appointed chairman of the State Council, was at work on legislation reforming that body and on revision of the legislation dealing with the organization and powers of the forthcoming State Duma. Much of that work was based on Witte's ideas and was being done with his participation.

While preparations for duma elections were in progress, the country was experiencing revolutionary tremors that threatened to tear it apart. This heartened socialist leaders, who strove to harness this energy to overthrow the regime. At the same time, the extreme right, which was gaining strength, was mobilizing to undo the October Manifesto.

As Witte put it:

> In Petersburg, despite the quick return of comparative calm, the soviet continued to command the support of the workers. In Moscow, where the troops were unreliable, there was trouble. The Caucasus was still aflame. Much the same can be said of Finland, the Kingdom of Poland, and many parts of the Baltic provinces. Disorder was prevalent in the Southwestern provinces (Kiev, Volhynia, and Podolia). Unrest among the peasantry was on the rise. In Siberia the region served by the railroad was out of hand, and the bulk of our million-man force that had been sent to Manchuria was still east of Lake Baikal.[14]

The responsibility for the reestablishment of order lay on the shoulders of the military and the police, but Witte had to take part in the decision making as well as assume the onus in the eyes of the tsar for the failure of the October Manifesto to restore calm. Witte was on the horns of a dilemma: he still hoped that the "good sense" of "society" would prevail, and he preferred to see the use of force as a last resort, but staring him in the face was the fact that force had to be used if the government was to remain in control. The consequence was stress that took a heavy toll. His psychic and physical health declined as he continued to carry a staggering workload. He grew more irritable as well as less resolute. G.E. Afanasev, a fellow student of Witte's at the university, who in December visited him for the first time in many years, found him suffering from eczema and almost unrecognizable.[15]

Another visitor during this period was Kuzmin-Karavaev, whom we have met before. He found Witte in despair, almost ready to throw in the towel. Witte, as we know, was temperamental, often succumbing to depression, a trait suggested by the description of him as "the son of a Prussian sergeant-major and a wild Circassian princess." But this time he was so sunk in despair that Kuzmin-Karavaev felt moved to write the premier a letter urging him not to give in to his feelings, which could have disastrous consequences. He counseled Witte to act more boldly in carrying out reform.[16]

Witte was clearly a troubled man, feeling that Projects One and Two represented a kind of Hobson's choice. It was apparent that it was indecision that had led him to counsel the tsar to preside over a special conference to consider both projects. Invited to attend the conference, which opened on December 5 at Tsarskoe Selo, were, among others, Grand Duke Michael Aleksandrovich, members of the cabinet, several members of the State Council, Trepov, and, at Witte's suggestion, four public men: D.N. Shipov, A.I. Guchkov, Count V.A. Bobrinskii, and Baron N.A. Korff.

In his memoirs, Shipov relates that before the opening of the conference,

Witte expressed himself in favor of Project Two. The premier said that he had considered it impolitic to support the project openly, thinking that it would be better for Shipov to be its spokesman.[17] Shipov's account suggests that Witte was speaking out of both sides of his mouth. There is no reason to question Shipov's reliability, but it is possible that the story grew in the telling, and it is possible too that his recollection was affected by Witte's performance at the conference. As will be seen, the premier was ambivalent about the projects as well as being under great stress. The fact that he had suggested that Shipov and the other public men be invited indicated both ambivalence and the desire to show that public men would be listened to.

The conference opened on December 5, did not meet on the following day, the name day of the tsar, a holiday, and met again on the seventh and ninth. It met amidst very disturbing news, about which more later: briefly, the St. Petersburg Soviet issued a manifesto calling for financial war against the government and a few days later issued a call for a general strike, while in Moscow armed uprising was in the making. Tsarskoe Selo was worlds away from the rest of the country, but the news from the outside was most unsettling, particularly to Witte, who would give what was probably the worst performance of his career, that of a man who seemed uncharacteristically uncertain of himself.

Witte spoke at some length and on several occasions. The burden of his remarks was that the country was in the midst of revolution, one in which organized labor represented the dangerous element. As he then saw it, the fact was that the peasantry, although restive, was still the foundation of Russia and was still loyal. The government, he declared, lacked sufficient military to regain control everywhere and therefore had to look to "moral suasion," particularly the forthcoming State Duma, but what kind of a duma? If Russia was to regain equilibrium, it would have to look to the duma as satisfying the demand of the people to be heard, but not, as one speaker said, a body that would stand "side by side" with the tsar. What was necessary, he insisted, was a body that would serve as a buffer between the tsar and the duma. That body should be the reconstituted State Council, which would have the role of a second legislative chamber.

As for elections to the State Duma, he saw flaws in both Project One and Project Two and spoke at length about them. His conclusion was that if he had to make a choice, he would cross himself and select the second one.

Each project received support, often of a passionate kind, with the tsar seeking to hurry things along. At the third session he declared that he had been ambivalent about the projects but had become convinced that Project

One would serve Russia better than Project Two, which would lead to the creation of a democratic republic. He then led the consideration of the details of the proposed legislation.[18]

Two days later, on December 11, an imperial decree was issued that altered the requirements for suffrage established for the abortive Bulygin Duma. The decree extended the right to vote in State Duma elections to virtually all males over twenty-five, but the election system remained indirect and complex, and votes were weighted so as to favor the upper classes over the lower ones and predominantly Russian areas over predominantly non-Russian ones. Nonetheless, the promise made in the October Manifesto that the State Duma, which would be popularly known as the Witte Duma, would be a legislative body was being adhered to.[19] The following day the tsar set the coming April 27 as the date for the State Duma to convene. What the public did not anticipate was that there would be a second legislative chamber in the form of a reorganized State Council.

With electoral law enacted and the date for the convening of the State Duma set, there remained the routine tasks of selecting the election dates, drawing up electoral rolls, and drafting a statute delineating the structure and powers of the State Duma and another statute reorganizing the State Council, the last proving to be a contentious one. Early in February, Count Solskii submitted a draft of a law reorganizing the State Council, a draft that incorporated Witte's views. The tsar then summoned a special conference for February 14 to meet at his residence under his chairmanship, expecting it to finish its work in one session. As it turned out, another session would be required.

Among those invited to attend were Witte and his cabinet, Solskii and other members of the State Council, and Trepov. The agenda was review of the draft statutes concerning the State Duma and the State Council. Nicholas, obviously resigned to accepting change but not to prolonged debate, prodded movement from one article to the next but was not entirely successful.

Chief among the moot points was the proposed composition of the State Council, that half of the members be appointed by the tsar, the other half elected, caused the most debate, pitting the conservative minority against the more liberal majority. The conservatives feared that the elected members would be oppositional. Witte countered that the limited electorate would guarantee that the council would be what it was meant to be, a conservative buffer between the duma and the tsar.

Yet at the same time he argued that if the State Council rejected a bill that had been passed by the State Duma, the tsar should have the authority to send the bill back to the duma and, if the duma passed it once more, should have the authority to sign it into law. He argued that the peasants, being heavily represented in the duma but not at all in the council, would look to the duma as their avenue to the tsar, and the arrangement he proposed would make them feel that they could thus speak to their ruler. The argument was consistent with Witte's philosophy and was likely to please the tsar.

It did not please Kokovtsev, who argued that such an arrangement would, in effect, mean a unicameral legislature. That, in turn, gave the premier an opportunity to taunt Kokovtsev and play up to the tsar. He insisted that the legislature should not be thought of in Western terms as a parliament with a lower house and an upper one and suggested that Kokovtsev spoke as if the October Manifesto were a constitutional document, which it was not, and that the tsar had issued the manifesto on his own initiative, a somewhat disingenuous position on Witte's part. His argument in turn served to provoke lengthy arguments that served little purpose other than to prolong the conference.

Witte, anxious to leave considerable power in the tsar's hands and thus the premier's, provoked further argument by proposing that the monarch have the right to issue decrees without having to go through the council and the duma. Solskii argued that this would be counter to the letter of the October Manifesto, to which the premier replied that a decree was not a law.

The tsar hurried proceedings along, indicating approval or disapproval of each point, on the whole supporting majority positions. Finally, in the early evening of the sixteenth, he closed the meeting, assigning the task of editing the proposed legislation to Witte, Solskii, and two others.[20]

Four days later, the tsar issued a manifesto concerning the State Council and State Duma, as well as decrees dealing with each of these. The manifesto consisted of broad outlines, and the decrees contained the details.

The legislation provided, as Witte had sought, that membership in the State Council be equally divided between members appointed by the tsar and members indirectly elected by the Russian Orthodox clergy, provincial zemstvos, the nobility, academe, and organizations representing commerce and industry. The council would share legislative power with the duma, and no bill approved by both chambers could become law without the signature of the tsar. On the other hand, no law could go into effect without the approval of both chambers.

However, if the duma was not in session at a time when "extraordinary circumstances" impelled the cabinet to propose temporary legislation, the tsar could give his approval providing that the legislation did not change the Fundamental Laws (about which more later) or change the legislative system. Such legislation had to be placed before the duma within two months and could be nullified by either chamber. As will be seen, this power would later prove a significant one.

The decree concerning the structure of the State Duma simply revised the law of August 6 to convert the body into a legislative one. It provided that deputies would be elected for five-year terms. The decree concerning the State Council stipulated that the elected councilors serve nine-year terms.[21]

Russia now had a legislature. The tsar had referred to aspirations for a lesser body as "senseless dreams." What had come to pass exceeded his fears but was short of realizing the hopes of most of the opposition. Witte hoped that the legislature would be a cooperative body, making it possible to continue the work of giving life to the October Manifesto.

Chapter 18

Revolution and Counterrevolution

Witte's declaration that Russia was in the midst of a revolution reflected a searing personal crisis over the use of force in the restoration of calm. In his October 8 memorandum, he had advised that the government adhere to the principle that: "countermeasures, based on law and in harmony with the ideas of the moderate majority of society [be used] against activities that do clearly threaten society and the state." By now, in December, such advice seemed milksoppish. Witte now reluctantly accepted the necessity of using whatever means seemed necessary to bring an end to disorder. Never before in his career had he faced a challenge of such a magnitude.

That challenge was magnified by sniping from the Black Hundreds, an epithet applied to mass organizations of the extreme right. Before 1905 right-wing organizations were a rarity in Russia. The monarchy had not needed help from the political arena to defend itself except at such a time as the assassination of Alexander II, when, as has been seen, the Holy Brotherhood was formed. But in 1905, and particularly as a result of the October general strike and the October Manifesto, there arose among those who supported the tsar the feeling that the regime required organized support, a feeling shared by some in the government. This manifested itself in the appearance of numerous organizations such as the Union of the Russian People, the Union of Russian Men, the Russian Monarchist Union, and the Union of the Archangel Michael, organizations that considered themselves "patriotic" and which the left referred to as "the Black Hundreds."

Although these organizations differed among themselves on specifics, they shared several basic views, namely, that the revolution Russia was witnessing was the work of non-Russians, mainly the "kikes" (*zhidy*), as they chose to call Jews, and to a lesser extent Poles, Finns, and students, who, even if they were Russian, were alien at heart. Further, they tended to believe in the fantasy of an "international kikish-Masonic plot" to dominate the world and that Witte was linked to that plot. What was needed, they argued, was to reestablish the primacy of "true Russians" and to return to the "verities" of "autocracy, Orthodoxy, and nationality."[1]

The largest and most clamorous of these organizations turned out to be the Union of the Russian People, established early in November and led by

Dr. A.I. Dubrovin. Like others of the extreme right, he sought to co-opt the support of the tsar and the Russian Orthodox Church.

Toward this end, Dubrovin sought a meeting with Grand Duke Nicholas Nikolaevich, commander of the St. Petersburg Military District. On December 16 he and an associate called on General G.O. von Rauch, the grand duke's adjutant, to make their case for a meeting with the tsar, as well as to make the point that as long as Witte, "pawn of the Jews," "member of a Jewish Masonic lodge," remained in office, the country was at risk. The general informed his visitors that, as a military man, the grand duke could not engage in politics and that the only practical result of a meeting would be to advise that they see Trepov, the man in charge of the tsar's security.

A secret meeting with the grand duke was arranged at Rauch's quarters in the English Club. Rauch was not present but was informed after the meeting by Dubrovin that the grand duke had told him not to take any actions without permission.[2] The grand duke was probably moved to do so by the fact that a few days earlier Dubrovin had seen the minister of war with an offer to fetch twenty thousand Old Believers from Vitebsk who would, when given arms, restore calm in the factory districts of the capital! The minister of war had put Dubrovin off by promising to look into the matter.[3]

What Nicholas Nikolaevich thought about the allegations against Witte is not on record, but Rauch's thoughts are. He considered the premier to be a "sphinx," a power-hungry man who might easily be the traitor depicted by Dubrovin. A few days later, the general was told by P.I. Rachkovskii, head of the secret police, that there were no Masonic lodges in Russia.[4] That should have destroyed Dubrovin's credibility. Not so. Arrangements were made for the tsar to receive Dubrovin.

On December 23 Nicholas welcomed a large delegation headed by Dubrovin, who, among others, read addresses urging the sovereign to hold fast to autocracy. The tsar's reply was warm. He thanked those who had joined the Union of the Russian People and stated that with their help "I and the Russian people will succeed in defeating Russia's enemies."[5] This was typical of his remarks, which surely brought joy to Dubrovin but not to Witte. The tsar was hungry for expressions of support, but he still remained committed to the course that had been set on October 17 even though his confidence in Witte was eroding. As long as Witte remained in office, the central government, except for one official, gave no succor to the Black Hundreds, but many local officials did.[6]

The Black Hundreds had the same mixed results in their effort to co-opt the established church with which they identified themselves. With Prince Obolenskii as overprocurator of the Holy Synod and Metropolitan Antonii as a member of the synod, the Black Hundreds could not hope for support from the church's governing body. On the contrary, the Holy Synod gave its unambiguous support to the October Manifesto, called for love for non-Christians as well as Christians, and cautioned the clergy against political activity.[7]

Nonetheless, the Black Hundreds found some moral and practical support among certain parish priests, monks, and the church hierarchy. Particularly prominent in this respect was Archbishop Antonii of Volhynia, who a few days after the October Manifesto wrote to a colleague: "Woe to us if the people do not arise for themselves and the Tsar; otherwise Witte will bring him to the scaffold."[8] A few months later, also in a letter, he argued that the first step in the fight against revolution should be the execution of Witte.[9] Interestingly enough, a later secret police survey found that about one-third of the members of the Union of the Russian People resided in the province of Volhynia.[10]

Before leaving the subject of the threat from the right, note should be made of the virulent animosity toward Witte in and around the court. As has been seen, even before October 17 there were many at court who believed that he was working hand in glove with the Jews to make himself president of a republic. After October 17 the animosity grew even more virulent and irrational, fueled by the belief that revolution had to be the product of conspiracy. Guards officers undertook to keep Witte under surveillance, a strange undertaking given the limitations on his movements. Grand Duke Michael Alexandrovich, the tsar's brother, a man whom Witte had tutored and believed to be a friend, was approached for help against his former teacher. He expressed sympathy but offered nothing more, saying that, as a grand duke, he could not engage in politics.[11] And then there was the foreign minister, Lamsdorff, who, although still on Witte's side, believed that the revolutionary movement had to be the work of foreign Masonic lodges and international Jewry. Despite the lack of evidence to support this view, he considered seeking the cooperation of other conservative monarchies and the Vatican in the struggle against foreign Masonic influence.[12] And there was Grand Duke Nicholas Nikolaevich, who placed a general under surveillance on the suspicion that he was part of a plot to overthrow the tsar, a suspicion that the war minister thought to be absurd.[13] Such was the surreal atmosphere in which Witte worked and sought to bring the country back to normal. Yet be it noted that, according to A.A. Lopukhin, who had been head of the Department of Police, Witte appeared to believe that there existed an international Jewish organization that could persuade the Jewish masses to refrain from revolutionary activity. He relates that he told Witte that the notion was "an anti-Semitic legend," that Jews were no more clannish than Christians.[14]

And now to the revolutionary threat. It came from all sides—from the peasantry, from industrial workers, from white-collar workers, including government employees, and from the armed forces. In the non-Russian borderlands, the movement for national minority rights exacerbated anti-governmental hostility. Not unexpectedly, fear of anarchy mounted among the propertied classes, prompting demands that the government, headed by Witte, regain control. The premier's inclination, at least through November, was to counsel restraint, to hope that good sense would prevail. The tsar, on the other hand, wanted quick action in dealing with disorder. In this he was supported by Durnovo, Trepov, and Grand Duke Nicholas Nikolaevich. As the days passed, the need for action became more pressing.

In late October and early November, what Witte had predicted and feared, peasant unrest, came to pass, although not on the scale he had foreseen. The October general strike, as has been seen, was an urban phenomenon. Its impact on the countryside took some time to be felt because of slowness of communication and the isolation of the peasantry, but felt it was. Peasant unrest was not as intense as it had been in the days of Pugachev, as Witte had feared, but it was widespread.

In European Russia nineteen provinces were the sites of severe peasant outbreaks, and of these, seven saw action close to open revolt. The most common actions were traditional ones in times of unrest: cutting of landlord-owned timber and harvesting of landlord-owned grain for peasant use. In many districts there were looting and burning of landlords' homes. Even more disturbing to the government and the landlords was the politicization of peasant unrest. To be sure, the more common peasant demands were usually purely economic, including the demand for more land. But in some places, inspired by peasants who had worked in the cities, by zemstvo workers, and by theological seminary students, peasants were coupling political demands, such as the call for a constituent assembly, with economic demands.[15] As indicated earlier, peasant unrest in the borderlands was linked to national minority concerns. Nonetheless, the Russian peasantry, on the whole, was not in the mainstream of the revolutionary movement and still appeared to believe that the tsar was their "Little Father."

Labor unrest continued to be a major concern because of the power of mass strikes. In cities with large labor forces the industrial districts, where workers tended to be militant, often equipped with knives and clubs and an occasional revolver, listening to their leaders, were virtually off limits to the authorities. The leaders sought to maintain revolutionary momentum, to keep the struggle for new concessions from industrial management and the government alive, and, more important, to continue the fight to overthrow the government and have a constituent assembly that would establish a democratic republic. The St. Petersburg Soviet played the leading role in the labor movement, a movement that was far from united. The soviet's leaders hoped that their calls would be heeded and their example followed throughout the land. And to some extent that proved to be the case, with workers' soviets and councils being formed in various cities, although most would turn out to be ephemeral.

Even more threatening to the government was the situation in the armed forces, particularly the navy. In his letter of November 17 to his mother, the tsar provides a sense of how the government perceived ongoing events:

> Another unhappy week has passed.
>
> For the most part the peasant disturbances are still going on—in some places they are over, but in others only just beginning. They are difficult to put down because there are not enough troops or Cossacks to go around.
>
> But the worst thing is another mutiny of the naval establishments in Sebastopol and part of the garrison there.
>
> How it hurts and how ashamed one is of it all. . . .
>
> A strong wave of subversive propaganda is sweeping through the Army now.[16]

He was right to be worried about the army: it was beset by severe mutinies, particularly along the Trans-Siberian line, on which movement was still at a halt, stranding hordes of soldiers returning from Manchuria. As for the navy, its utility as a fighting force was now nil.

Clearly the situation was becoming chaotic, with problems coming from all directions. What to do? Witte continued to give priority to carrying out the promise of the October Manifesto. The tsar, while accepting the need for reform, was more concerned with the restoration of order. Thus, as agrarian unrest burst out toward the end of October, the tsar ordered several of the generals-adjutant in his suite to proceed with small detachments to provinces where unrest was most severe. They could commandeer all military and police forces in their jurisdictions and could exercise other broad powers. Witte was not left out of the process, with the generals reporting to him. It would be some time before they accomplished their missions.[17]

At the same time Witte was using "suasion" to soothe peasant discontent. He and his cabinet drafted an imperial manifesto addressing the peasant question. This was in response to the growing feeling in higher circles that, given the fact that the October Manifesto had not held out any specific promises to the peasantry, something should be done to appease that class. On November 3, Nicholas signed the manifesto and a decree promising first a deduction and subsequently the cancellation of the redemption dues owed by the peasantry for the land they had received when they were emancipated. It also promised that the way would be eased for poorer peasants to buy land.[18]

Peasant unrest was but one sign of the revolutionary mood gripping the country. In the Baltic provinces, urban and rural unrest was so serious that this region was placed under martial law in late November, and Nicholas would advise his mother not to attempt to return home because she would have to travel through this area.[19] In portions of the Caucasus the rebels were, at times, able to cut telegraphic and railroad communications between that region and the interior.

There was no general staff directing the revolutionary forces at work, but there were links supplied by the socialist parties and other organizations. Moreover, what happened in St. Petersburg and Moscow produced a ripple effect. Nor was there anything resembling a general staff directing counter-revolutionary efforts. Not that there should have been, but what might have been expected was that Witte, as head of government, working with the tsar, would have overseen the coordination of efforts to deal with unrest. This was not the case, what with conflicts of authority and attitude. The major conflict was between Witte and Durnovo. Witte sought to avoid the use of force as long as possible and to plead for faith in the government's good intentions. It was typical that he would respond favorably to an attempt to revive the Father Gapon labor organization as an ally of the government, an effort that would end tragically, with the assassination of the priest, who had returned secretly to Russia. Durnovo was cast from a different mold. Although he had earned the reputation of taking a liberal line on occasion, he was a conservative nationalist who believed that Russia could survive only under a firm government that tolerated no nonsense. He had only contempt for those in the cabinet whom he called "dreamers," and he was constantly in disagreement with Witte.[20] The burgeoning revolutionary movement in November and December would impel Witte, willy-nilly, to favor the show and use of force.

On the first day of November, the St. Petersburg Soviet issued a call for a general strike to protest several governmental repressive acts. The next day, in the spirit of "suasion," communicating with the workers through management, Witte urged workers, whom he addressed in what he considered the spirit of comradeship, to ignore the call, assuring them that the problems of labor were being addressed by the government. His words were greeted with derision, but the strike call would be poorly heeded. On the same day, November 2, the premier began work on legislation to prohibit strikes of a nature to affect the interests of the state or cause widespread distress.[21] That legislation would require a month to gestate, while the need for it proved immediate, although the prospects for its effectiveness were slight.

That need was sharply illustrated by the effort at a congress being held in Moscow to form a postal and telegraph workers' union. Durnovo warned that since government employees were forbidden to unionize, those who sought to do so were subject to dismissal, and he was as good as his word. The dismissals in turn prompted the call for a postal-telegraph strike on November 15. The resulting strike, which led to the arrest of several leaders, encouraged strikes on a few railroad lines. Trouble kept erupting, especially in the borderlands. Thus, in Vilna a Lithuanian nationalist congress called for refusal to perform military service.

The St. Petersburg Soviet, trying, with some success to provide leadership to the revolutionary movement, felt pressure to take dramatic steps in the effort to force the pace of events. Left-wing liberals were still committed to pushing ahead in the struggle against the government, but more moderate ones were worrying about the growth of anarchy. A sign of the mood in those days was the bon mot that appeared in Suvorin's *Novoe vremia* that the country had two governments, one led by Witte, the other by Khrustalev-Nosar, head of the St. Petersburg Soviet, the question being who would arrest the other. The premier took umbrage and told Suvorin that there were in fact four governments, without specifying what he meant.[22] Perhaps he was referring to Trepov and Durnovo.

In his memoirs Witte writes that he intended to have Khrustalev-Nosar arrested when the time seemed propitious; that turned out to be November 26. The premier may not have had a hand in the act, however. Reportedly, the decision to act was made at the imperial palace by a group close to the tsar, a group that felt Witte had outlived his usefulness.[23] Be that as it may, the arrest was the opening salvo in a confrontation with the revolutionary opposition.

The soviet responded by electing a three-man presidium, which included the future Bolshevik leader Leon Trotsky, and mapping out a counterattack. There was inconclusive talk about calling for an armed uprising. Then the soviet hit upon a nonviolent method, which was expressed in a manifesto signed by the leading socialist parties and the Peasants' Union on December 1 and published the following day in several of the St. Petersburg newspapers. The document declared the government was "on the brink of bankruptcy" and could and should be sent over the edge by striking at what was left of its financial capacity. This was to be done by such methods as refusal "to make land redemption payments and all other payments to the Treasury," by insisting that wages above five rubles be paid in gold, and by withdrawing all money on deposit in government banks, demanding that payments be made in gold.[24] One can easily imagine Witte's reaction to the proposed assault on the edifice he had helped create.

On December 3, with Witte's approval, Durnovo had his police surround the Free Economic Society building, in which the soviet was meeting, and arrest the whole lot. Those who were able to escape sought to carry on, but the soviet was as good as dead. The center of revolutionary fury now moved to Moscow.

By this time Witte had experienced a wrenching change of heart with respect to unrest. Reluctantly, he accepted the view that force must be met with force without any regard for niceties. This was reported by the tsar in a letter written to his mother on December 1. He wrote that there was considerable public demand for strong measures in dealing with unrest and went on to say:

> It is just what Witte has been waiting for—he will now begin to deal with the revolutionary movement energetically—at least that is what he assures me. He understands that the well-disposed elements in the country are not pleased with him and are getting impatient at his inaction. He is now prepared to order the arrest of all the principal leaders of the outbreak. I have been trying for some time past to get him to do it—but he always hoped to be able to manage without drastic measures.[25]

The tsar was simplifying, but he did put his finger on Witte's change in attitude, which became dramatically clear as the center of revolutionary unrest shifted to Moscow. The premier had already expressed concern about what was called the second capital, primarily because its governor-general had shown himself to be a weak and ineffective administrator in a city that was the hotbed of the liberal movement. He had urged the tsar to replace the incumbent with General-Adjutant Dubasov, who was doing an effective job in dealing with peasant unrest. Belatedly, in late November, Nicholas had transferred Dubasov to the Moscow post. Also, Witte writes that he had advance information about the bloody events that beset the city, this from a woman for whom he had once done a favor. She was in love with a revolutionary, who told her of a plan for an uprising, and she was sharing her knowledge with Witte because of both her antipathy for the plan and her concern that her lover would suffer the consequences of participation in such an action. Unfortunately, Witte does not say what he did with this information.[26]

The action now moved to Moscow, where the mood among socialists was even more militant than among their comrades in St. Petersburg, expressed in considerable support for an armed uprising. And the recently formed Moscow Soviet could count on a workers' militia, armed with revolvers and bombs—no match, to be sure, for the city's garrison if the troops obeyed orders to attack insurgents, but a mutiny among part of the Rostov Grenadier Regiment on December 2 raised the hope that the Moscow garrison would either refuse orders to suppress an uprising or even support it.

Word of the arrest on December 3 of the St. Petersburg Soviet prompted the Moscow Soviet to take action in the belief that the government was on the offensive and that inaction on its part would dash any hope of overthrowing the regime.

Accordingly, on December 6, the soviet issued a call for a general strike for the following day, with the unstated expectation that it would turn into an armed uprising. As will be recalled, the special conference dealing with the electoral law was in session, with Witte declaring that Russia was in the midst of a revolution.

Only a few cities other than Moscow answered the call. In Moscow the strike succeeded in paralyzing civilian life. Factories, municipal services, retail stores, and schools closed down. All the railroad lines, except the one to St. Petersburg, were idled. The soviet appeared to be master of the city. Aside from making a few arrests, Governor-General Dubasov, who was not confident that he could count on the troops in Moscow to obey orders, took no action to regain control other than to telephone Witte asking for reinforcements.[27] Witte passed on the request to the minister of war, who said that he was ordering the dispatch of a regiment from the Warsaw Military District. As it turned out, that unit was held up by a derailment, the work of revolutionaries.

Within a few days the Moscow strike did turn into an armed uprising when action was taken to break up a union meeting and disarm those present. In the resulting fracas the troops shelled the building in which the meeting was being held. Workers replied by building barricades and engaging in gunfire with the troops. The battle was on. A desperate Dubasov phoned Witte for the quick dispatch of help, declaring that his pleas had not been answered.

The premier informed the tsar of the problem and was told to ask Grand Duke Nicholas Nikolaevich for troops. As Witte tells it, the grand duke balked, insisting that he could not spare any troops from the task of guarding the capital and that as far as he was concerned, Moscow, the source of so much of the troubles, could go to the devil. In the end, the tsar directed the grand duke to send some troops to Moscow. Accordingly, the elite Semenovskii Guard Regiment, together with some cavalry and light artillery, was detailed to Moscow, with orders to Colonel Min, the commander, to use deadly force when necessary.[28]

Difficult as the situation in Moscow was, its gravity was overblown in St. Petersburg. On the fifteenth, Nicholas was writing to his mother that the first news about the uprising provided a figure of ten thousand killed or wounded; later news reduced the figure to three thousand, which would subsequently prove a bit high.[29] Witte, who feared that it would be a calamity if Moscow fell into the insurgents' hands, was urging Dubasov to be "merciless," a sentiment also expressed by his cabinet.[30]

By the time Colonel Min and his men arrived in Moscow on December 15, Dubasov, using what forces he could rely on, had regained control of much of the city except for Presnia, a heavily barricaded industrial district. Acting under orders from the governor-general to be ruthless, Min mounted a major attack on Presnia, shelling some factories, storming barricades, and making free use of deadly force. In the process many women and children were among the casualties. The insurgents soon saw that their cause was hopeless. On the eighteenth, the Moscow Soviet called for an end to the uprising, but Min continued to act with savage fury in the process of cleaning up the insurgency.

Colonel Min's brutal behavior aroused widespread disgust. Grand Duchess Elizabeth Fedorovna complained bitterly about the colonel to the tsar, her nephew. Grand Duke Nicholas Nikolaevich suggested that the colonel be either dismissed or assigned to a post in the hinterland. The tsar, however, on Dubasov's recommendation, promoted Min.[31] Witte, in his memoirs, wrote that he "approved" of Min's actions, asserting that "force should be met with force, with no sentimentality, no quarter." But he argued that "as soon as the revolutionary activity or outbreak is put down, the spilling of the blood of innocent people is cruel and brutish" and that it was in this that Min was at fault.[32]

Shortly after the end of the uprising the tsar wrote to his mother:

> As for Witte, since the happenings in Moscow he has radically changed his views; now he wants to hang and shoot everybody.
>   I have never seen such a chameleon of a man. That, naturally, is the reason why no one believes in him anymore. He is absolutely discredited with everybody, except the Jews abroad.[33]

Chameleon? True, many thought of Witte as a man devoid of principles. True, he could be devious in his dealings, but he did stick to his convictions as long as facts did not force him to change, as happened in October. In this case what occurred was a change in tactics rather than in convictions. Mounting unrest and growing revolutionary fervor moved him to shift from counseling patience whenever possible to opting for the use of the iron fist and doing so with a vehemence that shocked observers, including the tsar, who had no empathy for his premier to start with. At this time Witte seemed almost hysterical. Here he was, finding the sea far rougher than he had ever expected, suffering massive blows to his self-esteem and his hopes for his motherland, all the while in poor health.

Yet he tempered his calls for the use of the iron fist. As indicated, he argued that once an insurgency was crushed, it was time to act with restraint. Thus, he agreed with Dubasov that those arrested for their roles in the Moscow uprising should be tried by regular courts rather than by courts martial, as was proposed.[34] On another occasion, when he received a report that an officer in the punitive forces in the Baltic provinces was summarily hanging or shooting insurgent leaders who had surrendered, he sent the document on to the tsar. The tsar's comment was that the officer was a "fine chap."[35] Comments such as this gave Witte cause to be circumspect in how he presented matters to his sovereign. For example, in the case of the naval officer Lieutenant P.P. Schmidt, who had been sentenced to death for leading a mutiny, Witte sent a note to the tsar in which he stated that experts had informed him that Schmidt was insane, adding that he did not feel competent to say yea or nay about the matter. The tsar's reply was that if the man were insane, the fact would have been established at the trial.[36]

None of this is to say that Witte did not throw himself into the attack on revolutionary activities after the Moscow uprising, an uprising that was the high-water mark of the revolutionary upsurge. The tsar and those around him were determined on a full-scale offensive against insurgency and other acts and threats of violence. Many men known to be decisive were appointed temporary governors-general in troubled areas, and given broad powers to deal with disorder. New punitive expeditions were sent to various areas with the same purpose. Two such expeditions were formed to end the long delay in opening traffic on the Trans-Siberian line so that the troops from the Manchurian front could return home. Witte claimed credit for that idea, as did several generals. The dispute is moot.[37]

Responsibility for dealing with unrest was divided, and Witte's role in this effort was far from clear-cut, all the more so because early in December, Durnovo stopped working closely with him.[38] This could only hamper Witte in his energetic, often frenetic efforts to cope with disorder. He met frequently with his cabinet, sent directives to governors-general, reported frequently to the tsar, and collected what information he could about the state of the country—all this while he was being criticized and attacked from various quarters.

The weeks following the beginning of the Moscow uprising were particularly bloody. The uprising inspired strikes and bloody clashes in some two dozen cities. Where revolutionary sentiment was already strong, there were armed uprisings and temporary seizures of power. The government answered with unsparing force. For example, the temporary governor-general of Kharkov reported to Witte that on December 12 his troops employed small arms and artillery, killing or wounding 120 insurgents.[39]

On the twenty-third, reporting to the tsar about the campaign to deal with revolutionary movement, Witte wrote that strikes were coming to an end except in the Baltic provinces, in the Caucasus, and along the Trans-Siberian line. He considered the situation in the Baltic provinces the most serious, noted that there were not enough troops in the Caucasus to cope, and alluded to the planned expeditions on the Trans-Siberian line.[40] It should be noted that the twenty-third was the day on which Nicholas received a delegation from the Union of the Russian People, an event that could only add to the weight of Witte's burden.

Predictably, Witte was deeply concerned with agrarian disorders. On the very same day, December 23, a day in which the cabinet was especially busy, we find Witte reporting to the tsar that serious agrarian disorder in the spring was likely; accordingly, he recommended preparatory measures of two kinds. One was reform, but that would have to be of a limited kind, since major change should be left to the State Duma. The other was repression, which would require that troops be in place in good time.[41] We find Witte returning to the subject many times in the next weeks. His communications to Nicholas about this and other pressing matters were so numerous that the tsar was led to complain that he could not cope with the volume.[42] It was in this period that the tsar told his mother that he was having Trepov summarize Witte's communications.

By the end of December the government had the upper hand, but the revolutionary surge was far from over, and Witte's "blood and iron" disposition was to continue for many weeks. He was particularly concerned about the lack of troops to deal with disorder and his lack of authority in getting troops to where they were needed and when they were needed. Witte complained to the tsar that neither he nor Durnovo was being kept up to date by the minister of war about the location of troops; he also disingenuously suggested that the tsar consider replacing him in the post of premier with a military man, a suggestion that the tsar did not take seriously.[43] Witte was hammering away on the theme that the positioning of troops should be guided during this period of turmoil by domestic rather than strategic considerations (such as a possible war with Germany) and that a commission should be formed in which he and the military would consider the problem. Nicholas acted slowly, and it was not until early March that the issue was settled.[44]

By February the country was calming down, albeit at an uneven pace, and it would not be until well into the following year that pacification could be considered complete. Regaining of the upper hand came at a predictably high cost to the country and to Witte. The measures taken were often egregiously brutal, leaving a legacy of hatred in many elements of the population. Witte was widely discredited, widely considered a lame duck. Empress Alexandra later put it: "Everyone said Witte was so clever, but in the end the Cossacks once more had to save the state."[45]

Witte was discouraged, felt himself isolated, and was ready to leave office, but Nicholas told him that he still needed him to accomplish several tasks, most importantly the securing of a huge loan abroad.[46] Indeed, the premier's agenda was a full one. There was, of course, the loan, but there was also the need to continue work on carrying out the promises of the October Manifesto, among them the election of a State Duma. But now he had to labor under the most dispiriting of conditions.

Chapter 19

"The Loan That Saved Russia"

Arranging a loan, as we have seen, had been weighing on Witte's mind for many a month.[1] As will be recalled, the chief obstacle to French participation in the loan was the Moroccan crisis, which threatened to lead to war with Germany. The French high command feared that without Russian military assistance their army would be defeated, but such help was then out of the question. What the French sought was Russian help in persuading Germany to agree to a negotiated settlement of their differences. Witte provided what help he could. Berlin finally gave its consent, and preparation was begun for an international conference to meet in the Moroccan city of Algeciras in January. Until the conference would reach a settlement satisfactory to France, it would not give the go-ahead to its bankers to arrange a loan, adding to Witte's anxieties.

This did not keep him from doing what preparatory work he could. This he began by inviting a group of bankers from several countries, headed by Edouard Noetzlin, chief of a syndicate of French bankers interested in the proposed loan, to a meeting in St. Petersburg. The formal invitation was issued by Kokovtsev, who was still minister of finance.

The bankers arrived just as the full force of the October general strike was being felt. The circumstances, as one can imagine, were not conducive to negotiations but the bankers were willing to go on. Witte, however, advised them to return home, saying that for Russia to negotiate at such a time was inappropriate. Obviously, he would be in a weak bargaining position and expected to see it improve soon.[2]

But the Algeciras conference was months away and fiscal needs were becoming more pressing by the day. The recent war had proved, as was to be expected, a huge financial drain. Moreover, as the revolution grew more intense, there was a flight of capital from the country, while tax revenues declined. So acute was the situation that in early December, the Finance Committee, an interagency body that dealt with domestic and foreign loans, heard talk of a temporary suspension of the gold standard. Rather than take that traumatic step, Witte and others suggested soliciting France for an advance on the major loan that was under consideration.

The premier was, of course, unable to go to Paris to seek a loan, and his minister of finance declared himself unable to carry out such a task. He then took a step that he must have considered distasteful, asking Kokovtsev, a member of the Finance Committee, to go to Paris. Artfully, he expressed his regrets for his past hostility toward the man, appealed to his sympathy by saying that he was at his wits' end, sometimes "ready to commit suicide." Kokovtsev was persuaded, leaving St. Petersburg amid the echoes of the Moscow uprising. With the help of pressure by Premier Rouvier on French bankers, a modest short-term loan was arranged. Kokovtsev then stopped off in Berlin, where he succeeded in having the date for repayment of a loan postponed. Russia now had a financial breathing space.[3]

During the period of negotiations for the major loan that Witte was seeking, diplomacy was tightly entwined with finance. France was deeply anxious for Russian support at the approaching conference in Algeciras, anxious too to strengthen the alliance with Russia. England was coming around to the idea of supplementing her entente with France by an entente with Russia and was therefore willing to signal her desire by encouraging her bankers to participate in a loan. Germany, for her part, was interested in bringing Russia into her fold, as was shown in the Treaty of Björkö, but that treaty had become a dead letter after the tsar was brought about to the view that the treaty was incompatible with the French alliance. Nonetheless, Germany was willing to support participation in the loan if Russia aided the German cause at Algeciras.

Witte sought to win support for the loan from as many sources as possible for two reasons: first, to ensure enough participation to realize the huge sum that was sought, and second, to keep from being too beholden to France. He was put out by the fact that Jewish bankers, notably the Rothschilds, indicated that they would not participate in the loan in protest against Russian persecution of the Jews. That attitude did not come as a surprise to Witte, but that did not deter him from making an effort to win the support of these bankers. In that spirit he had A.G. Rafalovich, the Ministry of Finance's financial agent in Paris and a member of a family with which he was well acquainted, call on Lord Nathan Rothschild, head of the House of Rothschild, to no avail.[4] At about the same time, Witte summoned A.A. Lopukhin for advice on how to bring Jewish bankers around, assuming that the man's police experience with the Jewish question would be of some help. It was not, for Lopukhin told the premier that the answer was to grant Russian Jews equality with the rest of the tsar's subjects, something that Witte was not prepared to support.[5]

With the opening of the conference early in January, the pressures on Witte mounted. The opening of the State Duma was scheduled for late April, and there was much for him to do. As soon as the conference opened he pressed the French to get the preliminaries out of the way, but they said that much of the work would have to wait for the conference to swing their way. However, they indicated that it would be proper for some of the preparatory work to be done provided that it was done in secret.[6]

This enabled Witte to invite Noetzlin to St. Petersburg. The banker's visit was shrouded in secrecy, so much so that he traveled incognito, using his valet's name. He stayed at a grand duke's guest house and was able to come and go without the fact of his presence becoming publicly known.

In the course of the negotiations several thorny problems arose. Among these were the size and terms of the loan. Witte talked about a sum of nearly three billion francs, a staggering amount. The Frenchman thought that a bit unrealistic, given the fact that some of the governments that had indicated support were wavering. Then there was disagreement about the rate of interest. And there was the thorny question, raised by Noetzlin, of whether or not the Russian government had the right to contract a loan without the consent of the soon-to-be-elected State Duma. Given the fact that it was considered vital for the Russian government to get the loan before the State Duma convened, the question was of the utmost importance. Witte provided written expert confirmation of his government's right to act in this matter without the legislature. As for the terms and size of the loan, final details would be worked out later.[7]

The question of legality did not die there. Although negotiations were secret, the fact that Russia was seeking a loan was not, and many hostile voices were raised, both at home and abroad, some objecting to a loan without the State Duma's consent, others objecting to a loan to the existing government of Russia. Many of these voices came from France, where loathing for the tsarist government was widespread and expressed forcefully by such men as Anatole France, the eminent author.

In the midst of all this, a complex situation was made all the more complex when a new government came into power in France. To be sure, it seemed most likely that the new government, under Jean Sarrien, would support the idea of a loan, for France needed Russia as much as Russia needed France. But there were some in the new cabinet who were unfavorably disposed to the idea of a loan. And two Kadets, acting on their own, undertook to journey to Paris to persuade the French government that a loan without State Duma approval would be invalid. In the end the French remained true to their commitment to Russia.

The question now was how long it would take for the conference to reach an outcome that the French found satisfactory. Witte informed Lamsdorff that the country's finances could not "hold out" if there was too long a delay.[8] To speed things along he availed himself of the privilege of communicating with

Kaiser William through Eulenberg, but to no avail: German stubbornness continued to prolong the proceedings.[9]

Finally, by mid-March, the conferees were near the end of their deliberations and were ready to agree on terms acceptable to France. Witte and Noetzlin had already settled the major terms, but there were still bankers other than the French whose commitment to participate was in question, and there was, of course, the need to settle the last details of the loan agreement and sign it.

Witte was very much on edge both because of his country's pressing financial needs and because of the imminent opening of the State Duma. Also, he was very concerned that the consortium of bankers who would participate in the loan be as broad as possible, both to ensure that the loan would be as large as he hoped and to avoid giving the impression that Russia was little more than a ward of the French. Toward this end he used whatever channels he could. Thus, he prevailed on his country's diplomats in Austria-Hungary, Italy, and the Netherlands to persuade these countries to support the loan. In his eyes it was of particular importance for both financial and diplomatic reasons that Germany participate, for if Germany did not, Russia would be drawn closer to the Anglo-French entente, and he was still attached to the idea of a Franco-Russo-German entente despite his willingness to show friendliness to the British at this point. At the same time he sought to convince the kaiser that the cause of monarchism would benefit greatly if Germany took part in the loan.[10]

As the days dragged on, Witte became more fretful, fearful that the French government was playing a dodgy game. At last, on March 18, a week before the close of the Algeciras conference, Poincaré, the French foreign minister, gave Noetzlin the go-ahead for final negotiations. Obviously, Witte could not go to Paris to do the work that was entailed. So he proposed sending Timashev, head of the State Bank, who had long served him in one capacity or another, but the tsar overruled him, selecting Kokovtsev instead, as a sop to the latter's feelings. The premier agreed, remarking, so he tells us, that what remained to be done was a mere formality.[11] Years later would find them arguing over credit for the loan.

Kokovtsev's task proved more complex than merely signing the loan agreement, as Witte had professed it to be. By the time Kokovtsev reached Paris, the German government, employing a rather transparent pretext, forbade its bankers to participate in the loan, and J.P. Morgan, representing a group of American bankers, had also decided not to participate in the undertaking. Moreover, Kokovtsev found the French bankers with whom he dealt less than enthusiastic about the loan, albeit willing to participate under pressure from their government.[12] Austrian bankers reluctantly agreed to participate on a small scale in return for some concessions on terms.

Finally, on April 3/16, the loan agreement was signed, providing for a sum of two and a quarter billion francs, considerably less than Witte had come to hope for. The French assumed the major part of the loan, which was to be repaid within fifty years. British, Dutch, Austrian, and Russian bankers took up the slack.[13]

Witte boasted that the loan saved Russia, boasting as well about the size of the loan. He was making a virtue out of a necessity, for Russia was now saddled with a huge addition to its indebtedness. But it was a necessity. The loan secured, at least for a time, the country's financial stability, and this included the gold standard. It strengthened the government's hand in its efforts to restore order. It would strengthen the government's hand with respect to the State Duma, for which elections were being held at the time.

No question that the loan was a great achievement for which Witte deserved the major credit, a fact that was widely recognized. Among the kudos he received, he especially prized the one from the tsar, who, in a handwritten letter, declared, "The successful conclusion of the loan represents the finest page [in the record] of your achievements. It represents a great moral success for the government as well as a guarantee of Russia's peaceful development in the years to come."[14]

But in addition to the burden of the debt itself, there were other costs. Russia now found herself more bound to France than ever. First, because Russian support of France at Algeciras, something Witte had sought to avoid, embittered Germany. Second, because at this time, the French renegotiated their military convention with Russia to their advantage. Also, the growing closeness between Russia and England, while promising elimination of some of the issues that had divided the two countries, would tie Russia closely to the Anglo-French entente and would soon result in the Anglo-Franco-Russo Triple Entente, a result far different from Witte's dream, a result that would increase the likelihood of a major war.

Ironically, but not unexpectedly, the conclusion of the loan agreement came at almost the precise moment that Witte's career was coming to an end. This will be addressed in a subsequent chapter.

Chapter 20

Implementing the October Manifesto

With the opening of the new year in 1906, Witte found himself increasingly isolated, under attack from both right and left. For good reason, he felt that he was losing the tsar's confidence and support. A striking sign of his declining position came when Nicholas informed him that he considered the role of premier to be "limited to coordinating rather than directing the ministers" and that the ministers "continued to be responsible to the tsar."[1] Another sign of the tsar's attitude can be found in a letter that he wrote to his mother in January, earlier referred to, in the course of which he commented that Witte "is absolutely discredited with everybody, except perhaps the Jews abroad." In the same letter he expressed approval of M.G. Akimov, who had replaced Manukhin, whom the tsar had found too liberal, as justice minister, and Durnovo. Of the other ministers he said that they "are people without importance."[2]

Given the tsar's attitude, it is easy to see that the premier had his work cut out for him, work made more difficult by the divisions within the cabinet. Far from being the homogeneous body Witte had sought, it was deeply divided, its members holding views ranging from quite liberal to quite conservative. Moreover, as Witte's star dimmed, it became increasingly difficult for him to ride herd on his colleagues, but he was determined to get on with the task of reform. Some of the work entailed preparing material and drafts of proposals for the State Duma, and some required immediate enactment—all this as he was working on the loan and coping with the revolutionary threat.

The threat was abating and the government appeared to have the upper hand, but the threat was still there and weighed heavily on Witte.[3] He was still in favor of the use of force but was becoming more temperate, now urging curbs on its unnecessary use. Meanwhile, he was seeking means to sway public opinion. He was able to establish a new government newspaper, *Russkoe gosudarstvo,* which, unlike the existing government newspaper, would devote itself to articles and editorials that would present the official position.[4] Also, he supported the use of counterpropaganda in the form of tracts and leaflets to expound the official position on matters of current concern.[5] And when an opportunity presented itself to win support among industrial workers, he embraced it.

That opportunity, earlier referred to, was provided by the notorious George Gapon, who, it will be recalled, fled abroad after Bloody Sunday. There he was lionized by Russian revolutionary émigrés. By the autumn he had suffered a change of heart, or so he said, and secretly returned to Russia, where he planned to revive his organization and direct it toward supporting the government's reform efforts. Witte unwisely responded favorably to his feelers. What resulted is a convoluted story, told in many versions,[6] much of the detail unverifiable. It is a story that involves intrigue, several adventurers, embezzlement and murder. The relevant details of the episode are as follows.

Witte arranged for the publication of a leaflet, to which Gapon attached his name, calling on workers to support the reform effort. In addition, Witte gave his support to an effort to revive Gapon's labor organization, an effort that died aborning. In the course of the negotiations involving Gapon, an unsavory agent acting in his name received a considerable sum of money on the authorization of V.I. Timiriazev, minister of trade and industry. Instead of turning over all the money to the intended recipient, the agent pocketed most of it, a fact that was soon uncovered by the radical press. The juicy scandal that ensued contributed to the departure from office of Timiriazev on February 18, 1906. Over a month later Gapon was put to death as a traitor by revolutionaries. Although Witte dissociated himself from the Gapon episode, his reputation suffered, particularly in the eyes of the tsar, who received a lengthy, slanted report about the episode from Durnovo.[7]

It was under these disheartening circumstances that the premier continued to give flesh to the promise of the October Manifesto. The liberals, to whom Witte was appealing, expected and demanded bold reforms, but that was not to be. The tsar was one obstacle. Then there was the State Council, which still had a voice in the making of laws. An additional obstacle was the stifling weight of bureaucratic tradition. A striking example occurred immediately after the October Manifesto was issued, when I.V. Hessen, a major liberal leader, called on Witte. When Hessen brought up the question of freedom of the press, the premier replied that he had just spoken to Professor Tagantsev, a noted jurist, who had told Witte that a statute on freedom of the press would require a good deal of time and effort. Hessen did not demur but said that there was one bold step the premier could take that would not require more than five minutes, and that was to write out a statement abolishing preliminary censorship.[8] This Witte did not do, limiting himself to issuing instructions to the censors to act with restraint.

A dark shadow over Witte's efforts was the law on exceptional measures, referred to earlier, which was totally inconsistent with the rule of law. The opposition called for its repeal and saw in the October Manifesto an implicit promise to do so. Both Witte and Durnovo recognized the law's evil effects.[9]

Leo Tolstoy, that immensely influential novelist, had appealed to the tsar to repeal the law, but it was still in effect, and its provisions were being applied in nearly half the provinces of the empire.[10] The December 12, 1904, decree called for mitigation of the law. A special conference to deal with it was formed, but the tsar's appointment of the highly conservative Count A.P. Ignatev as its chairman guaranteed that it would produce nothing.[11] However, the law had been enacted as temporary legislation, requiring renewal at three-year intervals. The time for renewal was at hand, and it could simply have been permitted to lapse, but because it was a convenient weapon for dealing with disorder it was renewed by the moribund Committee of Ministers, on Witte's watch, in the expectation that there would be no need for renewal in the future.[12]

The conditions that led to the renewal of the law on exceptional measures also made for temporizing in dealing with the promise of freedom of conscience, speech, assembly, and association, and the guarantee of personal inviolability, of which Witte was keenly aware. He was under public pressure to deal with all the civil rights. High on his list was freedom of speech, which he considered to mean primarily freedom of the press.

That subject had already been touched on in the December 12, 1904, decree, which had promised the removal of "unnecessary" restrictions on the press. The special conference on this subject, under the chairmanship of D.F. Kobeko, who was close to Witte, had not completed its work when the October Manifesto, which changed its mission, was issued. The task of the conference was challenging, given the voluminous legislation on the books dealing with the press, the extensive bureaucracy overseeing the press, and the ongoing challenges to government press control. Kobeko concluded that there was not enough time before the convening of the State Duma to prepare permanent legislation, and he accordingly prepared temporary press rules, which were approved by the State Council, then by Witte and his cabinet, and then by the tsar.[13]

These temporary regulations, issued in November 1905, represented a timid step toward press freedom. They ended preliminary censorship of the press in the cities but left in force legislation forbidding certain kinds of language. The rationale behind the regulations was that the press should be free to say anything it wished that was not defined as criminal—for example, incitement to violence—and that legal actions against the press should be taken by judicial action, in accordance with the law, rather than by administrative action, often capricious in practice. However, exceptions would be allowed in areas where the law on exceptional measures applied.[14]

It soon became apparent that many publishers were ignoring such regulations as the one requiring them to provide the authorities who supervised the press with copies of their publications. Consequently, supplementary regulations were issued on March 18 to strengthen press controls.[15] In practice, the Ministry of Interior dealt high-handedly with the press, taking action against many newspapers that did not violate the law. Freedom of the press, as experienced in the West, had yet to come about, but the press was freer, and more defiant, than it had been.

Much the same fate befell the promises of freedom of assembly and freedom of association. The right to assemble freely had not existed before 1905, although laws concerning assembly had been occasionally ignored, usually resulting in police action. After Bloody Sunday, defiance of these laws became frequent, as did police action. It was not until the law establishing a consultative legislature was issued that the question of the right to hold meetings during the election campaign—more broadly, the question of freedom of assembly—was addressed by the government.

The result was a decree providing for temporary regulations, issued on October 12, 1905, in the midst of the escalating general strike. The regulations did not provide for freedom of assembly but did permit meetings to be held with prior consent of the authorities. As can be surmised from what has been said earlier on, the regulations were widely ignored during the so-called freedom days. It was against this background that Witte and the cabinet worked to fulfill the promise of freedom of assembly, balancing that promise against the need to maintain order in a time of great disorder.

This was the sense of a cabinet meeting in early January 1906, at which it was argued that freedom of assembly could be allowed only under conditions of normalcy. This view was reflected in the temporary regulations concerning the right to assemble, issued on March 4. These followed the same lines as the October 12 regulations, permitting the authorities to close any gathering that strayed from the subject for which it had been called.[16]

On the same day, March 4, the cabinet issued temporary regulations concerning freedom of association. Previously, associations such as learned societies and trade associations could be established with governmental permission and could be shut down if they ventured into forbidden activity. But trade unions and political parties had been forbidden. Under the March 4 regulations, it became legal to form associations of various kinds, including trade unions and political parties, on condition that they registered with the government and provided full information about their nature. In practice, the right to register was denied to many trade unions and political parties, even those committed to peaceful tactics. Limited though they were, the regulations recognized the accomplished fact that the Russian people were beginning to organize and participate widely in public life.

When it came to the promise made in the October Manifesto of freedom of conscience, Witte assumed that religious toleration was already a fact as a result of the decree of April 17, 1905.[17] In fact, the decree extended the limits of religious toleration but left intact the rule that a person born into the Orthodox faith could not leave it.

But if he was not ready to broaden the April 17 decree, he was ready and anxious to renew the effort, referred to earlier, to reform the established church. In this he was aided by Prince Obolenskii, the overprocurator of the Holy Synod, and the majority of the Holy Synod itself. In March a commission was formed to prepare the way for the first convocation of a church council since 1666. It was expected that the council would restore church autonomy, but that was not to be under the monarchy.[18]

With respect to the promise of inviolability of person, Witte gilded the lily by asserting in his memoirs, "The promise of inviolability of person was assured because the law on exceptional measures could not be applied without consent of the State Duma and the State Council."[19] Even if that law had been repealed or permitted to lapse, the fact remained that the Russian legal system did not provide the kind of protection implicit in the notion of inviolability of person.

The October Manifesto implicitly promised removal of laws that discriminated against Jews and other minorities. The question of granting equal rights to Jews was quickly raised after October 17 by Jewish leaders who called on Witte. His response had been that while legal equality for Jews was inevitable, it was not imminent, because the Russian people were not ready to accept it peacefully. Equally galling was his advice that Jews should leave the struggle for equal rights to those of "Russian blood."[20]

The "Jewish question" was indeed a most delicate one for Witte to deal with, and he did not deal with it head-on. But even when he seemed to be doing so, he received a cold blast from the tsar. Thus, when he submitted a recommendation from the cabinet regarding the infamous quota system, which severely limited admission of Jews to universities and other higher schools, the tsar's reaction was terse and unequivocal: "The Jewish question should be considered in its entirety only when I consider it appropriate."[21] That time would never come.

Aside from increasing the number of villages open to Jews within the infamous Jewish Pale of Settlement and the recommendation mentioned above, Witte and the cabinet dealt only incidentally with Jewish matters. In February they advised the tsar of measures recommended for anticipating and forestalling rumored pogroms.[22] A few days later they reported on the complicity of a police officer in a pogrom in Homel, to which the tsar responded that the matter was none of his business.[23] But he did respond favorably to a recommendation from the cabinet in a very minor matter, the granting of permission to Jews in need of the cure, to visit a spa outside the Pale of Settlement but very close to its border.[24]

Nor did Witte and the cabinet find it possible to deal seriously with the task of improving the lot of labor, as had been promised in the December 12, 1904, decree. As I.I. Tolstoi, the minister of education, noted: "This period of the activity of the cabinet was devoted to the struggle with the hydra of strikes and rebellion."[25] But one major step forward was taken with the granting of the right of association.

Although Witte gave much attention to the struggle against agrarian disorder, he also spent much effort and political capital on finding a solution to the agrarian problem. Why? As has been noted, he felt that agrarian revolt represented a greater danger to the state than even the mass strikes. Moreover, there was support in higher circles for agrarian reform, provided it did not harm the interests of the large landowners. There were even some landowners who were willing to give up some land then if this would spare them greater sacrifices later on. In addition, as will be recalled, Witte had amassed a huge amount of materials and recommendations earlier on in seeking remedies for agrarian ills. And it was vitally important to convince the peasantry that they too would benefit from the promised reforms, for, at the moment, it was more important to give the peasantry some of what they wanted, even though it was not necessarily what they needed.

Witte had firm views about a solution to the peasant problem, a solution that would benefit the state as well as those peasants who were diligent. These views had been energetically presented in his 1898 letter to the tsar (see page 89) in which he asserted that the poor state of the peasantry was "the most pressing question facing Russia." At the time he ascribed that state not to lack of land but to the social and legal fetters that undermined peasant initiative, but he was frustrated in his efforts to have his views accepted. The task he now faced was to implement ameliorative measures that would placate the peasantry while preparing measures for State Duma consideration that would get to the heart of the peasant question.

What did the disaffected peasants want, as expressed by word and deed? They felt that they had been cheated in the postemancipation settlement, that they had not received as much as was their due, that they had been made to pay (in the form of redemption dues) for land that was theirs by right, and that they had been unjustly denied logging rights in the woods adjoining the land they tilled. Redemption dues had been abolished. In addition, they sought reduction in their tax burden and, more important, additional land, even through confiscation without compensation of the holdings of the landed nobility and other large landowners. It was the demand for land that sent chills through the bones of those in power.

On November 3, 1905, Nicholas had signed a manifesto and a decree intended to show his concern for the welfare of the peasantry. This gesture was accompanied by instructions to the Peasants' Land Bank to make more land available for purchase and to ease purchase conditions.[26] The tsar's instructions assumed that landowners would be urged to sell land to the bank. About the same time that the cabinet was considering the manifesto, it was also considering a proposal submitted by Professor P.P. Migulin and transmitted by the tsar to Witte that called for bold measures, for a large pool of land available for peasant purchase to come from such sources as land owned by the government, the imperial family, and large landowners, mainly those who rented land to peasants. Landowners whose lands were designated for sale would have no choice about complying but would be compensated. This was expropriation, a word that struck fear in the hearts of the upper classes. The cabinet rejected the Migulin proposal but did decide to create a commission under N.N. Kutler to consider the land question.[27]

Out of its deliberations came a proposal, much like Migulin's, that speeded the undermining of Witte's career and ended Kutler's long government service. Failure, as we know, is often an orphan, as was the case this time, with Witte placing responsibility for the proposal on Kutler and vice versa. According to the premier, the proposal came to him as a bolt from the blue, while Kutler claimed that he had acted on Witte's instructions.[28] Disinterested sources to support one side or the other are lacking, but what is not at issue is the fact that the most contentious part of the proposal was the one calling for expropriation, with compensation, of some large landholdings as a last resort.

The Kutler proposal came at a time when the mood in the country's upper circles was becoming more confident and therefore firmer in resisting challenges to their privileges. As Witte put it in his memoirs: "By January, as quiet began to return to the countryside, noble landowners began to recover from their fears and to have second thoughts about the wisdom of expropriation, even with compensation. In the end they denounced the whole idea as criminal."[29]

The tsar's reaction to the Kutler proposal reflected this shifting attitude. Although Witte was not in favor of expropriation, the idea did not make him apoplectic, as it did in the case of many large landowners, but it did seem most inopportune. In his report of January 10 to the tsar, he dealt critically with the Kutler proposal, prompting the tsar to write in a marginal note that he disapproved of it and in another marginal note that "private property should remain inviolable," underlining the word "should."[30] Soon thereafter he told the premier that he wished that Kutler be replaced, about which more later.

Word about the Kutler proposal had already spread, arousing bitter and vehement opposition among the upper classes. A good example of this opposition was a petition from landowners addressed to the tsar that made the Kutler proposal out to be something like Gracchian land laws, one of many "utopian legislative proposals emanating from Count Witte's office . . . secretly designed to spread revolution." The petition went on to call for the premier's replacement. Witte sent on a copy of the petition together with a heated letter, which prompted Nicholas to write a note to Trepov that said, sarcastically, "The count is angry."[31] So much for the count!

The Kutler proposal even caused waves abroad. When Kokovtsev called on Kaiser William in connection with loan negotiations, the emperor chided him about the Kutler proposal, declaring that it represented pure Marxism and that if it was enacted, it would make it difficult for him to deal with his own socialists.[32]

The furor continued for several weeks while the question of Kutler's successor was being settled. Early February 1906 found Witte being badgered in the State Council about the contentious proposal, probably by the very men who had initiated the petition against him. He let his critics know that he was answerable not to the council, only to the tsar, but he also let them know that two of the generals-adjutant had shown willingness to give up some of their land to the peasants if that would guarantee their title to the remainder.[33]

Actually, the Kutler proposal had been "dead in the water" for some time. General Rauch, who had expressed fear that the tsar might approve, noted in his diary entry for January 3 that he had received a letter from Grand Duke Nicholas Nikolaevich assuring him that he had spoken to the tsar and could therefore say that "nothing of the kind would take place." The grand duke went on to say, "Thank God, with His help Russia and the Tsar will be saved."[34]

All that remained was to replace Kutler, and that took several nerve-wracking weeks. First, the tsar took it upon himself, probably at Trepov's suggestion, to propose that A.V. Krivoshein, who was serving under Kutler, be the replacement. Witte, disturbed by the usurpation of his prerogative and suspecting that Trepov was behind the act, branded the nominee unsuitable, but Nicholas continued to insist on Krivoshein. Witte, for his part, pressed the tsar about the need to find a replacement for Kutler, because the agrarian question was one of the major concerns of the cabinet in preparing legislative proposals for the coming State Duma.[35]

The issue was exacerbated when Timiriazev, using rather liberal language, informed the press that, because of disagreement with some of his colleagues, he wished to leave his post. Witte proposed that Timiriazev be replaced by Filosofov, the state controller. The tsar reacted by noting that he preferred S.V. Rukhlov. On the same day, February 12, Nicholas informed the premier that he was still set on Krivoshein.[36] This set off a storm.

It was no storm in a teacup, for what was at issue was the prerogative of the premier to nominate ministers and to work with a cabinet that he could, with some license, call cohesive. Witte wrote that he thought of asking to be relieved of his duties but that at a quickly summoned cabinet meeting he was dissuaded from doing so. Moreover, his colleagues supported his decision to send a report to the tsar stating his position on maintaining a unified cabinet, something that would not be possible with Krivoshein and Rukhlov as members.[37]

The tsar gave in, asking for a list of candidates for the two positions. Witte complied. Nicholas returned the list, asking the premier to talk to the men whose names he had underlined. Witte did as asked, meeting only with rebuffs, which he duly reported.[38] In the end, the tsar accepted Witte's new nominees, A.P. Nikolskii to replace Kutler and M.M. Fedorov, to replace Timiriazev, both of whom had worked under Witte. It was a victory for the premier, but of the Pyrrhic variety, which could only deepen the tsar's distaste for the man.

Kutler's fall did not bring an end to work on the peasant question. If anything, the work became more intense, in consonance with Witte's sense that the question was the most urgent one facing Russia. He hoped to produce some legislation on the subject before the opening of the State Duma, but that turned out to be unfeasible. However, he and his cabinet were able to produce comprehensive proposals to be laid before the new legislature, proposals that reflected his long-held views on what needed to be done.

Witte viewed the peasant question as the product of long-term historical forces as well as more recent ones, such as the manner in which serf emancipation had taken place and the reactionary measures taken in response to the assassination of Alexander II. The net result, as he saw it, was to deprive the peasant not only of initiative but also of human dignity. The tide of history, he argued, was running against communal forms and in favor of individualism.

What he sought was to give peasants the right to transform their holdings into separate and consolidated farms, prospering if they were diligent and efficient or suffering the consequences if they were not. It would be what Stolypin would later call "a wager on the strong and the sober." The benefits that Witte foresaw were a more productive peasantry, one that was contented and therefore conservative, one that would enrich the economy as well as provide a more substantial tax base, thus helping provide for the needs of a great power.

It was in this spirit that the set of bold proposals referred to was prepared for submission to the State Duma. Chief among these were proposals for permitting peasants to gain title to the strips of land they cultivated by traditional right but that they had not been permitted to sell, as well as to consolidate their holdings into farmsteads. What this meant was the ultimate demise of the village commune, something the tsar had refused to contemplate. But the times were changing, and the reverence in which that institution had been held was declining in the upper classes. Had Witte remained in office, he could have claimed credit when these proposals were turned into law, but the credit would fall to another premier, Stolypin.[39] Time was running out for Witte, but he had set the agenda for turning Russia into a constitutional monarchy.

Chapter 21

The Last Lap

On the day of the signing of the October Manifesto, Witte had told Vuich that if the government could "hold out until the convening of the State Duma all would be saved, but that if it turned out that it was impossible to hold elections he could guarantee nothing." Fortunately, the worst had not come to pass. In February the complex and extended electoral process began, with the date for convocation of the State Duma and State Council set for April 27. Witte hoped that the two bodies would cooperate with the government in addressing the country's needs and that the very existence of the State Duma would serve as assurance of the government's good intentions.

Over Durnovo's objections, the premier committed the government to refrain from seeking to influence the outcome of the elections, again as a sign of sincere intention to live up to the October Manifesto. The machinery for holding elections was set up efficiently and with reasonable speed. Witte provided firm backing for the policy of noninterference.

However, he showed little interest in the results of the elections as they began trickling in.[1] Why is not clear. It may be that, because of the complexities of the electoral process and because the vast majority of the mostly illiterate electorate was not affiliated with any of the fledgling parties, it would be a long time before a picture of the State Duma's composition would emerge. More often than not, it was not until the last stage of the electoral process that it became clear who would be elected deputy because it was necessary to form blocs of electors to secure the needed majority. Another factor may have been that the premier was also preoccupied with negotiations for the loan, which has been dealt with earlier. For the most part the election campaign and the elections themselves proceeded peacefully, but here and there socialists, who were boycotting the elections, tried to disrupt the proceedings. The cabinet responded by issuing temporary regulations making it a crime to engage in such tactics.[2]

In the midst of all this, Witte was forced to give much of his attention to revision of the Fundamental Laws, the part of the Code of Laws that dealt with such matters as the powers of the sovereign, succession to the throne, and the imperial family, and which required revision to take into account recent changes in the structure and scope of the government. He began to participate in the process when that workhorse Count Solskii turned a draft of the revised Fundamental Laws over to him for review.[3]

Witte's reaction to the draft was devastating. In his view the revision would reduce the ruler's power to roughly that of the president of France. In a report to the tsar dated March 2, 1906, he declared that the draft contained articles that undermined the power of the monarch and was devoid of certain articles necessary for the preservation of that power.[4] It is obvious from the views he expressed in the course of considering the revision, as well as from views he expressed earlier, that, while recognizing the necessity of having a legislative body such as the State Duma, he was deeply committed to preserving most of the powers traditionally enjoyed by the monarch, powers exercised through his ministers.

In preparing a new draft he picked the brains of several experts and assigned to Baron E.Iu. Nolde, one of his assistants, the task of combing through the constitutions of several conservative monarchies for useful ideas. He was particularly concerned to see how others dealt with the distinction between decrees and laws and how the power of issuing decrees was made the exclusive prerogative of the monarch.[5]

The baron drew heavily on the Japanese and Prussian constitutions in the findings that he submitted to Witte, who, in turn, submitted them to the cabinet together with his own comments. Witte and his cabinet devoted several heated sessions to preparation of a new draft, concentrating on key questions. Should the State Duma participate in revision of the Fundamental Laws? Should the article in the current Fundamental Laws describing the tsar as being an "autocratic and unlimited monarch" be altered? Should the tsar share control over foreign affairs and the military with the State Duma? Should the tsar have the right to dismiss civil servants for misconduct? Should the tsar have the right to remove judges under special circumstances? How to define the position of the Grand Duchy of Finland?

Debate over these issues was lively, as was to be expected, with Witte taking a strong position in favor of maintaining as many of the monarch's prerogatives as possible. At this stage he was especially concerned that an unruly State Duma would further damage the already weakened status of Russia as a great power. The result of the deliberations was a draft considerably more conservative than the Solskii document, one that gave more power to the tsar and showed less concern for the protection of individual rights, as will be seen shortly. On March 19 Witte was ready to hand over to the tsar the cabinet's draft accompanied by Witte's explanation of the rationale behind the draft.[6]

After looking it over and doubtless consulting with Trepov and others at court, the tsar called a special conference to be held at Tsarskoe Selo, with himself presiding. Its task would be to review the Solskii and cabinet drafts and to recommend final wording to the tsar. Invited to attend were Witte and fellow ministers, heads of State Council departments, Grand Duke Michael Aleksandrovich, the tsar's brother, Grand Duke Vladimir Aleksandrovich, an uncle, and Grand Duke Nicholas Nikolaevich, a cousin. Also present, by invitation, was O. Eichelmann, a professor of public law, presumably there for his expertise. He came with his own draft of the Fundamental Laws, which received only cursory attention, and he was given little opportunity by the tsar to speak. Significantly, public men were prominent by their absence for the public was to be kept in the dark.

The first meeting opened at 9 P.M. on April 7 and closed shortly after midnight. The next, on April 9, opened at 9 P.M. and closed at two the next morning. The last two sessions, on April 11 and 12, respectively, met at more civilized times, in the late afternoon and early evening. This schedule left the monarch time to engage in customary activities such as receiving reports, taking walks, reading, and dining with relatives.[7]

The conferees were aware that this was a historic occasion. To be sure, this was not a constituent assembly working with a tabula rasa. The range of choice was limited to the two drafts, but it was a range that permitted significant choices. Witte played an important and vigorous part in the discussions, sometimes being more conservative than the tsar. This was to be his last appearance as premier on the historical stage. At this time he felt that, although the government had the upper hand, the revolutionary threat was still there. Moreover, with disquieting State Duma election results coming in, he was more fearful than ever that it would be a hostile body, from which monarchical power required protection. It was in this spirit that he stated at one session that "it is necessary to reckon with the needs of the state, which are above logic."[8] It was in the same spirit that he replied to the question raised as to why it was necessary to revise the Fundamental Laws except with respect to legislation. Witte said that it was necessary to prevent the State Duma from going too far by including in it those laws on the powers of the tsar with respect to such matters as the armed forces. On the other hand, said the premier, it was not necessary to include the freedoms specified in the October Manifesto because their exclusion posed no danger.[9] In fact, the revised Fundamental Laws included some, but not all, of the civil rights proclaimed in the October Manifesto.

The article that received special attention, because the tsar so willed it, was the fourth article of the cabinet draft, which read: "To the Emperor of All the Russias belongs the supreme autocratic power. Fear as well as duty commanded by God Himself is the basis of obedience to His supreme power." This phrasing omitted the word *unlimited* from the traditional wording of the tsar's power as found in the 1832 edition of the Fundamental Laws. And it was omission of this word that caused Nicholas deep anguish.

On April 9 the tsar, in what was for him an unusually long statement, declared that the article was the most important one under consideration and that he had been agonizing over it for a month. He was convinced that only a fifth of his subjects—"the so-called educated element, the proletariat, the third estate"—would raise any objections to retention of the word *unlimited*, while the rest of his people would be solidly behind his decision. Two of the grand dukes argued that the October Manifesto had made "unlimited" redundant. Witte went further, insisting that the word had become redundant a century earlier, as a result of Alexander I's reforms. No decision was reached during this session. (Apparently, the word *autocratic* was considered no more than a formalism at this point.)[10]

It was at the end of the last session of the conference that Count Solskii asked Nicholas what his decision about omission of the word *unlimited* was. The tsar gave his agreement. When asked who should do the final editing of the Fundamental Laws, he named Solskii, Frisch, Pahlen, Witte, and Akimov.[11]

The document reflected Witte's commitment to protect the powers of the monarch. Only the tsar could initiate revision of the Fundamental Laws. No bill could become law without his approval. He could issue decrees without consulting the legislative bodies. He had the sole authority to apply the exceptional laws. The conduct of foreign affairs was his and his alone. He was in sole command of the armed forces. He could issue emergency legislation when the legislative bodies were not in session. These were but a few of his exclusive powers, which were usually exercised by his ministers in his name and with his approval.

Of course, he was still bound by the limits he had accepted in the October Manifesto. Did the revised Fundamental Laws amount to a constitution? The tsar did not think so. Witte professed at the time not to think so, although once out of office he wrote: "In essence they constitute a constitution, a constitution that is conservative—without parliamentarianism, one that preserves many of the prerogatives of the Emperor."[12] And the *Almanch de Gotha*, that who's who and what's what of royal and noble houses, agreed that Russia had become a constitutional monarchy, despite objections from St. Petersburg.

Witte was insistent that the Fundamental Laws be published before the State Duma convened in order to present it with a fait accompli that could not be changed without the tsar's consent. With this document in place and the foreign loan also a fait accompli, he felt confident that the government could proceed with the knowledge that it could not be hamstrung by a contentious State Duma. Meanwhile, before the opening of that body he would continue with the preparation of a program of legislative proposals for its consideration.

That effort had begun on January 24, when Witte asked the various ministries and the Chief Administration for Land Administration and Agriculture to prepare proposals. Apparently, the ministries of foreign affairs, navy, and the imperial court were freed of this obligation, for obvious reasons. Some proposals came in quickly, others trickled in, the last on April 22. Individually and in their sum they amounted to a substantial body of material to be used for moderate reform if the State Duma chose to work with the government.

The proposals for agrarian reform have already been dealt with: they constituted the major part of the proposals and were the most ambitious ones. Other proposals included institution of an income tax to replace several existing taxes, some changes in the judicial system, new regulations to make trade associations more effective, and new regulations for stock exchanges. The minister of trade and industry did not have any immediate proposals that dealt specifically with the welfare of the workers, but he promised that he would submit to the State Duma proposals for government health and disability insurance for industrial workers and miners as well proposals dealing with workers' housing and working hours for minors, women, and adult men. The cabinet had also approved a proposal from the Ministry of Education for the introduction of universal and compulsory primary schooling.[13]

The proposals, except for those dealing with the peasantry, were modest ones, not calculated to satisfy the left. On April 23 Witte submitted the set of proposals to the tsar, nine days after he had asked to be relieved of his duties, a request that was granted the following day, April 15. Given the fact that he was preparing a program for the State Duma, which was scheduled to open shortly, his request is surprising. Why did he act as he did?

In his letter to the tsar he gave several reasons for not being able to continue in office. He wrote, first of all: "I am worn out from all the badgering from all sides that I have experienced and have become so nervous that I cannot maintain the equilibrium required of a premier, particularly under new circumstances." The other reasons given derived largely from the "badgering." He cited the conflicts within his cabinet between liberals and conservatives, with particular emphasis on the difficulties created for him by Durnovo. Also, he mentioned his differences with Goremykin. He added:

"During my tenure I have been attacked by all those in Russian society who can scream and write, as well as by the extreme elements that have access to Your Imperial Majesty." He argued he wished to leave at a time when conditions were such that the government could turn its attention to normal development and that he had contributed to that state by concluding the huge international loan that would enable the government to deal with the State Duma from a position of strength. He felt, moreover, that the government would have to decide whether to "come to terms with it [the State Duma] or else follow a very firm and decisive policy toward it, being ready to use the most extreme measures." In either case, he stated, he would be a liability.[14]

Undoubtedly, health was a major factor in Witte's decision. He had been driving himself beyond endurance for months while feeling increasingly isolated, especially from the monarch. The tsar's readiness to say farewell to Witte once the loan was in hand (which was set for April 16) was buttressed by pressure from Trepov and Grand Duke Nicholas Nikolaevich to rid himself of the man.[15] Reportedly, the tsar was consulting with Durnovo and Goremykin on the same subject.[16] Given his sources, Witte surely had some sense that his days were numbered and likely felt that it was better to walk out than be pushed out. And it is easy to imagine that his wife, who had sought to keep him out of rough waters, was now urging him to get out while he could do so with dignity.

Clearly, Witte's decision to leave was also strongly influenced by the disappointing results of the elections to the State Duma, which showed that if he remained he would be facing a hostile body. Over 60 percent of the deputies would be in opposition to the government, with Kadets constituting the largest bloc. There was a large contingent of nonparty peasant deputies, the kind that Witte once expected to support the regime, but now he was uncertain. To make matters worse, the tsar, in his letter accepting Witte's request, placed much of the blame for the election results on the government's failure to influence the elections.[17]

The premier continued working until a successor was ready to take over. That man turned out to be Goremykin, conservative, ambitious but indolent, aged beyond his years, one with whom the tsar was comfortable but not the man to deal with difficult times. On April 17 the tsar asked Goremykin to assume office and form a new cabinet, but it was not until the twenty-second that an official announcement of the appointment of a new premier would be made.

In his last days in office Witte worked on the program of legislative proposals to be put before the State Duma. On the twentieth he was received by the tsar. As Witte tells it, after some talk about appointing Witte to the next available ambassadorial post, "the Emperor went on to tell me that he had decided to appoint one of my enemies as my successor, but that I was not to think that he was appointing the man because he was my enemy." When he learned who the man was, Witte wrote, he asked, "What kind of enemy is he?"[18] True, the premier considered Goremykin to be an enemy, and for good reason, but he had not lost his contempt for the man.

The following day he met with his cabinet, informing them that this was their last meeting and that it would be devoted to conversation, not business. He later had them to a dinner at his home, to which he had returned.[19]

On the twenty-second came the official announcement, in the form of a rescript, of Witte's departure. It was couched in mellifluent and friendly terms, ending with:

> In granting your most humble request, I feel obliged to express my sincere recognition of the many services you have rendered the fatherland, in recognition of which I appoint you knight of the order of Saint Alexander Nevskii with diamonds. I remain inalterably well disposed toward you and sincerely grateful.[20]

This was, of course, for public consumption. Nicholas had come to loathe the man, as indicated by his reluctance to appoint him to the State Council, which was the custom in dealing with outgoing ministers, but Count Solskii succeeded in persuading the tsar to adhere to custom.[21]

As the date for the opening of the State Duma and the reformed State Council approached, Witte became increasingly apprehensive that the Fundamental Laws would not be published in time. The delay, as it was later learned, was caused by Trepov, a man of erratic judgment, who was fiercely devoted to the tsar and who had decided to have the document "vetted" by an eminent liberal jurist.[22] On April 22, back in his home by now, Witte telephoned Trepov, imploring him to convince the sovereign that immediate publication was imperative. Two days later it was published. It is moot whether Witte's claim that he deserves the credit for the speedy action is true or not.[23]

On the twenty-seventh he attended the resplendent ceremonial opening at the Winter Palace of the State Duma and the State Council. The unhappy tsar, flanked by his mother, who was almost in tears, and his red-faced wife, with duma deputies standing to the left and council members to the right, delivered a short, colorless welcoming speech. Once the proceedings were over, the tsar and his party left for Peterhof, while the members of the two legislative bodies departed for their respective venues, the Tauride Palace for the State Duma and the Marie Palace for the State Council.[24] Russia's first legislature was now in session.

Witte attended several sessions of the State Council, then, with his wife, left for an extended vacation in western Europe. His departure from office was sensational news both at home and abroad. Some rejoiced at the news. Few, if any, wept. After all, he had come in like a lion and was going out, if not like a lamb, then at least like a wounded creature, his reputation frayed although not in tatters. Assessment of his tenure will be dealt with at the end of this work. His stature as a political figure was still very high, and there were expectations that it would not be long before he would return to Russian political life in a major role. The ex-premier, although anxious for a rest, did not think his career was at an end. For the time being he seemed to look forward to an ambassadorship, preferably in Paris, but it is hard to believe that he did not think of returning to a powerful post in the future.

Chapter 22

Exile? Assassination?
May 1906–June 1907

This was Witte's second fall from power. He could have chosen to be done with Nicholas and turned to the private sector, where there many opportunities waiting for someone with the experience and reputation that he had in financial matters and railroading. That would have required that he leave the political stage, but he would not. As long as he lived he would find his identity in being prominently involved in government service. He was still state councilor, one of the tsar's state secretaries, chairman of the Finance Committee, and actual privy councilor. None of these titles conferred real power, but they conferred prestige, as did his title of count. His hopes for the near future were, as noted, set on an ambassadorship, preferably to Paris, which would be a high honor as well as an opportunity to influence foreign policy and at the same time provide a respite from the pressures he had been enduring.

For the moment his plans were focused on visiting his daughter and her family and on taking the cure in French spas. Vera was married to C.V. Naryshkin, who was serving in the Russian legation in Brussels. It was there that he was able to see Lev, his infant grandson, upon whom he doted. The remainder of his stay abroad was complicated by the death of Vera's father-in-law and by his wife's illness and his own, which required a stay in Bad Homburg, and a letter from St. Petersburg from Baron Freedericksz, whom Witte considered rather dim, informing him that the tsar thought that, given the disturbed situation in Russia, Witte's "return to Russia at the present time would be most undesirable."

Witte was outraged and replied by asking that he be relieved of all governmental duties. He had second thoughts about the wisdom of his reply when he learned that the State Duma had been dissolved after a tempestuous session. So he wired the director of the St. Petersburg Post Office to return the letter. A few weeks, after the dust seemed to be settling back home, he sent a lengthy self-serving letter to Baron Freedericksz. In it he patted himself on the back, damned Goremykin, expressed conditional confidence in the new premier, P.A. Stolypin, and went on at length about the government-sanctioned verbal abuse he was receiving from the right wing, finally getting to the point about his abandoning government service. He left to the tsar the decision whether to have Witte return to private life and be free to act the gadfly or to agree to having him remain in government service and be an unpleasant but powerless presence.[1] This put the tsar in a nasty predicament.

After several weeks had passed without a response, Witte wrote once more to the baron, asking for a reply. Freedericksz complied, informing Witte that the he had conveyed the gist of the letter to the tsar, who had said that at this time he saw no hindrance to the ex-premier's return. The baron added: "I am particularly pleased to inform you that when you return you will be well received by the Emperor and that he is unequivocally in favor of your remaining in government service."[2]

This was, needless to say, pro forma. The last thing the tsar wished for was to have Witte return, much less to receive him. The extent to which his feelings were tied to a belief in the Jewish-Masonic conspiracy myth has already been alluded to. Had this been a century earlier, he had might have done as Alexander I had done to Count Speranskii, with whom Witte was often compared, and exiled his ex-premier to some city in the provinces. Had Witte accepted the suggestion of prolonging his stay abroad, it would have provided the tsar some comfort, but, given the man's reaction, the tsar had no choice but to bite the bullet and pretend that Witte was welcome to return.

Return he did, in time for the new session of the State Council. The tsar shared his feelings about the event in a letter to his mother, who was abroad:

> To my great regret Count Witte has returned from abroad. It would have more sensible of him and convenient for me if he had stayed away. As soon as he was back a peculiar atmosphere full of all sorts of rumors and gossip and insinuations began to form around him. Some of the wretched papers are already beginning to say he is coming back to power, and that only he can save the country. Evidently the Jewish clique is starting to sow sedition again, trying to undo all the good which my own and Stolypin's efforts for peace have been able to achieve. As long as I live, I will never trust that man again with the smallest thing. I had quite enough of last year's experiment. It is still like a nightmare to me.
>
> Thank God I have not seen him yet![3]

Nicholas was as good as his word and would never soften his distaste for his ex-premier.[4]

Once home, Witte began to attend sessions of the State Council, closely follow political developments, maintain social contacts, and work on documenting his career. First, a few words about Witte and the State Council. The reconstituted body consisted of ninety-eight members appointed by the tsar and ninety-eight elected by such groups as the zemstvos, industrial and commercial associations, the clergy, the universities and learned societies, and the nobility. It was intended to be a conservative body that would serve as a check on the State Duma. The appointed members were, for the most part, men with considerable experience in government service, providing much-needed expertise. Because there were more than ninety-eight persons who bore the title of state councilor, some had to be excluded from service in the State Council. This led to the annual rite of the issuance of a list of "active" state councilors, confirmed by the tsar, of those who would participate in the work of the State Council in the coming year. This permitted the chairman of the body and the tsar to exclude men they considered troublesome. Witte was keenly aware that he might be excluded, but that did not come to pass, permitting him to participate in that body's deliberations, but only as a tolerated has-been. When the possibility arose that he might be invited to join one of the many factions in the council, word was received that an invitation "would be received unfavorably in higher places."[5] Witte did not become a member.

He was still a very important personage whose comings and goings were the subject of much public interest, even to the point of his travels being noted in the London *Times* court circular, but in the State Council he was a cipher.[6] He took the floor on subjects about which he had expertise or about which he had strong feelings. He spoke often about financial matters, not forgetting to criticize Kokovtsev, now minister of finance. He tended to speak at length and often rambled; he was given to irony, also to quoting from Dante, Schiller, and Shakespeare. When he rose to speak, adherents of the extreme right would walk out, but those remaining would listen attentively without necessarily agreeing. When the impatient chairman would cut him off, he would angrily reply, "Yes sir."[7] His influence in the State Council was slight, in sharp contrast to the days when he had held high office. As a colleague wrote, Witte was like a Gulliver tied down by the Lilliputians.[8] Or, as one obituary would later put it, he was like a "war horse" put out to pasture.[9] So there he was, on the sidelines, down but far from out, in his own opinion or in the opinion of friends and foes.

The fact that he was a count conferred some benefit in polite society. He had been troubled by the fact that his wife, to whom he was greatly devoted, had been something of a social outcast. Above all, he had been troubled that she was not received at court. Once he received his title, many doors hitherto closed were now open to him and his wife. During his tenure as premier their social life had been necessarily restricted, but the story changed once he was out of office. We find them attending lunch at the home of Grand Duke

Vladimir Aleksandrovich and hosting a lunch attended by such guests as Bompard, the French ambassador, H. Leroy-Beaulieu, a French expert on Russia and director of the École des Sciences Politiques in Paris, and our old friend Joseph Dillon.[10]

Needless to say, a broadened social life would hardly fill the void left in Witte's life by his fall from power. Enervated though he was, attendance at the sessions of the State Council and the infrequent meetings of the Finance Committee were not much of a challenge to a man as hardworking and addicted to power as he was. But there was a challenge he could respond to, and that was all the rumors and charges circulating in the press, at court, and in society about his role in the momentous events of the past few years, specifically his role in the events leading to the war with Japan, in negotiating the peace, and in the proclamation of the October Manifesto. Also, there was the question of how he had performed as premier. There were, of course, those who supported the Jewish-Masonic myth. One of these was Baron von der Launitz, prefect of St. Petersburg, who supplied the city's prison libraries with copies of a Union of the Russian People pamphlet blaming Witte for all of Russia's woes.[11] Others, who did not go that far, were certain that he bore some responsibility for the outbreak of war, that Russia could have won the war, that the peace was a betrayal of Russian interests, that he had forced the October Manifesto on the tsar, and that he had not served his country well as premier.

A passionate collector of documents about his work and much given to having records of his work compiled, Witte kept pertinent materials cached away both at home and abroad. As long as he was in government service he could not publish under his own name, but he could and did find willing and sympathetic publicists to whom he would provide information for use in articles and books favorable to his view of events. Now he began preparing material for posthumous publication, and he would continue to keep his eye open for an ambassadorial vacancy that he could fill. While Witte, on rare occasion, admitted privately that he had been in error, he did not do so publicly. He was, as we know, an arrogant man who, whatever his inner thoughts, was like a tiger whenever his policies were in question. He reminds one of Marshal Lyautey, who when asked if he had ever been in error replied, after some reflection, that he could remember only one occasion when he doubted himself. Witte would spend much of his remaining years defending his record and, when he deemed it necessary, attacking his critics.

Very high on the list of topics concerning which he was anxious "to set the record straight" was the history of the October Manifesto. There were many at court who, as has already been mentioned, believed that Witte was working with Jewry to establish a republic with himself as president, and sought to persuade the tsar that such was the case. Once the October Manifesto was issued, a detail was added to this myth, that Witte had foisted the document on the tsar as part of his scheme to attain power.[12]

Not long after Witte left office he asked two men in a position to know the facts to prepare accounts of the events. They were N.I. Vuich and Prince N.D. Obolenskii, who between them could supply eyewitness evidence of what had occurred, to be used as ammunition for getting acknowledgment in the right places that he had behaved as a loyal subject. Ostensibly, these documents were for his files as a form of insurance for his reputation. In fact, he was planning to have the documents published posthumously.

By early January 1907 he had in hand the accounts of Vuich and Obolenskii, to which he appended his own version of the events leading to the October Manifesto. He then sent the papers to Baron Freedericksz, asking the baron to note any errors and to return the documents, which he wanted for his own files.[13] As Witte tells it, he suggested that the tsar not be "disturbed" by being shown the documents. The assertion is patently disingenuous. Witte writes that he was told that the baron found the account accurate, then turned it over to the tsar, who held on to it for two weeks before returning it to the baron, saying: "The memorandum prepared by Count Witte is correct, but do not tell him so in writing."[14] This left Witte fuming, but he had achieved something: oral confirmation that the tsar agreed with his version of events. In addition, he had obtained oral or written confirmation from several highly placed persons privy to the history of the manifesto. In the process he had acted the gadfly, a role he would continue to play for the rest of his life. Such behavior would earn him no good marks from the tsar, but it would satisfy his own sense of honor.

Equally important in "setting the record straight" was recording and, if possible, publicizing his version of the origins of the war with Japan, a war that, in his opinion, had brought on the revolution. In so doing, his aim was to fix responsibility on the tsar, Bezobrazov, Plehve, and to some extent Kuropatkin, at the same time absolving himself of any responsibility. It was a task that would take much of his attention and energy. Witte began his efforts to protect his role in Far Eastern affairs even while he was minister of finance.[15]

Once the war broke out, debate about responsibility flared up, with some putting the blame on Bezobrazov, others on Witte, who, restrained by his position, could not speak out publicly and had to rely on surrogates. There was, for example, A. Polly, a German journalist stationed in St. Petersburg, who in 1906 published a book about the war and the revolution, basing it on material supplied by Witte. Then there was I.I. Kolyshko, one of Witte's "hired pens," who entered the newspaper fray in support of the Witte position.

Also helping the Witte interpretation was the newspaper publisher Prince E.E. Ukhtomskii, who had worked with Witte on Far Eastern matters. The most active of all in proclaiming the Witte interpretation was N.A. Gurev, a publicist who had served in the Ministry of Finance under Witte.[16] Before more is said about Gurev, it is worthwhile to deal with Witte's efforts to gag Bezobrazov.

Shortly after the outbreak of war Bezobrazov prepared a booklet of documents concerning the outbreak of the war with Japan with the intention of publishing it under official auspices. It was intended to be like publications put out by other governments at war to bolster their versions of the road to war. Bezobrazov's booklet was already off the press when Witte learned about it and informed the foreign minister, Lamsdorff, who promptly had the booklets confiscated on the ground that publication had not been authorized. After he became premier, Witte learned that Bezobrazov was about to have his version of the causes of the war published. The premier had no trouble preventing publication of this work, which was not to see the light of day until long after Witte's death.[17]

Now, back to Gurev. During the course of the war he published several articles, using material supplied by Witte, in which he espoused the Witte interpretation of the origins of the conflict. After becoming premier, Witte established a new government newspaper, of which Gurev was appointed acting editor.[18] Soon Gurev found himself acting in an additional capacity.

After returning to Russia in the fall of 1906, Witte undertook to prepare his own version of the origins of the war, for posthumous publication. To this end he recruited several former associates in the Ministry of Finance, Gurev among them, to develop the account, working from material supplied by Witte. In April 1907, the work was completed, a lengthy typewritten diplomatic history in which Witte appears, prominently, in the third person. Not unexpectedly, it supports Witte's view of how Russia and Japan came to blows and ends with the breakdown of negotiations between the two in 1903. That it was not the kind of document that he would wish to fall into the tsar's hands can be judged from the last paragraphs, in which he writes that the tsar, in reply to a warning from the kaiser that "the Japanese were energetically preparing for war," replied that "there would be no war because he did not want to fight."[19]

While work on this project was under way, an effort to assassinate him was made by agents of the extreme right. The story of this effort and its aftermath is labyrinthine and gory. Witte's efforts to bring the culprits to justice would serve to intensify his alienation from the powers that be.

The story, in brief, begins on the night of January 29, 1907, when Gurev came to Witte's home to look at some documents that Witte did not wish to be taken out of the house. Gurev was at work when the arrival of a doctor to swab Witte's throat necessitated Gurev's transfer to an unused and unheated room. When a servant was about to start up the room's stove, he became alarmed when he noticed in it a package with a long piece of twine attached to it. He informed his master, who, suspecting something sinister, phoned the Okhrana (secret police). Officers arrived and opened the package to find an explosive device and a timer, which had obviously failed to do its job because it was set for 9 P.M. and it was now 11 P.M. The next day a similar device was found in another stove. With this a long and unproductive investigation began.[20]

From the beginning Witte suspected that the Union of the Russian People, which was responsible for the recent killing of M.Ia. Herzenstein, a fiery Kadet deputy to the State Duma, was behind the attempt. Ironically, the right-wing press took it upon itself to assert that Witte had staged the attempt to further his own career. The tsar was inclined to accept this view for a time. Interestingly, Premier Stolypin was informed by the head of the St. Petersburg Okhrana that the Union of the Russian People was the responsible party.[21] But this was not the scent that the investigation would follow, about which more later. Witte did not set aside work on the account of the origins of the war with Japan but could not help but divert his attention to the efforts to find and punish the would-be assassins.

Four months later a second effort to kill him was prepared, this time by a bomb to be thrown into his car on May 30, while he was en route to the State Council. The night before, he was warned that his life would be in danger if he went. As a matter of honor, he chose to go, but he took evasive action that proved to be unnecessary because of a bloody hitch in the conspirators' plans.

What had happened involved A.E. Kazantsev, an Okhrana agent, with connections to the Union of the Russian People, and V. S. Fedorov, a radical worker who had been duped into believing that Kazantsev was working for the revolutionary cause and had received orders to have Witte killed—and not only Witte, but also G.B. Iollos, a Jewish deputy in the State Duma. In the aftermath of the killing of Iollos, in which both Kazantsev and Fedorov had a hand, the latter discovered that he had been duped. Fedorov was so enraged that on May 29 he killed Kazantsev and then fled to France, where he received both asylum and an audience, creating a major furor.

Not long before this failed effort to do away with Witte, a public attempt to defame him appeared in *La Revue*, a Parisian periodical. It was an anonymous memorandum, but its author was soon revealed to be none other than P.K. Schwanebach, longtime foe of the ex-premier. And it was not long before the document was reprinted in the Russian press.[22]

Schwanebach had been supplying Baron von Aerenthal, the Austro-Hungarian ambassador to Russia, with material denigrating Witte. The baron, who shared Schwanebach's feelings, sent on such material to Berlin in the hope that the kaiser would turn against Witte and share his views with the tsar. The memorandum in question, written shortly after the October Manifesto, accused Witte of being responsible for the troubles being borne by Russia. According to Schwanebach, Witte's economic policies had helped create a revolutionary working class, one of the major elements in the revolution. Moreover, he claimed that Witte, thirsty for power, had used the critical circumstances of October to dragoon the tsar into issuing the October Manifesto. He did not accuse the man of "conscious plans to destroy Tsarism" but suggested that he had come to seek "the development of a terrorist army." This was strong stuff. The memorandum saw the light of day thanks to E.N. Schelking, a somewhat shady character, who had left the Russian foreign office under less than honorable circumstances.

On June 3, just as Witte and his wife were preparing to leave the country for their annual holiday, there occurred an event that the opposition referred to as a coup d'état, namely, the dissolution of the Second State Duma and the issuance, as an emergency measure, of a new electoral law that favored Russians over non-Russians and landed nobles over lesser beings. For Witte, this was a heavy blow to the work he had done.

The government's expectation that the Second State Duma would be more cooperative than the first proved unfounded, and no sooner had it opened, in April 1907, than demands from the political right for its dissolution were issued. Premier Stolypin and his colleagues quickly realized that any hope of a cooperative body was misplaced, and they began to work on revision of the electoral law of December 11, 1905, in secret. It was implicit that the revised law would have to be issued without the consent of the State Duma, in contravention of Article 87 of the Fundamental Laws, and that it would have to be done on the occasion of the dissolution of the State Duma on some pretext or other.

It goes without saying that Witte was not invited to participate in the revision, yet he became indirectly involved. Baron Freedericksz not only informed him that the electoral law was being revised but also asked him, unofficially, for advice on coping with current problems. With reference to the electoral law, Witte suggested that the government could follow either of two courses. It could follow the example of Japan and dissolve uncooperative State Dumas ad infinitum until an acceptable one was elected, or it could revise the electoral laws. If the latter course was taken, a "temporary law should be issued empowering representatives of municipal dumas and zemstvos to prepare a new electoral law, which would be submitted to the

State Council." He went on to suggest, "If such a step required a long time the representatives could fulfill the functions of the State Duma on a temporary basis."[23] Witte offered similar, gratuitous advice to Stolypin, who obviously ignored it.[24]

Shortly after the coup, on a farewell call on Suvorin, the publisher, before going abroad, Witte dubbed the new electoral law "a diseased tooth" and spoke bitterly about the tsar, whom he described as immature in his conduct of the affairs of state. Suvorin then reminded Witte that at the time of Nicholas's accession he had predicted that within a decade or so the tsar would develop into "a good ruler." Witte did not deny this but remarked that when he had made this prediction to I.N. Durnovo, then minister of interior, Durnovo said: "You are totally mistaken. This one will turn out to be a weak-willed despot."[25]

During Witte's visit with Suvorin, the publisher showed him a copy of a telegram from Nicholas to Dubrovin that he had refused to publish, mistakenly thinking the document a fake. In it, the tsar thanked the leader of the Union of the Russian People and his fellow members for their enthusiastic expressions of support for the dissolution of the State Duma and the new electoral law. The tsar thanked the members of the organization for their loyalty and devotion "to the throne" and "to holy Russia" and assured them," "The Union of the Russian People will be my reliable support, serving as an example to all of law and order."[26]

It is easy to imagine the impression that this remarkable document made on Witte and his angry and bitter mood when he and his wife left Russia that June, "on holiday," smarting from attacks on his person and name and from the undoing of his work.

Chapter 23

The Stolypin Years,
June 1907–September 1911

The Wittes were under severe stress as they left Russia in June 1907—the attempts on his life, the coup d'état of June 3, the tsar's telegram to Dubrovin. Poor health added to their burden. He had to undergo a throat operation in Frankfurt am Main, and she soon began to experience seizures, which were to be variously diagnosed by eminent doctors as epilepsy, gastrointestinal disorder, or tonsillitis, a reflection of the dubious state of the medical arts at the time. But they did not cut short their travels. Brussels was a major stop, to see family, the ultimate destination being Biarritz, a tiny spa and resort in the south of France, to stay at the Villa Naryshkine, the property of his daughter-in-law, to which they would return year after year.

It was in Frankfurt am Main, without any documentary material on hand, that he began to write his memoirs, continuing to work in five- and ten-minute snatches at the various places they stopped during their stay: Brussels, Cauteret, a spa not far from Biarritz, and Biarritz. Behind the decision to write his memoirs were anger and bitterness. He knew that he could not publish them during his lifetime. That would be the task of his heirs. He began not at the beginning of his life, but at the point where he concluded his account of the origins of the war with Japan, his departure from the office of minister of finance.

By mid-fall, when it was time to go home for the next session of the State Council, Witte had reached the early days of October 1905 in his memoirs. He left what he had written behind in Brussels with his son-in-law for safekeeping, well aware that the secret police might try to lay their hands on the material, in which he had expressed himself acerbically about Nicholas and Alexandra.

A good example is the following passage:

> Alexandra Fedorovna is pretty. She is a good mother and undoubtedly loves her husband and seeks her happiness through him. She might have been a suitable wife for a German prince or for a tsar with backbone. . . . But sad to say, this Tsar has no will, and Alexandra Fedorovna is the only person close to him who exercises a continuing influence on him. It is fatal for the Russian Empire that a person such as this should be adviser to its Autocratic Master, able to affect the fate of tens of millions of human beings.[1]

Nor did he spare others, notably Plehve, who, he believed, was chiefly responsible for his dismissal from the office of minister of finance. In the process of skewering Plehve he attributed to him the widely quoted statement made after the war with Japan had begun: ."we need a little, victorious war to stem the tide of revolution."[2]

As he and his wife returned to Russia in the fall for the new session of the State Council, he was hardly in the best of spirits, given his own position in the world to which he was returning and the unnerving fact that his wife was still subject to seizures for which no satisfactory diagnosis had yet been found.

It made matters worse that he was returning to what may rightly be called the Stolypin era of reaction. Stolypin had entered office with the intention of following a course that would win support from liberal as well as conservative elements, but had soon begun to swing to the right, largely as a result of growing violence on the part of the far left. Stolypin himself was the object of such violence in August 1906, when a bomb destroyed his official residence, sparing him but killing thirty-two and wounding twenty-two, his son and daughter among them. This trauma could not help but accelerate Stolypin's shift to the right.[3]

This shift was bolstered by the election of a new State Duma. Just about the time of the return of Witte and his wife to Russia, the Third State Duma began its meetings, on November 1. This one, thanks to the law of June 3, 1907, and some interference by authorities in the electoral process, produced a body considerably to the right of its predecessors, one that would work with Stolypin, at least for several years. The largest group of deputies belonged to the Union of October 17 and were usually called Octobrists. As their name implied, they were committed to the principles of the October Manifesto and to the development of a constitutional monarchy, but they had lurched somewhat to the right. Witte held a poor opinion of its leader, A.I. Guchkov, of whom he wrote that his initial enthusiasm for liberty changed markedly when he found his "class interests threatened by the masses."[4] The Octobrists could be said to be to the right of center in the State Duma. Much to the right of them were the Nationalists, a bloc of some ninety Russian deputies, mainly wealthy landowners representing areas with large non-Russian populations. They were bitterly hostile to the October Manifesto, bitterly chauvinistic.[5] It goes without saying that they detested Witte. One such deputy, V.M. Purishkevich, one of the founders of the Union of the Russian People, later to be notorious for his part in the assassination of Rasputin, even denounced Countess Witte from the floor of the State Duma.[6]

Supported by a majority in the State Duma, Stolypin was able to carry out his program. Even so, he relied heavily on the use of Article 87 of the Fundamental Laws, which permitted the issuance of legislation to deal with problems that required immediate action at a time when the legislative bodies were not in session. Such legislation required the subsequent approval of the legislative bodies to remain in force.

It was by use of Article 87 that Stolypin could have legislation issued in late 1906 intended to end the village commune and turn the peasantry into owners of farms similar to those in the West. The aim was to make the peasantry productive and economically secure and therefore resistant to sedition while helping the national economy. This and other agrarian legislation are considered the premier's major achievements and were based heavily on the work that Witte and his colleagues had done. They had intended that the peasantry make the necessary changes voluntarily, but, as Witte pointed out bitterly, under Stolypin the peasants were given no choice.

The agrarian legislation represented reform, but much of the premier's efforts, especially after the attempt on his life, undermined the spirit of the October Manifesto. In response to terrorism he adopted egregiously harsh repressive measures such as the establishment of special military courts for revolutionaries that could try, sentence, and execute the accused within a matter of days. These and other actions were in defiance of the October Manifesto. Also, Stolypin failed to complete the work of implementing the promise of civil liberties that Witte had begun but had been unable to finish. As time went by, the ex-premier became disenchanted and hostile toward Stolypin, whom he saw as the wrecker of his work.

This hostility was compounded by what Witte justifiably saw as the government's deliberate foot-dragging in its investigation of those responsible for the attempts on his life, an effort that limped along for three years, with the government pretending to be carrying out a vigorous investigation and Witte carrying on his own investigation as best he could and acting the role of unremitting irritant. In the process his personal relations with Stolypin grew increasingly chilly.

Witte was convinced that the attempts on his life were the work of the Union of the Russian People, aided and abetted by important officials, and that neither Stolypin nor the tsar had any interest in uncovering the facts.[7] Witte was not entirely correct, but he was certainly correct in the belief that there was a cover-up to prevent embarrassing facts from coming to light.[8]

Witte's case was aided by the revelations of Fedorov and by A.I. Prussakov, who after serving as Dubrovin's secretary defected and spilled some beans about the attempts on the life of the ex-premier. But by 1910 the investigators decided that they had reached a dead end and chose to consider the case closed. Not so Witte, who decided to appeal to the premier. He engaged a prominent lawyer to prepare a letter, twenty-three pages long, detailing what Witte had uncovered about the attempts on his life, naming persons involved in these efforts, and calling on Stolypin to put an end to the activities and organizations that engaged in such terroristic efforts. In an implied threat to go public, he pointed out that in his position he could not appeal to public opinion. Before sending the letter, dated May 3, 1910, he showed it to several prominent jurists who served in the State Council. Shortly thereafter he encountered Stolypin, who testily asked the ex-premier whether he considered him an "idiot" or an accomplice in the attempted assassinations, to which Witte replied that he didn't care to answer the question.[9]

In December, after Witte's return from abroad, he received a reply from Stolypin denying the allegations in the May 3 letter. Witte countered with an angry letter that was met with a letter from the premier stating that the cabinet had reviewed the case and found no reason to continue the investigation, a finding with which the tsar concurred.

In his memoirs Witte wrote about the correspondence: "This correspondence gives me the moral right to call Stolypin a great, big political scoundrel." Someone, probably his widow, erased the last word and replaced it with ellipsis points, but there is no question that he had come to consider the premier to be a scoundrel.[10] Witte had no choice but to end his efforts to get the government to act, but, as will be seen, he would make sure that the public would be informed about the case.

For his part, Stolypin considered Witte beyond the pale, as, of course, did the tsar. Yet Witte did not give up hope, counting on the possibility that there might be a turn of events that would force the tsar to turn to him with an important assignment or, at the very least, to fill an ambassadorial post. Such an occasion arose in 1908 with the death, under scandalous circumstances, of N.V. Muravev, the ambassador to Rome. On the basis of the tsar's earlier promise, Witte let his sovereign know of his availability, but this was greeted with silence.[11]

Although we know that Witte's chances of being offered any sort of post by the tsar were nil, such was the power of his name that he was the subject of frequent rumors either of his influence or of the possibility of his return to power. Thus, after the Bosnian crisis of 1908, with the possibility of war with Austria-Hungary looming, it was reported that when Nicholas had been ready to order troop mobilization, Witte had been able to change his mind.[12] Then, in 1911, at a time when Stolypin was encountering political difficulties, rumors were spread that Witte might succeed him, rumors that spurred the right-wing press to express alarm.[13] In the following year it was rumored that both Witte and the foreign minister had been summoned to see the tsar at his hunting lodge, a rumor that turned out to be true only with respect to the foreign minister.[14]

Meanwhile, Witte busied himself with recording his career. However, his resolve to continue writing his memoirs in St. Petersburg on his return in the fall of 1907 weakened under the weight of an oppressive political atmosphere as well as fear that the secret police might try to lay their hands on his memoirs. Thereafter he confined himself to writing his memoirs only while he was abroad and in the proper frame of mind. That was not the case during the 1908 stay, during which worry about his wife's health kept him from writing all but a few pages. Fortunately, surgery to remove a growth above an eye restored her to health, giving him the calm to write during later stays abroad.

But if he could not write while he was at home, there was much else he could do and did, avidly, both to record his career and to protect his reputation. He collected documents, including newspaper clippings, usually having copies made either for his archive at home or for the archive he maintained abroad. And no sooner did he learn that one of his former colleagues was writing his memoirs than he asked to become acquainted with the material.[15] As usual, he provided access to relevant materials to writers willing to support his version of events. Such was the case with B. Demchinskii, whose book on Russia in Manchuria was published in 1908.[16]

Another, more consequential person whom Witte used as a surrogate author was a publicist named Vladimir von Stein, who usually published under the pseudonym of A. Morskoi. In 1911 a sensational pamphlet by Morskoi appeared that accused Theodore Roosevelt of having been far less of an honest broker during the Portsmouth peace negotiations than claimed. The pamphlet caused a few hackles to rise and the suggestion to be made that Witte had inspired the work. That appears to have been the case, but Witte, who could set scruples aside, was quick to dissociate himself from it by asserting publicly that he was not the author of the work in question, begging the question of inspiration.[17] The incident obviously did not prevent von Stein from continuing to prepare pamphlets and books presenting the Witte interpretation of various events while Witte continued to work on his memoirs.

Then, late in 1910, back home, he began an additional undertaking, the dictation of another set of memoirs, this time covering his life from the beginning. Why this new direction? In the absence of information from him one can only surmise. He was in his sixty-second year and not in the best of health. Perhaps he had become or had been made aware of his mortality and had come to feel that it was necessary to leave a record of his whole life.

The decision to dictate and to do so while in St. Petersburg was apparently based on the belief that the stenographer, probably N.S. Pomorin, his secretary, was trustworthy and that the typescript could be protected from the secret police while he was in the capital. And it was not only the secret police he had to worry about. There was also the Union of the Russian People, which, in addition to having sought his life, had sought to get at his papers. When the time came to go abroad he would take what had been typed and store it in a safe place away from Russia.[18]

Although he had his personal archive at hand, Witte chose to dictate largely from memory, apparently because he felt a sense of urgency. He noted that this set of memoirs "makes no claim to being systematic, nor to complete accuracy, but that it is justified to claim that . . . all that is told is unquestionable truth and that the circumstances are presented here impartially and honestly."[19] He dictated at a steady and speedy clip, between twenty and thirty pages a day. In the process he showed far greater restraint in dealing with Nicholas and his family than in his handwritten memoirs, presumably as a hedge against the remote possibility that the tsar would be able to see the typescript while Witte was still alive.

In the meantime, the anti-Witte campaign of the far right continued unabated. Typical was the publication in 1908 of a thirty-five-page pamphlet dealing with a case involving a certain K.A. Durante, who claimed that he had been swindled out of his estate by a member of the Rafalovich family, who had been aided by Witte, a friend of the family. Although the case went back to the days of Alexander III, it was still being kept alive through the efforts of Durante, who had become a member of the Union of the Russian People. The thesis of the pamphlet, which was based on material that had appeared in several far right organs, was that the swindle was the work of a Jew (the Rafaloviches were converts to the Russian Orthodox faith, but in the eyes of the far right they remained Jews), aided by other Jews and, most important, by Witte.[20] Witte wrote that he had taken to carrying a revolver when he left the house because Durante had threatened to shoot him on sight, but the two never had occasion to meet.[21]

On the political front, Stolypin's position in the State Duma began to weaken by the end of 1909 when the Octobrists, aided by the Kadets, started opposing the premier on budgetary matters. He, in turn, began to rely on the Nationalist bloc and right-wing Octobrists to build a majority. Soon he would be in conflict with the State Council as well.

Witte did not feel that he could influence the course of events. He admitted as much in a speech in the State Council when he said he was not so "naive" as to believe that he could sway many of its members.[22] More important, he did not believe that the tide of history could be changed.

Typical of his thinking was his response to I.I. Tolstoi, who had served him as minister of education, a man deeply disturbed by the current spirit of reaction, particularly as reflected in the official attitude toward non-Russians. He wanted Witte to join with other men of goodwill in "the battle with evil." To this plea Witte replied with the lame excuse that history showed that the current reaction was "a natural response" to the turmoil that had swept Russia from 1904 to 1906, that reaction had not yet reached its apogee, and that there was nothing that could be done to change its course, which would inevitably lead to "a liberationist upsurge."

Witte insisted that the revolution of 1905 revealed the low level of political maturity and cultural development that prevailed. He blamed the moderate left for failing to understand its duty to support the government's effort at reform, and he was harsh toward the non-Russian leaders, particularly the Jewish ones, for demanding "full rights" for themselves even before Russians had received such rights.[23] What he did not say, but we know he thought, was that the tsar bore much of the responsibility for the dire events of 1904 to 1906.

Willy-nilly, Witte accepted the role of a bystander, expressing his anger in private, be it in conversation or in his memoirs. He did not use the State Council as a forum for denouncing Stolypin. Had he tried, he would have been cut off by the chairman. When he spoke, it was usually to make a point about the meaning of a relevant article in the Fundamental Laws or to twitch a tail or two.

Thus, during the course of a debate in the State Council in March 1909 concerning a bill dealing with the Naval General Staff, he not only spoke up on the relevant article in the Fundamental Laws but also used the occasion to remark that the army, which was trying to recover from its defeat at the hands of Japan, should be renamed "the army of happenstance and dilettantism."[24] Two years later, in March 1911, in the course of a furious debate concerning a bill to extend elective zemstvos to six western provinces, Witte remarked that the Russian landed nobles in the region mistakenly believed their peasants to be backward when, in fact, the landowners knew less about agriculture than their peasants. He characterized the Russian landowners, as distinguished from the Polish landowners in that region, as being absentee owners who should be dubbed "the Russian landowners' road company."[25]

This bill had passed in the State Duma but met fierce opposition in the State Council for a variety of reasons. Witte, who had successfully argued against extension of elective zemstvos to the western provinces while the minister of finance, found himself on the same side as P.N. Durnovo, his erstwhile bête noire and one of the chief leaders of the opposition. The defeat of the bill produced a ministerial crisis. Stolypin, who had been able to count on a majority in the State Council, was beside himself and asked the tsar to release him from his duties, but relented when Nicholas agreed to prorogue both legislative chambers and to enact the bill through the use of Article 87.

Although many thought that the tsar, who deeply resented having his hand forced, would soon find a successor to the premier, Witte thought otherwise.

On April 27, Count I.I. Tolstoi noted in his diary that Witte had called on him, that "Witte cursed Stolypin, referred to him as an insolent fool who had completely compromised himself, that only the devil knew where he was leading Russia and that Russia would be rid of him only by a chance event such as an automobile accident or a sudden illness."[26]

Among those who believed that the tsar would part with Stolypin was the notorious Rasputin, who claimed to have considerable influence with Nicholas and Alexandra. In July, while in Biarritz, Witte received a letter, through "secure" channels, from an unsavory character named George P. Sazonov, who was very close to Rasputin, suggesting that Witte would be a good choice to replace Stolypin.[27] Witte replied, through the same channels, with a withering letter. We will hear more about Rasputin subsequently. In any event, the need for a replacement for the premier arose in September 1911, thanks to the ineptitude of the secret police, which permitted a double agent named Bogrov to assassinate Stolypin.

Chapter 24

Last Years, 1911–1915

Witte felt less hostile toward Kokovtsev, Stolypin's successor as premier, than he had toward the late premier. He expected the new premier to follow much the same line as Stolypin but with a lighter touch. Witte did not hold a high opinion of Kokovtsev's abilities and, as we know, had treated him shabbily, but the two were on superficially proper terms. Moreover, Witte felt that he had aided Kokovtsev's career earlier on and was not above asking for a favor.[1]

The request came in April 1912. A month earlier Witte had reached 1912 in his dictated memoirs and had decided to call a temporary halt to this phase of his work; on March 2, in St. Petersburg, he dictated the following: "Thus I have reached 1912 in my stenographic memoirs. For the time being, I am discontinuing this work."[2] With time on his hands, he complained about being underemployed. When the chance of a well-paying post as adviser to a bank arose, he accepted it provisionally because by law he could not take on outside employment while remaining in government service. Leaving government service was unacceptable; forgoing the income and challenge of the position offered was distasteful. A bank officer asked Kokovtsev, who had retained the finance portfolio, for a waiver of the legal prohibition but was rebuffed. Waiver denied, Witte decided to opt for government largesse, but chose, so it seems, not to face Kokovtsev and instead let his wife take on the task. This she did, on April 11. There followed a drawn-out period of give-and-take, in the course of which Witte wrote a whining letter to the tsar, complaining of the difficulty of maintaining his standard of living. In the end, the tsar, obviously still anxious to keep Witte on a tether in government service, made him a grant of 200,000 rubles.[3]

It was at this time that Witte learned that the tsar might soon be looking for a new ambassador to Rome, which could entail some shuffling of envoys, and took the news as an occasion to remind Nicholas of his availability. This he did in a letter in which he said that he would be glad to serve anywhere but China or Japan and added some unsolicited advice that Russia would be better served than she had been by having ambassadors with some knowledge of how to influence public opinion. He added coyly that although he did not know English he would be able to create a favorable climate in the United States for loans to Russia. The letter went unanswered.[4]

Thus he remained underemployed and dissatisfied. All he could do was to continue work on his memoirs while abroad, collecting documents about his career, helping to get good press and engaging in polemics when he felt it necessary.

On July 20, 1911, in a letter to Herman Bernstein, the journalist referred to earlier, Witte wrote:

> I am writing my memoirs, but I am writing very lazily. My memoirs cannot be published so soon. Under no circumstances can they be published before my death. But if we meet next year in St. Petersburg I can let you have some very important documents.[5]

Apparently Witte was referring to a query in Bernstein's letter, which is not extant, about publication. Reportedly, the American banker Jacob Schiff had offered Witte a million dollars for publishing rights for the memoirs but was rebuffed. That report cannot be verified, but it is the case that in 1919 Countess Witte would travel to New York to call on Schiff, who would help her find a publisher.[6]

Witte was adamant that his memoirs be published posthumously, and his wish would be respected. On October 12, 1912, while in Biarritz, evidently feeling that he was not likely to resume work on either the manuscript or typescript, he added a note to the manuscript instructing his heirs to publish these works after his death, but without some "references to living persons."[7] Joseph Dillon, whose contacts with Witte were frequent, advised him to edit his memoirs so that they would be ready for publication, but to no avail.[8]

While shielding the memoirs from the world, he made no secret about their existence, as his letter to Bernstein indicates. Apparently, this was done out of a need for self-promotion as well as a desire to tantalize the tsar, who was sure to get wind of what his former premier was up to. It was in Nicholas's interest to prevent publication of what was certain to be a damning work by keeping Witte in government service and, when the opportunity presented itself, to get his hands on it.

Although Witte stopped work on the memoirs, he was busier than ever in his defense of his record, usually from behind the scenes and, when it seemed unavoidable, in public polemic. He seemed like a man possessed, abnormally sensitive to any question raised about his role during the preceding troubled years, and this was a time when the debate of who was responsible for what raged with fiery intensity. In many ways he was behaving like another man of outsize ego and outsize ability in forced retirement, Bismarck, unwilling or unable to accept what could not be changed, hardening rather than mellowing.

Witte continued supplying von Stein with material supporting the Witte version of recent events, be it the Zubatov episode or the St. Petersburg Soviet. Also, he continued to use the services of I.I. Kolyshko, one of what were called his "hired pens," to write newspaper articles favorable to the ex-premier. In these last years he came to rely more and more on a new ally, B.B. Glinskii, editor of *Istoricheskii vestnik*, a popular historical journal.[9]

Witte provided Glinskii with considerable material for articles on various events as well as material for a biography. In addition, Witte abandoned his decision not to have his work on the origins of the Russo-Japanese War published during his lifetime. He permitted Glinskii to publish a slightly edited version of the work in *Istoricheskii vestnik* during 1914, but without attribution. Two years later, after Witte's death, the work would appear in book form, with Witte acknowledged as the source of the information in it.[10] Shortly after Witte's death Glinskii's biography of the ex-premier appeared in *Istoricheskii vestnik* in serial form.[11]

As if this were not enough, Witte arranged for the publication of new editions of earlier writings. Thus, in 1912 there appeared a second edition of the synopses of lectures on economics and government finance he had read to Grand Duke Michael Aleksandrovich as well as a new edition of his work about Freidrich List. In 1914 there appeared, with Witte's authorization, a new edition of his musings about the compatibility of autocracy and zemstvos.

What all this meant, aside from satisfying his ego, is a matter of conjecture. Did he seek to return to a position of power, and did he think that publicity would help him in his quest? It was widely assumed that such was the case. Witte himself asserted that he had little expectation of returning to the limelight. In October 1911, in response to a letter from Herman Bernstein, he wrote, among other things: "With regard to the rumor as to my accepting the post of Minister of Foreign Affairs, it is too late for me to start my career anew. I have long ended it. Only extraordinary circumstances could compel me to change my viewpoint on this subject."[12] Two years later, in reply to a query from another American journalist about the rumor that he might soon be named premier, Witte replied that such an appointment would not "suit my personal affairs" and that, in any case, the country was not in such dire straits that he would be recalled to power.[13]

How much of such disclaimers should be taken as posing and how much as sincere expression is an unanswerable question. But that he was seeking some sign from the sovereign that his contributions to the realm were recognized seems evident from the little evidence there is and from the nature of the man. Take the case of Witte and Rasputin. Witte shared a belief in the myth that Rasputin, through his influence on Nicholas and Alexandra, was able to make and break political careers, an illusion created by Rasputin's self-advertising, which inspired many in high places to call on this disreputable person.[14] Witte was one of them.

The evidence is spotty, but there is enough to support the view that between 1911 and 1913 Witte attempted to gain the favor of a man he despised and considered to be a corrupting influence.[15] True, he would not receive Rasputin, but he called on him more than once, apparently unaware that the so-called holy man was under constant surveillance.[16] There is also evidence that when Anna Vyrubova, go-between of Rasputin and Alexandra, was in a hospital asking to see Rasputin, it was Countess Witte who provided him with the necessary transportation.[17] Reportedly, Rasputin referred to Witte as "the cleverest man" in Russia, but one lacking in respect for "Papa and Mama," as he called Nicholas and Alexandra.[18] This was in 1913, when rumors were floating about that Witte might be the next premier. Whether or not Rasputin attempted to persuade the tsar to recall to power the man he had vowed never to trust again is a mystery. All that can be said is that Witte demeaned himself, as did so many others, by showing any attention to that despicable character, and that he did so for the sake of his career.

When Kokovtsev was dismissed at the end of January 1914, many, including the premier, believed that Witte had contributed to his fall.[19] Indeed he had. Earlier that month Witte had raised a storm by his harsh and sustained criticism in the State Council of Kokovtsev's handling of the liquor monopoly. This was in connection with proposed legislation concerning the sale of liquor. The incident came to the attention of the tsar, who was concerned about the weakness of the government's efforts to curb intemperance. But this was only one of the factors in the premier's fall. Witte had no reason to expect to benefit from the appointment of Goremykin, his rapidly aging foe, to succeed Kokovtsev as premier. But he did expect to benefit from the appointment of P.I. Bark as the new minister of finance.

Witte thought of Bark as one of the many whose careers he had advanced, and believed that he would enjoy some influence with the new minister of finance. In this he would be disappointed, as he would be in his expectation that he would named to negotiate renewal of the commercial treaty with Germany that he had negotiated in 1904 for a ten-year term.[20] There was virtually nothing left for him to hope for other than that the tenth anniversary of the signing of the Portsmouth Treaty would be marked by the unveiling of a commemorative monument in Portsmouth, presumably with him as a guest of honor. But this, too, was not to be.[21] Even if such a monument had been contemplated, Witte would not have lived to participate in the unveiling. And even had he lived that long, war would have prevented his attending.

Egocentric though he might be, he was deeply concerned with matters of

war and peace, continuing to believe that Russia required at least a generation of peace to recover from the war with Japan. He maintained the belief
that the continuing arms race was a threat to all, and he could express himself eloquently on the subject of armed peace as well as on the subject of the
horrors of the next major war.[22]

Also, he continued to believe that a Franco-German-Russian entente was
in the best interests of Russia and Europe as a whole. He was convinced that
had he been appointed ambassador to France, such an entente would have
come into being, an unrealistic expectation. As might be expected, he was
critical of the Anglo-Russian Convention of 1907, which had the effect of
creating the Anglo-Franco-Russian Triple Entente, directed against the Triple
Alliance of Austria-Hungary, Germany, and Italy.[23]

As is quite evident from what has been said about Witte's views in concluding peace with Japan, he was convinced that it was in Russia's interest to
establish friendly relations with Tokyo, which meant settling any differences
between the two as well as refraining from any expansionist activities in the
Far East. It was in this spirit that he approved of foreign minister Izvolskii's
dealings with Japan, not that he had any voice in his country's diplomacy.[24]
In fact, although he had some sources of inside information about what was
afoot at court and in the various ministries, there was much that he did not
know—quite a comedown.

There were some Far Eastern developments that disturbed him. First, there
was the proposal to build the so-called Amur Railroad. It will be recalled that
in 1896 plans for the Trans-Siberian Railroad were altered by eliminating a
proposed section north of the Amur River in favor of a shortcut through
Manchuria, which became the Chinese Eastern Railroad. The vulnerability
of this line in the war with Japan prompted the plan to build the section that
had been eliminated. When the proposal came before the State Council in
1908, Witte opposed it vigorously on several grounds, the chief of them being that such construction would alarm both Japan and China. He lost that
battle.[25] Also, Witte was surely aware that there were negotiations afoot to
sell his beloved Chinese Eastern Railroad. Had that occurred, the need to
build the Amur Railroad would have been overwhelming. In any event, construction of the proposed line was begun soon after the debate.

Another Far Eastern development that troubled the ex-premier arose out
of the 1911 revolution in China, which further weakened that country's ability to withstand imperialistic threats. By this time St. Petersburg had abandoned ambitions in Manchuria but had been gaining influence in Outer
Mongolia. With China weakened by revolution, Russia increased her efforts
in that area, much to Witte's dismay.[26]

Of more immediate concern was the Eastern Question, a term used with respect to the continuing decline of the Ottoman Empire and the problems arising from that condition. He had, as we know, spent his boyhood close to the border of that empire and had later actively supported the Serbian effort to gain independence from Turkish rule. By the time of the Young Turk revolt in 1908, which accelerated the process of Ottoman decay, he had become disenchanted with the aspirations of the Serbs and other Balkan Slavs who focused on expelling the Turks from the Balkans. Also, he had long been opposed to Russian threats to the Ottoman Empire, out of fear that they would result in war.

The Young Turk revolt of 1908 opened a new chapter in the history of the decline of the Ottoman Empire, whetting the appetites of the many who sought to profit from new opportunities. The first was Austria-Hungary, whose annexation of Bosnia and Herzegovina nearly provoked war with Russia, as has been noted earlier. Then, in 1911, Italy went to war with the Turks in a successful effort to annex Tripoli. In the same year Russia sought unsuccessfully to secure the opening of the Straits by diplomatic means.

Meanwhile, the Russian envoys to Serbia and Bulgaria, acting largely on their own, helped these two countries and Greece and Montenegro to form an alliance against the Ottoman Empire. In October 1912, this alliance, called the Balkan League, went to war against the Turks, a war that none of the great powers wanted. In Russia Sazonov was sharply criticized for poor leadership, and it was shortly after the outbreak of hostilities that the rumor, referred to earlier, was spread that Witte and Sazonov were being summoned to see the tsar.

As for Witte, he was quite critical of Sazonov as well as pessimistic about the consequences of war in the Balkans.[27] In January 1913, during a lull in the fighting, he wrote the following prescient lines to Bernstein:

> With regard to the Balkan situation, it appears to me that in the near future there will be no general European war as a result of this important world question, because all the great countries, or rather their Governments, are either unprepared for war or afraid of it. But the renewal of operations in the Balkans is possible though hardly probable. In this way the historical Eastern question will not be settled, and within a few years (a year hence or perhaps ten years or more) this universal question will arise again. Then the question will in all probability be solved through a general European war. At present such a war will probably not break out, not because the nations have come to the conclusion that war is in principle a terrible affair, but merely because the Governments want either to prepare themselves the better, or are waiting for a more favorable juncture.[28]

Fighting did resume in the Balkans and was not brought to a close until the end of July 1913. The Ottoman Empire was now virtually out of Europe, but the Eastern Question was far from solved, and other forces making for a general European war were still at work. As indicated, Witte did not foresee war in the immediate future, but he was apprehensive. At a meeting of the Finance Committee in March 1914, he said: "At the present time we are less prepared financially than we were ten years ago."[29]

As was often the case, Witte was willing to share his views with journalists while trying not to say anything for the record that could hurt him at court. Sometimes he slipped. In the spring of 1914 a Berlin newspaper reported that he had spoken critically of Kokovtsev after the latter had left office. Witte hastened to send a letter to the tsar disingenuously assuring him that he avoided speaking to journalists and that in speaking to acquaintances he avoided saying anything that could harm "the fatherland or the government." Also, he assured Nicholas of his undying loyalty. And to explain why he had been leaving the country for Biarritz in the off-season he cited "family reasons."[30]

Then he slipped once more. On July 2, a Moscow newspaper reported, "Witte in a serious conversation with representatives of foreign newspapers said that Rasputin had a definite influence on some questions of foreign policy."[31] One can imagine the tsar's outrage at being told of such a lapse.

During his spring and early summer stay abroad in 1914 Witte had many an occasion to speak to journalists, given the dramatic events of that time. The assassination of Archduke Franz Ferdinand at Sarajevo on June 28 found Witte, his wife, and their grandson at Bad Salzschlirf, in central Germany, a spa of which they had grown fond. Witte was treated there as a major celebrity, catered to by the director of the spa, ogled by the guests, sought out by journalists.

One of these was A.E. Kaufman, who broached the subject of the ex-premier's alleged Germanophilism, referring to the rumor of his having millions on deposit in German banks. Witte dismissed such talk as fantasy. As a matter of fact, he did have over a million marks deposited with the banker Robert Mendelssohn. (The banker also handled accounts of the imperial family.)[32] Rumor had it that Witte had accumulated a fortune by dubious means. There is no evidence to support such an accusation. The million marks did not represent a fortune and may have come from the large grants by the tsar, stowed away to produce income and to provide for his widow, as would prove to be the case. True, he had pleaded poverty to the tsar and can fairly be accused of being less than candid. But he was not a Germanophile; if anything, he could be classified as an Anglophobe.

In the days following Sarajevo the newspapers were full of speculation and what purported to be news about the probable consequences of the assassination. Witte did not trust what he read and therefore, using "discreet channels," queried a family friend in the diplomatic service about the true state of affairs. The reply, couched "in a veiled manner" and sent through the same channels, prompted Witte to cut short his stay abroad.[33]

He, his wife, and their grandson made their way back to Biarritz, where he made sure that the papers there were in order and then placed them in a bank safe deposit vault in Bayonne under an assumed name, where they were to remain untouched until his widow could reclaim them after the war. As they were waiting in Biarritz to return home, he harked back to the conversation he had had with William II in 1897 (see page 78). With some emotion he stressed that had his idea of a Franco-German-Russo entente been adopted, Europe would be united and mistress of the world.[34]

From Biarritz the party traveled to Odessa by way of Italy. Once back on Russian soil, Witte sounded an optimistic, patriotic note to reporters, but his private thoughts were quite another matter.[35] They were private but were shared, off the record, with many who could be counted on to hold their tongues, men such as M. Paléologue, the French ambassador, and Grand Duke Constantine Konstantinovich, with whom he was on good terms.

Witte was certain that the war was a great mistake, that it was likely to end in revolution in Germany and then in Russia. He was willing to concede that war between England and Germany had some rationale, but he did not think that France had any vital interest to protect in this war.[36] As for Russia, her participation in it was insane. He was particularly upset by the official line that Russia was at war to save Serbia and even more annoyed by the proclamation addressed to the Poles that Russia would annex Prussian and Austrian Poland, unite them with Russian Poland, and grant the Poles freedom of religion, language, and local administration.

Illustrative of Witte's views about the war and his country's war aims were remarks he addressed to Paléologue a few weeks after the beginning of hostilities. The war, he said, was stupid and should be ended as soon as possible. He described Russian interest in the Balkans as a "romantic, old-fashioned chimaera." Those Balkan peoples who considered themselves Slavs were "only Turks christened by the wrong name." And the Serbs, in his view, deserved to be taught a lesson, this from a man who had so ardently helped the Serb cause a generation earlier. He went on to say that Russia had no need of more territory, least of all Austrian and German Poland. If they were annexed, a united Poland would try to secede from Russia. Moreover, Austrian Poland was "full of Jews," and German Poland would only add more Germans, of whom the realm had more than enough.[37]

In a letter to Grand Duke Constantine Konstantinovich, who had just lost a son in the war, Witte asserted that Russia had been dragged into war to serve the purposes of "perfidious Albion," which, having destroyed the naval power of France and Spain, now wanted to fight, in the words of one Russian diplomat, "to the last drop of Russian blood" to do the same to German naval power. In presenting this view Witte had reason to believe that the grand duke would agree with him.[38]

Witte went further than expressing his feelings about the war by an effort to promote a separate peace with Germany, this when Russia was committed by treaty to do nothing of the kind. In October, in a letter to Robert Mendelssohn, sent through secure channels, he dealt not only with the matter of having his account transferred to a neutral country but also with the possibility of a separate peace. He obviously and correctly believed that Mendelssohn would inform the German foreign office of the letter. The foreign office was interested and so was the chancellor, who authorized discreet probes that led nowhere, but it is worth noting that in a later letter to Mendelssohn, Witte expressed his willingness to serve as a delegate to a conference to negotiate a separate peace.[39] Here, he was serving his country's interests at some risk to his own.

About the same time, the Finance Committee authorized Witte to go to the United States to obtain a loan. This put him in the anomalous position of aiding the war effort while seeking to end the conflict. He had, of course, sought to get American bankers to participate in the 1906 loan and even earlier had tried unsuccessfully to enter the American money market. Under other circumstances such a mission would have suited him perfectly, for maintenance of his country's financial strength was dear to him and the need for monetary aid was pressing. What his feelings were about his new task we do not know. But we do know that Witte informed the tsar that to obtain a loan it would be necessary to deal with the question of Jewish rights, a question that had recently led to the chilling of relations with the United States. While he was at it he brought up another subject, the need to "improve the social and economic conditions of the laboring classes." And then there was the problem of reaching the United States under the conditions of war. As it turned out, he did not have long to live, and all that he was able to accomplish was to call on the American ambassador.[40]

Meanwhile Witte continued to beat his own drum. Notable was his attempt to have the report he had submitted to Alexander III about the competing proposals for a naval base, one at Libau, the other at Murmansk (see page 58) published in *Istoricheskii vestnik*. Witte had recommended Murmansk, but Libau, located on the Baltic, had been chosen and a formidable naval base had been constructed there. Now it was evident that this base was useless in the face of superior German naval power.

Witte had been proven right, and he obviously wanted that fact to be widely known even though publication of the report would be sure to embarrass the tsar without serving any useful purpose at the moment other than enhancing Witte's reputation. As it turned out, publication was prohibited by military censorship, which was upheld by the naval minister, to whom the ex-premier sent a protest. Witte then arranged to have the report read as a scholarly paper at a session of a historical society he attended a few weeks before his death. The report was finally published in 1924.[41]

This episode is illustrative of Witte's state of mind in his last years, particularly after the outbreak of war: a desperate man, desperate about the state of the country, desperate about his career, beset by consciousness of his own mortality. Koni, his colleague in the State Council, writes that during the last two years of his life, and increasingly so toward the end, Witte seemed out of sorts and distant; during breaks in the council sessions, Witte would pace the corridor outside the chamber, speaking to no one. To Koni it seemed as if "Witte were some kind of Gulliver, tied down hand and foot, in the land of the Lilliputians."[42]

In the last year of his life, Witte thought increasingly about the end. He had premonitions of death to which he gave credence. During his daily automobile rides he would stop at a chapel to pray. He wished that his gravestone should have a black base topped by a black cross with the inscription "Count Witte, 17 October 1905."[43] To ensure that his title and surname did not die with him, he wrote a fawning letter to be delivered to the tsar after his death asking that "Count Witte" be added to his grandson's surname. He signed the letter "Count Witte—now your *bogomolets*," signifying that beyond the grave he was praying for the tsar. The request was not to be honored.[44]

Death came more quickly than he had anticipated. Late in February 1915 he came down with an ear infection that quickly led to a condition so acute that his doctors had him transferred from his bedroom to a downstairs living room, where he was isolated to prevent contamination. This gave rise to a series of notes between Witte and his beloved grandson, who was staying with the Wittes. During the morning of February 28, Witte died, the cause generally given as infection of the brain, although some said it was the prostate gland.[45] Given the low state of medical knowledge in 1915, one guess is probably as good as another.

The tsar, who was away from home at the time, wrote to his wife that he was experiencing "a feeling of Pascal peace," the source of which was either an optimistic prediction about the war from Rasputin or the news of Witte's death.[46] He obviously had not softened in his view of the man.

Nonetheless, propriety was observed. The official government newspaper printed a long and complimentary obituary.[47] Witte was buried, as was his wish, in the cemetery of the prestigious St. Alexander Nevskii Monastery. The services were conducted by a bishop, assisted by several archpriests. Higher officialdom was well represented, as was the general public. It was not as elaborate a funeral as would have been the case if he had been as rich as alleged, but it was a proper one.[48]

The news of Witte's death created a major sensation that went on for days, even though the country was at a critical point in the war. The Odessa Stock Exchange closed to honor the city's favorite son. Most newspapers recognized that the most important governmental figure of the last generation had died, and they devoted much space to his accomplishments, so much so that the organ of the Union of the Russian People deplored "the unhealthy and undesirable popularization" that Witte was receiving in the press, declaring that with his passing the ranks of the enemies of Russia had been reduced by one.[49]

Witte's troubles were over, but not those of his heirs. As was customary after the death of a high official, his study was sealed and his papers examined. Those relating to official business, particularly those dealing with direct relations with the tsar, were removed, some to be destroyed, others placed in the proper archives. His study in Biarritz presented difficulties for the tsar's emissaries in that the villa was considered to enjoy extraterritorial immunity since it was owned by the wife of a diplomat. These difficulties were surmounted by an unauthorized and fruitless search by agents of the Russian secret police. Also, the French government was asked if there was a safe deposit box in Witte's name in any of the country's banks. Of course there was none. Nicholas was particularly interested in putting his hands on his ex-premier's memoirs.[50] When he was informed that these were not found but that the table of contents of the dictated memoirs had been, he sent an adjutant-general to call on Countess Witte to say that the tsar "would be interested in reading the memoirs," to which she replied that she could not comply "because they were being kept abroad."[51] Witte had won a posthumous victory over his sovereign.

Afterword

What with the world at war, Witte's death became yesterday's news and remained so until the appearance of his memoirs. Once the war was over Countess Witte set about retrieving her husband's papers. In May 1919 she sailed for New York to see Jacob Schiff. If there had been a million-dollar offer on his part, it was no longer binding given the fall of the monarchy, but he did help by directing her to an eager publisher, who arranged for the simultaneous publication in the spring of 1921 of abridged English, French, and Spanish translations of the memoirs. Subsequently there would appear abridged Czech, German, Hungarian, and Japanese translations as well three-volume editions in Russian. Interest in the memoirs remained high. Thus, in 1960 there appeared in the Soviet Union an edition of seventy-five thousand three-volume sets that sold out in three months. As late as 1994 a new Russian edition of ten thousand three-volume sets was published.[1]

Witte's instruction that there be no references to persons still living at the time of publication was ignored, igniting a series of replies by those he showed in an unfavorable light, replies that in one case seemed the work of a demented man, I.I. Kolyshko, whom Witte described as dishonest and, by implication, homosexual. The reply, published under a pseudonym, was entitled *Lozh Vitte* (The Witte Lie), which assumed that the count was residing in hell.[2] In addition to raising the hackles of those still living who received critical mention, the memoirs caused the hair of readers to rise with revelations and depictions of the last decades of the Romanov dynasty. Had the memoirs been published during Witte's lifetime, the monarchy would have suffered a serious blow.[3] To this day views of the reign of Nicholas II have been shaped by Witte's account of the period.

Soon after the appearance of the memoirs, the task of analyzing and evaluating Witte's work began and has continued to this day, chiefly, but not exclusively in Russia. In the Soviet Union scholars were, of course, constrained to wear the Marxist-Leninist mantle, which did not preclude serious work because the party line permitted considerable latitude when it came to Witte. Consider the following observations concerning Witte's place in history. In his introduction to the 1960 edition of the memoirs, A.L. Sidorov, who held a commanding position among Soviet historians, wrote:

Count S.Iu. Witte, the most eminent statesman of tsarist Russia during the latter part of the nineteenth century and the early part of the twentieth, did much for the development of capitalism in Russia. His great abilities were displayed during his tenure as minister of finance, chairman of the Committee of Ministers and chairman of the Council of Ministers, as well as in the diplomatic field.[4]

A.Ia. Avrekh, a less eminent Soviet scholar, placed much more emphasis on what he considered the shortcomings of Witte's career, and concluded:

That Witte won a place in history is beyond question. But in historical perspective he remains a reformer who sought to use all the forces of progress for the strengthening of autocratic Russia and her most reactionary product—the bureaucracy.[5]

Both Sidorov and Avrekh agreed that Witte was swimming against the tide of history and that they were swimming with it. There are no final verdicts in history.

In the post-Soviet age the obligation to follow the party line in Russia was, of course, lifted, but some Witte experts from the earlier time are still active, and writings of some deceased specialists are being reprinted. Study of Witte's work has continued, rising in volume with the marking of the 150th anniversary of his birth, in 1999.

New times have brought new perspectives. Consideration of the Soviet experience has strengthened doubts about the benefits of revolution, particularly the October Revolution, and, by the same token, has led to rejection of the Soviet view that Witte's major fault was his hostility toward the revolutionaries.[6] And the current state of affairs in Russia has prompted appreciation of the relevance of his views to such problems as the weakness of present-day agriculture and industry, the poor fiscal state of the government, and the prevalence of alcoholism.[7] Remarkable was the publication of a textbook entitled *Politiko-ekonomicheskaia sistema S. Iu. Vitte i sovremennaia Rossiia* (The Political-Economic System of S.Iu. Witte and Contemporary Russia), "intended for instructors, students, and postgraduate students of macroeconomics and management."[8] Drawing on Witte's writings, the author, N.V. Raskov, presents a sympathetic view of what Witte had to say on such subjects as civil rights, representative government, the rule of law, church and state, the state and the economy, and European integration, suggesting that Russia would be well served by following Witte's strictures.

What is my judgment of Witte's place in history? I consider him the most outstanding official to have served under the last two tsars and probably the ablest official in the last century of the Romanov dynasty. First, a few words about Nicholas II and Witte. It seems commonplace to assert that had Witte's career been spent under a monarch like William I of Germany, as Bismarck's had been, his record would have been of comparable magnitude. Be that as it may, most of Witte's years as minister were spent under Nicholas II and only three under Alexander III, who had some of the qualities of William I. Alexander, strong and self-assured, provided Witte with strong and consistent support, as William II did for Bismarck. True, for the first five years of his reign, Nicholas II, unsure of himself and under the influence of his mother, who was one of Witte's admirers, gave his minister of finance a relatively free hand. It is evident that from the beginning, the tsar did not find the rough-mannered and didactic Witte a sympathetic person, and as Nicholas matured he increasingly chafed at the role of figurehead. He was, after all, the unlimited sovereign of all the Russias, as his wife and others kept reminding him. Add to this the widespread criticism of Witte's policies among those with whom Nicholas identified himself and his growing doubts about the finance minister's loyalty and you have a formula for mischief, which was to become all too evident during Witte's tenure as premier.

What Witte did accomplish was formidable. The Trans-Siberian Railroad alone, one of the major creations of the nineteenth and early twentieth centuries, for which he deserves a major share of the credit, ranks high among his accomplishments. All that he did for the railroad system and industry speeded Russia's belated industrialization and modernization. Had there been no wars, no revolutions, and no civil war, the economy would have enjoyed robust growth, continuing to catch up with the already industrialized nations. And as industrialization advanced so did social change, both urban and rural. True, some aspects of his economic policies have been justly criticized, but, all in all, these have earned him a solid place in history. There is more to be added to his credit, however. This is not to say that sans World War I, sans 1917, all would have been rosy. There were many unsettling forces at work: minority nationalism, a growing working class, a growing capitalist class, and a declining landed nobility. Conflict was certain, but revolution was not inevitable.

The task Witte performed at Portsmouth was a major one. His charge from the tsar was to achieve peace without giving up "a single kopek or a single square inch of soil." He succeeded in the former, winning far better terms in the process than anyone expected, as was acknowledged on both sides. That Witte received the title of count, an honor usually given to generals for major victories and ministers for exceptional and very lengthy service, is a mark of his achievement. Both the tsar and Theodore Roosevelt deserve some credit, but without Witte the negotiations would surely have had a different ending—probably resumption of fighting, which would have made the revolutionary upheaval in Russia even worse than what did happen.

Also in the roster of Witte's major achievements were the October Manifesto and his service as his country's first premier, playing a crucial role in turning Russia into a constitutional monarchy. Granted that he received no laurels for these in his lifetime, but the fact is that the two rank high on his list of achievements. The October Manifesto was as much a turning point in Russia's history as Alexander II's edict freeing the serfs. And during his six months in office he did much to lay the foundations of a conservative constitutional monarchy. It is doubtful that anyone else could have done as well under the circumstances, even though Witte was in poor health, torn between his sympathy for autocracy and his recognition of the necessity for constitutionalism, and undermined by the tsar, all at a time when the country seemed out of control and when the liberals upon whom he had counted were acting as enemies rather than allies.

One does not usually think of Witte as a visionary because he was primarily a doer, but the fact is that his economic program was visionary in its breadth and depth, conceiving of an industrialized Russia that would in the long run benefit all. As a conscientious minister of finance, he realized that Russia needed peace. To be sure, he engaged in economic imperialism when little risk seemed involved. The war with Japan was a shock that made him realize Russia was far more vulnerable than he had ever imagined. While he denied any responsibility for the war, he embraced what he thought were its lessons: that Russia must accept the fact that she was no longer a great power, that she needed a generation of peace to recover her economic strength, that she should rebuild her armed forces for defensive purposes. This implied forsaking any thought of a "historic mission" such as annexing the Straits, annexing Constantinople, forming a Slavic federation, or expanding Russian holdings in the Far East. Had Witte's views won out, the tsar would not have ordered general mobilization in August 1914 even though it would lead to war, having been won over by the argument that Russia would lose all the influence in the Balkans she had amassed. The chance of Witte's views prevailing were virtually nil given the nature of so-called statecraft. It has been said that "for over a century the Russian political system bred pygmies not giants to staff its bureaucracy."[9] Witte was not bred by that system and was a giant, albeit a flawed one.

Notes

Notes to Chapter 1

1. E.J. Dillon, *The Eclipse of Russia* (New York, 1918), p. 187.
2. V.I. Gurko, *Features and Figures of the Past* (Palo Alto, CA, 1939), p. 115.
3. J. Melnik, "Witte," *Century Magazine*, September 1915, p. 684.
4. V. Vonliarliarskii, *Moi vospominaniia* (Berlin, 1939), p. 120.
5. S.Iu. Witte, *Memoirs* (Armonk, NY, 1990), pp. 604, 775 n. 6, 783 n. 20; G.O. Raukh, "Dnevnik," *Krasnyi arkhiv* 19 (1926), pp. 98–100.
6. A.M. Fadeev, *Vospominaniia* (Odessa, 1897), Part 2, p. 200; P. Nikolaev, "Vospominaniia o kniaze A.I. Bariatinskom," *Istoricheskii vestnik* 22 (1885), p. 623.
7. Nikolaev, "Vospominaniia o kniaze A.I. Bariatinskom," p. 723.
8. Ibid., p. 623
9. Witte, *Memoirs*, p. 4.
10. Sophia Iu. Witte, *My Love Affair* (Burlington, VT, 1903). A novel, translated from the Russian.
11. T.H. von Laue, *Sergei Witte and the Industrialization of Russia* (New York, 1969), p. 39.
12. Witte, *Memoirs*, pp. 29–30.
13. De Witt Mackenzie Wallace papers, box 3, Cambridge University Library; St. Petersburg, May 10, 1896.
14. J. Curtin, *The Memoirs of Jeremiah Curtin* (Madison, WI, 1940), p. 153.
15. Witte, *Memoirs*, p. 31.

Notes to Chapter 2

1. S.Iu. Witte, *Memoirs* (Armonk, NY, 1990), p. 31.
2. A. Rumanov, "Shtrikhi k portretam," *Vremia i my*, no. 95 (1987), p. 216.
3. A.J.P. Taylor, *Bismarck* (New York, 1955), p. 12.
4. J. Curtin, *The Memoirs of Jeremiah Curtin* (Madison, WI, 1940), p. 250.
5. S. Harcave, *Russia, a History* (Philadelphia, 1968), p. 297.
6. F. Venturi, *Roots of Revolution* (New York, 1964), pp. 220–21.
7. N. Hans, *The Russian Tradition in Education* (London, 1963), p. 63; P.P. Semeniuta, "Iz vospominanii ob A.I. Zheliubove," *Byloe*, no. 4 (1906), p. 216.
8. Witte, *Memoirs*, p. 33.
9. B.B. Glinskii, "Graf Sergei Iulevich Vitte," *Istoricheskii vestnik* 140 (1915), p. 235.
10. Semeniuta, "Iz vospominanii ob A.I. Zheliubove"; G.E. Afanasev, "K konchine Grafa S.Iu. Vitte," *Volny*, no. 3 (1915), col. 97; V.V. Kirkhner, "K biografii S.Iu. Vitte," Iu. Witte, *Volny*, no. 4 (1915), col. 18; V.N. Pisnaia, "Studencheskie gody Zheliubova," *Byloe*, no. 22 (1925), p. 171.

11. Afanasev, "K konchine Grafa S.Iu. Vitte," col. 99; Kirkhner, "K biografii S.Iu. Vitte," col. 118.

12. Afanasev, col. 99.

13. Witte, *Memoirs*, p. 40.

14. Russia, Ministerstvo Finansov, *Ministerstvo Finansov, 1802–1902*, Part 2 (St. Petersburg, 1902), pp. 323–25.

15. Witte, *Memoirs*, p. 41.

16. S.Iu. Witte, *Vospominaniia* (Moscow, 1960) 1, p. 518 n. 19.

17. B.V. Ananich and R.Sh. Ganelin, *Sergei Iulevich Vitte i ego vremia* (St. Petersburg, 1999), p. 12.

18. *Ministerstvo Finansov, 1802–1902*, pp. 323–25; Witte, *Memoirs*, p. 40.

19. A.M. Soloveva, *Zheleznyi transport Rossii vo vtoroi polovine XIX v.* (Moscow, 1975), pp. 90–92; J.N. Westwood, *A History of Russian Railways* (London, 1964), pp. 99–101.

20. Afanasev, "K konchine Grafa S.Iu. Vitte," col. 97; Witte, *Memoirs*, p. 49.

21. Witte, *Memoirs*, pp. 82, 328, 329–30, 413, 545, 787 n. 21.

22. Witte, *Memoirs*, p. 42.

23. A.E. Kaufman, "Cherty iz zhizni grafa S.Iu. Vitte," *Istoricheskii vestnik* 140 (1915), p. 226.

24. Witte, *Memoirs*, p. 46.

25. L. Tolstoy, *Anna Karenina* (New York, n.d.), p. 1075.

26. Witte, *Memoirs*, p. 47.

27. Soloveva, *Zheleznyi transport Rossii vo vtoroi polovine XIX v.*, p. 113.

28. Witte, *Memoirs*, p. 47.

29. Ibid., pp. 48–49.

30. Ibid., pp. 49–51.

Notes to Chapter 3

1. J.N. Westwood, *A History of Russian Railways* (London, 1964), pp. 103–4; S.Iu. Witte, *Memoirs* (Armonk, NY, 1990), p. 52.

2. Witte, *Memoirs,* pp. 52–53. Someone, probably Matilda Witte, removed the pages of the dictated memoirs upon which the translated item referred to here is based and squirreled them away elsewhere in the typescript. Why is not evident.

3. A.M. Soloveva, *Zheleznyi transport Rossii vo vtoroi polovine XIX v.* (Moscow, 1975), pp. 153–55.

4. Witte, *Memoirs*, p. 53.

5. Ibid.

6. A.F. Koni, "Sergei Iulevich Vitte," *Sobranie sochinenii*, V (Moscow, 1968), pp. 239–42, 468n.; Soloveva, *Zheleznyi transport Rossii vo vtoroi polovine XIX v.* (Moscow, 1975), pp. 155–57; Westwood, *A History of Russian Railways,* pp. 80–81, 95; Witte, *Memoirs*, pp. 54–55.

7. *Ministerstvo Finansov, 1802–1902*, Part 2 (St. Petersburg, 1902), p. 324; Witte, *Memoirs*, pp. 54–55, 75–76. Witte was responsible for the preparation of the volume dealing with the proceedings.

8. Witte, *Memoirs*, p. 55.

9. N.D. Chubaty, "The Meaning of 'Russia' and 'Ukraine,'" *Readings in Russian History*, ed. by S. Harcave (New York, 1962), I, p. 11.

10. P.A. Zaionchkovskii, *Krizis samoderzhaviia na rubezhe 1870–1880 godov* (Moscow, 1964), p. 148.

11. Institut Istorii Akademii Nauk SSSR, *Istoriia Kieva* 1 (Kiev, 1963), p. 375; Witte, *Memoirs*, pp. 72–73.

12. B.V. Ananich and R. Sh. Ganelin, "R.A. Fadeev, S.Iu. Vitte i ideologicheskie iskaniia 'Okhranitelei' v 1881–1882 gg.," in *Issledovaniia po sotsialno-politicheskoi istorii Rossii: sbornik statei pamiati Borisa Aleksandrovicha Romanova* (Leningrad, 1971), p. 299.

13. M. Kleinmichel, *Bilder aus einer versunkten Welt* (Berlin, 1922), p. 107; Witte, *Memoirs*, pp. 68–69.

14. B.V. Ananich and R. Sh. Ganelin, "S.Iu. Vitte, M.P. Dragomanov i 'Volnoe slovo,'" in *Issledovaniia po otechestvennomu istochnikovedeniia: sbornik statei posviashchenykh 75-letiiu professora S.N. Valka*, no. 7 (1964) trudy Leningradskoi otdeleniia Instituta Istorii, p. 166n; V. Vonliarliarskii, *Moi vospominaniia* (Berlin, 1939), p. 106; Witte, *Memoirs*, p. 69.

15. Witte, *Memoirs*, pp. 69–70.

16. Ananich and Ganelin, "S.Iu. Vitte, M.P. Dragomanov i 'Volnoe Slovo,'" p. 166.

17. S. Lukashevich, "The Holy Brotherhood, 1881–1888," *American Slavic and East European Review* 18 (1959), pp. 494, 498.

18. Ibid., p. 503.

19. Ananich and Ganelin, "S.Iu. Vitte, M.F. Dragomnov i 'Volnoe Slovo,'" pp. 166–70.

20. Ananich and Ganelin, "R.A. Fadeev, S.Iu. Vitte i ideologicheskie iskaniia 'Okhranitelei' v. 1881–1882 gg.," pp. 323–24.

21. Witte, *Memoirs*, p. 70.

22. Lukashevich, "The Holy Brotherhood, 1881–1888," p. 492.

23. Ibid., p. 509.

24. Witte, *Memoirs*, pp. 143–45, 150–51, 170–75.

25. Ananich and Ganelin, "S.Iu. Vitte, M.F. Dragomanov i 'Volnoe Slovo,'" p. 175 n. 36.

26. B.B. Glinskii, "Graf Sergei Iulevich Vitte," *Istoricheskii vestnik* 142 (1915), p. 895.

27. Ananich and Ganelin, "S.Iu. Vitte, M.F. Dragomanov i 'Volnoe Slovo,'" p. 175.

28. G.E. Afanasev, "K konchine Grafa S.Iu. Vitte," *Volny*, no. 3 (1915), cols. 98–99; Glinskii, "Graf Sergei Iulevich Vitte," *Istoricheskii vestnik* 140 (1915), p. 245; Koni, "Sergei Iulevich Vitte," p. 406n.; *Ministerstvo finansov, 1802–1902*, p. 324.

29. Afanasev, "K konchine Grafa S.Iu. Vitte," cols. 98–99.

30. Witte, *Memoirs*, p. 84.

31. A.E. Kaufman, "Cherty iz zhizni grafa S.Iu. Vitte," *Istoricheskii vestnik* 140 (1915), pp. 226, 229; Witte, *Memoirs*, pp. xvi–xvii, 84.

32. Witte, *Memoirs*, pp. xvii, xxvi, 32.

33. Ibid., p. xxvi.

34. Ibid., p. 64.

35. Ibid., p. 65.

36. Koni, "Sergei Iulevich Vitte," p. 242; Witte, *Memoirs*, p. 96.

37. Westwood, *A History of Russian Railways,* p. 106; Witte, *Memoirs*, p. 165.

38. *Ministerstvo finansov, 1802–1902*, p. 324.

39. Ibid.; Soloveva, *Zheleznyi transport Rossii vo vtoroi polovine XIX v.*, pp. 164–45; Westwood, *A History of Russian Railways*, pp. 84–85; Witte, *Memoirs*, pp. 96–98.

40. Witte, *Memoirs*, p. 93.

41. Koni, "Sergei Iulevich Vitte," p. 243. Witte and others accepted the legend that Alexander III, thanks to his Herculean strength, prevented the dining car's roof from collapsing until all in the car could escape. Koni disposes of that legend.

42. Koni, "Sergei Iulevich Vitte," pp. 244–46.

43. J. Melnik, "Witte," *Century Magazine*, September 1915, pp. 684–90.

44. *Ministerstvo finansov, 1802–1902*, p. 323; Witte, *Memoirs*, pp. 97–98.

45. Witte, *Memoirs*, p. 99.

46. Glinskii, "Graf Sergei Iulevich Vitte," *Istoricheskii vestnik* 140 (1915), p. 293.

Notes to Chapter 4

1. V.N. Lamsdorff, *Dnevnik, 1891–1892* (Hague, 1970), pp. 279–80.

2. V.V. Vodovozov, *Graf S.Iu. Vitte i Imperator Nikolai II* (Petrograd, 1922), pp. 124–25.

3. N.E. Wrangel, *The Memoirs of Baron N. Wrangel* (Philadelphia, 1927), p. 99.

4. A.A. Polovtsov, *Dnevnik gosudarstvennogo sekretaria A.A. Polovtsova* (Moscow, 1966) 2, p. 343.

5. A.V. Bogdanovich, *Tri poslednikh samoderzhtsa* (Moscow, 1924), p. 102.

6. Ibid.

7. A.M. Soloveva, *Zheleznyi transport Rossii vo vtoroi polovine XIX v.* (Moscow, 1975), pp. 165–66; *Ministerstvo finansov, 1802–1902*; J.N. Westwood, *A History of Russian Railways* (London, 1964), pp. 83–84.

8. S.Iu. Witte, *Memoirs* (Armonk, NY, 1990), p. 103.

9. Soloveva, *Zheleznyi transport Rossii vo vtoroi polovine XIX v.*, pp. 196–98; Westwood, *A History of Russian Railways*, pp. 125–26.

10. Witte, *Memoirs*, p. 272.

11. Ibid., pp. 107, 111.

12. P.I. Lyashchenko, *History of the National Economy of Russia* (New York, 1949), pp. 557–58; Witte, *Memoirs*, pp. 26–27, 174.

13. T.H. von Laue, *Sergei Witte and the Industrialization of Russia* (New York, 1969), pp. 31–32.

14. Polovtsov, *Dnevnik gosudarstvennogo sekretaria A.A. Polovtsova* 2, p. 351.

15. Ibid., p. 421.

16. Lamsdorff, *Dnevnik, 1891–1892*, p. 279.

17. Bogdanovich, *Tri poslednikh samoderzhtsa*, pp. 152, 156, 157.

18. Polovtsov, *Dnevnik gosudarstvennogo sekretaria A.A. Polovtsova* 2, p. 424.

19. C.P. Pobedonostsev, *Reflections of a Russian Statesman* (Ann Arbor, MI, 1965), p. 32.

20. V.I. Mamontov, *Na gosudarevoi sluzhbe* (Tallinn, 1926), pp. 210–11.

21. Witte, *Memoirs*, pp. 377–78, 782 n. 16.

22. L.M. Aizenberg, "Velikii Kniaz Sergei Aleksandrovich, Vitte i evrei-moskovskie kuptsy," *Evreiskaia Starina* XIII (1930), pp. 80–89.

23. Bogdanovich, *Tri poslednikh samoderzhtsa*, p. 208, describes Witte's raising his voice in the presence of the tsar. There are other instances of Witte's arguing with the tsar.

24. Witte, *Memoirs*, pp. 170–78.

25. E. Amburger, *Geschichte der Behördenorganisation Russlands von Peter dem Grossen bis 1917* (Leiden, 1966), pp. 122–25; Witte, *Memoirs*, p. 353.

26. V.I. Gurko, *Features and Figures of the Past* (Palo Alto, CA, 1939), pp. 22–34.

27. S.M. Propper, *Was nicht in die Zeitung kam* (Frankfurt am Main, 1929), pp. 159–60.

28. K.A. Krivoshein, *A.V. Krivoshein (1857–1921 gg.)* (Paris, 1973), p. 154; A.S. Suvorin, *Dnevnik* (Moscow, 1922), p. 376; I. Vinogradoff, "Some Imperial Letters to Prince V.P. Meshchersky (1893–1914)," *Oxford Slavonic Papers* 10 (1962), pp. 105–58; Vodovozov, *Graf S.Iu. Vitte i Imperator Nikolai II*, pp. 56, 56n.

29. Polovtsov, *Dnevnik gosudarstvennogo sekretaria A.A. Polovtsova* 2, p. 463.

30. Ibid., p. 140; Vinogradoff, "Some Imperial Letters to Prince V.P. Meshchersky (1893–1914)," p. 121.

31. Witte, *Memoirs*, pp. 134–35, 757 XV n. 1.

32. Propper, *Was nicht in die Zeitung kam*, p. 177.

33. Witte, *Memoirs*, pp. 134–39.

34. J. Cantacuzene, *My Life Here and There* (New York, 1921), p. 267.

35. Propper, *Was nicht in die Zeitung kam*, pp. 168–72.

36. Witte, *Memoirs*, p. 72.

37. Ibid., p. 132.

38. Propper, *Was nicht in die Zeitung kam*, p. 248.

39. Lamsdorff, *Dnevnik, 1891–1892*, pp. 131, 143.

40. V. Vonliarliarskii, *Moi vospominaniia* (Berlin, 1939), pp. 161–62.

41. Suvorin, *Dnevnik,* p. 429.

42. Witte, *Memoirs*, p. 518.

43. Cantacuzene, *My Life Here and There*, pp. 267–68.

44. Propper, *Was nicht in die Zeitung kam*, p. 175; Witte, *Memoirs*, pp. 41n, 133.

45. Witte, *Memoirs*, pp. 121–24.

46. Ibid., pp. 125, 188.

47. Polovtsov, *Dnevnik gosudarstvennogo sekretaria A.A. Polovtsova,* II, pp. 440–42, 451.

48. Witte, *Memoirs*, p. 161.

49. Ibid.

50. Ibid., p. 163.

Notes to Chapter 5

1. V.I. Gurko, *Features and Figures of the Past* (Palo Alto, CA, 1939), pp. 22–34; G.B. Sliozberg, *Dorevoliutsionnyi stroi Rossii* (Paris, 1933), pp. 109–17.

2. A.S. Suvorin, *Dnevnik* (Moscow, 1922), pp. 314–15, 447.

3. F. List, *The National System of Political Economy* (New York, 1966), p. 115.

4. S.Iu. Witte, *Natsionalnaia ekonomiia i Fridrikh List*, appendix to A. Korelin and S. Stepanov's *S.Iu. Vitte* (Moscow, 1998), p. 314.

5. Ibid., p. 331.

6. Ibid., pp. 26–27 (Appendix).

7. S.Iu. Witte, *Memoirs* (Armonk, NY, 1990), pp. 155, 190.

8. Ibid., p. 330. An extensive review of the liquor monopoly will be found in *S.Iu. Vitte i Rossiia: kazennaia vinnaia monopoliia, 1894–1914*, ed. L.I. Zaitseva (Moscow, 2000).

9. Russia, Ministerstvo Finansov, *Ministerstvo Finansov, 1802–1902*, Part 2 (St. Petersburg, 1902), pp. 203, 507.

10. Ibid., p. 506.

11. Witte, *Memoirs*, p. 243.

12. Ibid., pp. 289–90.

13. L. Tolstoy, *Polnoe sobranie sochinenii* (Moscow, 1954) 19, pp. 205–6.

14. S.Iu. Witte, *Prolog Russko-Iaponskoi voiny* (Petrograd, 1916), p. 1.

15. S.G. Marks, *Road to Power* (Ithaca, NY, 1991), p. 47.

16. *Ministerstvo finansov, 1802–1902*, pp. 287–88.

17. Marks, *Road to Power*, pp. 170–95.

18. Witte, *Memoirs,* pp. 125–26.

19. Marks, *Road to Power*, pp. 179–85.

20. *Za kulisami tsarizma (arkhiv Tibetskogo vracha Badmaeva)*, ed. by V.P. Semmenikov (Leningrad, 1925), pp. 51–75.

21. Ibid., pp. 79–81.

22. Ibid., p. 81.

23. B.B. Glinskii, "Graf Sergei Iulevich Vitte," *Istoricheskii vestnik* 140 (1915), p. 256; A.V. Ignatev, *Vitte-diplomat* (Moscow, 1989), pp. 31–37; *Ministerstvo finansov, 1802–1902*, pp. 231–34; Witte, *Memoirs*, pp. 182–86.

24. Suvorin, *Dnevnik,* p. 17.

25. For an extensive account see E. Lvov (pseudonym of E.L. Kochetov), *Po studenomiu moriu* (St. Petersburg, 1898).

26. S.Iu. Witte, "Libava ili Murmansk," *Proshloe i nastoiashchee* (1924), pp. 25–39.

Notes to Chapter 6

1. V.N. Lamsdorff, *Dnevnik, 1894–1896* (Moscow, 1991), p. 54; A.S. Suvorin, *Dnevnik* (Moscow, 1922), p. 54; S.Iu. Witte, *Memoirs* (Armonk, NY, 1990), p. 208.

2. Nicholas II, *Dnevnik* (Berlin, 1923), p. 23.

3. *Krasnyi arkhiv* 17 (1926), pp. 219–20.

4. Suvorin, *Dnevnik*, p. 405.

5. *Krasnyi arkhiv* 52 (1932), pp. 78–83; B.A. Romanov, *Russia in Manchuria, 1892–1906* (Ann Arbor, MI, 1954), pp. 48–61; Witte, *Memoirs*, pp. 227–29.

6. A.V. Ignatev, *Vitte-diplomat* (Moscow, 1989), p. 44.

7. Ibid.

8. Ibid., p. 64; Romanov, *Russia in Manchuria, 1892–1906*, p. 397 n. 12.

9. Ignatev, *Vitte-diplomat*, p. 68.

10. Ibid., p. 96.

11. B.A. Romanov, "Likhunchangskii fond," *Borba klassov*, nos. 1–2 (1924), pp. 77–126.

12. *Sbornik dogovorov Rossii s drugimi gosudarstvenami, 1856–1917* (Moscow, 1952), pp. 292–94.

13. Ibid., pp. 297–302.

14. Romanov, *Russia in Manchuria*, p. 88.

15. J.J. Stephan, *The Russian Far East* (Palo Alto, CA, 1994), p. 59.

16. Ignatev, *Vitte-diplomat,* pp. 49–51.

17. Witte, *Memoirs*, p. 244.

18. B. Romanov, "Vitte kak diplomat," *Vestnik Leningradskogo universiteta*, nos. 4–5, 1946, pp. 151–72.

19. S.S. Oldenburg, *Tsarstvovanie Imperatora Nikolaia II* 1 (Belgrade, 1939), pp. 62–65.

Notes to Chapter 7

1. S.Iu. Witte, *Memoirs* (Armonk, NY, 1990), p. 249.
2. Russia, Ministerstvo Finansov, *Ministerstvo Finansov, 1802–1902*, Part 2 (St. Petersburg, 1902), pp. 409–19.
3. I.A. Blagikh, "Konvertiruemyi rubl Grafa Vitte," *Vestnik Rossiiskoi Akademii Nauk*, no. 2 (1992), pp. 109–24; *Ministerstvo Finansov, 1802–1902*, pp. 420–21.
4. D. Lieven, *Russia's Rulers Under the Old Regime* (New Haven, CT, 1989), p. 38; Witte, *Memoirs*, p. 247.
5. Ibid.
6. A.A. Polovtsov, "Iz dnevnika A.A. Polovtsova," *Krasnyi arkhiv* 46 (1931), p. 115; Witte, *Memoirs*, pp. 248–49.
7. Polovtsov, "Iz dnevnika A.A. Polovtsova," p. 116.
8. O. Crisp, "Russian Financial Policies and the Gold Standard," *Economic History Review* 6 (1953), p. 171.
9. S. Pushkarev, *The Emergence of Modern Russia* (New York, 1963), p. 228; S.S. Oldenburg, *Tsarstvovanie Imperatora Nikolaia II* 1 (Belgrade, 1939), p. 85.
10. *Ministerstvo Finansov, 1802–1902*, pp. 563–602.
11. M.V. Kovalevskii, ed., *La Russie à la fin du XIXe siècle* (Paris, 1900), p. 858; *Ministerstvo finansov, 1802–1902*, p. 581; A.M. Soloveva, *Zheleznyi transport Rossii vo vtoroi polovine XIX v.* (Moscow, 1975), p. 251.
12. Witte, *Memoirs*, p. 102.
13. *Ministerstvo Finansov, 1802–1902*, pp. 561–62.
14. Ibid., pp. 557–58; Witte, *Memoirs*, p. 168.
15. It was not until after the 1917 revolutions that the metric system and the Gregorian calendar were introduced.
16. V.B. Lopukhin, "Liudi i politika," *Voprosy istorii* 41 (1966), p. 120.
17. *Ministerstvo Finansov, 1802–1902*, pp. 603–15.
18. Ibid., p. 368; T.H. von Laue, *Sergei Witte and the Industrialization of Russia* (New York, 1969); pp. 98–99.
19. P.I. Lyashchenko, *History of the National Economy of Russia* (New York, 1949), p. 560.
20. *Ministerstvo Finansov, 1802–1902*, p. 369.
21. Akademiia Nauk, Institut Istorii, *Ocherki istorii Leningrada* 2 (1957), pp. 173–75.
22. W.L. Blackwell, *Industrialization of Russia* (New York, 1970), p. 42.
23. Witte, *Memoirs*, p. 321.
24. Crisp, "Russian Financial Policies and the Gold Standard," p. 157 n. 2; von Laue, *Sergei Witte and the Industrialization of Russia,* p. 97.
25. R. Portal, "The Problem of an Industrial Revolution in Russia in the Nineteenth Century," in *Readings in Russian History*, ed. by S. Harcave (New York, 1962), II, p. 28.
26. S.Iu. Witte, "Dokladnaia zapiska Nikolaiu II," *Istorik-Marksist* 42–43 (1935), pp. 131–38.
27. T. von L'aue, "Factory Inspection Under the Witte System," *American Slavic and East European Review,* 29 (1960), p. 69.
28. *Ministerstvo Finansov, 1802–1902*, p. 325.

Notes to Chapter 8

1. V.N. Lamsdorff, *Dnevnik, 1894–1896* (Moscow, 1991), pp. 250–51, 290–91, 295–96; "Proiekt zakhvata Bosfora v 1896 g.," *Krasnyi arkhiv*, XLVII–XLVIII (1931), pp. 50–55.

2. A.V. Ignatev, *Vitte-diplomat* (Moscow, 1989), p. 54.

3. Ibid., pp. 56–57.

4. Ibid.; *Krasnyi arkhiv*, XLVII–XLVIII, p. 54; S.Iu. Witte, *Memoirs* (Armonk, NY, 1990), pp. 250–51.

5. Witte, *Memoirs*, p. 252.

6. Ignatev, *Vitte-diplomat*, pp. 61–62; Witte, *Memoirs*, p. 268.

7. Witte, *Memoirs*, pp. 268–69.

8. I have this from the late H.F. MacNair, coauthor, together with H.B. Morse, of *Far Eastern International Relations*. He had no primary source for the quotation, nor do I, but it is in character.

9. B.A. Romanov, *Russia in Manchuria, 1896–1906* (Ann Arbor, MI, 1952), p. 139.

10. A.S. Suvorin, *Dnevnik* (Moscow, 1922), p. 209.

11. Ignatev, *Vitte-diplomat*, pp. 66–68; Romanov, *Russia in Manchuria*, pp. 130–37; Witte, *Memoirs*, pp. 273–74.

12. Ignatev, *Vitte-diplomat*, pp. 68–69; S.Iu. Witte, *Prolog russko-iaponskoi voiny* (Petrograd, 1916), pp. 47–48.

13. A. Malozemoff, *Russian Far Eastern Policy, 1881–1904* (Berkeley, CA, 1958), p. 101.

14. Witte, *Memoirs*, p. 275.

15. Ibid., p. 276.

16. Suvorin, *Dnevnik*, p. 209.

17. Ignatev, *Vitte-diplomat*, pp. 70–71; Witte, *Memoirs*, p. 276.

18. Witte, *Memoirs*, pp. 276–77.

19. *Sbornik dogovorov Rossii s drugimi gosudarstvenami, 1856–1917* (Moscow, 1952), pp. 309–12.

20. Malozemoff, *Russian Far Eastern Policy*, pp. 108–9.

21. D. Geyer, *Russian Imperialism* (Leamington Spa, UK, 1987), pp. 197–98.

22. A.N. Kuropatkin, "Dnevnik A.N. Kuropatkina," *Krasnyi arkhiv* 2 (1922), p. 191.

23. T.H. von Laue, *Sergei Witte and the Industrialization of Russia* (New York, 1969), p. 156.

24. "Novye materialy o Gaagskoi mirnoi konferentsii 1899 g.," 54–55 (1932), p. 55.

25. Ibid., p. 56; "K istorii pervoi Gaagskoi konferentsii," *Krasnyi arkhiv* 50–51 (1932), p. 72.

26. "Novye materialy o Gaagskoi mirnoi konferentsii 1899 g.," pp. 58–62; Witte, *Memoirs*, p. 107.

27. Montebello to Delcassé, September 1, 1898, France, Ministère des Affaires Étrangères, Archive, Russie, Politique Étrangère, Dossier Genérale, I.

28. "K istorii pervoi Gaagskoi konferentsii," p. 91 n. 3.

Notes to Chapter 9

1. A.A. Lopukhin, *Otryvki iz vospominanii* (Moscow, 1923), pp. 73–75.

2. A.N. Kuropatkina, "Dnevnik S.N. Kuropatkina," *Krasnyi arkhiv*, 18 (1926), p. 60.

3. M.A. Tkachenko, "Fond S.Iu. Vitte v TSGIA," in *Nekotorye voprosy istoriografii i istochnikovedeniia SSSR: sbornik statei* (Moscow, 1977), p. 193; Witte, *Memoirs* p. 770 n. 5.

4. S.Iu. Witte, *Samoderzhavie i zemstvo* (St. Petersburg, 1908), p. 210; Witte, *Memoirs*, p. 843; S.S. Oldenburg, *Tsarstvovanie Imperatora Nikolaia II*, I (Belgrade, 1939), p. 153n; S.E. Kryzhanovskii, *Vospominaniia* (Berlin, n.d.), p. 7.

5. V.I. Gurko, *Features and Figures of the Past* (Palo Alto, CA, 1939), pp. 82–88; *Krasnyi arkhiv* 18 (1926), pp. 31–32; Vauvineux to Delcassé, November 10, 1899, France, Ministère des Affaires étrangères, Archive, Russie, Politique Intérieure, I.

6. Witte, *Memoirs*, p. 287; A.S. Suvorin, *Dnevnik* (Moscow, 1922), p. 377.

7. B.B. Glinskii, "Graf Sergei Iulevich Vitte," *Istoricheskii vestnik* 132 (1915), pp. 573–76.

8. *Krasnyi arkhiv* 18 (1926), p. 46; P.I. Lyashchenko, *History of the National Economy of Russia* (New York, 1949), pp. 647–56.

9. V. Vonliarliarskii, *Moi vospominaniia* (Berlin, 1939), p. 120; Witte, *Memoirs*, pp. 319–20.

10. Suvorin, *Dnevnik,* p. 332.

11. *Khrestomatiia po istorii SSSR* 3 (Moscow, 1952), p. 454.

12. Ibid.

13. H. Löwe, *The Tsar and the Jews* (Chur, Switzerland, 1993), p. 108.

14. Suvorin, *Dnevnik*, pp. 340–41.

15. Iu.B. Solovev, *Samoderzhavie i dvorianstvo v kontse XIX veka* (Leningrad, 1973), pp. 291–93.

16. Witte, *Memoirs*, p. 333.

17. Ibid.

18. Ibid., pp. 342–47.

19. A.A. Polovtsov, "Dnevnik Polovtsova," *Krasnyi arkhiv* 3 (1923), p. 114.

20. Ibid., XLVI (1931), pp. 128–29.

21. *Polnoe sobranie rechei Imperatora Nikolaia II* (St. Petersburg, 1906), p. 32.

22. Oldenburg, *Tsarstvovanie Imperatora Nikolaia II*, I, pp. 173–88; Witte, *Memoirs*, pp. 336–41.

23. A. Malozemoff, *Russian Far Eastern Policy, 1881–1904* (Berkeley, CA, 1958), pp. 177–78; J.A. White, *The Diplomacy of the Russo-Japanese War* (Princeton, NJ, 1964), pp. 33–35.

24. B.V. Ananich and R. Sh. Ganelin, "S.Iu. Vitte, M.P. Dragomanov i 'Volnoe slovo,'" in *Issledovaniia po otechestvennomu istochnikovedeniia: sbornik statei posviashchenykh 75-letiiu professora S.N. Valka*, no. 7 (1964) trudy Leningradskoi otdeleniia Instituta Istorii, p. 171 n. 24; Malozemoff, *Russian Far Eastern Policy*, p. 179; Vonliarliarskii, *Moi vospominaniia, p.* 106.

25. B.A. Romanov, "Vitte nakanune Russko-Iaponskoi voiny," *Rossiia i zapad,* I (1923), p. 152.

26. A.V. Ignatev, *Vitte-diplomat* (Moscow, 1989), p. 150.

27. B.V. Ananich, "Memuary S.Iu. Vitte v tvorcheskoi sudbe B.A. Romanova," in *Problemy sotsialno-ekonomicheskoi istorii Rossii* (St. Petersburg, 1991), p. 34.

28. Ignatev, *Vitte-diplomat,* p. 132; Witte, *Memoirs*, pp. 278–82.

29. *Krasnyi arkhiv* 14 (1926), pp. 41–42.

30. *Krasnyi arkhiv* 63 (1934), p. 46.

31. Ignatev, *Vitte-diplomat*, pp. 147–49.

32. *Sbornik dogovorov Rossii s drugimi gosudarstvenami, 1856–1917* (Moscow, 1952), pp. 324–28.

33. B.A. Romanov, *Russia in Manchuria, 1896–1906* (Ann Arbor, MI, 1952) p. 296.

34. *Krasnyi arkhiv* 18 (1926), pp. 45–46.

35. Lopukhin, *Otryvki iz vospominanii,* pp. 11–14; Vonliariarskii, *Moi vospominaniia,* p. 164.

36. Suvorin, *Dnevnik,* p. 349.

37. Löwe, *The Tsar and the Jews,* p. 415.

38. Witte, *Memoirs,* pp. 372–73.

39. D.N. Shipov, *Vospominaniia i dumy o perezhitom* (Moscow, 1918), p. 178.

40. Witte, *Memoirs,* p. 309n.

41. Vonliarliarskii, *Moi vospominaniia,* pp. 133–36.

42. E. Amburger, *Geschichte der Behördenorganisation Russlands von Peter dem Grossen bis 1917* (Leiden, 1966), p. 263; Gurko, *Features and Figures,* pp. 263, 648 n. 14.

43. D. Geyer, *Russian Imperialism* (Leamington Spa, UK, 1987), pp. 209–10.

44. Ignatev, *Vitte-diplomat,* pp. 155–56; Witte, *Memoirs,* pp. 307–8.

45. Boutiron to Delcassé, December, 21, 1902, France, Ministère des Affaires Étrangére, Archive, Russie, Politique Intérieure, I; Ignatev, *Vitte-diplomat,* p. 164.

46. Suvorin, *Dnevnik,* p. 358.

47. Kuropatkina, "Dnevnik Kuropatkina," *Krasnyi arkhiv,* II (1922), p. 43; Malozemoff, *Russian Far Eastern Policy,* p. 207.

48. Ignatev, *Vitte-diplomat,* pp. 163–64; Malozemoff, *Russian Far Eastern Policy,*, pp. 206–14; B.A. Romanov, "Vitte nakanune Russkoi-Iaponskoi voiny," in *Rossiia i zapad* 1 (Petrograd, 1923), pp. 140–67.

49. A.M. Bezobrazov, "Les premières causes de l'effondrement de la Russie: le conflit russo-japonais," *Le Correspondant,* May 25, 1923, pp. 603–8; S.Iu. Witte, *Prolog Russko-Iaponskoi voiny* (Petrograd, 1916), pp. 282–87.

50. I. Vinogradoff, "Some Imperial Letters to Prince V.P. Meshchersky (1893–1914)," *Oxford Slavonic Papers* 10 (1962), p. 136.

51. Ignatev, *Vitte-diplomat,* p. 171.

52. Bezobrazov, "Les premières causes," p. 606.

53. A.F. Koni, "Sergei Iulevich Vitte," *Sobranie sochinenii* 5 (Moscow, 1968), p. 255.

54. Witte, *Prolog Russko-Iaponskoi voiny,* pp. 292–310.

55. Malozemoff, *Russian Far Eastern Policy,* pp. 224–25; S.Iu. Witte, *Voznikovenie Russko-Iaponskoi voiny,* Bakhmeteff Archive, Columbia University, p. 835.

56. Ignatev, *Vitte-diplomat,* pp. 176–77.

57. Bezobrazov to Nicholas II, August 2, 1903 in *Russko-Iaponskaia voina, iz dnevnikov A.N. Kuropatkina i N.P. Linevicha* (Leningrad, 1925), p. 157.

58. Ignatev, *Vitte-diplomat,* p. 178.

59. Kuropatkin, "Dnevnik Kuropatkina," *Krasnyi arkhiv* 2 (1922), pp. 60, 158–59.

60. Gurko, *Features and Figures,* p. 225.

61. Witte, *Memoirs,* p. 315.

62. S.M. Propper, *Was nicht in die Zeitung kam* (Frankfurt am Main, 1929), p. 248.

63. Ignatev, *Vitte-diplomat,* p. 180.

64. Nicholas II, *Dnevnik imperatora Nikolaia II* (Berlin, 1923), p. 124. This state-

ment does not appear as an entry in this edition, but is quoted by the editor, who simply dates it as being written in 1903. I am assuming that it was written after Witte's dismissal.

65. B. von Bülow, *Memoirs* 2 (Boston, 1931), p. 50.
66. Cf. Ignatev, *Vitte-diplomat*, p. 181.

Notes to Chapter 10

1. S.Iu. Witte, *Memoirs* (Armonk, NY, 1990), pp. 353–55, 362, 365.
2. Ibid., p. 354.
3. *The Times* (London), June 10, 1933. Witte, *Memoirs*, p. 430.
4. E.J. Dillon, *Leaves from Life* (London, 1932), title page.
5. B. Pares, *A Wandering Student* (Syracuse, NY, 1948), p. 132.
6. Witte, *Memoirs*, p. 399n.
7. A.V. Ignatev, *Vitte-diplomat* (Moscow, 1989), p. 186.
8. Sir S. Scott to Marquess of Landsdowne, January 20, 1904, *British Documents on the Origins of the War, 1898–1914*, II (London, 1927), pp. 237–38.
9. Nicholas II to William II, January 11/24, 1904, Germany, Auswärtiges Amt, *Russland*, vol. 82, no. 1, Geheim, vol. 5–6.
10. Nicholas II to William II, January 21, 1904, Germany, Auswärtiges Amt, *Russland*, vol. 82, no. 1, Geheim, vol. 5–6.
11. *Krasnyi arkhiv*, II (1922), p. 105; Witte, *Memoirs*, pp. 368–69.
12. Nicholas II, *Dnevnik imperatora Nikolain II* (Berlin, 1923), p. 130.
13. *Krasnyi arkhiv* 2 (1922), pp. 109–10.
14. Witte, *Memoirs*, p. 369.
15. Ibid.
16. *Krasnyi arkhiv* 2 (1922), pp. 83–93.
17. Ibid., p. 94.
18. *Krasnyi arkhiv* 17 (1926), p. 73.
19. *Krasnyi arkhiv* 19 (1926), p. 63.
20. S.G. Marks, *Road to Power* (Ithaca, NY, 1991), p. 202.
21. Witte, *Memoirs*, p. 107.
22. Ibid., p. 385.
23. *Krasnyi arkhiv* 19 (1926), p. 68.
24. Witte, *Memoirs*, p. 385.
25. Ibid., p. 384.
26. *Krasnyi arkhiv* 41–42, p. 72.
27. *Krasnyi arkhiv* 19, p. 68.
28. *Krasnyi arkhiv*, 19, p. 70.
29. *British Documents on the Origins of the War* 2, p. 2.
30. Ignatev, *Vitte-diplomat*, p. 190.
31. Germany, Auswärtiges Amt, *Die Grosse Politik der Europäischen Kabinette* 14 pt. 1 (Berlin, 1924), 182n.
32. B. von Bülow, *Memoirs* 2 (1931), p. 47.
33. Ignatev, *Vitte-diplomat*, p. 192; Witte, *Memoirs*, p. 399.
34. *Krasnyi arkhiv* 19 (1926), p. 70.
35. Nicholas II to William II, May 19, 1904, *Die Grosse Politik* 19 pt. 1, p. 182.
36. Witte, *Memoirs*, pp. 189–91.

37. *Die Grosse Politik* 19 pt. 1, pp. 194–96; Ignatev, *Vitte-diplomat*, p. 193.
38. Ignatev, *Vitte-diplomat*, pp. 194–95; Witte, *Memoirs*, pp. 390–91.
39. Witte, *Memoirs*, p. 392.
40. *Die Grosse Politik* 19 pt. 1, p. 197.
41. *Krasnyi arkhiv* 6 (1924), p. 6; ibid. 19 (1926), p. 79.
42. Witte, *Memoirs*, p. 391.
43. *Die Grosse Politik* 19 pt. 1, p. 198.
44. Witte, *Memoirs*, p. 391.
45. von Bülow, *Memoirs* 2, p. 54.
46. A.S. Suvorin, *Dnevnik* (Moscow, 1922), p. 371.
47. *Krasnyi arkhiv* 19 (1926), p. 71.
48. *Dnevniki imperatora Nikolaia II* (Moscow, 1992), p. 161.

Notes to Chapter 11

1. *Dnevniki imperatora Nikolaia II* (Moscow, 1992), p. 161; A.S. Suvorin, *Dnevnik* (Moscow, 1922), p. 374.
2. V.A. Gurko, *Features and Figures of the Past* (Palo Alto, CA, 1939), p. 292.
3. Suvorin, *Dnevnik*, p. 371.
4. "The Tsar," *Quarterly Review* 200 (1904), pp. 180–209.
5. Metternich to von Bülow, August 5, 1904, Germany, Auswärtiges Amt, *Russland*, vols. 51–52, no. 1.
6. Suvorin, *Dnevnik*, p. 383.
7. E.J. Dillon, *The Eclipse of Russia* (New York, 1918), p. 115.
8. Lopukhin, *Otryvki iz vospominanii*, pp. 12–14.
9. Ibid., pp. 66–67; S.Iu. Witte, *Memoirs* (Armonk, NY, 1990), p. 395.
10. Suvorin, *Dnevnik*, p. 383.
11. Witte, *Memoirs*, p. 381.
12. Suvorin, *Dnevnik*, p. 379.
13. E.A. Sviatopolk-Mirskaia, "Dnevnik na 1904–1905 gg.," *Istoricheskie zapiski* 77 (1965), pp. 240–42.
14. Witte, *Memoirs*, p. 392.
15. V.N. Kokovtsev, *Out of My Past* (Palo Alto, CA, 1935), p. 32.
16. Suvorin, *Dnevnik*, p. 364.
17. Sviatopolk-Mirskaia, "Dnevnik na 1904–1905 gg.," p. 244.
18. S. Harcave, *The Russian Revolution of 1905* (New York, 1970), pp. 54–55.
19. Witte, *Memoirs*, p. 394.
20. Suvorin, *Dnevnik*, p. 386.
21. Harcave, *The Russian Revolution of 1905*, pp. 279–81.
22. A.V. Bogdanovich, *Tri poslednikh samoderzhtsa* (Moscow, 1924), p. 313; Gurko, *Features and Figures*, pp. 307–8.
23. Sviatopolk-Mirskaia, "Dnevnik na 1904–1905 gg.," p. 255.
24. Ibid., pp. 250–58.
25. Ibid., p. 258.
26. D.N. Shipov, *Vospominaniia i dumy o perezhitom* (Moscow, 1918), p. 287.
27. Sviatopolk-Mirskaia, "Dnevnik na 1904–1905 gg.," p. 262; Witte, *Memoirs*, pp. 396–98.
28. Ibid., p. 399; A.M. Verner, *The Crisis of Russian Autocracy* (Princeton, NJ, 1990), pp. 133–39.

29. Suvorin, *Dnevnik*, pp. 395–96.
30. Witte, *Memoirs*, p. 389.
31. Harcave, *The Russian Revolution of 1905*, pp. 282–85.
32. I.V. Gessen, *V dvukh vekakh* (Berlin, 1937), p. 186.
33. S.Iu. Witte, *Zapiska po krestianskom dela* (St. Petersburg, 1904).
34. Sir Charles Hardinge to the Marquess of Lansdowne, January 1905, United Kingdom, Public Records Office, Foreign Office, 65/1698.
35. *Krasnyi arkhiv*, XIX (1926), p. 72.
36. Sviatopolk-Mirskaia, "Dnevnik na 1904–1905 gg.," p. 266.
37. Suvorin, *Dnevnik*, p. 376.
38. *Krasnaia letopis* 1 (1922), p. 292.

Notes to Chapter 12

1. A.S. Suvorin, *Dnevnik* (Moscow, 1922), p. 395; *Krasnyi arkhiv*, 38, p. 67.
2. S. Harcave, *The Russian Revolution of 1905* (New York, 1970), pp. 285–89.
3. S.Iu. Witte, *Memoirs* (Armonk, NY, 1990), p. 402.
4. Ibid., pp. 402–3.
5. Harcave, *The Russian Revolution of 1905*, p. 98.
6. *Krizis samoderzhaviia v Rossii* (Leningrad, 1989), p. 175; E.A. Sviatopolk-Mirskaia, "Dnevnik na 1904–1905 gg.," p. 278.
7. A.A. Lopukhin, *Otryvki iz vospominanii* (Moscow, 1923), p. 56.
8. Witte, *Memoirs*, p. 399n.
9. *Krasnyi arkhiv* 19 (1926), pp. 73–78.
10. Witte, *Memoirs*, pp. 404–5.
11. A.S. Gerasimov, *Na lezvi i terroristami* (Paris, 1935), pp. 36–37.
12. Witte, *Memoirs*, p. 405.
13. Sviatopolk-Mirskaia, "Dnevnik na 1904–1905 gg.," p. 275.
14. Nicholas II, *Dnevnik imperatora Nikolas II* (Berlin, 1923), p. 195.
15. Witte, *Memoirs*, p. 156.
16. *Krasnyi arkhiv* 8 (1925), p. 53.
17. *Krasnyi arkhiv* 11–12 (1925), pp. 28–28.
18. *Zhurnaly komiteta ministrov po ispolneniiu ukaza 12 dekabria 1904* (St. Petersburg, 1905).
19. Witte, *Memoirs*, p. 409.
20. Harcave, *The Russian Revolution of 1905*, p. 264.
21. R.F. Byrnes, *Pobedonostsev* (Bloomington, IN, 1968), pp. 364–66; J.S. Curtiss, *Church and State in Russia* (New York, 1965), pp. 212–15; Witte, *Memoirs*, pp. 411–13; *Zakonodatelnye akty perekhodnago vremeni, 1904–1908 gg.* (St. Petersburg, 1909), pp. 34–38.
22. Alvesleben to von Bülow, May 18, 1904, Germany, Auswärtiges Amt, *Russland*, no. 82, no. 1, vols. 53–54.
23. *Zakonodatelnye akty*, pp. 52–54, 63–67, 143–44.
24. M.H. Voskobynyk, "The Nationalities Question in Russia, 1905–1907," (Ph.D. dissertation, University of Pennsylvania, 1972), pp. 396, 397n; *Zakonodatelnye akty*, p. 24.
25. Witte, *Memoirs*, pp. 377–78, 782 n. 15.
26. *Zhurnaly komiteta ministrov*, pp. 439–57; *Zakonodatelnye akty*, p. 72.

27. *Krasnyi arkhiv*, XXVI (1928), p. 131; Witte, *Memoirs*, pp. 415–16.
28. Bompard to Delcassé, February 10, 1905, France, Ministère des Affaires Étrangères, Archive, Russie, Politique Intérieure, I.
29. P.A. Zaionchkovskii, *Krizis samoderzhaviia na rubezhe 1870–1880 godov* (Moscow, 1964), pp. 179–80; N.G. Koroleva, *Pervaia rossiiskaia revoliutsiia i tsarizm* (Moscow, 1982), pp. 29–32.
30. Witte, *Memoirs*, p. 340.
31. A.M. Verner, *The Crisis of Russian Autocracy* (Princeton, NJ, 1990), p. 188.
32. Witte, *Memoirs*, p. 339.
33. H.Löwe, *The Tsar and the Jews* (Chur, Switzerland, 1993), p. 276.
34. Bompard to Delcassé, April 22, 1905, France, Ministère des Affaires Étrangères, Archive, Russie, Politique Intérieure, I.
35. Witte, *Memoirs*, pp. 340–41.
36. Verner, *The Crisis of Russian Autocracy*, p. 197; Witte, *Memoirs*, p. 414.
37. Kokovtsev, *Out of My Past*, pp. 50–51; *Protokoly zasedanii soveshchaniia dlia obsuzhdeniia prednachertanii, ukazanykh v . . . reskript 18 fevralia 1905 goda 19, 21, 23, 25 i 26 iulia 1905 goda* (St. Petersburg, 1905), passim; Verner, *The Crisis of Russian Autocracy*, p. 210; Witte, *Memoirs*, p. 416.

Notes to Chapter 13

1. B.A. Romanov, *Russia in Manchuria, 1892–1906* (Ann Arbor, MI, 1954), p. 325–26.
2. V.N. Kokovtsev, *Out of My Past* (Palo Alto, CA, 1935), pp. 43–49.
3. S.Iu. Witte, *Vospominaniia* (Moscow, 1960) 2, pp. 572–74. This may be one of the letters referred to in S.Iu. Witte, *Memoirs* (Armonk, NY, 1990), p. 418.
4. A.V. Ignatev, *Vitte-diplomat* (Moscow, 1989), pp. 203–4.
5. C. Spring-Rice to the Marquess of Lansdowne, May 7, 1905, United Kingdom, Public Record Office, Foreign Office, 65/1700.
6. *Krasnyi arkhiv*, XXVIII, pp. 182–202.
7. Witte, *Vospominaniia*, I, XLVII.
8. Witte, *Memoirs*, p. 418. He mistakenly dates the letter as having been written before Tsushima.
9. *Krasnyi arkhiv* 19 (1926), pp. 79–80.
10. Ignatev, *Vitte-diplomat*, p. 265; I. Ia. Korostovets, "Mirnye peregovory v Portsmute v 1905 goda," *Byloe*, no. 1 (1918), p. 186.
11. A.P. Izvolsky, *The Memoirs of Alexander Izvolsky* (London, 1920), pp. 22–24.
12. Witte, *Memoirs*, p. 422.
13. Kokovtsev, *Out of My Past*, p. 53.
14. Ignatev, *Vitte-diplomat*, p. 206.
15. Izvolsky, *The Memoirs of Alexander Izvolsky*, p. 24.
16. Korostovets, "Mirnye peregovory v Portsmute v 1905 goda," p. 179.
17. W.B. Thorson, "American Public Opinion and the Portsmouth Peace Conference," *American Historical Review* 48 (1948), p. 442.
18. E.J. Dillon, *The Eclipse of Russia* (New York, 1918), p. 301; J.A. White, *The Diplomacy of the Russo-Japanese War* (Princeton, NJ, 1964), p. 229.
19. Von Bülow to William II, July 15, 1904, *Die Grosse Politik* 19, pt. 1, p. 204.

20. R.A. Esthus, *Double Eagle and Rising Sun* (Durham, NC, 1988), p. 64; Witte, *Memoirs*, pp. 423–24.

21. Witte, *Memoirs*, p. 426.

22. Ignatev, *Vitte-diplomat*, p. 215n.

23. Witte, *Memoirs*, p. 431.

24. Ibid., pp. 432–35.

25. Desportes de la Fosse to Rouvier, August 8, 1905, *Documents Diplomatiques Françaises*, series 2, VII, p. 384.

26. Korostovets, "Mirnye peregovory v Portsmute v 1905 goda," p. 202; Witte, *Memoirs*, p. 434.

27. Desportes de la Fosse to Rouvier, August 8, 1905.

28. Korostovets, "Mirnye peregovory v Portsmute v 1905 goda," p. 204; Witte, *Memoirs*, p. 434.

29. Korostovets, "Mirnye peregovory v Portsmute v 1905 goda."

30. Ibid., pp. 205–8; *New York Times*, August 7, 1905; Witte, *Memoirs*, pp. 434–46.

31. Esthus, *Double Eagle and Rising Sun*, p. 83.

32. Ignatev, *Vitte-diplomat*, pp. 206–8; White, *The Diplomacy of the Russo-Japanese War*, pp. 253–54.

33. *Krasnyi arkhiv* 6 (1926), pp. 31–32.

34. Esthus, *Double Eagle and Rising Sun*, pp. 85–87.

35. Ignatev, *Vitte-diplomat*, pp. 223–24.

36. Thorson, "American Public Opinion and the Portsmouth Peace Conference," pp. 439–64.

37. *Krasnyi arkhiv*, 6 (1924), p. 31; O. Strauss, *Under Four Administrations* (Boston, 1922), pp. 189–90; Witte, *Memoirs*, p. 438.

38. Ignatev, *Vitte-diplomat*, p. 225.

39. Esthus, *Double Eagle and Rising Sun*, p. 107; Ignatev, *Vitte-diplomat*, p. 227.

40. Ignatev, *Vitte-diplomat*, p. 227.

41. Ibid., p. 229.

42. Esthus, *Double Eagle and Rising Sun*, pp. 141–42.

43. Witte, *Memoirs*, p. 440.

44. Ignatev, *Vitte-diplomat*, p. 233; Korostovets, "Mirnye peregovory v Portsmute v 1905 goda," pp. 74–75.

45. Ignatev, *Vitte-diplomat*, p. 234.

46. *Dnevniki Imperatora Nikolaia II* (Moscow, 1992), p. 275.

47. J.O. Baylen, "The Tsar's 'Lecturer General,'" *Georgia State College of Arts and Sciences Research Papers*, no. 23 (July 1969); Ignatev, *Vitte-diplomat*, p. 234.

48. Witte, *Memoirs*, p. 443–44.

49. *New York Times*, September 3, 1905.

50. *Sbornik dogovorov Rossii s drugimi gosudarstvami, 1856–1917* (Moscow, 1952), pp. 337–44.

51. *New York Times*, September 7–12, 1905; Witte, *Memoirs*, pp. 445–49.

52. *Krasnyi arkhiv*, VI (1924), pp. 46–47; Witte, *Memoirs*, pp. 448–49.

53. *The Letters of Theodore Roosevelt*, ed. by E.E. Morison, V (Cambridge, MA, 1952), pp. 22–23.

54. Witte, *Memoirs*, pp. 442–43.

55. Ignatev, *Vitte-diplomat*, p. 238.

56. Witte, *Memoirs*, p. 450.

Notes to Chapter 14

1. S.Iu. Witte, *Memoirs* (Armonk, NY, 1990), p. 450.
2. Bompard to Rouvier, September 22, 1905. France, Ministère des Affaires Étrangères, Archive, Russie, Politique Intérieure, II.
3. Witte, *Memoirs*, pp. 451–52, 699.
4. *Die Grosse Politik*, XIX, pt. 2, pp. 503–4.
5. Ibid., pp. 505–7; V.N. Kokovtsev, *Out of My Past* (Palo Alto, CA, 1935), pp. 62–65. Radolin's dispatch to von Bülow and the latter's dispatch to the kaiser do not support Kokovtsev's assertion that von Bülow misstated what Witte had said.
6. Von Bülow to von Holstein, July 15, 1905, *Die Grosse Politik*, XIX pt. 2, p. 436.
7. *Sbornik dogovorov Rossii s drugimi gosudarstvami* (Moscow, 1952), pp. 335–36.
8. *Die Grosse Politik*, XIX, pt. 2, pp. 509–11.
9. M. Bompard, "Les Mémoires du Comte Witte," *La Revue de Paris*, XXVII (1921), pp. 28–29. See also Bihourd to Rouvier, September 28, 1905, *D.D.F.*, series 2, VII, p. 585.
10. Cf. Nicholas II to William II, September 24/October 7, 1905, *Die Grosse Politik*, XIX, pt. 2, pp. 512–13.
11. *Secret Letters of the Last Tsar*, ed. by E. Bing (New York, 1938), p. 175.
12. Witte, *Memoirs*, p. 460.
13. Boutiron to Rouvier, October 21, 1905, France, Ministère des Affaires Étrangères, Archive, Russie, Politique Intérieure, II.
14. B. von Bülow, *Memoirs* 2 (1931), pp. 192–93.
15. *Die Grosse Politik* 19, pt. 2, pp. 519–21.
16. C. Spring-Rice, *The Letters and Friendships of Sir Cecil Spring-Rice* (Boston, 1929) 1, p. 459.
17. *Krasnyi arkhiv* 4 (1923), pp. 63, 65.
18. Ibid., p. 77; N.G. Koroleva, *Pervaia rossiiskaia revoliutsiia i tsarizm* (Moscow, 1982), p. 35.
19. Koroleva, p. 75.
20. Witte, *Memoirs*, p. 466.
21. S. Harcave, *The Russian Revolution of 1905* (New York, 1970), p. 170.
22. *Krasnyi arkhiv* 4 (1923), p. 74.
23. Ibid., p. 71.
24. "K istorii sozdaniia manifesta 17 Oktiabria," *Sovetskie arkhivy* 5 (1985), p. 60.
25. Hardinge to Sanderson, October 8, 1905, United Kingdom, Public Records Office, Foreign Office, 65/1703.

Notes to Chapter 15

1. S.Iu. Witte, *Memoirs* (Armonk, NY, 1990), p. 479.
2. Nicholas II, *Dnevnik imperatora Nikolas II* (Berlin, 1923), p. 220.
3. Ibid., pp. 220–21; *Revoliutsia 1905 goda i samoderzhavie*, ed. by V.P. Semennikov, (Moscow, 1928), pp. 39–41; A.M. Verner, *The Crisis of Russian Autocracy* (Princeton, NJ, 1990), p. 228 n. 25.
4. Witte, *Memoirs*, pp. 479–80.
5. J.O. Baylen, "The Tsar's 'Lecturer General,'" *Georgia State College of Arts and Sciences Research Papers*, no. 23 (July 1969), pp. 6–7.

6. Witte, *Memoirs*, p. 480.

7. Cf. T.H. von Laue, "Count Witte and the Russian Revolution of 1905," *American Slavic and East European Review*, February 1958, pp. 25–46.

8. *Secret Letters of the Last Tsar*, ed. by E. Bing (New York, 1938), p. 183.

9. A. Ascher, *The Revolution of 1905* 1 (Palo Alto, CA, 1988), pp. 213–14; H. Reichman, "Tsarist Labor Policy and the Railroads, 1885–1914," *Russian Review* 42 (1983), p. 64.

10. *Krasnyi arkhiv* 11–12 (1925), p. 61.

11. *Dnevniki imperatora Nikolaia II* (Moscow, 1992), p. 284.

12. *Krasnyi arkhiv* 4 (1923), p. 76.

13. Witte, *Memoirs*, p. 481.

14. Ibid.; *Dnevniki Imperatora Nikolaia II*, p. 284.

15. V.A. Gurko, *Features and Figures of the Past* (Palo Alto, CA, 1939), pp. 206–24; D. Lieven, *Russia's Rulers Under the Old Regime* (New Haven, CT, 1989), pp. 267–68; Witte, *Memoirs*, p. 396.

16. A.A. Ignatev, *Piatdesiat let v strolu*, I (Moscow, 1967), p. 176.

17. Witte, *Memoirs*, p. 482.

18. Ibid.

19. Ibid., p. 483n.

20. *Krasnyi arkhiv* 45, p. 89; A.A. Mosolov, *At the Court of the Last Tsar* (London, 1935), p. 90.

21. *Krasnyi arkhiv* 45, p. 88; Witte, *Memoirs*, pp. 483–84, 612.

22. *Dnevniki Imperatora Nikolaia II*, p. 284.

23. "Neizvestnyi proekt manifesta 17 Oktiabria 1905 goda," *Sovetskie arkhivy*, no. 2 (1979), pp. 63–65.

24. Witte, *Memoirs*, p. 484.

25. *Byloe*, no. 18, 1919, pp. 110–11; *Krasnyi arkhiv* 11–12 (1925), pp. 92–93.26. *Krasnyi arkhiv* 45, p. 89; *Secret Letters of the Last Tsar*, p. 185.

27. Witte, *Memoirs*, p. 613.

28. English translations of the manifesto and the memorandum will be found in S. Harcave, *The Russian Revolution of 1905* (New York, 1970), pp. 195–96, 289–92.

29. Witte, *Memoirs*, p. 613.

30. Ibid., p. 488.

Notes to Chapter 16

1. S. Harcave, *The Russian Revolution of 1905* (New York, 1970), pp. 195–96, 289–92.

2. S.Iu. Witte, *Memoirs* (Armonk, NY, 1990), p. 369.

3. P. Miliukov, *Vospominaniia* 1 (New York, 1955), p. 329.

4. *Secret Letters of the Last Tsar*, ed. by E. Bing (New York, 1938), pp. 187–88.

5. An English translation of the program will be found in S. Harcave, *The Russian Revolution of 1905* (New York, 1970), pp. 202–300.

6. Witte, *Memoirs*, pp. 408, 491, 503–4.

7. K.F. Shatsillo, "Pervyi den svobody v Peterburge," *Arkhegraficheskii ezhegodnik za 1975 god* (Moscow, 1976), p. 273n.

8. V.I. Lenin, *Polnoe sobranie sochinenii* 12 (Moscow, 1976), p. 76.

9. Witte, *Memoirs*, p. 494.

10. Ibid., pp. 495–96; *Krasnyi arkhiv* 11–12 (1925), pp. 99–105.

11. Harcave, *The Russian Revolution of 1905*, p. 292.

12. R.F. Byrnes, *Pobedonostsev* (Bloomington, IN, 1968), pp. 364–66; J.S. Curtiss, *Church and State in Russia* (New York, 1965), p. 367.

13. N.S. Tagantsev, *Perezhitoe* (Petrograd, 1918), pp. 99–106.

14. Shatsillo, "Pervyi den svobody v Peterburge," p. 273.

15. D.N. Shipov, *Vospominaniia i dumy o perezhitom* (Moscow, 1918), pp. 334–37; Witte, *Memoirs*, pp. 501–2.

16. Shipov, *Vospominaniia i dumy o perezhitom*, pp. 338–41; Witte, *Memoirs*, p. 502.

17. I.I. Petrunkevich, "Iz zapisok obshchestvennago deatelia," *Arkhiv russkoi revoliutsii*, XXI (1934), p. 432.

18. I.V. Gessen, *V dvukh vekakh* (Berlin, 1937), pp. 207–8.

19. Shipov, *Vospominaniia i dumy o perezhitom*, p. 392.

20. Witte, *Memoirs*, p. 503.

21. S.Iu. Witte, "Moia polemika s A.I. Guchkovym," appendix to his *Vospominaniia* 3, pp. 595–607.

22. Witte, *Memoirs*, p. 503.

23. Shipov, *Vospominaniia i dumy o perezhitom*, p. 347.

24. Cf. V.A. Gurko, *Features and Figures of the Past* (Palo Alto, CA, 1939), p. 406.

25. P.N. Miliukov, *Vospominaniia*, 1, (New York, 1955), p. 326.

26. Ibid.; B.B. Glinskii, "Graf Sergei Iulevich Vitte," *Istoricheskii vestnik* 142 (1915), pp. 899–904.

27. *Byloe* 32, no. 4 (1925), p. 107; V.N. Kokovtsev, *Out of My Past* (Palo Alto, CA, 1935), pp. 76–78.

28. H. Reichman, "Tsarist Labor Policy and the Railroads, 1885–1914)," *Russian Review*, XLII (1983), p. 64.

29. L.I. Tolstaia, "Vospominaniia I.I. Tolstago kak istoricheskii istochnik," *Vspomogatelnye istoricheskie distsipliny* 19 (1987), pp. 205–6; Witte, *Memoirs*, p. 509.

30. *Secret Letters of the Last Tsar*, p. 188; Witte, *Memoirs*, p. 513.

31. "Graf S.Iu. Vitte i Leo Mekhelin," *Byloe* 30, no. 2 (1918), pp. 108–9; Witte, *Memoirs*, pp. 497–98. Witte was later accused by opponents of Finnish autonomy of being the author of the manifesto.

32. "The Years 1881–1894 in Russia," *Transactions of the American Philosophical Society* 71 (1981), p. 42.

33. *Tsarizm v borbe s revoliutsiei 1905–1907 gg.* (Moscow, 1936), pp. 150–51; Witte, *Memoirs*, pp. 524–26.

34. *Byloe*, no. 18 (1919), pp. 110–11.

35. S.M. Dubnow, *History of the Jews in Russia and Poland*, III (Philadelphia, 1920), pp. 130–31.

36. *Secret Letters of the Last Tsar*, p. 188.

37. Ibid., pp. 190–92.

Notes to Chapter 17

1. S.A. Stepanov, *Chernaia sotnia* (Moscow, 1992), p. 121.

2. *Secret Letters of the Last Tsar*, ed. by E. Bing (New York, 1938), pp. 191–92.

3. S.Iu. Witte, *Memoirs* (Armonk, NY, 1990), pp. 513–14.

4. *Secret Letters of the Last Tsar,* p. 215.

5. Witte, *Memoirs*, pp. 514–15.

6. A.A. Spasskii-Odynets, *Vospominaniia* (Bakhmetev Archive, Columbia University), p. 27.

7. *Krasnyi arkhiv* 45 (1931), p. 90.

8. L.I. Tolstaia, "Vospominaniia I.I. Tolstago kak istoricheskii istochnik," *Vospomogatelnye istoricheskie distsipliny*, XIX (1987), p. 209.

9. T.H. von Laue, "Count Witte and the Russian Revolution of 1905," *American Slavic and East European Review*, February 1958, pp. 25–46.

10. Tolstaia, "Vospominaniia I.I. Tolstago kak istoricheskii istochnik," p. 207; F.W. Wcislo, "Witte, Memory and the 1905 Revolution," *Revolutionary Russia*, VIII (1995), pp. 166–78.

11. S.M. Propper, *Was nicht in die Zeitung kam* (Frankfurt am Main, 1929), p. 262.

12. B.B. Glinskii, "Graf Sergei Iulevich Vitte," *Istoricheskii vestnik* 140 (1915), p. 609.

13. N.G. Koroleva, *Pervaia rossiiskaia revoliutsiia i tsarizm* (Moscow, 1982), pp. 71–72.

14. Witte, *Memoirs*, p. 522.

15. G.E. Afanasev, "K konchine Grafa S.Iu. Vitte," *Volny*, no. 3, 1915, col. 99.

16. A.M. Verner, *The Crisis of Russian Autocracy* (Princeton, NJ, 1990), pp. 266–67.

17. H.D. Mehlinger and J.M. Thompson, *Count Witte and the Tsarist Government in the 1905 Revolution* (Bloomington, IN, 1972), pp. 118–19.

18. N.S. Tagantsev, *Perezhitoe* (Petrograd, 1918), p. 82; "Tsarskoselskie soveshchaniia," *Byloe*, no. 3 (25) (1917), pp. 217–65; no. 4 (26) (1917), pp. 183–245.

19. *Gosudarstvennaia duma v Rossii: v dokumentakh i materialakh*, ed. by F.I. Kalinychev (Moscow, 1957).

20. Tagantsev, *Perezhitoe*, pp. 107, 151; "Tsarskoselskie soveshchaniia," *Byloe*, nos. 5/6 (27/28) (1917), pp. 292–318; Witte, *Memoirs*, pp. 577–78.

21. *Gosudarstvennaia duma v Rossii*, pp. 102–23; Witte, *Memoirs*, pp. 577–78.

Notes to Chapter 18

1. Cf. Iliodor (S.M. Trufanov), *Pravda o soiuze russkago naroda, soiuze russkago liudei i drugikh monarchicheskikh partiiakh* (Odessa, 1907).

2. "Dnevnik G.O. Raukha," *Krasnyi arkhiv* 19 (1926), pp. 88–90.

3. *Krasnyi arkhiv*, 45 (1931), 100n.

4. "Dnevnik G.O. Raukha," pp. 90, 100; B. Elkin, "Attempts to Revive Freemasonry in Russia," *Slavonic and East European Review* 44 (1966), pp. 454–72.

5. Nicholas II, *Dnevnik imperatora Nikolas II* (Berlin, 1923), p. 229.

6. A.A. Lopukhin, *Otryvki iz vospominanii* (Moscow, 1923), pp. 76–88; S.Iu. Witte, *Memoirs* (Armonk, NY, 1990), pp. 515–17.

7. A. Agursky, "Caught in a Cross Fire: The Russian Church Between Holy Synod and Radical Right (1905–1908)," *Orientalia Christiana Periodica* 50 (1984), pp. 168, 170.

8. J. Curtiss, *Church and State in Russia, 1900–1917* (New York, 1965), p. 259.

9. H. Löwe, *The Tsar and the Jews* (Chur, Switzerland, 1993), p. 217.

10. *Pravye partii: dokumenty i materialy*, I (Moscow, 1998), p. 613.

11. S.A. Stepanov, *Chernaia sotnia* (Moscow, 1992), p. 121.

12. A.V. Ignatev, *Vneshnaia politika Rossii v 1905–1907 gg.* (Moscow, 1986), p. 82.

13. *Krasnyi arkhiv* 60 (1933), p. 100.

14. Lopukhin, *Otryvki iz vospominanii,* pp. 82–83.

15. S. Harcave, *The Russian Revolution of 1905* (New York, 1970), pp. 216–20.

16. *Secret Letters of the Last Tsar,* ed. by E. Bing (New York, 1938), pp. 192–93.

17. *Tsarizm v borbe s revoliutsiei, 1905–1907 gg.: sbornik dokumentov* (Moscow, 1936), pp. 9, 116.

18. *Sovet ministrov Rossiiskoi Imperii, 1905–1906* (Leningrad, 1990), pp. 31–40.

19. *Secret Letters of the Last Tsar,* p. 200.

20. D. Lieven, *Russia's Rulers Under the Old Regime* (New Haven, CT, 1989), pp. 207–30.

21. H.D. Mehlinger and J.M. Thompson, *Count Witte and the Tsarist Government in the 1905 Revolution* (Bloomington, IN, 1972), p. 85; P.I. Potolov, "Ukaz 2 dekabria 1905 g.," *Vspomogatelnye distsipliny* 16 (1985), pp. 221–22; Witte, *Memoirs,* pp. 526–27.

22. Witte, *Memoirs,* p. 418; A.S. Suvorin, *Dnevnik* (Moscow, 1922), p. 418.

23. A. Ascher, *The Revolution of 1905,* I (Palo Alto, CA, 1988), pp. 298–99.

24. G. Garvy, "The Financial Manifesto of the Saint Petersburg Soviet," *International Review of Social History* 20, pt. 1 (1975), pp. 30–31.

25. *Secret Letters of the Last Tsar,* pp. 194–95.

26. Witte, *Memoirs,* pp. 531–35.

27. Ibid., pp. 535–36; Harcave, *The Russian Revolution of 1905,* pp. 233–34.

28. *Tsarizm v borbe s revoliutsiei, 1905–1907 gg.,* p. 18; Witte, *Memoirs,* p. 536.

29. *Secret Letters of the Last Tsar,* p. 201.

30. L. Engelstein, *Moscow, 1905* (Palo Alto, CA, 1982), p. 220; G. Vetlugin, "S.Iu. Vitte i dekabrskoe vosstanie v Moskve," *Byloe* 24 (1925), pp. 225–26.

31. *Secret Letters of the Last Tsar,* p. 21; A.A. Spasskii-Odynets, *Vospominaniia* (Bakhmeteff Archive, Columbia University), pp. 18–19.

32. Witte, *Memoirs,* pp. 537, 809–10.

33. *Secret Letters of the Last Tsar,* pp. 211–12.

34. *Revoliutsiia 1905 goda i samoderzhavie,* ed. by V. Semennikov (Moscow, 1928), pp. 41–43; Witte, *Memoirs,* p. 537.

35. Witte, *Memoirs,* pp. 529, 808 n. 12.

36. Ibid., p. 523; *Revoliutsiia 1905 goda i samoderzhavie,* p. 58.

37. Witte, *Memoirs,* pp. 541–42; *Tsarizm v borbe s revoliutsiei, 1905–1907 gg.,* p. 244 n. 6.

38. A.S. Gerasimov, *Na lezvii s terroristami* (Paris, 1935), pp. 50–52.

39. *Tsarizm v borbe s revoliutsiei, 1905–1907 gg.,* p. 100.

40. Akademiia Nauk SSSR, Institut Istorii, *Revoliutsiia 1905–1907 gg. v Rossii; vyshii podem revoliutsiei,* I (Moscow, 1955), pp. 162–63.

41. *Sovet ministrov,* pp. 117–18.

42. A.M. Verner, *The Crisis of Russian Autocracy* (Princeton, NJ, 1990), p. 277.

43. *Revoliutsiia 1905 goda i samoderzhavie,* pp. 30–32.

44. Mehlinger and Thompson, *Count Witte and the Tsarist Government in the 1905 Revolution,* p. 158.

45. Hintze to William II, January 28, 1909, Germany, Auswärtiges Amt, Archive, *Russland,* 82, no. 1, Geheim, vols. 6–7.

46. Witte, *Memoirs,* p. 597.

Notes to Chapter 19

1. The chapter title comes from the title of a pamphlet published by Witte in 1913.
2. V.N. Kokovtsev, *Out of My Past* (Palo Alto, CA, 1935), pp. 70–73; H.D. Mehlinger and J.M. Thompson, *Count Witte and the Tsarist Government in the 1905 Revolution* (Bloomington, IN, 1972), pp. 216–17; B.A. Romanov, *Russia in Manchuria, 1892–1906* (Ann Arbor, MI, 1952), pp. 360–61; S.Iu. Witte, *Memoirs* (Armonk, NY, 1990), p. 453.
3. Kokovtsev, *Out of My Past*, pp. 89–99; Witte, *Memoirs*, pp. 563–64.
4. Witte, *Memoirs*, p. 562.
5. O. Crisp, "The Russian Liberals and the 1906 Anglo-French Loan to Russia," *Slavonic and East European Review* 39 (1961), pp. 497–511; A.A. Lopukhin, *Otryvki iz vospominanii* (Moscow, 1923), p. 76–88.
6. Romanov, *Russia in Manchuria*, p. 364.
7. Kokovtsev, *Out of My Past*, pp. 107–11; Witte, *Memoirs*, pp. 564–65.
8. A.V. Ignatev, *Vitte-diplomat* (Moscow, 1989), p. 276.
9. Witte, *Memoirs*, p. 570.
10. Ignatev, *Vitte-diplomat*, p. 287.
11. Ibid., pp. 283–88; Witte, *Memoirs*, p. 568.
12. Ignatev, *Vitte-diplomat*, p. 288; Kokovtsev, *Out of My Past*, pp. 114–15; Witte, *Memoirs*, p. 569.
13. R. Girault, *Emprunts russes et investissements français en Russie, 1887–1914* (Paris, 1973), pp. 444 n. 69, 445.
14. Witte, *Memoirs*, pp. 571–72.

Notes to Chapter 20

1. S.Iu. Witte, *Memoirs* (Armonk, NY, 1990), pp. 595–96.
2. *Secret Letters of the Last Tsar*, ed. by E. Bing (New York, 1938), p. 211.
3. *Revoliutsiia 1905 goda i samoderzhavie*, ed. by V. Semennikov (Moscow, 1928), pp. 45–54.
4. Witte, *Memoirs*, p. 678.
5. *Krasnyi arkhiv* 105, 149–50; *Sovet ministrov rossiiskoi imperii, 1905–1906* (Leningrad, 1990), pp. 231–34.
6. B.V. Ananich and R. Sh. Ganelin, "Opyt kritiki memuarov S.Iu. Vitte," in *Voprosy istoriografii i istochnikovedeniia istorii SSSR: sbornik statei*, no. 5 (1963), Trudy Leningradskogo otdeleniia Instituta Istorii, pp. 347–50; E.J. Dillon, *The Eclipse of Russia* (New York, 1918), pp. 164–65; A.S. Gerasimov, *Na lezvii s terroristami* (Paris, 1935), pp. 61–63; *Krasnaia letopis* 1 (1922), pp. 302–3; W. Sablinsky, *The Road to Bloody Sunday* (Princeton, NJ, 1976), pp. 305–15.
7. N. Petrov, "Gapon i Graf Vitte," *Byloe*, no. 1 (29), 1925, pp. 15–27.
8. I.V. Gessen, *V dvukh vekakh* (Berlin, 1937), p. 207.
9. Witte, *Memoirs*, p. 410.
10. A. Ascher, *The Revolution of 1905*, I (Palo Alto, CA, 1988), p. 111; S. Harcave, *The Years of the Golden Cockerel: The Last Romanov Tsars, 1814–1917* (New York, 1968), p. 315.
11. Witte, *Memoirs*, pp. 410–11.
12. Ibid., p. 588.

13. *Sovet ministrov*, pp. 45–50; Witte, *Memoirs*, p. 589.

14. Witte, *Memoirs*, 589.

15. K.N. Mironenko, "Manifest 17 oktiabria 1905 g.," Iuridicheskii facultet Leningradskogo Universiteta, *Uchenye zapiski*, no. 255 (1958), pp. 166–68; *Sovet ministrov*, pp. 218–28; Witte, *Memoirs*, pp. 588–89.

16. Mironenko, "Manifest 17 oktiabria 1905 g.," pp. 168–69; *Sovet ministrov*, pp. 165–72.

17. Witte, *Memoirs*, pp. 590–91.

18. J.W. Cunningham, *A Vanquished Hope* (Crestwood, NY, 1981), pp. 208–321 passim.

19. Witte, *Memoirs*, p. 590.

20. Ibid., pp. 592–93.

21. *Sovet ministrov*, p. 196.

22. Ibid., pp. 279–80.

23. Ibid., p. 283.

24. Ibid., pp. 431–32.

25. N.G. Koroleva, *Pervaia rossiiskaia revoliutsiia i tsarizm* (Moscow, 1982), p. 87.

26. *Sovet ministrov*, pp. 30–40.

27. H.D. Mehlinger and J.M. Thompson, *Count Witte and the Tsarist Government in the 1905 Revolution* (Bloomington, IN, 1972), pp. 188–89; Witte, *Memoirs*, pp. 548–50.

28. V.N. Kokovtsev, *Out of My Past* (Palo Alto, CA, 1935), pp. 99–100; Witte, *Memoirs*, pp. 550–52.

29. Witte, *Memoirs*, p. 550.

30. *Sovet ministrov*, pp. 149–50.

31. *Revoliutsiia 1905 g. i samoderzhavie*, p. 57; Witte, *Memoirs*, pp. 554–55.

32. Kokovtsev, *Out of My Past,* p. 99.

33. A.V. Bogdanovich, *Tri poslednikh samoderzhtsa* (Moscow, 1924), pp. 364–65.

34. *Krasnyi arkhiv* 19 (1926), pp. 96–97.

35. *Sovet ministrov*, pp. 256–57.

36. Ibid.

37. Witte, *Memoirs*, pp. 555–56.

38. *Sovet ministrov*, p. 258.

39. Ibid., pp. 204–9, 449–59.

Notes to Chapter 21

1. H.D. Mehlinger and J.M. Thompson, *Count Witte and the Tsarist Government in the 1905 Revolution* (Bloomington, IN, 1972), p. 251.

2. *Gosudarstvennaia duma v Rossii: v dokumentakh i materialakh*, ed. by F.I. Kalinychev (Moscow, 1957), pp. 136–40.

3. S.Iu. Witte, *Memoirs* (Armonk, NY, 1990), p. 579.

4. *Sovet ministrov rossiiskoi imperii, 1905–1906* (Leningrad, 1990), pp. 331–32; Witte, *Memoirs*, p. 580.

5. I.V. Gessen, *V dvukh vekakh* (Berlin, 1937), p. 224; N.S. Tagantsev, *Perezhitoe* (Petrograd, 1918), pp. 157–58, 157–58n.

6. Mehlinger and Thompson, *Count Witte and the Tsarist Government in the 1905 Revolution*, pp. 336–44; *Sovet ministrov*, pp. 336–44.

7. "Tsarskoselskie soveshchaniia," *Byloe 26*, no. 4 (1917), p. 189.

8. Ibid., p. 194.

9. Ibid., p. 202.

10. Ibid., pp. 204, 245.

11. Ibid., p. 245.

12. Witte, *Memoirs*, p. 586.

13. *Sovet ministrov*, pp. 211–12, 446–67.

14. A.A. Spasskii-Odynets, *Vospominaniia* (Bakhmeteff Archive, Columbia University), p. 22, states that two-thirds of the cabinet were hostile to Witte. Witte, *Memoirs*, pp. 599–601.

15. N.G. Koroleva, *Pervaia rossiiskaia revoliutsiia i tsarizm* (Moscow, 1982), p. 106.

16. A.V. Ignatev, *Vitte-diplomat* (Moscow, 1989), p. 297.

17. V.A. Gurko, *Features and Figures of the Past* (Palo Alto, CA, 1939), p. 456.

18. *Dnevniki Imperatora Nikolaia II* (Moscow, 1992), p. 239; Witte, *Memoirs*, pp. 602–3, 819 n. 15.

19. L.I. Tolstaia, "Vospominaniia I.I. Tolstago kak istoricheskii istochnik," *Vspomogatelnye istoricheskie distsipliny* 19 (1987), p. 213.

20. *Pravitelstvennyi vestnik*, April 22, 1906; Witte, *Memoirs*, p. 802.

21. Koroleva, *Pervaia rossiiskaia revoliutsiia i tsarizm,* p. 106n.

22. There are some unresolved questions concerning the issuance of the fundamental laws. See Witte, *Memoirs*, p. 817 n. 25.

23. M. Szeftel, *The Russian Constitution of April 23, 1906* (Brussels, 1976), pp. 77–78.

24. Nicholas II, *Dnevnik imperatora Nikolas II* (Berlin, 1923), p. 240; Szeftel, *The Russian Constitution of April 23, 1906,* p. 106.

Notes to Chapter 22

1. S.Iu. Witte, *Memoirs* (Armonk, NY, 1990), pp. 624–26.

2. Ibid., p. 627.

3. *Secret Letters of the Last Tsar*, ed. by E. Bing (New York, 1938), pp. 219–20; see also *Pravye partii: dokumenty i materialy*, I, ed. by O.V. Volubnev et al. (Moscow, 1998), p. 211.

4. A.V. Ignatev, *Vitte-diplomat* (Moscow, 1989), p. 298, asserts that the idea of an ambassadorship for Witte was opposed by the foreign service and that the tsar chose not to pursue the matter, but he gives no details or sources.

5. A.F. Koni, "Sergei Iulevich Vitte," *Sobranie sochinenii* 5 (Moscow, 1968), pp. 258–59.

6. *The Times* (London), June 22, 1907, p. 12.

7. Koni, "Sergei Iulevich Vitte," pp. 260–62.

8. Ibid.

9. B.B. Glinskii, "Graf Sergei Iulevich Vitte," *Istoricheskii vestnik* 117 (1915), p. 899.

10. I.I. Tolstoi, *Dnevnik* (St. Petersburg, 1997), pp. 94–95, 115.

11. A. Agursky, "Caught in a Cross Fire: The Russian Church Between Holy Synod and Radical Right (1905–1908)," *Orientalia Christiana Periodica* 50 (1984), p. 177.

12. *Krasnyi arkhiv* 38 (1930), p. 67; Witte, *Memoirs*, pp. 604, 617.

13. *Krasnyi arkhiv* 11–12 (1925), p. 23.

14. Ibid.; Witte, *Memoirs*, pp. 604, 609–10.

15. Witte, *Memoirs*, p. 608.

16. B.V. Ananich and R. Sh. Ganelin, "Opyt kritiki memuarov S.Iu. Vitte," in *Voprosy istoriografii i istochnikovedeniia istorii SSSR: sbornik statei,* no. 5 (1963), Trudy Leningradskogo otdeleniia Instituta Istorii, pp. 309–13.

17. Ibid., pp. 317–18.

18. Ibid., p. 312.

19. Witte, *Memoirs*, p. 349.

20. S.A. Stepanov, *Chernaia sotnia v Rossii* (Moscow, 1992), pp. 154–64; E.J. Dillon, *The Eclipse of Russia* (New York, 1918), pp. 187–95; Witte, *Memoirs*, pp. 629–35.

21. A.S. Gerasimov, *Na lezvii s terroristami* (Paris, 1935), pp. 152–53.

22. H. Heilbronner, "An Anti-Witte Conspiracy, 1905–1906," *Jahrbücher für Geschichte Osteuropas* 14 (1966), pp. 331–61; A.S. Suvorin, *Dnevnik* (Moscow, 1922), pp. 41–13; Witte, *Memoirs*, pp. 704–7.

23. Witte, *Memoirs*, pp. 827–28 n. 2.

24. Suvorin, *Dnevnik,* p. 406.

25. Ibid.

26. Ibid., pp. 404–5.

Notes to Chapter 23

1. S.Iu. Witte, *Memoirs* (Armonk, NY, 1990), p. 375.

2. Ibid., p. 369. See also p. 109 of this text.

3. Witte, *Memoirs*, pp. 656–57.

4. Ibid., p. 677.

5. H. Jablonowski, "Die russischen Rechtsparteien," in *Russland Studien* (Stuttgart, 1957), pp. 42–55.

6. Witte, *Memoirs*, p. 645.

7. S.A. Stepanov, *Chernaia sotnia v Rossii* (Moscow, 1992), pp. 180, 184; A.S. Gerasimov, *Na lezvii s terroristami* (Paris, 1935), p. 153; Witte, *Memoirs*, pp. 639–42.

8. Gerasimov, *Na lezvii s terroristami,* p. 153.

9. A. Chernovskii, *Soiuz russkogo naroda* (Moscow, 1924), pp. 107–30; A.F. Koni, "Sergei Iulevich Vitte," *Sobranie sochinenii,* V (Moscow, 1968), pp. 275–76; L. Lvov (A.M. Kliachko) "Perepiska Grafa S.Iu. Vitte i P.A. Stolypina," *Russkaia mysl* 36 (1915), pp. 134–52; Witte, *Memoirs*, pp. 629–41.

10. Witte, *Memoirs*, pp. 823–24 n. 10.

11. B.V. Ananich and R. Sh. Ganelin, "Opyt kritiki memuarov S.Iu. Vitte," in *Voprosy istoriografii i istochnikovedeniia istorii SSSR: sbornik statei,* no. 5 (1963), Trudy Leningradskogo otdeleniia Instituta Istorii, p. 372.

12. A. Markow, *Rasputin und die um ihm* (Königsberg, 1928), p. 98.

13. A. Tager, *The Decay of Tsarism* (Philadelphia, 1925), p. 16.

14. *The Times* (London), October 14 and 17, 1912.

15. I.I. Tolstoi, *Dnevnik* (St. Petersburg, 1997), pp. 45, 60–61.

16. Ananich and Ganelin, "Opyt kritiki," p. 321.

17. Ibid., pp. 327–30; *New York Times,* August 18, 1911.

18. S. Harcave, "The Hessen Redaction of the Witte Memoirs," *Jahrbücher für Geschichte Osteuropas* 36 (1988), p. 269.

19. S.Iu. Witte, *Vospominaniia. Rasskazy v stenograficheskoi zapisi*, p. 1423. Bakhmeteff Archive, Columbia University.

20. *Byvshii ministr finansov Sergei Iulevich Vitte kak glavnyi vinovnik . . . v dele ogrableniia krymskago pomeshchika K.A. Durante . . .* (Odessa, 1908).

21. Witte, *Memoirs*, p. 755.

22. Russia, Gosudarstvennyi sovet, *Stenograficheskie otchety 1910–1911 gg., sessiia VI* (St. Petersburg, 1911), col. 1308.

23. Tolstoi, *Dnevnik*, p. 301.

24. Russia, Gosudarstvennyi sovet, *Stenograficheskie otchety 1908–1909 gg., sessiia IV* (St. Petersburg, 1909), cols. 1343, 1359.

25. Russia, Gosudarstvennyi sovet, *Stenograficheskie otchety 1910–1911 gg., sessiia VI* (St. Petersburg, 1911), col. 318.

26. I.I. Tolstoi, *Dnevnik*, p. 363.

27. V.N. Kokovtsev, *Out of My Past* (Palo Alto, CA, 1935), p. 291; Witte, *Memoirs*, p. 738. The two accounts differ slightly in detail.

Notes to Chapter 24

1. S.Iu. Witte, *Memoirs* (Armonk, NY, 1990), pp. 306, 742.

2. S.Iu. Witte, *Zapisi Grafa Witte*, p. 363, Bakhmeteff Archive, Columbia University.

3. V.N. Kokovtsev, *Out of My Past* (Palo Alto, CA, 1935), pp. 328–32; the text of Countess Witte's letter will be found in Kokovtsev's *Iz moego proshlago*, II (Paris, 1933), p. 91.

4. Kokovtsev, *Out of My Past*, p. 333.

5. H. Bernstein, *Celebrities of Our Times* (Freeport, NY, 1968), p. 33.

6. I.V. Gessen, *Gody iznaniia* (Paris, 1979), pp. 18–19. The Schiff papers in the American Jewish Archive do not contain any reference to such an offer according to a letter from F. Zelcher to S. Harcave, December 1, 1977. Nonetheless, Gessen is apparently reporting what Countess Witte told him. See also B.V. Ananich and R. Sh. Ganelin, "Opyt kritiki memuarov S.Iu. Vitte," in *Voprosy istoriografii i istochnikovedeniia istorii SSSR: sbornik statei*, no. 5 (1963), Trudy Leningradskogo otdeleniia Instituta Istorii, p. 299.

7. Witte, *Memoirs*, p. 742.

8. B.V. Ananich and R. Sh. Ganelin, *S.Iu. Vitte-Memuarist* (St. Petersburg, 1994), p. 3; Witte, *Memoirs*, p. 845.

9. E.J. Dillon, "Two Russian Statesmen," *Quarterly Review* 236 (1921), p. 408.

10. S.Iu. Witte, *Prolog Russko-Iaponskoi voiny* (Petrograd, 1916).

11. Glinskii, "B.B. Graf Sergei Iulevich Vitte," *Istoricheskii vestnik* 140 (1915), pp. 232–79; 141 (1915), pp. 520–55, 893–906; 142 (1915), pp. 592–609, 893–907.

12. Bernstein, *Celebrities of Our Times,* pp. 34–35.

13. J. Melnik, "Witte," *Century Magazine*, September 1915, p. 690.

14. M. Kulikowski, *Rasputin and the Fall of the Romanovs* (Ph.D. dissertation, 1982, SUNY Binghamton).

15. Witte, *Memoirs*, pp. 625n., 662, 681, 739.

16. I.V. Gessen, *V dvukh vekakh* (Berlin, 1937), p. 320.

17. B. Pares, *The Fall of the Russian Monarchy* (New York, 1961), p. 223; Russia, Chrezvychainaia sledstvennaia komissiia, *Padenie tsarskogo rezhima* (Leningrad and Moscow, 1924–1927), 4, pp. 501–2.

18. B.V. Ananich, *Bankirskie doma v Rossii, 1860–1914 gg.* (Leningrad, 1991), pp. 140–42.

19. Kokovtsev, *Out of My Past*, p. 409.

20. B.B. Glinskii, "Graf Sergei Iulevich Vitte," *Istoricheskii vestnik* 142 (1915), p. 907.

21. Ibid.; Bernstein, *Celebrities of Our Times*, p. 38.

22. Bernstein, *Celebrities of Our Times*, pp. 27–31; Witte, *Memoirs*, pp. 27–31.

23. A. Izvolsky, "Le Comte Witte," *Revue de Paris* 29 (1922), pp. 703–20; Witte, *Memoirs*, pp. 699–701.

24. Witte, *Memoirs*, pp. 697–98.

25. Kokokovtsev, *Out of My Past*, pp. 209–12; Witte, *Memoirs*, p. 698.

26. Ibid., pp. 698–99.

27. I.I. Tolstoi, *Dnevnik* (St. Petersburg, 1997), p. 417.

28. Bernstein, *Celebrities of Our Times*, pp. 29–30.

29. A.V. Ignatev, *Vitte-diplomat* (Moscow, 1989), p. 312.

30. Witte to Nicholas II, May 11, 1914, *Monarkhiia pered krusheniem*, pp. 99–100.

31. *Moskovskii listok*, July 2, 1914.

32. A.E. Kaufman, "Cherty iz zhizni grafa S.Iu. Vitte," *Istoricheskii vestnik*, CXXXX (1915), pp. 230–31; B. M. Vitenberg, "K istorii lichnogo arkhiva S.Iu. Vitte," *Vospomogatelnye istoricheskie distsipliny*, XVII (1986), 257 n. 35. B.V. Ananich and R.Sh. Ganelin, *Sergei Inlevich Vitte i ego vremia* (St. Petersburg, 1999), p. 392 n. 20.

33. N. de Basily, *Memoirs* (Palo Alto CA, 1973), p. 101n.

34. V. Naryshkin-Witte, *Souvenirs de fillette russes* (Paris, 1925), pp. 229–36.

35. Kaufman, "Cherty iz zhizni grafa S.Iu. Vitte," p. 230.

36. A. Rumanov, "Shtrikhi k portretam," *Vremia i my*, no. 95 (1987); B.B. Glinskii, "Graf Sergei Iulevich Vitte," *Istoricheskii vestnik*, CXL (1915), p. 593.

37. M. Paléologue, *An Ambassador's Diary* I, (New York, 1923), pp. 122–23.

38. A.F. Koni, "Sergei Iulevich Vitte," *Sobranie sochinenii*, V (Moscow, 1968), p. 277.

39. Ananich and Ganelin, *Sergei Iulevich Vitte i ego vremia*, pp. 387–88.

40. Ibid., p. 387.

41. Ibid., pp. 391–92 n. 12; S.Iu. Witte, "Libava ili Murmansk," *Proshloe i nastoiashchee*, Vyp. 1 (1924), pp. 25–39; Witte, *Memoirs*, pp. 193–97, 210–11.

42. Koni, "Sergei Iulevich Vitte," p. 262.

43. B.B. Glinskii, "Graf Sergei Iulevich Vitte," *Istoricheskii vestnik* 141 (1915), p. 609; CXLII (1915), p. 907.

44. *Monarkhiia pered krusheniem*, pp. 100–1.

45. B.B. Glinskii, "Graf Sergei Iulevich Vitte," *Istoricheskii vestnik* 142 (1915), p. 905; Tolstoi, *Dnevnik*, p. 610.

46. *Perepiska Nikolaia i Aleksandry Romanovikh*, III (Moscow, 1923), p. 116.

47. *Pravitelstvennyi vestnik*, March 3, 1915.

48. Ignatev, *Vitte-diplomat*, p. 314; Tolstoi, *Dnevnik*, p. 612.

49. Ananich and Ganelin, "Opyt kritiki," p. 299.

50. M.A. Tkachenko, "Fond S.Iu. Vitte v TSGIA," in *Nekotorye voprosy istoriografii i istochnikovedeniia SSSR: sbornik statei* (Moscow, 1977), pp. 186–97; Vitenberg, "K istorii lichnogo arkhiva S.Iu. Vitte," pp. 248–60.

51. Witte, *Memoirs*, p. 24. Countess Witte asserts that the search in Biarritz began after she said no to the tsar. Vitenberg provides a different sequence.

Notes to Afterword

1. S. Harcave, "The Hessen Redaction of the Witte Memoirs," *Jahrbücher für Geschichte Osteuropas*, XXXVI (1988), pp. 270–72.

2. Baian (I.I. Kolyshko), *Lozh Vitte* (Berlin, n.d.).

3. V.V. Vodovozov, *Graf S.Iu. Vitte i Imperator Nikolai II* (Petrograd, 1922), p. 126.

4. S.Iu. Witte, *Vospominaniia* (Moscow, 1960), III.

5. A. Ia. Avrekh, "Politicheskaia kontseptsiia S.Iu. Vitte," in *Rossiiskaia Akademiia Nauk. Institut Ekonomiki. Sergei Iulevich Vitte—gosudarstvennyi deiatel, reformator i ekonomist* (Moscow, 1999), pt. 1, p. 152.

6. L.M. Abalkin, "Ekonomicheskie vozzreniia S.Iu. Vitte i ego gosudarstvennaia deiatelnost," in *Rossiiskaia Akademiia Nauk. Institut Ekonomiki. Sergei Iulevich Vitte—gosudarstvennyi deiatel, reformator i ekonomist*, pp. 5–48.

7. L.I. Zaitseva, *S.Iu. Vitte i Rossiia* (Moscow, 2000).

8. N.V. Raskov, *Politiko-ekonomicheskaia sistema S.Iu. Vitte i sovremennaia Rossiia* (St. Petersburg, 2000).

9. A. Kahan, *Russian Economic History* (Chicago, 1989), p. xi.

Bibliography

Books and Articles About Witte

Abalkin, L. *Ekonomicheskie vozzreniia i gosudarstvennaia deiatelnost S. Iu. Vitte* (The Economic Outlook and Governmental Practice of S. Iu. Witte). Moscow, 1999.

Aizenberg, L. M. "Velikii Kniaz Sergei Aleksandrovich, Vitte i evrei-moskovskie kuptsy" (Grand Duke Sergei Aleksandrovich, Witte and Jewish Muscovite Merchants). *Evreiskaia starina* 13 (1930), pp. 80–89.

Ananich, B. V. "Memuary S. Iu. Vitte v tvorcheskoi sudbe B. A. Romanova" (Memoirs of S. Iu. Witte in the Creative Work of B. A. Romanov). In *Problemy sotsialno-ekonomicheskoi istorii Rossii*, pp. 30–40. St. Petersburg, 1991.

———. "O rukopisakh i tekste memuarov S. Iu. Vitte" (Concerning the Manuscripts and Text of the Memoirs of S. Iu. Vitte). *Vspomogatelnye istoricheskie distsipliny* 12, pp. 188–204. Leningrad, 1981.

———. "S. Iu. Vitte v Portsmute." In *Problemy vsemirnoi istorii*, pp. 339–46. St. Petersburg, 2000.

Ananich, B. V., and R. Sh. Ganelin. "Opyt kritiki memuarov S. Iu. Vitte" (An Attempt at a Critique of the Memoirs of S. Iu. Witte). In *Voprosy istoriografii i istochnikovedeniia istorii SSSR: sbornik statei*. Vypusk 5, pp. 298–374. Trudy Leningradskogo otdeleniia Instituta Istorii, 1963.

———. "S. Iu. Vitte, M. P. Dragomanov i 'Volnoe slovo'" (S. Iu. Vitte, M. P. Dragomanov and *Volnoe slovo*). In *Issledovaniia po otechestvennomu istochnikovedeniia: sbornik statei posviashchennykh 75—letiiu professora S. N. Valka*, pp. 163–78. Trudy Leningradskoi otdeleniia Instituta Istorii, no. 7. Moscow-Leningrad, 1964.

———. "R. A. Fadeev, S. Iu. Vitte i ideologicheskie iskaniia 'Okhranitelei' v 1881–1882 gg." (R. A. Fadeev, S. Iu. Vitte and the Ideological Quests of the "Guardians" in 1881–1882). In *Issledovniia po sotsialno-politicheskoi istorii Rossii: sbornik statei pamiati Borisa Aleksandrovicha Romanova*, pp. 299–326. Leningrad, 1971.

———. "Vitte i izdatelskaia deiatelnost 'Bezobrazovogo klika'" (Witte and the Publishing Activity of the Bezobrazov Clique). *Knizhnoe delo v Rossii vo vtoroi polovine XIX–nachale XX veka; sbornik nauchnykh trudov*, no. 4 (1989), pp. 59–78.

———. *S. Iu. Vitte—memuarist* (S. Iu. Witte—Memoirist). St. Petersburg, 1994.

———. *Sergei Iulevich Vitte i ego vremia* (Sergei Iulevich Witte and His Times). St. Petersburg, 1999.

Anspach, A. *La Russie économique et l'oeuvre de M. de Witte.* Paris, 1904.

Asheshkov, N. "Nikolai II i ego sanovniki v vospominaniiakh grafa S. Iu. Vitte" (Nicholas II and His High Officials in the Memoirs of Count S. Iu. Witte). *Byloe*, no. 18 (1922), pp. 164–210.

Baian (I. I. Kolyshko). *Lozh Vitte* (Witte's Lie). Berlin, n.d.

Bernstein, H. *Celebrities of Our Time.* Freeport, NY, 1968.
Blagikh, I. A. "Konvertiruemyi rubl grafa Vitte" (Count Witte's Convertible Ruble). *Vestnik Rossisskoi Akademii Nauk*, no. 2 (1992), pp. 109–24.
Bompard, M. "Les Mémoires du Comte Witte." *La Revue de Paris* 28, no. 17 (1921), pp. 19–33.
Dillon, E. J. "Two Russian Statesmen." *Quarterly Review* 236 (1921), pp. 407–17.
Enden, M. N. de. "The Roots of Witte's Thoughts." *Russian Review* 29 (1970), pp. 6–24.
Gindin, I. F. "S. Iu. Vitte als Staatsmann." *Jahrbüch für Geschichte der sozialistischen Länder Europas*, 27 (1983), pp. 7–52.
———. "Kak otsenival S. Iu. Vitte svoiu ekonomicheskuiu politiku?" (How Did S. Iu. Witte Evaluate His Own Economic Policies?). *Iz istorii ekonomicheskoi mysli i narodnogo khoziaistva Rossii*, no. 1 (1993), pp. 57–69.
Glinskii, B. B. "Graf Sergei Iulevich Vitte (materialy dlia biografii)" (Count Sergei Iulevich Vitte [Materials for a Biography]). *Istoricheskii vestnik* 140 (1915), pp. 232–279, 573–89; 141 (1915), 520–55, 893–906; 142 (1915), 592–609, 893–907.
Grimm, C. *Graf Witte und die deutsche Politik.* Freiburg, 1930.
Gurko, V. I. "Chto est i chego net v 'Vospominaniiakh S. Iu. Vitte'" (What Is in Witte's Memoirs and What Is Not). *Russkaia starina*, no. 2 (1922), pp. 59–153.
Harcave, S. "The Hessen Redaction of the Witte Memoirs." *Jahrbücher für Geschichte Osteuropas* 36 (1988), pp. 268–76.
Heilbronner, H. "An Anti-Witte Diplomatic Conspiracy, 1905–1906: The Schwanebach Memorandum." *Jahrbücher für Geschichte Osteuropas* 14 (1966), pp. 347–61.
Ignatev, A. V. *S. Iu. Vitte—diplomat.* Moscow, 1989.
Izvolsky, A. "Le Comte Witte." *Revue de Paris* 29 (1922), pp. 703–20.
Kaufman, A. E. "Cherty iz zhizni grafa S. Iu. Vitte" (Aspects of the Life of Count S. Iu. Witte). *Istoricheskii vestnik* 140 (1915), pp. 220–31.
Klein, A. *Der Einfluss des Grafen Witte auf die deutsch-russischen Beziehungen.* Bethel/Bielefeld, 1932.
Koni, A. F. "Sergei Iulevich Vitte." In *Sobranie sochinenii* 5, pp. 238–77. Moscow, 1968.
Korelin, A. P., and Stepanov, S. A. *S. Iu. Vitte.* Moscow, 1988.
Korostowetz, W. von. *Graf Witte.* Berlin, 1929.
Kutler, N., and L. Slonimskii. "Vitte." *Novyi entsiklopedicheskii slovar* 9, pp. 827–50.
Laue, T. H. von. "Count Witte and the Russian Revolution of 1905." *American Slavic and East European Review* (February 1958), pp. 25–46.
———. *Sergei Witte and the Industrialization of Russia.* New York, 1963.
Lopukhin, A. A. *Otryvki iz vospominanii (po povodu "Vospominanii" Gr. S. Iu. Vitte)* (Fragments from My Memoirs [Concerning the Memoirs of Count S. Iu. Witte]). Moscow, 1923.
Lutokhin, D. A. *Graf S. Iu. Vitte kak ministr finansov* (Count S. Iu. Witte as Minister of Finance). Petrograd, 1915.
Lvov, E. *Po studenomu moriu* (Over the Frozen Sea). St. Petersburg, 1895. Description of Witte's trip to the Murman coast.
Lvov, L. "Sem let nazad" (Seven Years Ago). *Russkaia mysl* 35 (1914), pp. 48–84. About the attempt on Witte's life.
Mehlinger, H. D., and J. M. Thompson. *Count Witte and the Tsarist Government in the 1905 Revolution.* Bloomington, 1972.

Mellor, J. "Modernization Theory and Count Witte's Russia in the 1890's." *Slovo: A Journal of Contemporary Soviet and East European Affairs* 1, no. 2 (1988), pp. 8–34.

Melnik, J. "Witte." *Century Magazine* 58 (1915), pp. 684–90.

Mironenko, K. N. "Manifest 17 Oktiabria 1905 g." (The Manifesto of October 17, 1905). *Uchenye zapiski Leningradskogo universiteta* 255 (1958). Seriia iuridicheskoi nauki, no. 10. Voprosy gosudarstva i prava, pp. 158–79.

Naryshkin-Witte, V. *Souvenirs d'une fillette Russe*. Paris, 1925. Recollections of Witte's adopted daughter.

Nötzold, J. *Wirtschaftspolitische Alternativen der Entwicklung in der Ära Witte und Stolypin*. Berlin, 1966.

Petrov, N. "Gapon i Graf Vitte" (Gapon and Count Witte). *Byloe* 29, no. 1 (1925), pp. 15–27.

Pokrovskii, M. N. "O memuarakh Vitte" (Witte's Memoirs). *Pechat i revoliutsiia* (January–March 1922), pp. 54–58; (September 1922), pp. 11–21.

Raskov, N. V. *Politiko-eknomicheskaia sistema S. Iu. Vitte i sovremennaia Rossiia* (S. Iu. Witte's Political-Economic System and Contemporary Russia). St. Petersburg, 2000.

Rieber, A. "Patronage and Professionalism: The Witte System." In *Problemy vsemirnoi istorii*, pp. 286–98. St. Petersburg, 2000.

Rohrbach, P. "Das Finanzsystem Witte." *Preussische Jahrbücher* 109 (1902), pp. 90–121, 305–36.

Romanov, B. A. "Vitte nakanune Russkoi-Iaponskoi voiny" (Witte on the Eve of the Russo-Japanese War). In *Rossiia i zapad* 1, pp. 140–67. Petrograd, 1923.

———. "Likhungchangskii fond" (The Li Hung-chang Fund). *Borba klassov*, nos. 1–2 (1924), pp. 77–126. A commentary on Witte's memoirs.

———. "Vitte kak diplomat" (Witte as a Diplomat). *Vestnik Leningradskogo universiteta*, nos. 4–5 (1946), pp. 151–72.

Russian Academy of Sciences, Institute of Economics. *Sergei Iulevich Vitte—gosudarstvennyi deiatel, reformator, ekonomist* (Sergei Iulevich Witte—Statesman, Reformer, Economist), 2 parts. Moscow, 1999.

Rusov, A. A. "S. Iu. Vitte i ukrainskoe slovo" (S. Iu Witte and the Ukrainian Language). *Utro zhizni*, nos. 3–4 (1915), pp. 95–97.

Savitsky, N. "Serge Witte." *Le Monde Slav* 3 (1932), pp. 161–91, 321–48.

Seraphim, E. "Zar Nikolaus II und Graf Witte." *Historische Zeitschrift* 161 (1940), pp. 277–308.

Sidorov, A. L. "K voprosu o kharaktere teksta i istochnikov 'Vospominanii' S. Iu. Vitte" (The Problem of the Text and Sources of S. Iu. Witte's Memoirs). In Sidorov, *Istoricheskie predposylki velikoi oktiabrskoi sotsialisticheskoi revoliutsii*, pp. 187–216. Moscow, 1970.

Sirotkin, V. "Graf Vitte—tsivilizovannyi industrializator strany" (Count Witte—A Civilizing Industrializer of the Country). *Svobodnaia mysl*, no. 18 (1992), pp. 73–82.

Struve, P. "Graf S. Iu. Vitte: opyt kharakteristiki" (Count S. Iu. Witte: Attempt at a Characterization). *Russkaia mysl* 36 (1915), pp. 129–52.

Szeftel, M. "Nicholas II's Constitutional Decisions of October 17–19, 1905 and Sergius Witte's Role." In *Album J. Balon*, pp. 461–93. Namur, 1968.

———. "The Parliamentary Reforms of the Witte Administration." *Parliaments, Estates and Representation*, no. 1 (1981), pp. 71–94.

Tagantsev, N. S. "V pechatleniia ot vospominanii grafa S. Iu. Vitte" (My Impressions of Count S. Iu. Witte's Memoirs). In *Intelligentsiia i rossiiskoe obshchestvo v nachale XX veka*, pp. 184–99. St. Petersburg, 1996.

Tarle, E. V. *Graf S. Iu. Vitte: opyt kharakteristiki vneshnei politiki* (Count S. Iu. Vitte: Attempt at a Characterization of His Foreign Policy). Leningrad, 1927.

Tsion (Cyon), E. M. *M. Witte et les finances russes*. 5th ed. Lausanne, 1895.

Vetlugin, G. "S. Iu. Vitte i dekabrskoe vosstanie v Moskve" (S. Iu. Witte and the December Uprising in Moscow). *Byloe* 34, no. 6 (1925), pp. 225–26.

Vitenberg, B. M. "K istorii lichnogo arkhiva S. Iu. Vitte" (The History of S. Iu. Witte's Personal Archive). *Vspomogatelnye istoricheskie distsipliny* 17 (1986), pp. 248–60.

Vodovozov, V. V. *Graf S. Iu. Vitte i Imperator Nikolai II* (Count S. Iu. Witte and Emperor Nicholas II). Petrograd, 1922.

Wcislo, F. W. "Witte, Memory and the 1905 Revolution." *Revolutionary Russia* 8 (1995), pp. 166–78.

Wegner-Korfes, S. "Die Rolle von S. Iu. Vitte beim Abschluss des russisch-deutschen Handelsvertrages von 1894," *Jahrbüch für Geschichte der sozialistischen Länder* 22 (1978), pp. 119–46.

Zaitseva, L. I. *S. Iu. Vitte i Rossiia*, Part 1, *Kazennaia vinnaia monopoliia, 1894–1914* (S. Iu. Witte and Russia, Part 1, The Governmental Liquor Monopoly, 1894–1914). Moscow, 2000.

Books, Articles, and Pamphlets by Witte

Konspekt lektsii o narodnom i gosudarstvennom khoziaistve, chit. ego Imperatorskomu Vysochestvu Velikomu Kniaziu Mikhailu Aleksandrovichu (Synopsis of Lectures on Economics and Government Finance Read to His Imperial Highness Grand Duke Michael Aleksandrovich), 2d ed. St. Petersburg, 1912.

"Libava ili Murman?" (Libau or Murman?). *Proshloe i nastoiashchee* 1 (1924), pp. 25–39.

The Memoirs of Count Witte, trans. and ed. by S. Harcave. Armonk, NY, 1990.

Natsionalnaia ekonomiia i Fridrikh List (The National Economy and Frederick List). Kiev, 1889.

Printsipy zheleznodorozhnykh tarifov po perevozke gruzov (Principles of Railroad Freight Rate Determination). Kiev, 1883.

Prolog russko-iaponskoi voiny (Prologue to the Russo-Japanese War). Petrograd, 1916. This work is an abridged and edited version of a three-volume typescript entitled *Vozniknovenie russko-iaponskoi voiny* (The Origin of the Russo-Japanese War), which was prepared under Witte's direction. The typescript is in the Witte Collection of the Bakhmeteff Archive at Columbia University. The editor of the published work, B. B. Glinskii, does not credit Witte as the author, but does note that it comes from his archive.

Samoderzhavie i zemstvo (Autocracy and the Zemstvo). St. Petersburg, 1908.

Spravka o tom, kak byl zakliuchen vneshnii zaem 1906 goda, spasshi finansovoe polozhenie Rossii (How the Foreign Loan of 1906, Which Saved Russia's Financial Position, Was Concluded). St. Petersburg, 1913.

Vospominaniia (Memoirs), ed. by A. L. Sidorov. 3 vols. Moscow, 1960. The most useful of the five Russian editions.

Vynuzhdennye raziasnenniia Grafa Vitte po povodu otcheta Gen.-Adiut. Kuropatkina o voine s Iaponiei (Unavoidable Comments by Count Witte Concerning General-

Adjutant Kuropatkin's Account of the War with Japan). St. Petersburg, 1909.
Zapiska po krestianskomu delu (Memorandum Concerning the Peasant Problem). St. Petersburg, 1904.

Witte's Published Letters, Reports, *et sim.*

"Borba S. Iu. Vitte s agrarnoi revoliutsiei" (The Struggle of S. Iu. Witte Against Agrarian Revolution). *Krasnyi arkhiv* 31 (1928), pp. 81–102.
"Dokladnaia zapiska Vitte Nikolaiu II" (Report of Witte to Nicholas II). *Istorik-marksist*, 2–3 (1935), pp. 131–38."
Doklady S. Iu. Vitte Nikolaiu II" (Reports of S. Iu. Vitte to Nicholas II). *Krasnyi arkhiv* 11–12 (1925), pp. 144–58.
"Graf S. Iu. Vitte i Leo Mekhelin" (Count S. Iu. Witte and Leo Mekhelin). *Byloe* 30, no. 2 (1918), pp. 108–9.
"Graf S. Iu. Vitte i Nikolai II v oktiabre" (Count S. Iu. Witte and Nicholas II in October). *Byloe* 32, no. 4 (1925), p. 107.
"Graf Vitte v borbe s revoliutsiei" (Count Witte at War with the Revolution). *Byloe* 31, no. 3 (1918), pp. 3–10.
"Iz arkhiva S. Iu. Vitte" (From S. Iu. Witte's Archive). *Krasnyi Arkhiv* 11–12 (1925), pp. 107–43.
"Iz arkhiva S. Iu. Vitte" (From S. Iu. Witte's Archive). St. Petersburg (2003), 3 vols.
"K istorii manifesta 17 oktiabria" (Concerning the History of the October 17 Manifesto). *Krasnyi arkhiv* 4 (1923), pp. 411–17.
"K istorii 'Sobranie russkikh fabrichno-zavodskikh rabochikh g. S. Peterburga'" (Concerning the History of the Assembly of Russian Factory Workers of St. Petersburg). *Krasnaia letopis* 1 (1922), pp. 288–329.
"Manifest 17 oktiabria" (The October 17 Manifesto). *Krasnyi arkhiv* 11–12 (1925), pp. 39–106.
"Ob osnovakh ekonomicheskoi politiki tsarskogo pravitelstva v kontse XIX–nachale XX v." (The Principles of the Tsarist Government's Economic Policy at the End of the Nineteenth and the Beginning of the Twentieth Centuries). In *Materialy po istorii SSSR* 6, pp. 157–222. Moscow, 1959. Text of Witte report to Nicholas II.
"Perepiska Grafa S. Iu. Vitte i P. A. Stolypina" (The Correspondence of Count S. Iu. Vitte and P. A. Stolypin). *Russkaia mysl* 36 (1915), pp. 134–52. "Perepiska o podkupke kitaiskikh sanovnikov Li-khun-chzhana i Chzhan-in-khuana" (Correspondence Concerning the Bribing of the High Chinese Officials Li Hung-chang and Chang In-huan). *Krasnyi arkhiv* 2 (1922), pp. 287–93.
"Perepiska S. Iu. Vitte i A. M. Kuropatkina v 1904–1905 gg." (The Correspondence of S. Iu. Witte and A. M. Kuropatkin 1904–1905). *Krasnyi arkhiv* 19 (1926), pp. 64–82. "Perepiska Vitte i Pobedonostseva" (The Correspondence of Witte and Pobedonostsev). *Krasnyi arkhiv* 30 (1928), pp. 89–116.
"Pisma S. Iu. Vitte k D. S. Sipiaginu" (S. Iu. Witte's Letters to D. S. Sipiagin). *Krasnyi arkhiv* 18 (1926), pp. 30–48.
"S. Iu. Vitte, frantsuzskaia pechat i russkie zaimy" (S. Iu. Witte, the French Press, and Russian Loans). *Krasnyi arkhiv* 10 (1925), pp. 36–40.
"Trebovaniia dvorianstva i ekonomicheskaia politika pravitelstva" (Demands of the Nobility and the Economic Policy of the Government). *Istoricheskii arkhiv*, no. 4 (1954), pp. 122–55. Witte's reply to a statement by marshals of the nobility in 1896 concerning the needs of noble landowners.

Other Sources

Agursky, M. "Caught in a Cross Fire: The Russian Church Between Holy Synod and Radical Right, 1905–1908." *Orientalia Christiana Periodica* 50 (1984), pp. 163–96.

Akademiia Nauk SSSR. Institut Istorii. *Revoliutsiia 1905–1907 gg. v Rossii: dokumenty i materialy* (The Revolution of 1905–1907 in Russia: Documents and Materials). 15 vols. Moscow, 1955–1963.

Alexander Mikhailovich, Grand Duke. *Once a Grand Duke*. New York, 1932.

Ananich, B. V. *Bankirskie doma v Rossii, 1860–1914 gg.* (Banking Houses in Russia, 1860–1914). Leningrad, 1991.

Ascher, A. *The Revolution of 1905*. 2 vols. Stanford, CA, 1988.

Avrekh, A. Ia. *Masony i revoliutsiia* (Masons and Revolution). Moscow, 1990.

Basily, N. de. *Memoirs*. Stanford, CA, 1973.

Baylen, J. "The Tsar's 'Lecturer-General' W. T. Stead and the Russian Revolution of 1905." *Georgia State College of Arts and Sciences Research Papers*, no. 23 (July 1969).

Bezobrazov, A. "Les premières causes de l'effondrement de la Russie: le conflit russo-japonais." *Le Correspondent*, May 25, 1923.

Bing, E. J., ed. *The Secret Letters of the Last Tsar*. New York, 1938.

Bogdanovich, A. V. *Tri poslednikh samoderzhtsa: dnevnik A. V. Bogdanovich* (The Three Last Autocrats: Diary of A. V. Bogdanovich). Moscow, 1924.

Bompard, M. *Mon ambassade en Russie, 1903–1908*. Paris, 1937.

Bülow, B. von. *Memoirs*. 3 vols. Boston, 1931–1932.

Bunge, A. Kh. "The Years 1881–1894 in Russia, a Memorandum," tr. and ed. by G. E. Snow. *Transactions of the American Philosophical Society* 71, pt. 6 (1981).

Byrnes, R. F. *Pobedonostsev*. Bloomington, IN, 1968.

Cantacuzene, J. *My Life Here and There*. New York, 1921.

"Church Reform in Russia: Witte versus Pobedonostsev." *Contemporary Review* 77 (1905), pp. 712–26.

Crisp, O. "The Russian Liberals and the 1906 Anglo-French Loan to Russia." *Slavonic and East European Review* 39 (1961), pp. 497–511.

———. "Russian Financial Policy and the Gold Standard." *Economic History Review* 6 (1953), pp. 156–72.

Cunningham, J. W. *A Vanquished Hope: The Movement for Church Renewal in Russia, 1905–1906*. Crestwood, NY, 1981.

Curtin, J. *Memoirs of Jeremiah Curtin*. Madison, WI, 1940. A twenty-four page section covering Curtin's conversation with Witte at Portsmouth was omitted from the published work and is now in the archive of the Wisconsin State Historical Society.

Dillon, J. *The Eclipse of Russia*. New York, 1918.

Dnevniki Imperatora Nikolaia II (The Diaries of Emperor Nicholas II). Moscow, 1992.

Drezen, A., ed. *Tsarizm v borbe s revoliutsiei, 1905–1907 gg.: sbornik dokumentov* (Tsarism's Struggle Against Revolution, 1905–1907: Collection of Documents). Moscow, 1936.

Dubnow, S. M. *History of the Jews of Russia and Poland*. 3 vols. Philadelphia, PA, 1916–1920.

Elkin, B. "Attempts to Revive Freemasonry in Russia." *Slavonic and East European Review* 44 (1960), pp. 454–72.

Emmons, T. *The Formation of Political Parties and the First National Elections in Russia*. Cambridge, MA, 1983.

Esthus, R. A. *Double Eagle and Rising Sun*. Durham, NC, 1988.

Fadeev, A. R. *Vospominaniia* (Memoirs). Odessa, 1897.

"Finansovoe polozhenie tsarskogo samoderzhaviia v period russko-iaponskoi voiny i pervoi russkoi revoliutsii" (The Financial Situation of the Tsarist Autocracy During the Russo-Japanese War and the First Russian Revolution). *Istoricheskii arkhiv*, no. 2 (1955), pp. 121–49.

France. Archives de Ministère des Affaires Étrangères. Russie, Politique Intérieure, I, II, X; Politique Extérieure, Dossier Générale, I.

———. *Documents diplomatique françaises*, Series 2, I,VII, XII. Paris, 1930, 1937.

Gerasimov, A. A. *Na lezvii s terroristami* (The Struggle Against the Terrorists). Paris, 1985.

Germany. Auswärtiges Amt, Arkhiv, Russland 53, no. 1, Geheim, V–VI.

———. *Die Grosse Politik der Europäischen Kabinette, 1871–1914*, XIV, pt. 1, XIX, pt. 2. Berlin, 1924, 1928.

Gessen, I. V. *Gody izgnaniia* (Years of Exile). Paris, 1979.

———. *V dvukh vekakh* (In Two Centuries). Berlin, 1937.

Geyer, D. *Russian Imperialism*. Leamington Spa, UK, 1987.

Girault, R. *Emprunts Russes et investissements français en Russie, 1887–1914*. Paris, 1973.

Gooch, G. P., and H. Temperley, eds. *British Documents on the Origins of the War, 1898–1914*. London, 1927.

Gosudarstvennaia duma v Rossii: v dokumentakh i materialakh (The Russian State Duma: Documents and Materials). Moscow, 1957.

Gurko, V. I. *Features and Figures of the Past*. Stanford, CA, 1939.

Hamburg, G. M. *Politics of the Russian Nobility, 1881–1905*. New Brunswick, NJ, 1984.

Harcave, S. *The Russian Revolution of 1905*. New York, 1964.

Iliodor (Trufanov, S. M.). *Pravda o Soiuz Russkago Naroda, Soiuz Russkikh Liudei i dr. monarkhicheskikh partiiakh* (The Truth About the Union of the Russian People, the Union of Russian Men, and Other Monarchist Parties). Odessa, 1907.

Izvolsky, A. *The Memoirs of Alexander Izvolsky*. London, 1920.

Jablonowski, H. "Die russischen Rechtsparteien, 1905–1907." In *Russland-Studien: Gedenkschrift für Otto Hoetzsch*, pp. 42–55. Stuttgart, 1957.

"K istorii sozdaniia manifesta 17 oktiabria" (Concerning the History of the Creation of Manifesto of 17 October). *Sovetskie arkhivy*, no. 5 (1985), pp. 62–63.

"K istorii 'Sobranie russkikh fabrichno-zavodskikh rabochikh g. S. Peterburga'" (Concerning the History of the "Assembly of Russian Factory and Mill Workers of St. Petersburg"). *Krasnaia letopis* 1 (1922), pp. 288–329.

Kleinmichel, M. *Bilder aus einer versunkten Welt*. Berlin, 1922.

Kokovtsev, V. N. *Out of My Past*. Stanford, CA, 1939.

Koroleva, N. G. *Pervaia rossiiskaia revoliutsiia i tsarizm: sovet ministrov Rossii v 1905–1907 gg.* (The First Russian Revolution and Tsarism: The Russian Council of Ministers 1905–1907). Moscow, 1982.

Korostovets, I. Ia. "Mirnye peregovory v Portsmute v 1905 godu" (The Peace Negotiations in Portsmouth in 1905). *Byloe*, no. 1 (1918), pp. 177–220; no. 2 (1918), pp. 110–46; no. 3 (1918), pp. 58–85; no. 12 (1918), pp. 154–82.

Kovalevskii, M. M. "Moia zhizn" (My Life). *Istoriia SSSR*, July/August (1969), pp. 59–79.

Krasnyi arkhiv, 1922–1941. Various volumes.

Krivoshein, K. A. *A. V. Krivoshein*. Paris, 1973.

Krizis samoderzhaviia v Rossii, 1895–1917 (The Crisis of Autocracy in Russia 1895–1917). Leningrad, 1984.

Kryzhanovskii, S. E. *Vospominaniia* (Memoirs). Berlin, n.d.

Kurlov (Komarov-Kurlov), P. G. *Das Ende des russischen Kaisertums*. Berlin, 1920.

Lamsdorff, V. N. *Dnevnik, 1891–1892* (Diary, 1891–1892). Hague, 1970.

———. *Dnevnik, 1894–1896* (Diary, 1894–1896). Moscow, 1991.

Lieven, D. *Russia's Rulers Under the Old Regime*. New Haven, CT, 1989.

List, F. *The National System of Political Economy*. New York, 1966.

Long, J. W. "Organized Protest Against the 1906 Russian Loan." *Cahiers du monde russe et sovietique* 13 (1972), pp. 24–39.

Louis, G. *Les Carnets de George Louis*. 2 vols. Paris, 1926.

Löwe, H. D. *The Tsars and the Jews*. Langhorne, PA, 1993.

Lukashevich, S. "The Holy Brotherhood, 1881–1883." *American Slavic and East European Review* 18 (1959), pp. 491–510.

Lyashchenko, P. I. *History of the National Economy of Russia*. New York, 1949.

Malozemoff, A. *Russian Far Eastern Policy, 1881–1904*. Berkeley, CA, 1958.

Mamontov, V. I. *Na gosudarevoi sluzhbe: vospominaniia* (In the Tsar's Service: Memoirs). Tallinn, 1926.

Markov, A. *Rasputin und die um ihn*. Königsberg, 1928.

Marks, S. *Road to Power: The Trans-Siberian Railroad and the Colonization of Asian Russia, 1850–1917*. Ithaca, NY, 1991.

McDonald, D. M. *United Government and Foreign Policy, 1900— 1914*. Cambridge, MA, 1992.

McReynolds, L. "Autocratic Journalism: The Case of the St. Petersburg Telegraph Agency." *Slavic Review* 48 (1990), pp. 48–57.

Miliukov, P. N. *Vospominaniia* (Memoirs). 2 vols. New York, 1955.

Mironenko, K. N. "Manifest 17 Oktiabria 1905 g." (The Manifesto of October 17, 1905). *Uchenye zapiski Leningradskogo universiteta, seriia iuridicheskikh nauk* 255, no. 10 (1958), pp. 158–79.

Monarkhiia pered krusheniem, 1914–1917: bumagi Nikolaia II i drugie dokumenty (The Monarchy on the Eve of Its Fall, 1914–1917: The Papers of Nicholas II and Other Documents). Moscow, 1927.

Morison, E. E., ed. *The Letters of Theodore Roosevelt*. Cambridge, MA, 1952.

Mosolov, A. A. *At the Court of the Last Tsar*. London, 1925.

"Neizvestnyi proekt manifesta 17 Oktiabria 1905 goda" (An Unknown Draft of the Manifesto of October 17, 1905). *Sovetskie arkhivy*, no. 2 (1979), pp. 63–65.

Nicholas II. *Dnevnik imperatora Nikolas II* (The Diary of Emperor Nicholas II). Berlin, 1923.

———. *Polnoe sobranoe rechei imperatora Nikolaia II, 1894–1906* (Complete Collection of the Speeches of Emperor Nicholas II, 1894–1906). St. Petersburg, 1906.

Nikolaev, P. "Vospominaniia o kniaze A. I. Bariatinskom" (Recollections Concerning Prince A. I. Bariatinskii). *Istoricheskii vestnik* 22 (1885), pp. 618–44.

Novitskii, V. D. *Iz vospominaniia zhandarma* (From the Memoirs of a Gendarme). Moscow, 1929.

Oldenburg, S. S. *Tsarstvovanie imperatora Nikolaia II* (The Reign of Emperor Nicholas II). 3 vols. Belgrade-Munich, 1939–1949.

Paléologue, M. *An Ambassador's Memoirs*. 3 vols. New York, 1924–1925.

Petrunkevich, I. I. "Iz zapisok obshchestvennago deiatelia" (From the Notebooks of a Public Man). *Arkhiv russkoi revoliutsii* 21 (1934), pp. 5–467.

Pisnaia, V. N. "Studencheskie gody Zheliabova" (Zheliabov's Student Years). *Byloe*, no. 4 (1925), pp. 171–201.

Pobedonostev, K. P. *Pisma Pobedonostseva k Aleksandru III* (Letters of Pobedonostseva to Alexander III). 2 vols. Moscow, 1925–1926.

———. "Iz pisem K. P. Pobedonostseva k Nikolaiu II (1898–1905)" (From the Letters of Pobedonostsev to Nicholas II). *Religii mira: istoriia i sovremennost. Ezhegodnik, 1983*, pp. 163–93. Moscow, 1983.

Polovtsev, A. A. "Dnevnik A. A. Polovtseva," *Krasnyi arkhiv* 3 (1923), pp. 75–172; 4 (1923), pp. 63–128; 46 (1931), pp. 110–32; 67 (1934), pp. 163–86).

———. *Dnevnik gosudarstvennogo sekretaria A. A. Polovtsova (Polovtseva)* (Diary of Imperial Secretary A. A. Polovtsov [Polovtsev]). 2 vols. Moscow, 1966.

Portal, R. "The Problem of an Industrial Revolution in Russia in the Nineteenth Century." In *Readings in Russian History*, ed. S. Harcave, vol. 2, pp. 22–29. New York, 1962.

"Portsmut" (Portsmouth). *Krasnyi arkhiv* 6 (1924), pp. 3–47; 7 (1924), pp. 3–31.

Pravye partii: dokumenty i materialy (Rightist Parties: Documents and Materials), ed. O. V. Volubuev et al., vol. 1. Moscow, 1998.

Propper, S. M. *Was nicht in die Zeitung kam.* Frankfurt am Main, 1929.

Rauch, G. O. "Dnevnik G. O. Raukha" (Diary of G. O. Rauch). *Krasnyi arkhiv* 18 (1926), pp. 83–109.

Reichman, H. "Tsarist Labor Policy and the Railroads." *Russian Review* 42 (1983), pp. 51–72.

Rhinelander, A. L. H. *Prince Michael Vorontsov: Viceroy to the Tsar.* Montreal, 1990.

Rödiger, A. F. "Iz zapisok A. F. Redigera" (From the Memoirs of A. F. Rödiger). *Krasnyi arkhiv* 45 (1931), pp. 86–111; 60 (1933), pp. 42–111.

Rogger, H. "Russian Ministers and the Jewish Question, 1881–1917." *California Slavic Studies* 8 (1975), pp. 15–76.

Romanov, B. A. "Likhungchangskii fond" (The Li Hung-chang Fund). *Borba klassov*, nos. 1–2 (1924), pp. 77–126.

———. *Russia in Manchuria, 1892–1906.* Ann Arbor, MI, 1952.

Rosen, R. R. *Forty Years of Diplomacy.* 2 vols. New York, 1922.

Russia, Gosudarstvennyi Soviet. *Stenografichsekie otchety, sozyv 3* (Stenographic Reports, Session 3). 15 vols. St. Petersburg 1907–1912.

Russia, Komitet Ministrov. *Zhurnaly Komiteta Ministrov po ispolneniiu ukaza 12 dekabria 1904 g.* (Journals of the Committee of Ministers Concerning Implementation of the Decree of December 12, 1904). St. Petersburg, 1908.

Russia, Ministerstvo Finansov. *Ministerstvo Finansov, 1802–1902*, pt. 2. St. Petersburg, 1902.

Russko-iaponskaia voina iz dnevnikov A. N. Kuropatkina i N. P. Linevicha (The Russo-Japanese War in the Diaries of A. N. Kuropatkin and N. P. Linevich). Leningrad, 1925.

Ruud, C. A. "The Printing Press as an Agent of Political Change in Early Twentieth Century Russia. *Russian Review* 40 (1981), pp. 378–95.

Sablinsky, W. *The Road to Bloody Sunday: Father Gapon and the St. Petersburg Massacre of 1905.* Princeton, NJ, 1976.

Sazonov, S. *Fateful Years: 1909–1916.* London, 1928.

Sbornik dogovorov Rossii s drugimi gosudarstvenami, 1856–1917 (Collection of Treaties Between Russia and Other States). Moscow, 1952.

Semeniuta, P. P. "Iz vospominanii ob A. I. Zheliabova" (Recollections Concerning A. I. Zheliabov). *Byloe*, no. 4 (1906), pp. 216–25.

Semennikov, V. P., ed. *Za kulisami tsarizma (arkhiv tibetskogo vracha Badmaeva)*, (Behind the Scenes of Tsarism: The Archive of the Tibetan Doctor Badmaev). Leningrad, 1925.

———. *Revoliutsiia 1905 goda i samoderzhavie* (The Revolution of 1905 and the Autocracy), ed. by V. Semennikov. Moscow, 1928.

Shepelev, L. E. *Tsarizm i burzhuaziia vo vtoroi polovine XIX veka* (Tsarism and the Bourgeoisie in the Second Half of the Nineteenth Century). Leningrad, 1981.

Shipov, D. *Vospominaniia i dumy o perezhitom* (Recollections and Thoughts About the Past). Moscow, 1918.

Smelskii, V. N. "Sviashchennaia druzhina (iz dnevnika eia chlena V. N. Smelskago)" (The Holy Brotherhood [From the Diary of V. N. Smelskii, a Member]). *Golos minuvshago*, no. 1 (1916), pp. 222–56; no. 2 (1916), pp. 135–63; no. 3 (1916), pp. 155–76.

Soiuz russkago naroda (Union of the Russian People), ed. by A. Chernovskii. Moscow, 1924.

Solovev, Iu. B. *Samoderzhavie i dvorianstvo v kontse XIX veka* (Autocracy and the Nobility at the End of the Nineteenth Century). Leningrad, 1973.

———. *Samoderzhavie i dvorianstvo v 1902–1907 gg.* (Autocracy and the Nobility in 1902–1907). Leningrad, 1981.

Soloveva, A. M. *Zheleznodorozhnyi transport Rossii v vtoroi polovine XIX v.* (Russian Railroads in the Second Half of the Nineteenth Century). Moscow, 1975.

Sovet ministrov rossisskoi imperii, 1905–1906 gg.: dokumenty i materialy (The Council of Ministers of the Russian Empire, 1905–1906, Documents and Materials). Leningrad, 1990.

Spasskii-Odynets, A. A. *Vospominaniia* (Memoirs). Ms., Bakhmeteff Archive, Columbia University.

Spiridovich, A. *Les dernières années de la cour de Tzarskoié Sélo*. Paris, 1928–1929.

Spring-Rice, C. *The Letters and Friendships of Sir Cecil Spring-Rice*. Boston, 1929.

Startsev, V. I. *Russkaia burzhuaziia i samoderzhavie v 1905–1917 gg.* (The Russian Bourgeoisie and Autocracy, 1905–1917). Leningrad, 1977.

Stepanov, S. A. *Chernaia sotnia v Rossii: 1905–1914 gg.* (The Russian Black Hundreds, 1905–1914). Moscow, 1992.

Stephan, J. J. *The Russian Far East*. Stanford, CA, 1994.

Strauss, O. S. *Under Four Administrations*. Boston, MA, 1922.

Suvorin, A. S. *Dnevnik* (Diary). Moscow, 1922.

Sviatopolk-Mirskaia, E. A. "Dnevnik Kn. Ekateriny Alekseevny Sviatopolk-Mirskoi za 1904–1905 gg." (Diary of Princess Catherine Alekseevna Sviatopolk-Mirskaia 1904–1905). *Istoricheskie zapiski* 77 (1965), pp. 240–93.

Szeftel, M. *The Russian Constitution of April 23, 1906*. Brussels, 1976.

Tagantsev, N. S. *Perezhitoe: uchrezhdenie Gosudarstvennoi dumy v 1905–1906 gg.* (Experiences: The Establishment of the State Duma in 1905–1906). Petrograd, 1918.

Thorson, W. B. "American Public Opinion and the Portsmouth Peace Conference." *American Historical Review* 53 (1948), pp. 439–64.

Tolstaia, L. I. "Vospominaniia I. I. Tolstogo kak istoricheskii istochnik" (The Memoirs of I. I. Tolstoi as Historical Source). *Vspomogatelnye istoricheskie distsipliny*, XIX (1987), pp. 201–16.

Tolstoi, I. I. *Dnevnik, 1906–1916* (Diary, 1906–1916). St. Petersburg, 1997.

"The Tsar." *Quarterly Review*, CC (1904), pp. 180–209. Published without attribution; the author is Joseph Dillon.

"Tsarskoselskie soveshchaniia" (Conferences at Tsarskoe Selo). *Byloe*, no. 25 (1917), pp. 217–65; no. 26 (1917), pp. 183–245; no. 27/28 (1917), pp. 289–318.

United Kingdom. Public Record Office, Foreign Office, 65/1700 (1905).

Verner, A. M. *The Crisis of Russian Autocracy: Nicholas II and the 1905 Revolution*. Princeton, NJ, 1990.

Vinogradoff, I. "Some Russian Imperial Letters to Prince V. P. Meshchersky (1839–1914)." *Oxford Slavonic Papers* 10 (1962), pp. 105–58.

Vonliarliarskii, V. *Moi vospominaniia* (My Memoirs). Berlin, 1939.

Westwood, J. N. *A History of Russian Railways*. London, 1964.

White, J. A. *The Diplomacy of the Russo-Japanese War*. Princeton, NJ, 1964.

Witte, S. *My Love Affair*. Burlington, VT, 1903. A novel by Witte's sister, translated from the Russian.

Zaionchkovskii, P. A. *Samoderzhavie i russkaia armiia na rubezhe XIX–XX stoletii* (Autocracy and the Russian Army at the Turn of the Twentieth Century). Moscow, 1973.

Zakonodatelnye akty perekhodnago vremeni, 1904–1908 gg. (Legislation Enacted During the Transitional Period of 1904–1908), ed. by N. Lazarevskii. St. Petersburg, 1909.

Name Index

Subject Index

About the Author

Sidney Harcave is professor emeritus of history at the State University of New York at Binghamton, where he taught for thirty years. Among his many books issued in numerous editions are: *Russia: A History; First Blood: The Russian Revolution of 1905; Years of the Golden Cockerel: The Last Romanov Tsars, 1814–1917;* and *The Memoirs of Count Witte.*